Discourse in Machine Translation (DiscoMT 2015)

Held at EMNLP 2015

Lisbon, Portugal
17 September 2015

ISBN: 978-1-5108-1192-8

Printed from e-media with permission by:

Curran Associates, Inc.
57 Morehouse Lane
Red Hook, NY 12571

Some format issues inherent in the e-media version may also appear in this print version.

Printed by Curran Associates, Inc. (2015)

Association for Computational Linguistics
209 N. Eighth Street
Stroudsburg, Pennsylvania 18360

Phone: 1-570-476-8006
Fax: 1-570-476-0860

acl@aclweb.org

Additional copies of this publication are available from:

Curran Associates, Inc.
57 Morehouse Lane
Red Hook, NY 12571 USA
Phone: 845-758-0400
Fax: 845-758-2634
Email: curran@proceedings.com
Web: www.proceedings.com

DiscoMT 2015

Discourse in Machine Translation

Proceedings of the Workshop

17 September 2015
Lisbon, Portugal

Preface

It is well-known that texts have properties that go beyond those of their individual sentences and that reveal themselves in the frequency and distribution of words, word senses, referential forms and syntactic structures, including:

- document-wide properties, such as style, register, reading level and genre;
- patterns of topical or functional sub-structure;
- patterns of discourse coherence, as realized through explicit and/or implicit relations between sentences, clauses or referring forms;
- anaphoric and elliptic expressions, in which speakers exploit the previous discourse context to convey subsequent information very succinctly.

By the end of the 1990s, these properties had stimulated considerable research in Machine Translation, aimed at endowing machine-translated texts with similar document and discourse properties as their source texts. A period of ten years then elapsed before interest resumed in these topics, now from the perspectives of Statistical and/or Hybrid Machine Translation. This led to the *First Workshop on Discourse in Machine Translation* (DiscoMT) in 2013, held in Sofia, Bulgaria, in connection with the annual ACL conference.

Since then, SMT has itself evolved in ways that reflect more interest in and provide more access to needed linguistic knowledge. This evolution is charted in this *Second Workshop on Discourse in Machine Translation (DiscoMT 2015)*, held in Lisbon, Portugal, in connection with EMNLP. Part of this evolution has been the growth of interest in one particular problem: the translation of pronouns whose form in the target language may be constrained in challenging ways by their context. This shared interest has created an environment in which a shared task on pronoun translation or prediction from English–to–French was able to stimulate responses from groups in China, the Czech Republic, Malta, Sweden, Switzerland, and the UK.

In addition to nine papers describing shared task submissions and an overview of the shared task, the submitted systems and the findings (Hardmeier et al., 2015), twelve submissions were accepted for presentation (five as long papers, three as short papers, and four as posters). The papers and posters span the topics of: pronoun translation between languages which differ in pronoun usage (Novák et al., 2015; Guillou and Webber, 2015); explicitation/implicitation in translating discourse connectives (Hoek et al., 2015; Yung et al., 2015); context-aware translation of ambiguous terms (Mascarell et al., 2015; Zhang and Ittycheriah, 2015); assessing document-level properties of MT output, including coherence (Sim Smith et al., 2015; Gong et al., 2015); preserving document-level properties characteristic of register, genre, and other types of text variation (Lapshinova-Koltunski and Vela, 2015; van der Wees et al., 2015; Lapshinova-Koltunski, 2015); and difficulties in preserving them in a purely alignment-based MT framework (Hardmeier, 2015). We hope that workshops such as this one will continue to stimulate work on these aspects of Discourse and Machine Translation, as well as in the many areas not yet represented.

We would like to thank all the authors who submitted papers to the workshop, as well as all the members of the Program Committee who reviewed the submissions and delivered thoughtful, informative reviews.

The Organizers
August 15, 2015

References

Zhengxian Gong, Min Zhang, and Guodong Zhou. 2015. Document-level machine translation evaluation with gist consistency and text cohesion. In *Proceedings of the Second Workshop on Discourse in Machine Translation*, pages 33–40, Lisbon, Portugal. Association for Computational Linguistics.

Liane Guillou and Bonnie Webber. 2015. Analysing ParCor and its translations by state-of-the-art SMT systems. In *Proceedings of the Second Workshop on Discourse in Machine Translation*, pages 24–32, Lisbon, Portugal. Association for Computational Linguistics.

Christian Hardmeier, Preslav Nakov, Sara Stymne, Jörg Tiedemann, Yannick Versley, and Mauro Cettolo. 2015. Pronoun-focused MT and cross-lingual pronoun prediction: Findings of the 2015 DiscoMT shared task on pronoun translation. In *Proceedings of the Second Workshop on Discourse in Machine Translation*, pages 1–16, Lisbon, Portugal. Association for Computational Linguistics.

Christian Hardmeier. 2015. On statistical machine translation and translation theory. In *Proceedings of the Second Workshop on Discourse in Machine Translation*, pages 168–172, Lisbon, Portugal. Association for Computational Linguistics.

Jet Hoek, Jacqueline Evers-Vermeul, and Ted J.M. Sanders. 2015. The role of expectedness in the implicitation and explicitation of discourse relations. In *Proceedings of the Second Workshop on Discourse in Machine Translation*, pages 41–46, Lisbon, Portugal. Association for Computational Linguistics.

Ekaterina Lapshinova-Koltunski and Mihaela Vela. 2015. Measuring 'registerness' in human and machine translation: A text classification approach. In *Proceedings of the Second Workshop on Discourse in Machine Translation*, pages 122–131, Lisbon, Portugal. Association for Computational Linguistics.

Ekaterina Lapshinova-Koltunski. 2015. Exploration of inter- and intralingual variation of discourse phenomena. In *Proceedings of the Second Workshop on Discourse in Machine Translation*, pages 158–167, Lisbon, Portugal. Association for Computational Linguistics.

Laura Mascarell, Mark Fishel, and Martin Volk. 2015. Detecting document-level context triggers to resolve translation ambiguity. In *Proceedings of the Second Workshop on Discourse in Machine Translation*, pages 47–51, Lisbon, Portugal. Association for Computational Linguistics.

Michal Novák, Dieke Oele, and Gertjan van Noord. 2015. Comparison of coreference resolvers for deep syntax translation. In *Proceedings of the Second Workshop on Discourse in Machine Translation*, pages 17–23, Lisbon, Portugal. Association for Computational Linguistics.

Karin Sim Smith, Wilker Aziz, and Lucia Specia. 2015. A proposal for a coherence corpus in machine translation. In *Proceedings of the Second Workshop on Discourse in Machine Translation*, pages 52–58, Lisbon, Portugal. Association for Computational Linguistics.

Marlies van der Wees, Arianna Bisazza, and Christof Monz. 2015. Translation model adaptation using genre-revealing text features. In *Proceedings of the Second Workshop on Discourse in Machine Translation*, pages 132–141, Lisbon, Portugal. Association for Computational Linguistics.

Frances Yung, Kevin Duh, and Yuji Matsumoto. 2015. Crosslingual annotation and analysis of implicit discourse connectives for machine translation. In *Proceedings of the Second Workshop on Discourse in Machine Translation*, pages 142–152, Lisbon, Portugal. Association for Computational Linguistics.

Rong Zhang and Abraham Ittycheriah. 2015. Novel document level features for statistical machine translation. In *Proceedings of the Second Workshop on Discourse in Machine Translation*, pages 153–157, Lisbon, Portugal. Association for Computational Linguistics.

Organizing Committee

Bonnie Webber, University of Edinburgh (chair)
Marine Carpuat, University of Maryland (co-chair)
Andrei Popescu-Belis, Idiap Research Institute, Martigny (co-chair)

Mark Fishel, University of Zurich
Christian Hardmeier, Uppsala University
Lori Levin, Carnegie Mellon University
Preslav Nakov, Qatar Computing Research Institute
Ani Nenkova, University of Pennsylvania
Lucia Specia, University of Sheffield
Jörg Tiedemann, Uppsala University
Min Zhang, Soochow University

Program Committee

Beata Beigman Klebanov, Educational Testing Service
Liane Guillou, University of Edinburgh
Francisco Guzmán, Qatar Computing Research Institute
Shafiq Joty, Qatar Computing Research Institute
Thomas Meyer, Google, Zürich
Michal Novák, Charles University in Prague
Lucie Poláková, Charles University in Prague
Maja Popovic, DFKI, Berlin
Sara Stymne, Uppsala University
Yannick Versley, Heidelberg University
Marion Weller, University of Stuttgart

Shared Task Organizers

Christian Hardmeier, Uppsala University
Preslav Nakov, Qatar Computing Research Institute
Sara Stymne, Uppsala University
Jörg Tiedemann, Uppsala University
Yannick Versley, Heidelberg University

Table of Contents

Pronoun-Focused MT and Cross-Lingual Pronoun Prediction: Findings of the 2015 DiscoMT Shared Task on Pronoun Translation
Christian Hardmeier, Preslav Nakov, Sara Stymne, Jörg Tiedemann, Yannick Versley and Mauro Cettolo 1

Comparison of Coreference Resolvers for Deep Syntax Translation
Michal Novák, Dieke Oele and Gertjan van Noord 17

Analysing ParCor and its Translations by State-of-the-art SMT Systems
Liane Guillou and Bonnie Webber 24

Document-Level Machine Translation Evaluation with Gist Consistency and Text Cohesion
Zhengxian Gong, Min Zhang and Guodong Zhou 33

The Role of Expectedness in the Implicitation and Explicitation of Discourse Relations
Jet Hoek, Jacqueline Evers-Vermeul and Ted J.M. Sanders 41

Detecting Document-level Context Triggers to Resolve Translation Ambiguity
Laura Mascarell, Mark Fishel and Martin Volk 47

A Proposal for a Coherence Corpus in Machine Translation
Karin Sim Smith, Wilker Aziz and Lucia Specia 52

Part-of-Speech Driven Cross-Lingual Pronoun Prediction with Feed-Forward Neural Networks
Jimmy Callin, Christian Hardmeier and Jörg Tiedemann 59

Automatic Post-Editing for the DiscoMT Pronoun Translation Task
Liane Guillou 65

A Document-Level SMT System with Integrated Pronoun Prediction
Christian Hardmeier 72

Predicting Pronoun Translation Using Syntactic, Morphological and Contextual Features from Parallel Data
Sharid Loáiciga 78

Rule-Based Pronominal Anaphora Treatment for Machine Translation
Sharid Loáiciga and Eric Wehrli 86

Pronoun Translation and Prediction with or without Coreference Links
Ngoc Quang Luong, Lesly Miculicich Werlen and Andrei Popescu-Belis 94

Predicting Pronouns across Languages with Continuous Word Spaces
Ngoc-Quan Pham and Lonneke van der Plas 101

Baseline Models for Pronoun Prediction and Pronoun-Aware Translation
Jörg Tiedemann 108

A Maximum Entropy Classifier for Cross-Lingual Pronoun Prediction
Dominikus Wetzel, Adam Lopez and Bonnie Webber 115

Measuring 'Registerness' in Human and Machine Translation: A Text Classification Approach
Ekaterina Lapshinova-Koltunski and Mihaela Vela 122

Translation Model Adaptation Using Genre-Revealing Text Features
Marlies van der Wees, Arianna Bisazza and Christof Monz 132

Crosslingual Annotation and Analysis of Implicit Discourse Connectives for Machine Translation
Frances Yung, Kevin Duh and Yuji Matsumoto 142

Novel Document Level Features for Statistical Machine Translation
Rong Zhang and Abraham Ittycheriah 153

Exploration of Inter- and Intralingual Variation of Discourse Phenomena
Ekaterina Lapshinova-Koltunski 158

On Statistical Machine Translation and Translation Theory
Christian Hardmeier 168

Workshop Program

Thursday, September 17, 2015

09:00–10:30 Session 1

09:00–09:05 *Introduction*

09:05–09:35 *Pronoun-Focused MT and Cross-Lingual Pronoun Prediction: Findings of the 2015 DiscoMT Shared Task on Pronoun Translation*
Christian Hardmeier, Preslav Nakov, Sara Stymne, Jörg Tiedemann, Yannick Versley and Mauro Cettolo

09:35–09:50 *Comparison of Coreference Resolvers for Deep Syntax Translation*
Michal Novák, Dieke Oele and Gertjan van Noord

09:50–10:15 *Analysing ParCor and its Translations by State-of-the-art SMT Systems*
Liane Guillou and Bonnie Webber

10:15–10:30 *Poster Boaster*

10:30–11:00 *Coffee Break*

11:00–12:30 Session 2a: Regular Track Posters

Document-Level Machine Translation Evaluation with Gist Consistency and Text Cohesion
Zhengxian Gong, Min Zhang and Guodong Zhou

The Role of Expectedness in the Implicitation and Explicitation of Discourse Relations
Jet Hoek, Jacqueline Evers-Vermeul and Ted J.M. Sanders

Detecting Document-level Context Triggers to Resolve Translation Ambiguity
Laura Mascarell, Mark Fishel and Martin Volk

A Proposal for a Coherence Corpus in Machine Translation
Karin Sim Smith, Wilker Aziz and Lucia Specia

Thursday, September 17, 2015 (continued)

11:00–12:30 Session 2b: Posters Related to Oral Presentations

On Statistical Machine Translation and Translation Theory
Christian Hardmeier

Exploration of Inter- and Intralingual Variation of Discourse Phenomena
Ekaterina Lapshinova-Koltunski

Measuring 'Registerness' in Human and Machine Translation: A Text Classification Approach
Ekaterina Lapshinova-Koltunski and Mihaela Vela

Translation Model Adaptation Using Genre-Revealing Text Features
Marlies van der Wees, Arianna Bisazza, Christof Monz

Crosslingual Annotation and Analysis of Implicit Discourse Connectives for Machine Translation
Frances Yung, Kevin Duh, Yuji Matsumoto

11:00–12:30 Session 2c: Shared Task Posters

Part-of-Speech Driven Cross-Lingual Pronoun Prediction with Feed-Forward Neural Networks
Jimmy Callin, Christian Hardmeier and Jörg Tiedemann

Automatic Post-Editing for the DiscoMT Pronoun Translation Task
Liane Guillou

A Document-Level SMT System with Integrated Pronoun Prediction
Christian Hardmeier

Predicting Pronoun Translation Using Syntactic, Morphological and Contextual Features from Parallel Data
Sharid Loáiciga

Rule-Based Pronominal Anaphora Treatment for Machine Translation
Sharid Loáiciga and Eric Wehrli

Pronoun Translation and Prediction with or without Coreference Links
Ngoc Quang Luong, Lesly Miculicich Werlen and Andrei Popescu-Belis

Thursday, September 17, 2015 (continued)

Predicting Pronouns across Languages with Continuous Word Spaces
Ngoc-Quan Pham and Lonneke van der Plas

Baseline Models for Pronoun Prediction and Pronoun-Aware Translation
Jörg Tiedemann

A Maximum Entropy Classifier for Cross-Lingual Pronoun Prediction
Dominikus Wetzel, Adam Lopez and Bonnie Webber

12:30–14:00 ***Lunch Break***

14:00–15:30 **Session 3**

14:00–14:25 *Measuring 'Registerness' in Human and Machine Translation: A Text Classification Approach*
Ekaterina Lapshinova-Koltunski and Mihaela Vela

14:25–14:50 *Translation Model Adaptation Using Genre-Revealing Text Features*
Marlies van der Wees, Arianna Bisazza and Christof Monz

14:50–15:15 *Crosslingual Annotation and Analysis of Implicit Discourse Connectives for Machine Translation*
Frances Yung, Kevin Duh and Yuji Matsumoto

15:15–15:30 *Novel Document Level Features for Statistical Machine Translation*
Rong Zhang and Abraham Ittycheriah

15:30–16:00 ***Coffee Break***

16:00–17:30 **Session 4**

16:00–16:25 *Exploration of Inter- and Intralingual Variation of Discourse Phenomena*
Ekaterina Lapshinova-Koltunski

16:25–16:40 *On Statistical Machine Translation and Translation Theory*
Christian Hardmeier

16:40–17:30 ***Final Discussions and Conclusions***

Pronoun-Focused MT and Cross-Lingual Pronoun Prediction: Findings of the 2015 DiscoMT Shared Task on Pronoun Translation

Christian Hardmeier
Uppsala University
Dept. of Linguistics and Philology
first.last@lingfil.uu.se

Preslav Nakov
Qatar Computing Research Institute
HBKU
pnakov@qf.org.qa

Sara Stymne
Uppsala University
Dept. of Linguistics and Philology
first.last@lingfil.uu.se

Jörg Tiedemann
Uppsala University
Dept. of Linguistics and Philology
first.last@lingfil.uu.se

Yannick Versley
University of Heidelberg
Institute of Computational Linguistics
versley@cl.uni-heidelberg.de

Mauro Cettolo
Fondazione Bruno Kessler
Trento, Italy
cettolo@fbk.eu

Abstract

We describe the design, the evaluation setup, and the results of the DiscoMT 2015 shared task, which included two subtasks, relevant to both the machine translation (MT) and the discourse communities: (*i*) *pronoun-focused translation*, a practical MT task, and (*ii*) *cross-lingual pronoun prediction*, a classification task that requires no specific MT expertise and is interesting as a machine learning task in its own right. We focused on the English–French language pair, for which MT output is generally of high quality, but has visible issues with pronoun translation due to differences in the pronoun systems of the two languages. Six groups participated in the pronoun-focused translation task and eight groups in the cross-lingual pronoun prediction task.

1 Introduction

Until just a few years ago, there was little awareness of discourse-level linguistic features in statistical machine translation (SMT) research. Since then, a number of groups have started working on discourse-related topics, and today there is a fairly active community that convened for the first time at the Workshop on Discourse in Machine Translation (DiscoMT) at the ACL 2013 conference in Sofia (Bulgaria). This year sees a second DiscoMT workshop taking place at EMNLP 2015 in Lisbon (Portugal), and we felt that the time was ripe to make a coordinated effort towards establishing the state of the art for an important discourse-related issue in machine translation (MT), the translation of pronouns.

Organizing a shared task involves clearly defining the problem, then creating suitable datasets and evaluation methodologies. Having such a setup makes it possible to explore a variety of approaches for solving the problem at hand since the participating groups independently come up with various ways to address it. All of this is highly beneficial for continued research as it creates a well-defined benchmark with a low entry barrier, a set of results to compare to, and a collection of properly evaluated ideas to start from.

We decided to base this shared task on the problem of pronoun translation. Historically, this was one of the first discourse problems to be considered in the context of SMT (Le Nagard and Koehn, 2010; Hardmeier and Federico, 2010); yet, it is still far from being solved. For an overview of the existing work on pronoun translation, we refer the reader to Hardmeier (2014, Section 2.3.1). The typical case is an *anaphoric* pronoun – one that refers to an entity mentioned earlier in the discourse, its *antecedent*. Many languages have agreement constraints between pronouns and their antecedents. In translation, these constraints must be satisfied in the target language. Note that source language information is not enough for this task. To see why, consider the following example for English–French:[1]

> The *funeral* of the Queen Mother will take place on Friday. *It* will be broadcast live.
>
> Les *funérailles* de la reine-mère auront lieu vendredi. *Elles* seront retransmises en direct.

[1] The example is taken from Hardmeier (2014, 92).

Proceedings of the Second Workshop on Discourse in Machine Translation (DiscoMT), pages 1–16,
Lisbon, Portugal, 17 September 2015.

Here, the English antecedent, *the funeral of the Queen Mother*, requires a singular form for the anaphoric pronoun *it*. The French translation of the antecedent, *les funérailles de la reine-mère*, is feminine plural, so the corresponding anaphoric pronoun, *elles*, must be a feminine plural form too. Note that the translator could have chosen to translate the word *funeral* with the French word *enterrement* 'burial' instead:

> L'*enterrement* de la reine-mère aura lieu vendredi. *Il* sera retransmis en direct.

This time, the antecedent noun phrase (NP) is masculine singular and thus requires a masculine singular anaphoric pronoun and singular verb forms. Therefore, correctly translating anaphoric pronouns requires knowledge about a pronoun's antecedent and its translation in the target language.

Early SMT research on pronoun translation focused exclusively on agreement in the target language (Le Nagard and Koehn, 2010; Hardmeier and Federico, 2010). While this is one of the main issues with pronoun translation, it soon became clear that there were other factors as well. On the one hand, the same source language pronoun can have both anaphoric and non-anaphoric functions, with different constraints. On the other hand, anaphoric reference can be realized through different types of referring expressions, including personal pronouns, demonstrative pronouns, zero pronouns, full noun phrases, etc., with different languages exploiting these means in different ways. The precise mechanisms underlying these processes in various language pairs are not well understood, but it is easy to see that pronoun translation is not a trivial problem, e.g., by noting that the number of pronouns on the source and on the target side of the same parallel text may differ by up to 40 % (Mitkov and Barbu, 2003).

2 Task Description

The shared task had two subtasks. The first subtask, *pronoun-focused translation*, required full translation of texts from one language into another with special attention paid to the translation of pronouns. The second, *cross-lingual pronoun prediction*, was a classification task requiring only the generation of pronouns in the context of an existing translation. Its purpose was to lower the entrance barrier by allowing the participants to focus on the actual pronoun translation problem without having to worry about the complexities of full MT.

Experiments on discourse-related aspects of MT are unlikely to be successful unless a strong MT baseline is used. Also, evaluation is much easier if there are clear, relevant, measurable contrasts in the translation task under consideration (Hardmeier, 2012). For the DiscoMT shared task, we chose to study translation from English into French because this language pair is known from other evaluations such as WMT or IWSLT to have good baseline performance. Also, there are interesting differences in the pronoun systems of the two languages. French pronouns agree with the *grammatical* gender of their antecedent in both singular and plural. In English, the singular pronouns *he* and *she* agree with the *natural* gender of the referent of the antecedent, and the pronoun *it* is used with antecedents lacking natural gender; the plural pronoun *they* is not marked for gender at all.

The text type, or "domain", considered in the shared task is that of public lectures delivered at TED conferences. This choice was motivated by the ready availability of suitable training data in the WIT^3 corpus (Cettolo et al., 2012), together with the fact that this text type is relatively rich in pronouns compared to other genres such as newswire (Hardmeier et al., 2013b).

In the *pronoun-focused translation* task, participants were given a collection of English input documents, which they were asked to translate into French. As such, the task was identical to other MT shared tasks such as those of the WMT or IWSLT workshops. However, the evaluation of our shared task did not focus on general translation quality, but specifically on the correctness of the French translations of the English pronouns *it* and *they*. Since measuring pronoun correctness in the context of an actual translation is a very difficult problem in itself, the evaluation of this task was carried out manually for a sample of the test data.

The *cross-lingual pronoun prediction* task was a gap-filling exercise very similar to the classification problem considered by Hardmeier et al. (2013b). Participants were given the English source text of the test set along with a full reference translation created by human translators. In the reference translations, the French translations of the English pronouns *it* and *they* were substituted with placeholders. For each of these placeholders, the participants were asked to predict a correct pronoun from a small set of nine classes (see Table 1), given the context of the reference translation.

ce	The French pronoun *ce* (sometimes with elided vowel as *c'*) as in the expression *c'est* 'it is'
elle	feminine singular subject pronoun
elles	feminine plural subject pronoun
il	masculine singular subject pronoun
ils	masculine plural subject pronoun
ça	demonstrative pronoun (including the misspelling *ca* and the rare elided form *ç'*)
cela	demonstrative pronoun
on	indefinite pronoun
OTHER	some other word, or nothing at all, should be inserted

Table 1: The nine target pronoun classes predicted in the *cross-lingual pronoun prediction task.*

The evaluation for the cross-lingual pronoun prediction task was fully automatic, comparing the predictions made by the participating systems with the translations actually found in the reference.

3 Datasets

As already noted, the corpus data used in the DiscoMT shared task comes from the TED talks. In the following, the datasets are briefly described.

3.1 Data Sources

TED is a non-profit organization that "invites the world's most fascinating thinkers and doers [...] to give the talk of their lives". Its website[2] makes the audio and video of TED talks available under the Creative Commons license. All talks are presented and captioned in English, and translated by volunteers world-wide into many languages. In addition to the availability of (audio) recordings, transcriptions and translations, TED talks pose interesting research challenges from the perspective of both speech recognition and machine translation. Therefore, both research communities are making increased use of them in building benchmarks. TED talks address topics of general interest and are delivered to a live public audience whose responses are also audible on the recordings.[3] The talks generally aim to be persuasive and to change the viewers' behaviour or beliefs. The genre of the TED talks is transcribed planned speech.

[2]`http://www.ted.com`

[3]The following overview of text characteristics is based on work by Guillou et al. (2014).

Dataset	segs	tokens		talks
		en	fr	
IWSLT14.train	179k	3.63M	3.88M	1415
IWSLT14.dev2010	887	20,1k	20,2k	8
IWSLT14.tst2010	1664	32,0k	33,9k	11
IWSLT14.tst2011	818	14,5k	15,6k	8
IWSLT14.tst2012	1124	21,5k	23,5k	11
DiscoMT.tst2015	2093	45,4k	48,1k	12

Table 2: Statistics about the bilingual linguistic resources for the shared task.

Table 2 provides statistics about the in-domain tokenized bitexts we supplied for training, development and evaluation purposes.

Note that TED talks differ from other text types with respect to pronoun use. TED speakers frequently use first- and second-person pronouns (singular and plural): first-person pronouns to refer to themselves and their colleagues or to themselves and the audience, and second-person pronouns to refer to the audience, to the larger set of viewers, or to people in general. Moreover, they often use the pronoun *they* without a specific textual antecedent, in phrases such as "This is what they think", as well as deictic and third-person pronouns to refer to things in the spatio-temporal context shared by the speaker and the audience, such as props and slides. In general, pronouns are abundant in TED talks, and anaphoric references are not always very clearly defined.

3.2 Selection Criteria

The training and the development datasets for our tasks come from the English-French MT task of the IWSLT 2014 evaluation campaign (Cettolo et al., 2014). The test dataset for our shared task, named *DiscoMT.tst2015*, has been compiled from new talks added recently to the TED repository that satisfy the following requirements:

1. The talks have been transcribed (in English) and translated into French.
2. They were not included in the training, development, and test datasets of any IWSLT evaluation campaign, so *DiscoMT.tst2015* can be used as held-out data with respect to those.
3. They contain a sufficient number of tokens of the English pronouns *it* and *they* translated into the French pronouns listed in Table 1.
4. They amount to a total number of words suitable for evaluation purposes (e.g., tens of thousands).

To meet requirement 3, we selected talks for which the combined count of the rarer classes *ça*, *cela*, *elle*, *elles* and *on* was high. The resulting distribution of pronoun classes, according to the extraction procedure described in Section 5.1, can be found in Table 8 further below.

We aimed to have at least one pair of talks given by the same speaker and at least one pair translated by the same translator. These two features are not required by the DiscoMT shared task, but could be useful for further linguistic analysis, such as the influence of speakers and translators on the use of pronouns. Talks 1756 and 1894 were presented by the same speaker, and talks 205, 1819 and 1825 were translated by the same translator.

Once the talks satisfying the selection criteria were found, they were automatically aligned at the segment level and then manually checked in order to fix potential errors due to either automatic or human processing. Table 3 shows some statistics and metadata about the TED talks that are part of the *DiscoMT.tst2015* set.

talk id	segs	tokens		speaker
		en	fr	
205	189	4,188	4,109	J.J. Abrams
1756	186	4,320	4,636	A. Solomon
1819	147	2,976	3,383	S. Shah
1825	120	2,754	3,078	B. Barber
1894	237	5,827	6,229	A. Solomon
1935	139	3,135	3,438	S. Chandran
1938	107	2,565	2,802	P. Evans
1950	243	5,989	6,416	E. Snowden
1953	246	4,520	4,738	L. Page
1979	160	2,836	2,702	M. Laberge
2043	175	3,413	3,568	N. Negroponte
2053	144	2,828	3,023	H. Knabe
total	2,093	45,351	48,122	–

Table 3: Statistics about the talks that were included in DiscoMT.tst2015.

4 Pronoun-Focused Translation

4.1 Baseline System

For comparison purposes and to lower the entry barrier for the participants, we provided a baseline system based on a phrase-based SMT model. The baseline system was trained on all parallel and monolingual datasets provided for the DiscoMT shared task, namely aligned TED talks from the WIT^3 project (Cettolo et al., 2012), as well as Europarl version 7 (Koehn, 2005), News Commentary version 9 and the shuffled news data from WMT 2007–2013 (Bojar et al., 2014).

The parallel data were taken from OPUS (Tiedemann, 2012), which provides sentence-aligned corpora with annotation. The latter is useful for finding document boundaries, which can be important when working with discourse-aware translation models. All training data were pre-processed with standard tools from the Moses toolkit (Koehn et al., 2007), and the final datasets were lower-cased and normalized (punctuation was unified, and non-printing characters were removed). The pre-processing pipeline was made available on the workshop website in order to ensure compatibility between the submitted systems.

The parallel data were prepared for word alignment using the cleaning script provided by Moses, with 100 tokens as the maximum sentence length. The indexes of the retained lines were saved to make it possible to map sentences back to the annotated corpora. The final parallel corpus contained 2.4 million sentence pairs with 63.6 million words in English and 70.0 million words in French. We word-aligned the data using fast_align (Dyer et al., 2013) and we symmetrized the word alignments using the *grow-diag-final-and* heuristics. The phrase tables were extracted from the word-aligned bitext using Moses with standard settings. We also filtered the resulting phrase table using significance testing (Johnson et al., 2007) with the recommended filter values and parameters. The phrase table was provided in raw and binary formats to make it easy to integrate it in other systems.

For the language model, we used all monolingual datasets and the French parts of the parallel datasets and trained a 5-gram language model with modified Kneser-Ney smoothing using KenLM (Heafield et al., 2013). We provided the language model in ARPA format and in binary format using a trie data structure with quantization and pointer compression.

The SMT model was tuned on the IWSLT 2010 development data and IWSLT 2011 test data using 200-best lists and MERT (Och, 2003). The resulting baseline system achieved reasonably good scores on the IWSLT 2010 and 2012 test datasets (Table 4).

test set	BLEU	
IWSLT 2010	33.86	(BP=0.982)
IWSLT 2012	40.06	(BP=0.959)

Table 4: Baseline models for English-French machine translation: case-insensitive BLEU scores.

We experimented with additional datasets and other settings (GIZA++ instead of fast_align, unfiltered phrase tables), but could not improve.

All datasets, models and parameters were made available on the shared task website to make it easy to get started with new developments and to compare results with the provided baseline. For completeness, we also provided a recasing model that was trained on the same dataset to render it straightforward to produce case-sensitive output, which we required as the final submission.

4.2 Submitted Systems

We received six submissions to the pronoun-focused translation task, and there are system descriptions for five of them. Four submissions were phrase-based SMT systems, three of which were based on the baseline described in Section 4.1. One was a rule-based MT system using a completely different approach to machine translation.

The IDIAP (Luong et al., 2015) and the AUTO-POSTEDIT (Guillou, 2015) submissions were phrase-based, built using the same training and tuning resources and methods as the official baseline. Both adopted a two-pass approach involving an automatic post-editing step to correct the pronoun translations output by the baseline system, and both of them relied on the Stanford anaphora resolution software (Lee et al., 2011). They differed in the way the correct pronoun was assigned: the IDIAP submission used a classifier with features that included properties of the hypothesized antecedent together with the output of the baseline system, whereas the AUTO-POSTEDIT system followed a simpler rule-based decision procedure.

The UU-TIEDEMANN system (Tiedemann, 2015) was another phrase-based SMT system extending the official baseline. In contrast to the other submissions, it made no attempt to resolve pronominal anaphora explicitly. Instead, it used the Docent document-level decoder (Hardmeier et al., 2013a) with a cross-sentence *n*-gram model over determiners and pronouns to bias the SMT model towards selecting correct pronouns.

The UU-HARDMEIER system (Hardmeier, 2015) was yet another phrase-based SMT using Docent, but built on a different baseline configuration. It included a neural network classifier for pronoun prediction trained with latent anaphora resolution (Hardmeier et al., 2013b), but using the Stanford coreference resolution software at test time.

ITS2 (Loáiciga and Wehrli, 2015) was a rule-based machine translation system using syntax-based transfer. For the shared task, it was extended with an anaphora resolution component influenced by Binding Theory (Chomsky, 1981).

For the sixth submission, A3-108, no system description paper was submitted. Its output seemed to have been affected by problems at the basic MT level, yielding very bad translation quality.

4.3 Evaluation Methods

Evaluating machine translations for pronoun correctness automatically is difficult because standard assumptions fail. In particular, it is incorrect to assume that a pronoun is translated correctly if it matches the reference translation. If the translation of an anaphoric pronoun is itself a pronoun, it has to agree with the translation of its antecedent, and a translation deviating from the reference may be the only correct solution in some cases (Hardmeier, 2014, 92). Doing this evaluation correctly would require a working solution to the cross-lingual pronoun prediction task, the second challenge of our shared task. Given the current state of the art, we have little choice but to do manual evaluation.[4]

Our evaluation methodology is based on the gap-filling annotation procedure introduced by Hardmeier (2014, Section 9.4). We employed two annotators, both of whom were professional translators, native speakers of Swedish with good command of French. Tokens were presented to the annotators in the form of examples corresponding to a single occurrence of the English pronouns *it* or *they*. For each example, the sentence containing the pronoun was shown to the annotator along with its machine translation (but not the reference translation) and up to 5 sentences of context in both languages. In the MT output, any French pronouns aligned to the pronoun to be annotated were replaced with a placeholder. The annotators were then asked to replace the placeholder with an item selected from a list of pronouns that was based on the classes of the cross-lingual pronoun prediction task (Table 1).

Compared to the perhaps more obvious methodology of having the annotators judge examples as good or bad, treating evaluation as a gap-filling task has the advantage of avoiding a bias in favour of solutions generated by the evaluated systems.

[4] While discourse-aware MT evaluation metrics were proposed recently (Guzmán et al., 2014b; Joty et al., 2014; Guzmán et al., 2014a), they do not specifically focus on pronoun translation.

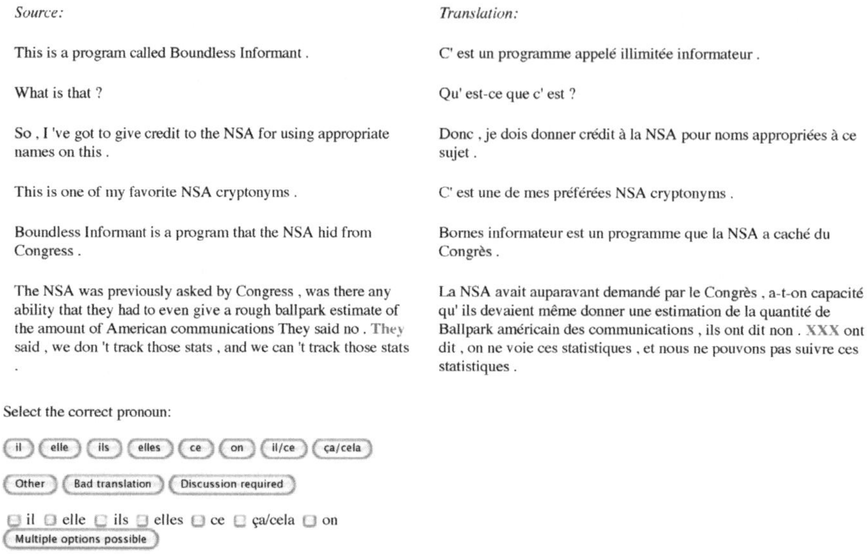

Figure 1: The web interface used for annotation.

This is particularly relevant when the overall quality of the translations is imperfect and the evaluators might be tempted to accept the existing solution if it looks remotely plausible. Moreover, this form of annotation creates a dataset of correct pronoun translations in the context of MT output that can be used in future work and that would be very difficult to obtain otherwise.

In the annotation interface, the pronouns *ça* and *cela* were merged into a single class because the annotators found themselves unable to make a consistent and principled distinction between the two pronouns, and the grammar books we consulted (Grevisse and Goosse, 1993; Boysen, 1996) did not offer enough guidance to create reliable guidelines. Moreover, the annotation interface allowed the annotators to select BAD TRANSLATION if the MT output was not sufficiently well-formed to be annotated with a pronoun. However, they were instructed to be tolerant of ill-formed translations and to use the label BAD TRANSLATION only if it was necessary to make more than two modifications to the sentence, in addition to filling in the placeholder, to make the output locally grammatical.

In earlier work, Hardmeier (2014) reported an annotation speed of about 60 examples per hour. While our annotators approached that figure after completed training, the average speed over the entire annotation period was about one third lower in this work, mostly because it proved to be more difficult than anticipated to settle on a consistent set of guidelines and reach an acceptable level of inter-annotator agreement.

We believe there are two reasons for this. On the one hand, the MT output came from a number of systems of widely varying quality, while previous work considered different variants of a single system. Achieving consistent annotation turned out to be considerably more difficult for the lower-quality systems. On the other hand, unlike the annotators used by Hardmeier (2014), ours had a linguistic background as translators, but not in MT. This is probably an advantage as far as unbiased annotations are concerned, but it may have increased the initial time to get used to the task and its purpose.

We computed inter-annotator agreement in terms of Krippendorff's α (Krippendorff, 2004) and Scott's π (Scott, 1955), using the NLTK toolkit (Bird et al., 2009), over 28 examples annotated by the two annotators. After two rounds of discussion and evaluation, we reached an agreement of $\alpha = 0.561$ and $\pi = 0.574$. These agreement figures are lower than those reported by Hardmeier (2014, 149), which we believe is mostly due to the factors discussed above. Some of the disagreement also seems to stem from the annotators' different propensity to annotate examples with demonstrative pronouns. This point was addressed in discussions with the annotators, but we did not have time for another round of formal annotator training and agreement evaluation. We do not believe this had a major negative effect on the MT evaluation quality since, in most cases where the annotators disagreed about whether to annotate *ça/cela*, the alternative personal pronoun would be annotated consistently if a personal pronoun was acceptable.

In case of insurmountable difficulties, the annotators had the option to mark an example with the label DISCUSSION REQUIRED. Such cases were resolved at the end of the annotation process.

In total, we annotated 210 examples for each of the six submitted systems as well as for the official baseline system. The examples were paired across all systems, so the same set of English pronouns was annotated for each system. In addition, the sample was stratified to ensure that all pronoun types were represented adequately. The stratification was performed by looking at the pronouns aligned to the English pronouns in the *reference* translation and separately selecting a sample of each pronoun class (according to Table 1) in proportion to its relative frequency in the complete test set. When rounding the individual sample sizes to integer values, we gave slight preference to the rarer classes by rounding the sample sizes upwards for the less frequent and downwards for the more frequent classes.

After completing the human evaluation, we calculated a set of evaluation scores by counting how often the output of a particular system matched the manual annotation specific to that system. This is straightforward for the annotation labels corresponding to actual pronouns (*ce*, *ça/cela*, *elle*, *elles*, *il*, *ils* and *on*). The examples labelled as BAD TRANSLATION were counted as incorrect. The label OTHER leads to complications because this label lumps together many different cases such as the use of a pronoun not available as an explicit label, the complete absence of a pronoun translation on the target side, the translation of a pronoun with a full noun phrase or other linguistic construct, etc. As a result, even if the MT output of an example annotated as OTHER contains a translation that is compatible with this annotation, we cannot be sure that it is in fact correct. This must be kept in mind when interpreting aggregate metrics based on our annotations.

The evaluation scores based on manual annotations are defined as follows:

Accuracy with OTHER (Acc+O) Our primary evaluation score is accuracy over all 210 examples, i.e., the proportion of examples for which the pronouns in the MT output are compatible with those in the manual annotation. We include items labelled OTHER and count them as correct if the MT output contains any realisation compatible with that label.

Accuracy without OTHER (Acc–O) This is an accuracy score computed only over those examples that are not labelled OTHER, so it does not suffer from the problem described above. However, the set of examples annotated as OTHER differs between systems, which could in theory be exploited by a system to increase its score artificially, e.g., by predicting OTHER for all hard cases. In practice, it is very unlikely that this happened in this evaluation since details about the evaluation modalities were not known to the participants at submission time.

Pronoun-specific F_{max}-score To permit a more fine-grained interpretation of the evaluation results, we also computed individual precision, recall and F-score values for each of the pronoun labels available to the annotators (excluding OTHER and BAD TRANSLATION). Since multiple correct choices are possible for each example, an example need not (and cannot) match each of the annotated pronouns to be correct. To account for this, we operate with a non-standard definition of recall, which we call R_{max} because it can be interpreted as a sort of upper bound on the "intuitive" notion of recall. R_{max} for a given type of pronoun counts as matches all correct examples labelled with a given pronoun type, even if the actual pronoun used is different. To illustrate, suppose an example is annotated with *il* and *ce*, and the MT output has *ce*. This example would be counted as a hit for the R_{max} of *both* pronoun types, *il* and *ce*. The F_{max} score in Table 6 is the harmonic mean of standard precision and R_{max}.

Pron-F The fine-grained precision and recall scores give rise to another aggregate measure, labelled Pron-F in Table 6, which is an F-score based on the micro-averaged precision and recall values of all pronoun types.

In addition to the above manual evaluation scores, we also computed automatic scores (Table 5). This includes the pronoun precision/recall scores as defined by Hardmeier and Federico (2010), as well as four standard MT evaluation metrics: BLEU (Papineni et al., 2002), NIST (Doddington, 2002), TER (Snover et al., 2006), and METEOR (Denkowski and Lavie, 2011).

	Pronoun Evaluation			Standard MT Evaluation Metrics			
	P	R	F	BLEU	NIST	TER	METEOR
BASELINE	0.371	0.361	0.366	37.18	8.04	46.74	60.05
IDIAP	0.346	0.333	0.340	36.42	7.89	48.18	59.26
UU-TIEDEMANN	0.386	0.353	0.369	36.92	8.02	46.93	59.92
UU-HARDMEIER	0.347	0.333	0.340	32.58	7.66	49.04	57.50
AUTO-POSTEDIT	0.329	0.276	0.300	36.91	7.98	46.94	59.70
ITS2	0.184	0.187	0.188	20.94	5.96	60.95	47.90
A3-108	0.054	0.045	0.049	4.06	2.77	88.49	25.59

Table 5: Pronoun-focused translation task: automatic metrics.

				F_{max} Scores for Individual Pronouns						
	Acc+O	Acc–O	Pron-F	*ce*	*ça/cela*	*elle*	*elles*	*il*	*ils*	*on*
BASELINE	0.676	0.630	0.699	0.832	0.631	0.452	0.436	0.522	0.900	∅
IDIAP	0.657	0.617	0.711	0.842	0.703	0.336	0.545	0.600	0.848	∅
UU-TIEDEMANN	0.643	0.590	0.675	0.781	0.573	0.516	0.462	0.402	0.891	∅
UU-HARDMEIER	0.581	0.525	0.580	0.765	0.521	0.207	0.421	0.254	0.882	∅
AUTO-POSTEDIT	0.543	0.473	0.523	0.496	0.238	0.304	0.396	0.422	0.869	∅
ITS2	0.419	0.339	0.396	∅	∅	0.256	0.353	0.373	0.782	∅
A3-108	0.081	0.081	0.188	0.368	0.149	0.000	0.000	∅	0.271	∅

Acc+O: Accuracy with OTHER Acc–O: Accuracy without OTHER Pron-F: micro-averaged pronoun F-score
∅: this pronoun type that was never predicted by the system

Table 6: Pronoun-focused translation task: manual evaluation metrics.

4.4 Evaluation Results

The standard automatic MT evaluation scores (BLEU, NIST, TER, METEOR; Table 5) do not offer specific insights about pronoun translation, but it is still useful to consider them first for an easy overview over the submitted systems. They clearly reveal a group of systems (IDIAP, UU-TIEDEMANN and AUTO-POSTEDIT) built with the data of the official BASELINE system, with very similar scores ranging between 36.4 and 37.2 BLEU points. The baseline itself achieves the best scores, but considering the inadequacy of BLEU for pronoun evaluation, we do not see this as a major concern in itself. The other submissions fall behind in terms of automatic MT metrics. The UU-HARDMEIER system is similar to the other SMT systems, but uses different language and translation models, which evidently do not yield the same level of raw MT performance as the baseline system. ITS2 is a rule-based system. Since it is well known that n-gram-based evaluation metrics do not always do full justice to rule-based MT approaches not using n-gram language models (Callison-Burch et al., 2006), it is difficult to draw definite conclusions from this system's lower scores. Finally, the extremely low scores for the A3-108 system indicate serious problems with translation quality, an impression that we easily confirmed by examining the system output.

The results for the manual evaluation are shown in Table 6: we show aggregate scores such as accuracy, with and without OTHER, as well as F_{max} scores for the individual pronouns. We have chosen Acc+O to be the primary metric because it is well defined as it is calculated on the same instances for all participating systems, so it cannot be easily exploited by manipulating the system output in clever ways. It turns out, however, that the rankings of our participating systems induced by this score and the Acc–O score are exactly identical. In both cases, the BASELINE system leads, followed relatively closely by IDIAP and UU-TIEDEMANN. Then, UU-HARDMEIER and AUTO-POSTEDIT follow at a slightly larger distance, and finally A3-108 scores at the bottom. The micro-averaged Pron-F score would have yielded the same ranking as well, except for the first two systems, where IDIAP would have taken the lead from the BASELINE. This is due to the fact that the IDIAP system has a higher number of examples labelled BAD TRANSLATION, while maintaining the same performance as the baseline for the examples with acceptable translations. Rather than implying much about the quality of the systems, this observation confirms and justifies our decision to choose a primary score that is not susceptible to effects arising from excluded classes.

The low scores for the ITS2 system were partly due to a design decision. The anaphora prediction component of ITS2 only generated the personal pronouns *il*, *elle*, *ils* and *elles*; this led to zero recall for *ce* and *ça/cela* and, as a consequence, to a large number of misses that would have been comparatively easy to predict with an *n*-gram model.

There does not seem to be a correlation between pronoun translation quality and the choice of (a) a two-pass approach with automatic post-editing (IDIAP, AUTO-POSTEDIT) or (b) a single-pass SMT system with some form of integrated pronoun model (UU-TIEDEMANN, UU-HARDMEIER). Also, at the level of performance that current systems achieve, there does not seem to be an inherent advantage or disadvantage in doing explicit anaphora resolution (as IDIAP, UU-HARDMEIER, AUTO-POSTEDIT and ITS2 did) as opposed to considering unstructured context only (as in UU-TIEDEMANN and the BASELINE).

One conclusion that is supported by relatively ample evidence in the results concerns the importance of the *n*-gram language model. The BASELINE system, which only relies on *n*-gram modelling to choose the pronouns, achieved scores higher than those of all competing systems. Moreover, even among the submitted systems that included some form of pronoun model, those that relied most on the standard SMT models performed best. For example, the IDIAP submission exploited the SMT decoder's translation hypotheses by parsing the search graph, and UU-TIEDEMANN extended the baseline configuration with additional *n*-gram-style models. By contrast, those systems that actively overrode the choices of the baseline *n*-gram model (UU-HARDMEIER and AUTO-POSTEDIT) performed much worse.

Based on these somewhat depressing results, one might be tempted to conclude that all comparison between the submitted systems is meaningless because all they managed to accomplish was to "disfigure" the output of a working baseline system to various degrees. Yet, we should point out that it was possible for some systems to outperform the baseline at least for some of the rarer pronouns. In particular, the IDIAP system beat the baseline on 4 out of 6 pronoun types, including the feminine plural pronoun *elles*, and the UU-TIEDEMANN system performed better on both types of feminine pronouns, *elle* and *elles*. Results like these suggest that all hope is not lost.

5 Cross-Lingual Pronoun Prediction

5.1 Data Preparation

For the second task, *cross-lingual pronoun translation*, we used the same bitext as for the MT baseline in the first task (Section 4.1); we pre-processed it like before, except for lowercasing. Then, we generated the following two resources: (*i*) a bitext with target pronouns identified and their translations removed, and (*ii*) word alignments between the source and the target sentences in the bitext.

Since the word alignments in the training and in the testing datasets were created automatically, without manual inspection, we performed a small study in order to investigate which alignment method performed best for pronouns. We followed the methodology in Stymne et al. (2014), by aligning English–French data using all IBM models (Brown et al., 1993) and the HMM model (Vogel et al., 1996) as implemented in GIZA++ (Och and Ney, 2003), as well as fast_align (Dyer et al., 2013), with a number of different symmetrization methods. IBM models 1, 2 and 3 yielded subpar results, so we will not discuss them.

To evaluate the alignments, we used 484 gold-aligned sentences from Och and Ney (2000).[5] We used the F-score of correct *sure* and *possible* links (Fraser and Marcu, 2007) for a general evaluation, which we will call F_{all}.[6] In order to specifically evaluate pronoun alignment, we used the F-score of the subset of links that align the two sets of pronouns we are interested in, F_{pro}. For all alignment models, *grow-diag-final-and* symmetrization performed best on the pronoun metric, followed by *grow-diag* and *intersection*, which also performed best for general alignments.

Table 7 shows the results for different models with *grow-diag-final-and* symmetrization. We can see that, for all three models, the results on pronoun links are better than those on all links. Moreover, IBM model 4 and HMM are better than fast_align both for general alignments and for pronoun alignments. In the final system, we chose to use IBM model 4 since it finds slightly more *possible* links than HMM. Overall, we find the results very good. In the best system, all pronoun links except for one *possible* link were found, and there are only four pronoun links that are not in the gold standard.

[5]Downloaded from `http://www.cse.unt.edu/~rada/wpt/index.html`

[6]F_{all} is equivalent to $1 - \text{AER}$, Alignment Error Rate (Och and Ney, 2003).

Alignment	F_{all}	F_{pro}
GIZA++, HMM	0.93	0.96
GIZA++, Model 4	0.92	0.96
fast_align	0.86	0.93

Table 7: F-score for *all* alignment links (F_{all}), and for *pronoun* links (F_{pro}), for different alignment models with *grow-diag-final-and* symmetrization.

Ultimately, we applied GIZA++ with *grow-diag-final-and* symmetrization and we used fast_align as a backoff alignment method for the cases that could not be handled by GIZA++ (sentences longer than 100 tokens and sentence pairs with unusual length ratios). This was necessary in order to align the full bitext without missing any sentence pair in the discourse, as all sentences may contain valuable information for the classifier.

We developed a script that takes the word-aligned bitext and replaces the tokens that are aligned with the English target pronouns *it* and *they* with placeholders, keeping the information about the substitutions for training and evaluation purposes. Note that the substitutions are always single words. Pronouns corresponding to one of the target classes were preferred among the aligned tokens. If none of the tokens matched any of the classes, we kept the shortest aligned word as the substitution and set the class to OTHER. We marked the unaligned words with the substitution string "NONE". Figure 2 shows two examples of training instances that we created.

The final data contains five TAB-separated columns for each aligned segment pair from the bitext: (1) the classes to be predicted in the same order as they appear in the text (may be empty), (2) the actual tokens that have been substituted, (3) the source language segment, (4) the target language segment with placeholders, and (5) the word alignment. The placeholders have the format REPLACE_XX where XX refers to the index (starting with 0) of the English token that is aligned to the placeholder. We normalized instances of *c'* and *ca* to *ce* and *ça*, respectively. The substituted tokens are case-sensitive and the class OTHER also includes empty alignments. For the latter, we developed a strategy that inserts placeholders at a reasonable position into the target language segment by looking at the alignment positions of the surrounding words of the selected English pronoun and then putting the placeholder next to the closest link in the target sentence.

In the unlikely case that there is no alignment link in the neighbourhood of the pronoun, the placeholder will be inserted at a similar position as the source language position or at the end of the segment before any punctuation.

The test data were prepared in the same way but with empty columns for the classes and the substitution strings. We also provided information about the document boundaries in each dataset. For Europarl, we included file names, sentence IDs and annotations such as SPEAKER and paragraph boundaries. For the News Commentaries, we supplied document IDs and paragraph boundaries. Finally, the IWSLT data included the TED talk IDs.

Table 8 shows the distribution of classes in the three training datasets and the official test dataset. We can see that there are significant differences between the different genres with respect to pronoun distributions.

class	DiscoMT 2015	IWSLT14	Training Europarl	News
ça	102	4,548	412	39
ce	184	14,555	52,964	2,873
cela	27	2,256	13,447	1,025
elle	83	2,999	50,254	4,363
elles	51	2,888	18,543	1,929
il	104	8,467	166,873	8,059
ils	160	14,898	45,985	7,433
on	37	1,410	9,871	566
OTHER	357	25,394	231,230	14,969

Table 8: Distribution of classes in the DiscoMT 2015 test set and the three training datasets.

5.2 Baseline System

The baseline system tries to reproduce the most realistic scenario for a phrase-based SMT system assuming that the amount of information that can be extracted from the translation table is not sufficient or is inconclusive. In that case, the pronoun prediction would be influenced primarily by the language model.

Thus, our baseline is based on a language model. It fills the gaps by using a fixed set of pronouns (those to be predicted) and a fixed set of non-pronouns (which includes the most frequent items aligned with a pronoun in the provided test set) as well as NONE (i.e., do not insert anything in the hypothesis), with a configurable NONE penalty that accounts for the fact that n-gram language models tend to assign higher probability to shorter strings than to longer ones.

classes	*ils ce*
substitutions	*ils c'*
source	Even though they were labeled whale meat , they were dolphin meat .
target	Même si REPLACE_2 avaient été étiquettés viande de baleine , REPLACE_8 était de la viande de dauphin .
alignment	0-0 1-1 2-2 3-3 3-4 4-5 5-8 6-6 6-7 7-9 8-10 9-11 10-16 11 -13 11-14 12-17
classes	*ils* OTHER
substitutions	*ils* NONE
source	But they agreed to go along with it for a while .
target	Mais REPLACE_1 ont accepté de suivre REPLACE_7 pendant un temps .
alignment	0-0 1-1 1-2 2-3 3-4 4-5 5-5 6-5 7-6 8-7 9-8 10-9 11-10

Figure 2: Examples from the training data for the cross-lingual pronoun prediction task.

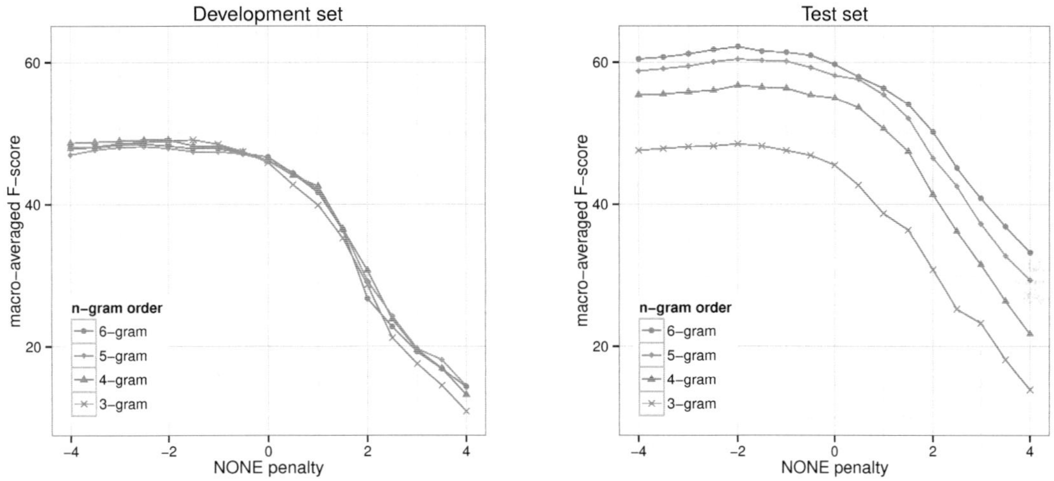

Figure 3: Performance of the baseline cross-lingual pronoun prediction system as a function of the NONE penalty and the n-gram order. Shown are results on the development and on the test datasets.

The official baseline score was computed with the NONE penalty set to an unoptimized default value of 0. We used the same 5-gram language model that was part of the baseline for the pronoun-focused translation task, constructed with news texts, parliament debates, and the TED talks of the training/development portion.

After completing the evaluation, we ran additional experiments to analyze the effect of the NONE penalty and the order of the n-gram model on the performance of the baseline system. The results are shown on Figure 3, where we can see that the optimal value for the NONE penalty, both for the development and for the test set, would have been around -2. This is expected, since a negative penalty value penalizes the omission of pronouns in the output. The system works robustly for a wide variety of negative penalty values, but if the penalty is set to a positive value, which encourages pronoun omission, the performance degrades quickly.

It is interesting that the performance of a 3-gram model is very similar on the development and on the test set. Increasing the n-gram order has almost no effect for the development set, but for the test set it yields substantial gains in terms of both macro-averaged F-score (see Figure 3) and accuracy (not shown here). We plan a detailed analysis of this in future work, but one hypothesis is that it is due to the test set's better coverage of infrequent pronouns.

Overall, the language model baseline is surprisingly strong since the following (or preceding) verb group often contains information about number, gender, obliqueness, and animacy. It goes without saying that much of this information is not present in an actual MT system, which would have as much difficulty reconstructing number and gender information in verb groups as in argument pronouns. Thus, to achieve a good score, systems have to use both source-side and target-side information.

5.3 Submitted Systems

For the cross-lingual pronoun prediction task, we received submissions from eight groups. Some of them also submitted a second, contrastive run. Six of the groups submitted system description papers, and one of the two remaining groups formally withdrew its submission after evaluation.

All six groups with system description papers used some form of machine learning. The main difference was whether or not they explicitly attempted to resolve pronominal coreference. Two systems relied on explicit anaphora resolution: UEDIN and MALTA. They both applied the Stanford coreference resolver (Lee et al., 2011) on the source language text, then projected the antecedents to the target language through the word alignments, and finally obtained morphological tags with the Morfette software (Chrupała et al., 2008). The UEDIN system (Wetzel et al., 2015) was built around a maximum entropy classifier. In addition to local context and antecedent information, it used the NADA tool (Bergsma and Yarowsky, 2011) to identify non-referring pronouns and included predictions by a standard n-gram language model as a feature. The MALTA system (Pham and van der Plas, 2015) was based on a feed-forward neural network combined with word2vec continuous-space word embeddings (Mikolov et al., 2013). It used local context and antecedent information.

The other systems did not use explicit anaphora resolution, but attempted to gather relevant information about possible antecedents by considering a certain number of preceding, or preceding and following, noun phrases. They differed in the type of classifier and in the information sources used. UU-TIEDEMANN (Tiedemann, 2015) used a linear support vector machine with local features and simple surface features derived from preceding noun phrases. WHATELLES (Callin et al., 2015) used a neural network classifier based on work by Hardmeier et al. (2013b), but replacing all (explicit or latent) anaphora resolution with information extracted from preceding noun phrases. The IDIAP system (Luong et al., 2015) used a Naïve Bayes classifier and extracted features from both preceding and following noun phrases to account for the possibility of cataphoric references. The GENEVA system (Loáiciga, 2015) used maximum entropy classification; unlike the other submissions, it included features derived from syntactic parse trees.

5.4 Evaluation

For the automatic evaluation, we developed a scoring script that calculates the following statistics:

- confusion matrix showing (*i*) the count for each gold/predicted pair, and (*ii*) the sums for each row/column;
- accuracy;
- precision (P), recall (R), and F-score for each label;
- micro-averaged P, R, F-score (note that in our setup, micro-F is the same as accuracy);
- macro-averaged P, R, F-score.

The script performs the scoring twice:

- using coarse-grained labels (*ce*, {*cela*+*ça*}, *elle*, *elles*, *il*, *ils*, {OTHER+*on*});
- using fine-grained labels (*ce*, *cela*, *elle*, *elles*, *il*, *ils*, *on*, *ça*, OTHER).

The official score was the macro-averaged F-score using fine-grained labels.

5.5 Discussion

The results for the cross-lingual pronoun prediction task are shown in Table 9. The table includes the scores for both the primary and the secondary submissions; the latter are marked with 2. The three highest scores in each column are marked in boldface. The official score was the macro-averaged F-score, which is reported in the second column.

As in the first subtask (the pronoun-focused translation task), we find that the baseline system, BASELINE-NP0 (here a simple n-gram-based model) outperformed all the participating systems on the official macro-averaged F-score. Note that the performance of the baseline depends on the NONE penalty; we set this parameter to 0, a default value which we did not optimize in any way.

Immediately following the baseline, there are several systems with macro-averaged F-scores ranging between 0.55 and 0.58 (Table 9). This seems to mark the level of performance that is achievable with the methods currently at our disposal.

We should note that while our baseline system outperformed all submissions, both primary and secondary, in terms of macro-averaged F-score, several systems performed better in terms of accuracy.

2: secondary submission				F-score								
		Macro-F	Accuracy	*ce*	*cela*	*elle*	*elles*	*il*	*ils*	*on*	*ça*	OTHER
BASELINE-NP0		**0.584**	0.663	0.817	**0.346**	**0.511**	**0.507**	0.480	0.745	**0.571**	0.539	0.739
UU-TIED		**0.579**	**0.742**	**0.862**	**0.235**	0.326	0.389	0.558	0.828	**0.557**	**0.557**	**0.901**
UEDIN		**0.571**	0.723	0.823	**0.213**	**0.417**	**0.479**	0.544	**0.834**	0.475	0.497	0.855
MALTA	2	0.565	**0.740**	**0.875**	0.111	0.378	0.359	**0.588**	0.828	**0.537**	0.494	**0.917**
MALTA		0.561	0.732	0.853	0.071	0.368	0.420	**0.579**	0.829	0.448	**0.585**	0.898
WHATELLES		0.553	0.721	**0.862**	0.156	0.346	0.436	0.561	**0.830**	0.451	0.452	0.882
UEDIN	2	0.550	0.714	0.823	0.083	**0.382**	**0.451**	**0.573**	0.823	0.448	0.523	0.840
UU-TIED	2	0.539	**0.734**	0.849	0.125	0.283	0.242	0.545	**0.838**	0.516	**0.551**	**0.902**
GENEVA		0.437	0.592	0.647	0.197	0.365	0.321	0.475	0.761	0.340	0.075	0.757
GENEVA	2	0.421	0.579	0.611	0.147	0.353	0.313	0.442	0.759	0.310	0.092	0.759
IDIAP		0.206	0.307	0.282	0.000	0.235	0.205	0.164	0.429	0.000	0.149	0.391
IDIAP	2	0.164	0.407	0.152	0.000	0.000	0.000	0.065	0.668	0.000	0.072	0.518
A3-108		0.129	0.240	0.225	0.000	0.020	0.033	0.132	0.246	0.047	0.067	0.391
(WITHDRAWN)		0.122	0.325	0.220	0.000	0.000	0.000	0.187	0.134	0.000	0.000	0.555

Table 9: Results for the cross-lingual pronoun prediction task.

The reason why we chose macro-averaged F-score rather than accuracy as our primary metric is that it places more weight on the rare categories: we wanted to reward efforts to improve the performance for the rare pronouns such as *elles*. This choice was motivated by the findings of Hardmeier et al. (2013b), who observed that the performance on the rare classes strongly depended on the classifier's capacity to make use of coreference information. It is worth noting that none of their classifiers used target language *n*-gram information. Yet, in our shared task, we observed that our *n*-gram baseline, despite having no access to antecedent information beyond the extent of the *n*-gram window, performed better than systems that did have access to such information; this was especially true for classes such as *elle* and *elles*, which supposedly require knowledge about antecedents.

While a detailed analysis of this observation must be deferred to future work, we can think of two possible explanations. On the one hand, even after removing the pronoun translations, there remains enough information about gender and number in the inflections of the surrounding words, and *n*-gram models are very good at picking up on this sort of information. Thus, the presence of a nearby adjective or participle with feminine inflection may be enough for an *n*-gram model to make the right guess about the translation of a pronoun.

On the other hand, there is evidence that *n*-gram models are very good at recognising the *typical*, rather than the *actual*, antecedent of a pronoun based on context features (Hardmeier, 2014, 137–138). This may be another factor contributing to the good performance of the *n*-gram baseline.

Finally, it is interesting to note that systems with similar overall performance perform very differently on individual pronoun classes. UU-TIEDEMANN, which is the second-best submission after the baseline in terms of both macro-averaged F-score and accuracy, is very strong on all classes *except* for personal pronouns, that is, the classes *ce*, *cela*, *on*, and *ça*. In contrast, the third-best system, UEDIN is much stronger on *elle* and *elles*. Without additional experiments, it is impossible to say whether this is due to its use of anaphora resolution or to some other factors.

6 Conclusions

We have described the design and evaluation of the shared task at DiscoMT 2015, which included two different, but related subtasks, focusing on the difficulty of handling pronouns in MT. We prepared and released training and testing datasets, evaluation tools, and baseline systems for both subtasks, making it relatively easy to join. This effort was rewarded by the attention that the task attracted in the community. With six primary submissions to the pronoun-focused translation task, and eight to the cross-lingual pronoun prediction task, we feel that the acceptance of the task was high and that our goal of establishing the state of the art in pronoun-aware MT has been accomplished.

The results suggest that the problem of pronoun translation is far from solved. Even for cross-lingual pronoun prediction, where the entire translation of the input, except for the translations of the pronouns, is given, none of the participating systems reached an accuracy of more than 75 % or a macro-averaged F-score of more than 60 %.

In other words, even though the actual challenge of translating the source text was completely removed from the task, and despite the focused efforts of eight groups, we still find ourselves in a situation where one pronoun in four was predicted incorrectly by the best-performing system.

This tells us something about the difficulty of the task: In the real world, an MT system has to generate hypotheses not only for the translation of pronouns, but also for the full text. Many clues that are successfully exploited by the pronoun prediction systems, such as word inflections in the neighbourhood of the pronouns, cannot be relied on in an MT setting because they must be generated by the MT system itself and are likely to be absent or incorrect before the translation process is completed. If it is difficult to choose the correct pronoun given the entire target language context, this should be even more challenging in MT.

In both tasks, the baseline systems, whose strongest components are standard *n*-gram models, outperformed all submissions on the official metrics. This suggests that there are aspects of the pronoun generation problem, and possibly of *n*-gram models, that we do not fully understand. As a first step towards deeper analysis of the shared task results, it will be necessary to study why *n*-gram models perform better than systems specifically targetting pronoun translation. In the pronoun prediction task, they may exploit local context clues more aggressively, while the submitted classifiers, designed with MT applications and unreliable context in mind, tend to make incomplete use of this readily available information. However, while this may be a reason for the good performance of the baseline in the prediction task, it does not explain the results for the pronoun-focused translation task.

In any case, while this shared task has not revealed a substantially better method for pronoun translation than a plain *n*-gram model, we should certainly not conclude that *n*-gram models are sufficient for this task. In the pronoun-focused translation task, all systems, including the baseline, had error rates of 1 in 3 or higher, which confirms earlier findings showing that pronoun translation is indeed a serious problem for SMT (Hardmeier and Federico, 2010; Scherrer et al., 2011). We should therefore see the results of this shared task as an incentive to continue research on pronoun translation. We believe that our resources, methods and findings will prove useful for this endeavour.

Acknowledgements

The manual evaluation of the pronoun-focused translation task was made possible thanks to a grant from the European Association for Machine Translation (EAMT). We gratefully acknowledge the help of our annotators, Charlotta Jonasson and Anna Lernefalk, and we are indebted to Bonnie Webber for proofreading a draft of this paper. CH and JT were supported by the Swedish Research Council under project 2012-916 *Discourse-Oriented Machine Translation*. The work of CH, SS, and JT is part of the Swedish strategic research programme eSSENCE. MC was supported by the CRACKER project, which received funding from the European Union's Horizon 2020 research and innovation programme under grant no. 645357.

References

Shane Bergsma and David Yarowsky. 2011. NADA: A robust system for non-referential pronoun detection. In *Proceedings of the 8th Discourse Anaphora and Anaphor Resolution Colloquium*, volume 7099 of *Lecture Notes in Computer Science*, pages 12–23, Faro, Portugal.

Steven Bird, Edward Loper, and Ewan Klein. 2009. *Natural Language Processing with Python*. O'Reilly, Beijing.

Ondrej Bojar, Christian Buck, Christian Federmann, Barry Haddow, Philipp Koehn, Johannes Leveling, Christof Monz, Pavel Pecina, Matt Post, Herve Saint-Amand, Radu Soricut, Lucia Specia, and Aleš Tamchyna. 2014. Findings of the 2014 workshop on statistical machine translation. In *Proceedings of the Ninth Workshop on Statistical Machine Translation*, pages 12–58, Baltimore, Maryland, USA.

Gerhard Boysen. 1996. *Fransk grammatik*. Studentlitteratur, Lund.

Peter F. Brown, Stephen A. Della Pietra, Vincent J. Della Pietra, and Robert L. Mercer. 1993. The mathematics of statistical machine translation. *Computational Linguistics*, 19(2):263–311.

Jimmy Callin, Christian Hardmeier, and Jörg Tiedemann. 2015. Part-of-speech driven cross-lingual pronoun prediction with feed-forward neural networks. In *Proceedings of the Second Workshop on Discourse in Machine Translation*, pages 59–64, Lisbon, Portugal.

Chris Callison-Burch, Miles Osborne, and Philipp Koehn. 2006. Re-evaluating the role of BLEU in machine translation research. In *Proceedings of the 11th Conference of the European Chapter of the Association for Computational Linguistics*, pages 249–256, Trento, Italy.

Mauro Cettolo, Christian Girardi, and Marcello Federico. 2012. WIT^3: Web inventory of transcribed and translated talks. In *Proceedings of the 16th Conference of the European Association for Machine Translation (EAMT)*, pages 261–268, Trento, Italy.

Mauro Cettolo, Jan Niehues, Sebastian Stüker, Luisa Bentivogli, and Marcello Federico. 2014. Report on the 11th IWSLT evaluation campaign, IWSLT 2014. In *Proceedings of the International Workshop on Spoken Language Translation*, Hanoi, Vietnam.

Noam Chomsky. 1981. *Lectures on Government and Binding: The Pisa lectures*. Mouton de Gruyter.

Grzegorz Chrupała, Georgiana Dinu, and Josef van Genabith. 2008. Learning morphology with Morfette. In *Proceedings of the Sixth International Conference on Language Resources and Evaluation (LREC'08)*, pages 2362–2367, Marrakech, Morocco.

Michael Denkowski and Alon Lavie. 2011. Meteor 1.3: Automatic metric for reliable optimization and evaluation of machine translation systems. In *Proceedings of the Sixth Workshop on Statistical Machine Translation*, pages 85–91, Edinburgh, Scotland, UK.

George Doddington. 2002. Automatic evaluation of machine translation quality using n-gram cooccurrence statistics. In *Proceedings of the Second International Conference on Human Language Technology Research*, pages 138–145, San Diego, California, USA.

Chris Dyer, Victor Chahuneau, and Noah A. Smith. 2013. A simple, fast, and effective reparameterization of IBM model 2. In *Proceedings of the Conference of the North American Chapter of the Association for Computational Linguistics*, pages 644–648, Atlanta, Georgia, USA.

Alexander Fraser and Daniel Marcu. 2007. Measuring word alignment quality for statistical machine translation. *Computational Linguistics*, 33(3):293–303.

Maurice Grevisse and André Goosse. 1993. *Le bon usage: Grammaire française*. Duculot, Paris, 13e édition.

Liane Guillou, Christian Hardmeier, Aaron Smith, Jörg Tiedemann, and Bonnie Webber. 2014. ParCor 1.0: A parallel pronoun-coreference corpus to support statistical MT. In *Proceedings of the Tenth Language Resources and Evaluation Conference (LREC'14)*, pages 3191–3198, Reykjavík, Iceland.

Liane Guillou. 2015. Automatic post-editing for the DiscoMT pronoun translation task. In *Proceedings of the Second Workshop on Discourse in Machine Translation*, pages 65–71, Lisbon, Portugal.

Francisco Guzmán, Shafiq Joty, Lluís Màrquez, Alessandro Moschitti, Preslav Nakov, and Massimo Nicosia. 2014a. Learning to differentiate better from worse translations. In *Proceedings of the 2014 Conference on Empirical Methods in Natural Language Processing*, pages 214–220, Doha, Qatar.

Francisco Guzmán, Shafiq Joty, Lluís Màrquez, and Preslav Nakov. 2014b. Using discourse structure improves machine translation evaluation. In *Proceedings of the 52nd Annual Meeting of the Association for Computational Linguistics (Volume 1: Long Papers)*, pages 687–698, Baltimore, Maryland, USA.

Christian Hardmeier and Marcello Federico. 2010. Modelling pronominal anaphora in statistical machine translation. In *Proceedings of the Seventh International Workshop on Spoken Language Translation (IWSLT)*, pages 283–289, Paris, France.

Christian Hardmeier, Sara Stymne, Jörg Tiedemann, and Joakim Nivre. 2013a. Docent: A document-level decoder for phrase-based statistical machine translation. In *Proceedings of the 51st Annual Meeting of the Association for Computational Linguistics*, pages 193–198, Sofia, Bulgaria.

Christian Hardmeier, Jörg Tiedemann, and Joakim Nivre. 2013b. Latent anaphora resolution for cross-lingual pronoun prediction. In *Proceedings of the Conference on Empirical Methods in Natural Language Processing*, pages 380–391, Seattle, Washington, USA.

Christian Hardmeier. 2012. Discourse in statistical machine translation: A survey and a case study. *Discours*, 11.

Christian Hardmeier. 2014. *Discourse in Statistical Machine Translation*, volume 15 of *Studia Linguistica Upsaliensia*. Acta Universitatis Upsaliensis, Uppsala.

Christian Hardmeier. 2015. A document-level SMT system with integrated pronoun prediction. In *Proceedings of the Second Workshop on Discourse in Machine Translation*, pages 72–77, Lisbon, Portugal.

Kenneth Heafield, Ivan Pouzyrevsky, Jonathan H. Clark, and Philipp Koehn. 2013. Scalable modified Kneser-Ney language model estimation. In *Proceedings of the 51st Annual Meeting of the Association for Computational Linguistics*, pages 690–696, Sofia, Bulgaria.

Howard Johnson, Joel Martin, George Foster, and Roland Kuhn. 2007. Improving translation quality by discarding most of the phrasetable. In *Proceedings of the 2007 Joint Conference on Empirical Methods in Natural Language Processing and Computational Natural Language Learning*, pages 967–975, Prague, Czech Republic.

Shafiq Joty, Francisco Guzmán, Lluís Màrquez, and Preslav Nakov. 2014. DiscoTK: Using discourse structure for machine translation evaluation. In *Proceedings of the Ninth Workshop on Statistical Machine Translation*, pages 402–408, Baltimore, Maryland, USA.

Philipp Koehn, Hieu Hoang, Alexandra Birch, et al. 2007. Moses: Open source toolkit for Statistical Machine Translation. In *Annual Meeting of the Associ-*

ation for Computational Linguistics: Demonstration session, pages 177–180, Prague, Czech Republic.

Philipp Koehn. 2005. Europarl: A corpus for statistical machine translation. In *Proceedings of MT Summit X*, pages 79–86, Phuket, Thailand.

Klaus Krippendorff. 2004. Measuring the reliability of qualitative text analysis data. *Quality and Quantity*, 38(6):787–800.

Ronan Le Nagard and Philipp Koehn. 2010. Aiding pronoun translation with co-reference resolution. In *Proceedings of the Joint Fifth Workshop on Statistical Machine Translation and MetricsMATR*, pages 252–261, Uppsala, Sweden.

Heeyoung Lee, Yves Peirsman, Angel Chang, Nathanael Chambers, Mihai Surdeanu, and Dan Jurafsky. 2011. Stanford's multi-pass sieve coreference resolution system at the CoNLL-2011 shared task. In *Proceedings of the Fifteenth Conference on Computational Natural Language Learning: Shared Task*, pages 28–34, Portland, Oregon, USA.

Sharid Loáiciga and Eric Wehrli. 2015. Rule-based pronominal anaphora treatment for machine translation. In *Proceedings of the Second Workshop on Discourse in Machine Translation*, pages 86–93, Lisbon, Portugal.

Sharid Loáiciga. 2015. Predicting pronoun translation using syntactic, morphological and contextual features from parallel data. In *Proceedings of the Second Workshop on Discourse in Machine Translation*, pages 78–85, Lisbon, Portugal.

Ngoc Quang Luong, Lesly Miculicich Werlen, and Andrei Popescu-Belis. 2015. Pronoun translation and prediction with or without coreference links. In *Proceedings of the Second Workshop on Discourse in Machine Translation*, pages 94–100, Lisbon, Portugal.

Tomas Mikolov, Kai Chen, Greg Corrado, and Jeffrey Dean. 2013. Efficient estimation of word representations in vector space. In *International Conference on Learning Representations: Workshop Proceedings*.

Ruslan Mitkov and Catalina Barbu. 2003. Using bilingual corpora to improve pronoun resolution. *Languages in Contrast*, 4(2):201–211.

Franz Josef Och and Hermann Ney. 2000. Improved statistical alignment models. In *Proceedings of the 38th Annual Meeting of the Association for Computational Linguistics*, pages 440–447, Hongkong, China.

Franz Josef Och and Hermann Ney. 2003. A systematic comparison of various statistical alignment models. *Computational Linguistics*, 29(1):19–51.

Franz Josef Och. 2003. Minimum error rate training in Statistical Machine Translation. In *Proceedings of the 41st Annual Meeting of the Association for Computational Linguistics*, pages 160–167, Sapporo, Japan.

Kishore Papineni, Salim Roukos, Todd Ward, and Wei-Jing Zhu. 2002. BLEU: A method for automatic evaluation of machine translation. In *Proceedings of the 40th Annual Meeting of the Association for Computational Linguistics*, pages 311–318, Philadelphia, Pennsylvania, USA.

Ngoc-Quan Pham and Lonneke van der Plas. 2015. Predicting pronouns across languages with continuous word spaces. In *Proceedings of the Second Workshop on Discourse in Machine Translation*, pages 101–107, Lisbon, Portugal.

Yves Scherrer, Lorenza Russo, Jean-Philippe Goldman, Sharid Loáiciga, Luka Nerima, and Éric Wehrli. 2011. La traduction automatique des pronoms. Problèmes et perspectives. In Mathieu Lafourcade and Violaine Prince, editors, *Actes de la 18e conférence sur le Traitement Automatique des Langues Naturelles*, volume 2, pages 185–190, Montpellier, France.

William A. Scott. 1955. Reliability of content analysis: The case of nominal scale coding. *Public Opinion Quarterly*, 19(3):321–325.

Matthew Snover, Bonnie Dorr, Richard Schwartz, Linnea Micciulla, and John Makhoul. 2006. A study of translation edit rate with targeted human annotation. In *AMTA 2006: Proceedings of the 7th Conference of the Association for Machine Translation in the Americas*, pages 223–231, Cambridge, Massachusetts, USA.

Sara Stymne, Jörg Tiedemann, and Joakim Nivre. 2014. Estimating word alignment quality for SMT reordering tasks. In *Proceedings of the Ninth Workshop on Statistical Machine Translation*, pages 275–286, Baltimore, Maryland, USA.

Jörg Tiedemann. 2012. Parallel data, tools and interfaces in OPUS. In *Proceedings of the Eighth International Conference on Language Resources and Evaluation (LREC'12)*, pages 2214–2218, Istanbul, Turkey.

Jörg Tiedemann. 2015. Baseline models for pronoun prediction and pronoun-aware translation. In *Proceedings of the Second Workshop on Discourse in Machine Translation*, pages 108–114, Lisbon, Portugal.

Stephan Vogel, Hermann Ney, and Christoph Tillmann. 1996. HMM-based word alignment in statistical translation. In *Coling 1996: the 16th International Conference on Computational Linguistics*, pages 145–154, Copenhagen, Denmark.

Dominikus Wetzel, Adam Lopez, and Bonnie Webber. 2015. A maximum entropy classifier for cross-lingual pronoun prediction. In *Proceedings of the Second Workshop on Discourse in Machine Translation*, pages 115–121, Lisbon, Portugal.

Comparison of Coreference Resolvers for Deep Syntax Translation *

Michal Novák,* Dieke Oele,‡ Gertjan van Noord,‡
*Charles University in Prague, Faculty of Mathematics and Physics,
Institute of Formal and Applied Linguistics
mnovak@ufal.mff.cuni.cz
‡University of Groningen, The Netherlands
{d.oele,g.j.m.van.noord}@rug.nl

Abstract

This work focuses on using anaphora for machine translation with deep-syntactic transfer. We compare multiple coreference resolvers for English in terms of how they affect the quality of pronoun translation in English-Czech and English-Dutch machine translation systems with deep transfer. We examine which pronouns in the target language depend on anaphoric information, and design rules that take advantage of this information. The resolvers' performance measured by translation quality is contrasted with their intrinsic evaluation results. In addition, a more detailed manual analysis of English-to-Czech translation was carried out.

1 Introduction

Over the last years, the interest in addressing coreference-related issues in Machine Translation (MT) has increased. Multiple works focused on using information coming from a Coreference Resolution (CR) system to improve pronoun translation in phrase-based frameworks (Le Nagard and Koehn, 2010; Hardmeier and Federico, 2010; Guillou, 2012). A similar task was addressed in the TectoMT deep syntax tree-to-tree translation system (Žabokrtský et al., 2008). Novák et al. (2013a; 2013b) presented specialized models for the personal pronoun *it* and reflexive pronouns in English-Czech translation, which resulted in an improvement in terms of human evaluation. Although these models were tailored to pronoun translation, they only addressed cases where anaphora information is in fact not needed. For proper translation of other pronouns, however, coreference must be involved.

The present work concentrates on exploiting coreference for deep syntax MT. We integrate three coreference resolvers for English into TectoMT system, namely the Treex CR (Popel and Žabokrtský, 2010), the Stanford CR (Lee et al., 2013), and BART (Versley et al., 2008), and observe their effects on translation quality. Taking linguistic observations on the target languages into account, we design rules that make use of the information supplied by the CR systems. We apply this approach to English-Czech and English-Dutch translation.

This paper is structured as follows. In Section 2, we introduce the grammar of Czech and Dutch pronouns with a special emphasis on cases where form depends on anaphoric relations. Section 3 gives a brief description of the used CR systems. In Section 4, the TectoMT system is presented, along with our rules exploiting coreference information. In Section 5, the individual configurations of the MT system are evaluated using BLEU score and human evaluation. These evaluations are contrasted with intrinsic scores of the CR systems. The results of English-to-Czech translation are analyzed in a greater detail in Section 6. Ultimately, this paper is concluded in Section 7.

2 Pronouns in the target languages

The system of anaphoric pronouns is similar for Czech and Dutch, both containing personal, possessive, reflexive, relative, and demonstrative pronouns.[1]

In the present work, we mainly concentrate on a subset of anaphoric pronouns whose form cannot be reliably determined without knowing the closest co-referring mention (the antecedent) and its

*This work has been supported by the 7th Framework Programme of the EU grant QTLeap (No. 610516), SVV project 260 104 and the GAUK grant 338915. It is using language resources hosted by the LINDAT/CLARIN Research Infrastructure, Project No. LM2010013 of the Ministry of Education, Youth and Sports. We also thank Ondřej Dušek and Rudolf Rosa for their help with annotation and proof-reading.

[1] We omit demonstrative pronouns in this work as they are not consistently treated by any of the CR systems used here.

Proceedings of the Second Workshop on Discourse in Machine Translation (DiscoMT), pages 17–23,
Lisbon, Portugal, 17 September 2015.

grammatical properties. Grammatical properties (such as morphological gender, number, or syntactic position) and the agreement of such pronoun and its antecedent are the key factors that suggest to the reader which entity the pronoun refers to.

2.1 Pronouns in Czech

The typology of Czech pronouns is the following:

Personal pronouns. Their form depends on the person (cf. *já /I/* in 1st person and *ty /you/* in 2nd person), number (cf. *já /I/* in singular and *my /we/* in plural), gender (cf. masculine *on /he/*, feminine *ona /she/* and neuter *ono /it/*), and case (cf. *on /he/* in nominative and *jemu /to him/* in dative). In addition, some forms may have a short or a long variant. As Czech is a pro-drop language, pronouns in the subject can be even omitted from the surface.[2] Out of these features, only gender and number depend on anaphora – they must agree with antecedent's gender and number.

Possessive pronouns. Unlike personal pronouns, two types of gender and number are distinguished for possessives: one agreeing with the possessed object and one agreeing with the possessor (cf. feminine–masculine *s jeho ženou /with his wife/*, masculine–feminine *s jejím mužem /with her husband/* and feminine–feminine *s její ženou /with her wife/*). The latter type of gender and number depends on anaphora, as the antecedent of the possessive pronoun is in fact their possessor.

Reflexive pronouns. Their form is determined only by the case and variant. Unlike English, they carry no gender and number information. However, information on anaphora is still required to specify whether a reflexive or a personal pronoun should be used, since reflexive pronoun are used in case of coreference with the sentence subject.

Reflexive possessive pronouns. A special category of pronouns which is used instead of a possessive pronoun if its possessor is the sentence subject. They do not depend on other grammatical features of the antecedent than its syntactic position, as reflexives do.

Relative pronouns. Relative pronouns need to agree in gender and number[3] with their antecedent. However, their usage is limited by the nature of their antecedents, e.g., while the pronoun *který /which, that, who/* can be used in most cases where the antecedent is a noun phrase, the pronoun *což /which/* is required whenever referring to a clause or a longer utterance.

2.2 Pronouns in Dutch

The typology of Dutch anaphoric pronouns is the following:

Personal pronouns. The form of Dutch personal pronouns depends on person, case, number, and gender. They are used in a similar way as in English. Nouns are partitioned by the article they use: *de* or *het*. While *het-* nouns are referred to by the pronoun *het*, masculine pronouns are mostly used for *de-* nouns. Feminine pronouns can be used for abstract feminine nouns.

Possessive pronouns. Possessive pronouns differ with respect to person, gender, and number. In addition, some of them agree in gender with their head noun (e.g., *ons* versus *onze /our/*). They make no distinction based on whether they refer to a *het-* or *de-* noun.

Reflexive pronouns. Each Dutch personal pronoun has a reflexive form that can differ with respect to person and number, but not gender, i.e. *zich/zichzelf* is used for all genders.

Relative pronouns. The distinction between relative pronouns *die* and *dat* is determined by the type of the antecedent. *Die* is used when it refers to a *de-* noun or any plural form while *dat* is used for singular *het-* nouns. When the pronoun refers to a person with a direct object function, *wie* is used. *Wat* can refer to indefinite words, superlatives, or whole phrases while *welke* can solely refer to *de-* words but is mostly used in formal texts. A relative pronoun turns into a so-called pronominal adverb if it is part of a prepositional phrase (e.g., preposition+*die/dat* is replaced by *waar*+preposition).

3 Coreference resolution systems for English

We apply the Treex CR system, the BART system and the Stanford Deterministic CR system in our experiments[4]. As neither BART nor the Stanford

[2]In that case, some of the pronoun's properties can be reconstructed from the verb thanks to subject-verb agreement.

[3]Possessor's gender and number in case of possessive relative pronouns.

[4]The reasons for choosing the latter two systems are twofold: they are freely available and they perform close to the state of the art, as confirmed by the results of CoNLL-2012 Shared Task (Pradhan et al., 2012).

system target relative pronouns, we combine these two systems with a Treex module for relative pronouns (the *Treex-relat* module).

3.1 Treex Coreference Resolution System

This system is a part of the Treex framework (Popel and Žabokrtský, 2010) and has been used for English-to-Czech translation in the TectoMT system (Žabokrtský et al., 2008). It consists of several modules; each of them focuses on a specific type of coreferential relations in English:[5] anaphora of relative pronouns (the *Treex-relat* module) and personal, possessive, and reflexive pronouns (the *Treex-other* module). All the modules are rule-based, making use of syntactic representation of the sentence as well as simple context heuristics.

3.2 BART

BART 2.0 (Versley et al., 2008; Uryupina et al., 2012) is a modular toolkit for end-to-end coreference resolution. It is based on mention-pair model, which means that a classifier makes a decision for every pair of mentions whether they belong to the same coreference cluster or not. Subsequently, the mentions paired by pairwise decisions need to be partitioned into coreference chains. The model is trained using the WEKA machine-learning toolkit (Witten and Frank, 2005). Features for English are identical to those used in virtually all state-of-the-art coreference resolvers (Soon et al., 2001).

3.3 Stanford Deterministic Coreference Resolution System

The Stanford resolver (Lee et al., 2013) is a state-of-the-art rule-based system. Unlike BART, it is an entity-based system, meaning that in each step, the system decides on assigning a mention into one of the partially created coreference chains. It proceeds in multiple steps – *sieves*, starting with high-precision rules and ending with those with a lower precision but a higher recall. The version of the system used here consist of ten sieves including the sieve for pronominal mentions in quotations, sieves for string match, head match, proper head noun match, and the pronoun match applied at the end.

[5]A similar system for Czech pronouns is also a part of the Treex framework.

4 The TectoMT System and Coreference

TectoMT (Žabokrtský et al., 2008) is a tree-to-tree machine translation system whose translation process follows the analysis-transfer-synthesis pipeline.

In the analysis stage, the source sentence is transformed into a deep syntax dependency representation based on the Prague tectogrammatics theory (Sgall et al., 1986). At this point, CR systems are applied to interlink the tree representation with coreference relations.

The source language tree structure is transferred to the target language using three factors: translation models for deep lemmas, morpho-syntactic form labels, and a rule-based factor for other grammatical properties. For the most part, isomorphism of the tree representation in both languages is assumed, and the tree is translated node-by-node.

In the last step, the deep representation is transformed to a surface sentence in the target language.

English-to-Czech translation has been developed and tuned in TectoMT since its very beginning. Translation to other languages, including Dutch, was added only recently (Popel et al., 2015).

4.1 Rules Using Coreference

During the transfer and the synthesis stage, language-dependent rules that make use of the projected coreference relations are applied. The rules are based on linguistic observations presented in Section 2.

Even if a given grammatical property is ruled by the antecedent, it is not always necessary to use anaphora information. The correct form in the target language can be inferred from the source language word itself. For example, genders in English and Czech are of a different nature. While the gender of English pronouns is *notional*, reserving masculine and feminine gender exclusively for persons (Quirk et al., 1985), the Czech gender is *grammatical* with all gender values more evenly distributed. However, masculine and feminine pronouns mostly remain the same in English-to-Czech translation. Other similar phenomena can be observed in both Czech and Dutch.

Czech. Rules employing coreference resolution have been used in TectoMT English-Czech translation since its beginning, but their contribution has not been evaluated so far. The following rules are used:

- Impose agreement in gender and number for personal, possessive, and relative pronouns translated from English pronouns *it* and *its* as well as English relative pronouns.[6]
- Transform a possessive to a reflexive possessive pronoun if it refers to a sentence subject.
- Transform a relative pronoun referring to a verb phrase into the Czech relative pronoun *což*.

Dutch. In translation to Dutch, possessives can be inferred solely using the source pronoun. Therefore, only personal and relative pronouns are targeted with the following coreference-based rules:

- Impose agreement in gender (*het-* or *de-* type) for personal pronouns translated from the English pronoun *it*.
- For relative pronouns, a corresponding form is picked based on whether the pronoun is bound in a prepositional phrase, refers to a verb phrase, a person, or a *het-* or *de-* noun.

5 Automatic evaluation

The TectoMT translation models were trained on parallel data from CzEng 1.0 (Bojar et al., 2012) and a concatenation of Europarl (Koehn, 2005), Dutch parallel corpus (Macken et al., 2007) and KDE4 localizations (Tiedemann, 2009), for Czech and Dutch, respectively.

We tested the English-Czech and English-Dutch translation systems on datasets from two different domains: the news domain, represented by English-Czech test set for the WMT 2012 Translation Task (Callison-Burch et al., 2012) as well as the last 36 documents from English-Dutch News Commentary data set (Tiedemann, 2012),[7] and the IT domain, represented by the corresponding pairs of the QTLeap Corpus Batch 2 (Osenova et al., 2015).[8]

The evaluation was conducted for several configurations of TectoMT. The *Baseline* systems did not use any coreference-related rules while the remaining configurations apply all TectoMT coreference rules. They combine the Treex CR module for relative pronouns *Treex-relat* with the three resolvers detailed in Section 3: the *Treex-other* module, the Stanford system, and the BART system. Table 1 shows BLEU scores of all four configurations with respect to the domain and the target language. In addition, it presents an intrinsic evaluation of the CR – anaphora resolution F-scores measured on English parts of sections 20–21 of the Prague Czech-English Dependency Treebank (Hajič et al., 2012).

The results reveal that for every domain and language, there is at least a single coreference-aware configuration that outperforms the baseline.

In addition to the substantial BLEU difference between the Czech best system and the baseline, all the coreference-aware configurations improved upon the baseline translation into Czech. On the other hand, we observed a very small improvement of the best Dutch system over the baseline.

This disproportion reflects the fact that whereas English-to-Czech TectoMT has been developed and tuned over seven years, the English-to-Dutch translation was added only recently.

Comparable scores of Czech systems on the IT domain can be attributed to two aspects: TectoMT has mostly been tuned to the news domain, and the distribution of pronoun types may differ.

When contrasting BLEU scores with the intrinsic evalution of CR systems, one can see that although their performance is similar, their effect on translation quality varies across languages and domains. The results also show that out of all pronoun types, CR of relative pronouns is the most reliable. This is confirmed by consistent gains of the *Treex-relat* system over the baseline.

6 Manual analysis of the results

BLEU score has previously been shown not to be suitable for measuring small modifications such as changes in pronouns (Le Nagard and Koehn, 2010; Hardmeier and Federico, 2010; Guillou, 2012; Hardmeier, 2014). Despite these findings, we succeeded in getting a better BLEU score with coreference-aware systems for English-to-Czech translation. To reveal a reason for such behaviour, we conducted a detailed analysis of the translation results on the English-Czech news domain dataset.

The data-set comprising almost 64,000 English words contains 894 occurrences are relative pronouns, 770 possessive pronouns and 1950

[6] For other English pronouns, it appeared to be sufficient to copy their gender and number to the translated pronoun.

[7] Since the original dataset contains a substantial amount of neighboring words stuck together, we corrected it using a spellchecker.

[8] `http://metashare.metanet4u.eu/go2/qtleapcorpus`

	Czech		Dutch		Intrinsic			
	news	IT	news	IT	pers	poss	relat	total
Baseline	11.12	30.55	11.76	24.22	—			
Treex-relat	11.45	31.08	**11.78**	**24.25**	–	–	73.64	
Treex-relat+other	**11.54**	31.08	10.55	24.06	54.05	64.09	73.64	62.78
Stanford + Treex-relat	11.45	**31.10**	11.79	24.22	54.08	57.20	73.64	60.65
BART + Treex-relat	11.48	31.09	11.76	24.17	56.61	60.02	73.64	62.45

Table 1: BLEU scores of the TecotMT system for English-Czech and English-Dutch translation using various CR systems, contrasted with their intrinsic evaluation measured by F-score.

	pers	poss	relat
Treex-relat	–	–	337
Treex-relat+other	0	339	337
Stanford + Treex-relat	40	44	337
BART + Treex-relat	128	188	337
potential	1950	770	894

Table 2: Number of changed Czech pronoun translations if the Baseline system is replaced by each of the coreference-aware systems. The last line indicates number of English pronouns of a particular type in the dataset.

personal pronouns. Table 2 presents in how many cases the translation of these pronouns was changed when the baseline system was replaced by each of the coreference-aware systems. [9]

Not surprisingly, all the systems produced exactly the same amount of changes in relative pronouns. We randomly sampled and manually inspected 30 translation changes.[10] Most of the changes are caused by imposing agreement between the pronoun and its antecedent. Compared with the Baseline, in 24 cases the output is better, it is worse in 3 cases and in 3 cases equally bad. In 12 of the improved cases, the produced form of the Czech relative pronoun matches a unigram in the reference translation. Since the relative pronouns are often subjects of the clause, the form of the governing verb is also affected due to agreement rules in Czech. This typically results in matches longer than unigrams, justifying the BLEU score improvement.

Regarding possessive pronouns, the Stanford coreference resolver seems to be very conservative explaining the lack of change in BLEU score compared to the Treex-relat system. We sampled 30 changes of the Treex-relat+other system and observed 16 better, 7 worse, 4 equally good and 3 equally bad translations compared to the Baseline system. Most of the changes stem from the transformation of possessives to reflexive possessives. The improvement is less convincing for relative pronouns, which correlates with the measured BLEU scores.

As for personal pronouns, the Stanford system confirmed its conservative nature while surprisingly, the Treex coreference system produced no change at all. We sampled 30 translations produced by BART+Treex-relat system and compared it with the Baseline system: 14 translation were better, 7 worse, and 9 equally bad.

For English-to-Dutch translation, we carried out human evaluation with no pronoun type distinction, comparing 30 changed sentences randomly selected from the news domain dataset. The best system's output was considered better in 13 cases, worse in 11 cases, confirming the marginal BLEU changes.

7 Conclusion

In this work, we compared three systems for coreference resolution with regard to what effect they have on the quality of deep syntax machine translation. We found that the results are heavily affected by the quality of the used coreference rules as well as by the language they are applied to. While coreference is essential for better results in the well-tuned translation into Czech, it is so far disputable in translation into Dutch. The reliability of coreference resolution also plays a key role there as the most reliable resolver for relative pronouns was the only one that consistently improved the translation. Manual analysis of the results confirmed the outcomes of the automatic evaluation.

[9] If the subject pronoun is dropped from the surface, we decide on the verb properties.

[10] In manual evaluation, the source, automatic and reference translations of the current and two previous sentences were presented to the human judge.

References

Ondřej Bojar, Zdeněk Žabokrtský, Ondřej Dušek, Petra Galuščáková, Martin Majliš, David Mareček, Jiří Maršík, Michal Novák, Martin Popel, and Aleš Tamchyna. 2012. The joy of parallelism with CzEng 1.0. In *Proceedings of LREC 2012*. European Language Resources Association.

Chris Callison-Burch, Philipp Koehn, Christof Monz, Matt Post, Radu Soricut, and Lucia Specia. 2012. Findings of the 2012 Workshop on Statistical Machine Translation. In *Proceedings of the Seventh Workshop on Statistical Machine Translation*, pages 10–51. Association for Computational Linguistics.

Liane Guillou. 2012. Improving Pronoun Translation for Statistical Machine Translation. In *Proceedings of the Student Research Workshop at the 13th Conference of the EACL*, pages 1–10. Association for Computational Linguistics.

Jan Hajič, Eva Hajičová, Jarmila Panevová, Petr Sgall, Ondřej Bojar, Silvie Cinková, Eva Fučíková, Marie Mikulová, Petr Pajas, Jan Popelka, Jiří Semecký, Jana Šindlerová, Jan Štěpánek, Josef Toman, Zdeňka Urešová, and Zdeněk Žabokrtský. 2012. Announcing Prague Czech-English Dependency Treebank 2.0. In *Proceedings of the 8th International Conference on Language Resources and Evaluation (LREC 2012)*. European Language Resources Association.

Christian Hardmeier and Marcello Federico. 2010. Modelling Pronominal Anaphora in Statistical Machine Translation. In *Proceedings of the seventh International Workshop on Spoken Language Translation (IWSLT)*, pages 283–289. ISCA.

Christian Hardmeier. 2014. *Discourse in Statistical Machine Translation*. Ph.D. thesis, Uppsala University.

Philipp Koehn. 2005. Europarl: A Parallel Corpus for Statistical Machine Translation. In *Conference Proceedings: the tenth Machine Translation Summit*, pages 79–86. AAMT.

Ronan Le Nagard and Philipp Koehn. 2010. Aiding Pronoun Translation with Co-Reference Resolution. In *Proceedings of the Joint Fifth Workshop on Statistical Machine Translation and MetricsMATR*, pages 252–261. Association for Computational Linguistics.

Heeyoung Lee, Angel Chang, Yves Peirsman, Nathanael Chambers, Mihai Surdeanu, and Dan Jurafsky. 2013. Deterministic Coreference Resolution Based on Entity-centric, Precision-ranked Rules. *Comput. Linguist.*, 39(4):885–916.

Lieve Macken, Julia Trushkina, and Lidia Rura. 2007. Dutch parallel corpus: Mt corpus and translator's aid. In *In Proceedings of the Machine Translation Summit XI*, pages 313–320. European Association for Machine Translation.

Michal Novák, Anna Nedoluzhko, and Zdeněk Žabokrtský. 2013a. Translation of "It" in a Deep Syntax Framework. In *51st Annual Meeting of the Association for Computational Linguistics Proceedings of the Workshop on Discourse in Machine Translation*. Omnipress, Inc.

Michal Novák, Zdeněk Žabokrtský, and Anna Nedoluzhko. 2013b. Two Case Studies on Translating Pronouns in a Deep Syntax Framework. In *Proceedings of the 6th International Joint Conference on Natural Language Processing*, pages 1037–1041. Asian Federation of Natural Language Processing.

Petya Osenova, Rosa Del Gaudio, João Silva, Aljoscha Burchardt, Martin Popel, Gertjan van Noord, Dieke Oele, and Gorka Labaka. 2015. Interim report on the curation of language resources and tools for deep mt. Technical Report Deliverable D2.5, Version 2.0, QTLeap Project.

Martin Popel and Zdeněk Žabokrtský. 2010. TectoMT: Modular NLP framework. In *Lecture Notes in Artificial Intelligence, Proceedings of the 7th International Conference on Advances in Natural Language Processing (IceTAL 2010)*, volume 6233. Springer.

Martin Popel, Jaroslava Hlaváčová, Ondřej Bojar, Ondřej Dušek, António Branco, Luís Gomes, João Rodrigues, Andreia Querido João Silva, Nuno Rendeiro, Marisa Campos, Diana Amaral, Eleftherios Avramidis, Aljoscha Burchardt, Maja Popovic, Arle Lommel, Iliana Simova, Nora Aranberri, Gorka Labaka, Gertjan van Noord, Rosa Del Gaudio, Michal Novák, Rudolf Rosa, Aleš Tamchyna, and Jan Hajič. 2015. Report on the first mt pilot and its evaluation. Technical Report Deliverable D2.4, Version 1.8, QTLeap Project.

Sameer Pradhan, Alessandro Moschitti, Nianwen Xue, Olga Uryupina, and Yuchen Zhang. 2012. CoNLL-2012 Shared Task: Modeling Multilingual Unrestricted Coreference in OntoNotes. In *Proceedings of the Sixteenth Conference on Computational Natural Language Learning (CoNLL 2012)*, Jeju, Korea.

Randolph Quirk, Sidney Greenbaum, Geoffrey Leech, and Jan Svartvik. 1985. *A Comprehensive Grammar of the English Language*. Longman.

Petr Sgall, Eva Hajičová, and Jarmila Panevová. 1986. *The Meaning of the Sentence in Its Semantic and Pragmatic Aspects*. D. Reidel Publishing Company, Dordrecht.

Wee Meng Soon, Hwee Tou Ng, and Daniel Chung Yong Lim. 2001. A Machine Learning Approach to Coreference Resolution of Noun Phrases. *Comput. Linguist.*, 27(4):521–544.

Jörg Tiedemann. 2009. News from OPUS - A collection of multilingual parallel corpora with tools and interfaces. In *Recent Advances in Natural Language Processing*, volume V, pages 237–248. John Benjamins, Amsterdam/Philadelphia.

Jörg Tiedemann. 2012. Parallel Data, Tools and Interfaces in OPUS. In *Proceedings of the Eight International Conference on Language Resources and Evaluation (LREC'12)*. European Language Resources Association.

Olga Uryupina, Alessandro Moschitti, and Massimo Poesio. 2012. BART Goes Multilingual: The UniTN/Essex Submission to the CoNLL-2012 Shared Task. In *Joint Conference on EMNLP and CoNLL - Shared Task*, pages 122–128. Association for Computational Linguistics.

Yannick Versley, Simone Paolo Ponzetto, Massimo Poesio, Vladimir Eidelman, Alan Jern, Jason Smith, Xiaofeng Yang, and Alessandro Moschitti. 2008. BART: A Modular Toolkit for Coreference Resolution. In *Proceedings of the 46th Annual Meeting of the Association for Computational Linguistics on Human Language Technologies: Demo Session*, pages 9–12. Association for Computational Linguistics.

Ian H. Witten and Eibe Frank. 2005. *Data Mining: Practical Machine Learning Tools and Techniques, Second Edition (Morgan Kaufmann Series in Data Management Systems)*. Morgan Kaufmann Publishers Inc.

Zdeněk Žabokrtský, Jan Ptáček, and Petr Pajas. 2008. TectoMT: highly modular MT system with tectogrammatics used as transfer layer. In *Proceedings of the Third Workshop on Statistical Machine Translation*, page 167–170. Association for Computational Linguistics.

Analysing ParCor and its Translations by State-of-the-art SMT Systems

Liane Guillou
School of Informatics
University of Edinburgh
Scotland, United Kingdom
L.K.Guillou@sms.ed.ac.uk

Bonnie Webber
School of Informatics
University of Edinburgh
Scotland, United Kingdom
bonnie@inf.ed.ac.uk

Abstract

Previous work on pronouns in SMT has focussed on third-person pronouns, treating them all as anaphoric. Little attention has been paid to other uses or other types of pronouns. Believing that further progress requires careful analysis of pronouns as a whole, we have analysed a parallel corpus of annotated English-German texts to highlight some of the problems that hinder progress. We combine this with an assessment of the ability of two state-of-the-art systems to translate different pronoun types.

1 Introduction

Previous work on the translation of pronouns in Statistical Machine Translation (SMT) has focussed on the specific problem of translating *anaphoric* pronouns – i.e., ones that co-refer with an *antecedent* entity previously mentioned in the discourse (Le Nagard and Koehn, 2010; Hardmeier and Federico, 2010; Guillou, 2012; Novák et al., 2013; Hardmeier, 2014; Weiner, 2014). This is because languages differ in how an anaphoric pronoun relates to its antecedent, and the relationship does not fit naturally into the SMT pipeline. Some pronoun forms also have non-anaphoric uses, and there are other types of pronouns. Languages also differ as to what types of pronouns are used for what purposes.

To investigate similarities and differences in pronoun usage across languages, we conducted an analysis of the ParCor corpus[1] of pronoun annotations over a set of parallel English-German texts. The corpus contains a collection of texts from two different genres: 8 EU Bookshop[2] publications (written text) and 11 TED[3] Talks (transcribed planned speech). In the ParCor annotations, each pronoun is marked as being one of eight *types*: Anaphoric/cataphoric, event reference, extra-textual reference, pleonastic, addressee reference, speaker reference, generic reference, or other function[4]. Additional features are recorded for some pronoun types, for example anaphoric/cataphoric pronouns are linked to their antecedents. Full details of the annotation scheme are provided in Guillou et al. (2014).

Through analysing similarities and differences in pronoun use in these parallel texts, we hope to better understand the problems of translating different types of pronouns. This knowledge may in turn be used to build discourse-aware SMT systems in the future. In addition, through analysing translations produced by state-of-the art systems, we hope to understand how well current systems translate a range of pronoun types. This information may be used to identify the pronoun types where future efforts would be best directed.

The advantage of using the ParCor corpus is that it allows us to conduct part of the analyses automatically once we have word–aligned the parallel texts. The annotations also allow for the separation of ambiguous pronouns such as "it" which may serve as an anaphoric, event or pleonastic pronoun[5]. This allows for a more granular analysis than has been provided in other similar studies.

2 Previous Work

There has been previous work both on comparing pronoun usage in English and German (in the genre of business letters using comparable rather than parallel texts (Becher, 2011) and for the multi-genre GECCo corpus (Kunz and Lapshinova-Koltunski, 2015)) and on pronoun translation accuracy by SMT systems (Hardmeier and Federico, 2010; Novák et al., 2013;

[1] http://opus.lingfil.uu.se/ParCor/
[2] EU Bookshop: https://bookshop.europa.eu
[3] TED: WIT3 corpus: https://wit3.fbk.eu/
[4] Pronoun does not belong to any of the other categories
[5] Each pronoun type has different translation requirements

Proceedings of the Second Workshop on Discourse in Machine Translation (DiscoMT), pages 24–32,
Lisbon, Portugal, 17 September 2015.

Pronoun Type	TED Talks				EU Bookshop			
	English		German		English		German	
Anaphoric	*886*	*(27.71)*	*1,228*	*(40.52)*	*2,767*	*(20.32)*	*3,036*	*(22.72)*
Anaphoric (pronominal adverb)	N/A		N/A		70	(0.51)	84	(0.63)
Cataphoric	5	(0.16)	16	(0.53)	67	(0.49)	19	(0.14)
Event	264	(8.26)	331	(10.92)	239	(1.76)	255	(1.91)
Event (pronominal adverb)	N/A		N/A		0	(0.00)	78	(0.58)
Extra-textual reference	52	(1.63)	26	(0.86)	N/A		N/A	
Pleonastic (non-referential)	*61*	*(1.91)*	*224*	*(7.39)*	*191*	*(1.40)*	*391*	*(2.93)*
Addressee reference	499	(15.61)	525	(17.32)	112	(0.82)	76	(0.57)
Speaker reference	1,386	(43.35)	1,467	(48.41)	548	(4.02)	580	(4.34)
Generic	N/A		N/A		9	(0.07)	58	(0.43)
Pronoun (other)	N/A		N/A		135	(0.99)	126	(0.94)
Pronoun (unsure)	N/A		N/A		14	(0.10)	0	(0.00)
Total	3,153	(98.62)	3,817	(125.95)	4,152	(30.49)	4,703	(35.20)

Table 1: Pronoun **type** counts for English (source) and German (translation) texts in ParCor. Counts per 1000 tokens are provided in parentheses. *N/A* indicates that the type is not marked for one of the corpora

Weiner, 2014), these being relatively small scale. The main focus, however, has been on building models to improve pronoun translation in SMT through targeting different stages of the translation process. These include pre-annotation of the source-language data (Le Nagard and Koehn, 2010; Guillou, 2012), decoder features (Hardmeier and Federico, 2010; Novák et al., 2013; Hardmeier, 2014; Weiner, 2014) and post-editing / re-ranking (Weiner, 2014). Despite these efforts, little progress has been made.

In the most comprehensive study to date, Hardmeier (2014) concludes that current models for pronoun translation are insufficient and that *"...future approaches to pronoun translation in SMT will require extensive corpus analysis to study how pronouns of a given source language are rendered in a given target language"*. This paper reports on such a corpus analysis.

3 Analysis of Manual Translation

Identifying and understanding systematic differences in pronoun use between a pair of languages may help inform the design of SMT systems. With this in mind, we compared original English texts and their human-authored German translations in the ParCor corpus, for both genres, at the corpus, document and sentence levels.

3.1 Corpus-level

Corpus-level comparison reveals the first differences between pronoun use in the two languages. (See Table 1. Some counts differ from those in (Guillou et al., 2014) due to minor changes prior to corpus release and the automatic addition of first person pronouns and German "man".) Specifically, the German translations contain more anaphoric and pleonastic pronouns than the original English texts. (A *pleonastic* pronoun does not refer to an antecedent, e.g. "**It** is raining" / "**Es** regnet".) Paired t-tests show that this difference is significant for pleonastic pronouns in both the TED corpus, $t(10)=-5.08$, $p < .01$, and the EU Bookshop corpus, $t(10)=-3.68$, $p < .01$. The difference in anaphoric pronoun use is significant for the TED corpus, t(7)=-3.52, p < .01, but not the EU Bookshop corpus, t(7)=-1.09, (p=0.31).

3.2 Document-level

Again, at the document-level we observe that the German translations typically contain more anaphoric and pleonastic pronouns than the original English texts. (See Table 2 for the pronoun counts of a randomly selected document, 767.)

Pronoun Type	English		German	
Anaphoric	*121*	*(22.53)*	*189*	*(39.58)*
Cataphoric	0	(0.00)	2	(0.42)
Event	49	(9.12)	59	(12.36)
Extra-textual ref.	5	(0.93)	6	(1.26)
Pleonastic	*8*	*(1.68)*	*54*	*(11.31)*
Addressee reference	102	(18.99)	91	(19.06)
Speaker reference	156	(29.04)	163	(34.14)
Pronoun (unsure)	3	(0.56)	0	(0.00)
Total	444	(82.67)	564	(118.12)

Table 2: Pronoun **type** counts for TED Talk 767. Counts per 1000 tokens provided in parentheses

Similar trends were observed for the other documents in the corpus which suggests that this is not simply a consequence of stylistic differences over authors or speakers. A presentation of the full analysis would, however, require a longer paper.

Documents in ParCor were originally produced in English and then translated into German. To ascertain whether similar patterns of pronoun use can be observed for the opposite translation direction, we annotated two German TEDx talks and their English translations, again using the guidelines described in Guillou et al. (2014).

We observed similar patterns, with more pleonastic pronouns used in German than in English (19 vs. 11 pleonastic pronouns in one document, and 15 vs. 2 in the other). For anaphoric pronouns, one document has 119 in the German original and 140 in the English translation, with near equal numbers (54 vs. 51) in the other document. With only two documents it is not possible to confirm whether German systematically makes use of more anaphoric and pleonastic pronouns, but cf. Becher (2011) who points to several patterns, in particular the insertion of explicit possessive pronouns in English-to-German translation and pronominal adverbs in the opposite direction.

3.3 Sentence-level

Pronoun counts at the corpus and document levels are simply raw counts. They do not tell us anything about cases in which a pronoun is used in the original text and dropped from the translation (deletions), or is absent from the original text but present in the translation (insertions). To discover this, we need to drill down to the sentence–level.

We start with the sentence–aligned parallel texts provided as part of the ParCor release. In order to identify the German translation of each pronoun in the original English text, we compute word alignments using Giza++ (`https://code.google.com/p/giza-pp/`) with *grow-diag-final-and* symmetrisation. To ensure robust alignments, we concatenated the ParCor texts and additional data – specifically, the IWSLT 2013 shared task training data (for TED and TEDx) and Europarl data (for EU Bookshop). We consider an English and German pronoun to be equivalent if the following conditions hold: (a) a word alignment exists between them, and (b) they share the same pronoun type label in the ParCor annotations.

To evaluate the word-alignment quality we examined a random sample of 100 parallel sentences from the TED corpus. The sentences contain 213 English and 241 German pronouns. We define a bad alignment as one where a pronoun is aligned to something that is not the corresponding pronoun in the other language, or should be unaligned but is not. We find that 6.57% of English and 9.12% of German pronouns are part of a bad alignment.

Taking TED talk 767 as an example and using the combination of pronoun type and alignments to identify a source-target pronoun match, we observe many mismatches. Table 3 shows that 412 pronouns are unique to either the English original or the German translation, with only 298 matching English-German pronoun pairs. The largest absolute difference lies in the number of anaphoric pronouns in the target for which there is no comparable pronoun in the source (*anaphoric* insertions), followed by *pleonastic* insertions.

Pronoun Type	**English (deletion)**	**German (insertion)**
Anaphoric	*49*	*117*
Cataphoric	0	2
Event	26	36
Extra-textual ref.	4	5
Pleonastic	*3*	*49*
Addressee reference	31	20
Speaker reference	30	37
Pronoun (unsure)	3	0
Total	146	266

Table 3: Sentence-level pronoun **type + alignment** mismatches for TED Talk 767

There is no single reason for *anaphoric* deletions: Anaphoric pronouns may be omitted from the German output for stylistic reasons, as a result of paraphrasing or possibly to conform with language-specific constraints. With respect to *anaphoric* insertions, intra-sententially, many correspond to relativizers in English. That is, while in English a relative clause is introduced with a *that-*, *wh-* or *null-relativizer*, an anaphoric pronoun serves as a relativizer in German.[6] For example, "that" in "The house **that** Jack built" is a relativizer and the corresponding "das" in "Das Haus, **das** Jack gebaut hat" is a relative pronoun. Manual analysis of the German translation for TED Talk 767 identified 42 cases where an anaphoric pronoun was inserted as a relative pronoun corresponding to a relativizer in English. While this does not explain all of the *anaphoric* insertions, it is frequent enough to deserve further attention.

[6]The ParCor corpus has not marked instances of *that* when used as a relativizer in English.

Several fixed expressions in English appear to trigger *pleonastic* insertions in German. A commonly observed pair is "There *+be*"/"Es gibt". These *existential there* constructions are not annotated in ParCor, but their presence accounts for some (not all) of the insertions of pleonastic pronouns in German. As the fixed expressions are short and occur frequently, phrase-based systems could be expected to provide accurate translations.

3.4 Discussion

We have observed differences in pronoun use in both genres of the ParCor corpus. Since SMT systems are trained on parallel data similar to that in ParCor, it is important to be aware that content words such as nouns and verbs are more likely to be faithfully translated as there are fewer ways to convey the same meaning. On the other hand, there is more variation in the translation of function words such as pronouns — for example in active to passive conversions (and vice versa). Where there is a lot of variation the SMT system may not be able to learn accurate mappings.

To this is added the problem of ambiguous pronouns such as "it", for which the anaphoric and pleonastic forms both translate as "es" in German. These frequent alignments in the training data may also bias the likelihood that "it" is incorrectly translated as "es" (neuter), even if a feminine or masculine pronoun is required in German.

4 Assessing Automated Translation

Analyses of the output of state-of-the-art SMT systems provide an indication of how well current systems are able to translate pronominal coreference — what they are good and bad at. We follow our analysis of manual translation and examine English-to-German translation for anaphoric pronouns ("it" and "its") and relativizers.

For our state-of-the-art systems, we selected two systems from the IWSLT 2014 shared task in machine translation (Birch et al., 2014). The first is a phrase-based system that incorporates factored models for words, part-of-speech tags and Brown clusters. The second is a syntax-based, string-to-tree, system. Both systems were trained using a combination of TED data and corpora provided for the WMT shared task. Here, TED talks are considered to be in-domain, with the EU Bookshop texts considered out-of-domain.

We are not interested in making direct comparisons between the two systems, as their different training makes such comparisons unfair. However, similarities in the translation accuracy of two systems can show that our findings are not specific to a single system or type of system.

For manual translation, we can assume that a pronoun is accurately translated, inserted or dropped, as part of a close translation of the original sentence or an acceptable paraphrase. As such, it is reasonable to use automated analysis based on the ParCor annotations and alignments between the texts. With automated translations, however, there is no guarantee that a source pronoun is translated correctly by the system. We therefore need to rely more heavily on manual analysis.

However, manual analysis can be aided by some automated pre-processing steps, to help select pronouns for further study. Using the source text and its translation together with word alignments output by the SMT systems, we can investigate which pronouns may be more difficult to translate than others – i.e. we can produce frequency distributions of the translations produced for each source pronoun surface-form (split by pronoun type).

4.1 Identifying Pronouns for Analysis

Examining the translation frequency distributions for the two state-of-the-art systems, we can observe the following. First, "it" can be translated into German, depending on the context, as either masculine singular (sg.), feminine sg. or neuter sg., or plural. As plural pronouns are not gendered, "they" has fewer translations. The possessive pronoun "its" has additional possible translation options due its multiple dependencies. That is, possessive pronouns in German must agree in number/gender with both the possessor and the object that is possessed. Different base forms are used depending on whether the possessor is feminine/plural ("ihr") or masculine/neuter ("sein"). Other anaphoric pronouns such as "he" and "she" have far fewer translation options and are therefore less interesting. Based on the possible translation options, we selected (anaphoric) "it" and "its".

Our analysis of manual translation (Section 3.3) showed that relativizers in English often corresponded to a relative pronoun inserted in the German translation. We wish to see how well SMT systems handle the translation of relativizers. We selected that-relativizers (explicit in English text) and null-relativizers (implicit). We exclude wh-relativizers, also explicit, but with many forms (what, who, etc.), to reduce the annotation effort.

4.2 Pronoun Selection Task

Our manual analysis of pronoun translation is framed as a pronoun selection task. In this setting a human annotator is asked to identify which pronoun(s) could validly replace a placeholder masking a pronoun at a specific point in the SMT output. By masking the pronoun, we remove the risk that the annotator is biased by the pronoun present in the SMT output. The annotator's selections may then be compared with the pronouns produced by the system in order to assess translation accuracy.

We used the tool described by Hardmeier (2014) for the pronoun selection task. The interface presents the annotator with the source sentence and its translation plus up to five previous sentences of history, as well as a number of pronoun options. The source pronoun in the final sentence of each example block is highlighted and its translation is replaced with a placeholder.

To determine how many sentences of history to present to the annotator (to help them identify the antecedent of an anaphoric pronoun), we used the manual annotations in ParCor. We calculated both the mean number of sentences between a pronoun and its antecedent, and two standard deviations from the mean (accounting for 95% of pronouns). (Intra-sentential pronouns have a distance of zero.) For the TED corpus the mean distance between pronoun and antecedent is 1.33 sentences, and two standard deviations from the mean is 4.95 sentences. For the EU Bookshop (whose sentences are longer), the distances between pronoun and antecedent are typically shorter, with a mean distance of 0.67 sentences and two standard deviations from the mean at 3.57 sentences. We nevertheless allow for up to five previous sentences of history for each example, regardless of genre.

4.3 Pronoun Selection Task: Guidelines

The following guidelines were adapted from those used by Hardmeier (2014) in order to cater for the requirements of English-German translation:

1) Select the pronoun that will create the most fluent translation, while preserving the meaning of the English sentence as much as possible. The latter means assigning correct number/gender to the pronoun that replaces the placeholder: Its case may be left "unknown".

- If the SMT output is sufficiently fluent to be able to determine the case of the pronoun, select the appropriate check-box.
- Use the plural options if the antecedent is translated as a plural, or in any other scenarios in which a plural might seem appropriate.
- If different, equally grammatical options are available, select all appropriate check-boxes.

2) Alternatively select "Other" if the sentence should be completed with a pronoun not included in the list, "Bad translation" if a grammatical and faithful translation cannot be created without making major changes to the surrounding text, or "Discussion required" if you are unsure what to do.

3) Ignore minor disfluencies (e. g., incorrect verb agreement or obviously missing words).

4) Always try to select the pronoun that best agrees with the antecedent in the SMT output, even if the antecedent is translated incorrectly, and even if this forces you to violate the pronoun's agreement with immediately surrounding words such as verbs, adjectives etc.

5) If the translation does not contain a placeholder, but a pronoun corresponding to the one marked in the English text should be inserted somewhere, indicate which pronoun should be inserted.

6) If the SMT output does not contain a placeholder, but already includes the correct pronoun, annotate the example as if a placeholder were present. This will mean selecting the same pronoun that is included in the SMT output.

4.4 Anaphoric "it"

The anaphoric pronoun "it" can co-refer either intra-sententially (i.e., to an antecedent in the same sentence) or inter-sententially (i.e., to an antecedent in a different sentence). While coreference imposes number–gender constraints on a pronoun and its antecedent, intra-sentential coreference imposes additional constraints.

We randomly selected 50 inter- and 50 intra-sentential tokens of "it" labelled anaphoric in the ParCor annotations. Tokens were selected from the TED Talks, as sentences there are typically shorter than those in the EU Bookshop and hence, potentially easier to work with. Additional guidelines are provided for "it":

- Select "Pronominal adverb" if the most fluent translation would come from using a German pronominal adverb[7]. (Selection of the pronominal adverb is not required.)

- If a demonstrative pronoun (e.g. "diese" or "jene") is possible, select whether it is **more** or **less** likely than the personal pronoun(s).
- Genitive options are not available as these are used for possessives.

The annotator is presented with a table of options for number/gender and case combinations. The number/gender options are masculine, feminine, neuter and plural. The case options are: "case unknown", and three German cases: nominative, accusative and dative. See Figure 1.

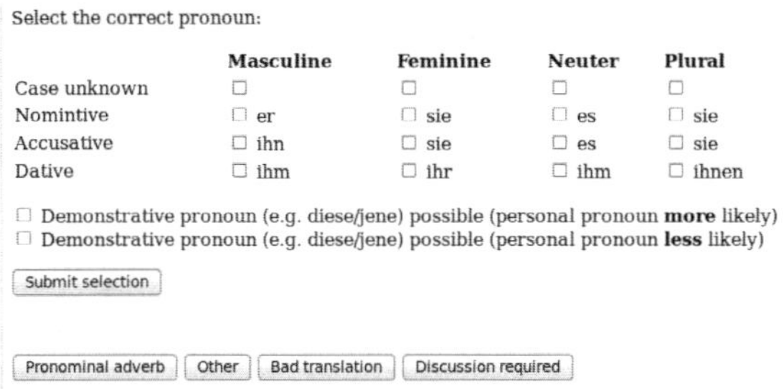

Figure 1: Annotator options for "it"

Although the ParCor annotations contain antecedent links for anaphoric pronouns, we did not display these to the annotator for any of the tasks.

4.5 Anaphoric possessive "its"

In German, *dependent* possessive pronouns (i.e. those that precede a noun) must agree not only with the number/gender of its antecedent (possessor) but also with the number/gender of its object (i.e. the noun that follows the pronoun). For example in: "**Der** Staat und **sein***e Einwohner*" ("The state and its inhabitants") the antecedent "Staat" ("state") is masculine (sg.) and so a "sein" form is required for the possessive pronoun. The ending "e" in "seine" is needed because the noun following the possessive pronoun is plural ("Einwohner/inhabitants").

We randomly selected 50 instances of "its" marked as anaphoric in ParCor. As "its" is uncommon in the TED corpus, all 50 instances came from the EU Bookshop corpus. Additional guidelines are provided for "its":

- Select the relevant combination of number/gender of possessor and object. Select the case of the pronoun if the quality of the SMT output permits this.
- Select "Pronoun not required" if the translation does not require a pronoun.

[7]Pronominal adverbs also exist in English (e.g. therefore, wherein, hereafter) but are used more frequently in German

The annotator is presented with a table of options capturing the number/gender of the possessor vs. the number/gender of the object. To reduce the number of options, a separate set of check-boxes is provided for case options, including "case unknown", nominative, accusative, dative and genitive.

4.6 Relativizers

English relativizers may be explicit (*that-* and *wh-relativizers*), or implicit (*null-relativizers*). Both may be translated as relative pronouns in German.

We randomly selected 50 instances of relativizers from the TED corpus; 25 that- and 25 null-relativizers. The selection was semi-automatic, based on identifying relative clauses in the output of the Berkeley Parser (Petrov et al., 2006) and manually selecting those that contained a that- or null-relativizer.

As null-relativizers are implicit, there are no tokens in the English text to highlight. To keep this task in line with the others, we manually insert symbols for the nulls, i.e. the "∅" in "The house ∅ Jack built", and (manually) align them to the corresponding token in the SMT output. (Unalignable tokens are left untranslated.) Instead of a pronoun in the English text, the annotator is presented with an instance of "that" or a symbol representing the null-relativizer. Placeholders are included in the translation as normal.

The options table captures pronoun number/gender and case. It is similar to the table for "it", but with relative pronoun forms and options for "case unknown" and all four German cases.

5 Results

The results of the three pronoun selection tasks are presented in Table 4. We automatically compared the translations produced by the systems with the selections made by the annotator. If the system-generated pronoun matches one of the annotator's selections, there is a "pronoun match". If it doesn't match any of the annotator's selections or the system did not generate a pronoun there is a "pronoun mismatch". Matches are recorded in terms of number/gender and case if the annotator supplied it, or number/gender only, if not.

Result	"it"				"its"		Relativizers			
	Inter		Intra				That		Null	
	PB	Syn	PB	Syn	PB	Syn	PB	Syn	PB	Syn
Pronoun match (number/gender + case)	20	8	14	15	15	9	14	12	13	12
Pronoun match (number/gender only)	0	1	1	0	8	10	0	0	2	0
Pronoun mismatch	14	28	27	26	24	28	2	3	1	1
Pronoun not translated (mismatch)	1	0	0	0	0	0	4	3	5	6
Pronominal adverb match	5	8	2	2	N/A	N/A	N/A	N/A	N/A	N/A
Pronominal adverb mismatch	2	0	0	1	N/A	N/A	N/A	N/A	N/A	N/A
Other	2	0	2	1	0	0	2	3	3	3
Bad translation	4	1	1	2	1	1	3	4	1	2
Pronoun not required	0	1	0	0	2	2	0	0	0	1
Anaphoric but could not find antecedent	0	1	0	0	0	0	0	0	0	0
Unsure: may not be anaphoric	2	2	3	3	0	0	0	0	0	0
Sub-total	50	50	50	50	50	50	25	25	25	25
Total	200				100		100			

Table 4: Pronoun selection task results for anaphoric "it", anaphoric possessive "its" and relativizers. PB=Phrase-based system, Syn=Syntax-based system, Inter=pronoun and antecedent are not in the same sentence. Intra=pronoun and antecedent in same sentence. Pronominal adverb is an option for "it" only

For most examples the annotator was able to determine the case of the pronoun as well as its number/gender. Recall that the annotator was specifically instructed to only select the case of the pronoun if the SMT output was sufficiently fluent so as to make this possible. It would therefore appear that our initial assumption that it might be difficult to identify syntactic role was not entirely correct.

"Pronominal adverb match" is used when the SMT output contains a pronominal adverb and the annotator had indicated that one would be appropriate. As the annotator was not asked to specify the pronominal adverb, we make no further comparison. "Pronominal adverb mismatch" is the opposite; the annotator indicated that a pronominal adverb should be used but the system did not output one. "Other", "Bad translation" and "Pronoun not required"[8] are used for those pronouns marked as such in the pronoun selection task.

Some instances of "it" were initially left for discussion. These were later assigned one of two new categories: "Anaphoric but could not find antecedent" where the antecedent could not be identified due to insufficient history or "Unsure: may not be anaphoric" where the annotator believed that the pronoun may not in fact be anaphoric, despite being labelled as such in the ParCor corpus.

Instead of comparing the systems, we use the results from both to assess how well state-of-the-art systems perform at pronoun translation. We find that both systems typically produce more incorrect translations than correct ones.

[8]Although "pronoun not required" was not initially provided for the "it" task, we added it later when the need arose.

Both systems regularly translate "it" as "es": 79/100 cases for the phrase-based and 78/100 for the syntax-based system. This reflects biases in the training data, where the use of "it" and "es" as both anaphoric and pleonastic pronouns leads to their frequent alignment. A similar bias is observed for relativizers, with both that- and null-relativizers commonly translated as "die". For example, both systems translate "that" as "die" in 13 of the 21 instances in which a translation is provided, though not the same 13 of 21 instances.

It is often acceptable to translate "it" using either a personal or demonstrative pronoun: 49/100 cases for the phrase-based and 59/100 cases for the syntax-based system. However, neither system generated demonstrative pronouns, perhaps due to the bias toward translating "it" as "es".

For "its" the systems often select an incorrect base form for the pronoun: i.e. "ihr" when "sein" should be used, and vice versa. The phrase- and syntax-based systems selected the incorrect base form for 17/50 and 15/50 instances respectively.

Both systems are able to insert relative pronouns when a null-relativizer is encountered in the English source text, with a similar accuracy to the translation of that-relativizers. One might have expected that translating an explicit source token would be easier (and more accurate) than inserting a token in the SMT output which has no explicit representation in the source.

6 Discussion: Anaphoric "it"

When annotating the English side of ParCor, deciding whether a pronoun was anaphoric, event-related or pleonastic was one of the major causes of annotator disagreement. It is therefore not surprising that problems might arise in identifying the pronoun's antecedent for the pronoun selection task. This ambiguity did not arise for the "its" or relativizers tasks. With "its", events are rarely (if ever) possessors and so rarely serve as antecedents. With relativizers, the relative pronoun and its antecedent (in German) are likely to be very close together, and certainly intra-sentential.

The syntax-based system is much better at translating intra-sentential pronouns than inter-sentential ones. Although this system contained no such enhancements, one might expect that pronoun-aware syntax-based systems could be designed to leverage the fact that intra-sentential pronouns are syntactically governed, and produce better translations. One possible option would be to combine two systems: a phrase-based system to translate inter-sentential pronouns, and an enhanced syntax-based system to translate intra-sentential pronouns.

7 Discussion: Relative pronouns

When the antecedent is not a noun, i.e. "something" ("etwas"), "anything" ("alles"/"jedes" etc.) or "nothing" ("nichts"), "was" should be used:

(1) Now , when I use the term miracle , I don 't mean something **that** 's impossible.

(2) Nun , wenn ich den Begriff Wunder verwenden , ich meine nicht etwas , **XXX** ist unmöglich .

As "was" is not provided as an option in the pronoun selection task, the annotator marked example 2 (and others like it) as "other". SMT systems must decide whether to use a relative pronoun that conveys the number/gender of the antecedent (i.e. der/die/das) or "was/wer/wo" (if the antecedent cannot be determined / there is no antecedent). As this decision depends on the antecedent, relative pronouns may therefore be treated as a more localised sub-set of anaphoric pronouns.

The translation of relativizers may require a preposition preceding the relative pronoun:

(3) That 's the planet ∅ we live on .

(4) Das ist die Welt , **XXX** wir leben .

The correct translation of example 3, which contains a null-relativizer (indicated by ∅), would be "Das ist die Welt, **in der** wir leben". However, in the SMT output the preposition "in" is missing, and so the annotator was required to select the correct pronoun as if the preposition had been present.

In German, the choice of preposition and case of the pronoun are determined by the verb of the clause. As these choices are connected, SMT systems could also consider the translation of prepositions when translating relative pronouns.

8 Conclusion

The analysis of manual translation revealed that pronouns are frequently dropped and inserted by human translators and that German translations contain many more pleonastic and anaphoric pronouns than the original English texts. Both of these differences can result in SMT systems learning poor translation mappings.

The analysis of state-of-the-art translation revealed that biases in the training data and incorrect selections of the base form pronoun (i.e. "ihr" vs. "sein" for "its") are both problems which SMT systems must overcome. For relative pronouns selecting the correct preposition is also important as it influences the case of the pronoun.

9 Future Work

Possible directions for future work include further analyses of manual and automated translation and applying the knowledge that is gained to build pronoun-aware SMT systems. Initial efforts could focus on syntax-based SMT — leveraging information within target-side syntax trees constructed by the decoder, to encourage pronoun-antecedent agreement for intra-sentential anaphoric pronouns (i.e. "it/its" and relative pronouns).

Pronoun-aware SMT systems could also address translation of the ambiguous second-person pronouns "you" and "your". In English, they have both deictic and generic use, while in German, different forms are used ("Sie/du" vs. "man").

Acknowledgements

Thanks to Christian Hardmeier for providing the pronoun-selection tool, to Susanne Tauber for completing the annotations and to Felix Suessenbach and Sam Gibbon for assisting with the significance testing. This project has received funding from the European Union's Horizon 2020 research and innovation programme under grant agreement n° 645452 (QT21).

References

Viktor Becher. 2011. *Explicitation and implicitation in translation. A corpus-based study of English-German and German-English translations of business texts*. Ph.D. thesis, Department of Applied Linguistics (Institut für Sprachlehrforschung), University of Hamburg.

Alexandra Birch, Matthias Huck, Nadir Durrani, Nikolay Bogoychev, and Philipp Koehn. 2014. Edinburgh SLT and MT System Description for the IWSLT 2014 Evaluation. In *International Workshop on Spoken Language Translation*, pages 49–56, Lake Tahoe, CA, USA.

Liane Guillou, Christian Hardmeier, Aaron Smith, Jörg Tiedemann, and Bonnie Webber. 2014. ParCor 1.0: A Parallel Pronoun-Coreference Corpus to Support Statistical MT. In *Proceedings of the Ninth International Conference on Language Resources and Evaluation (LREC'14)*, Reykjavik, Iceland. European Language Resources Association (ELRA).

Liane Guillou. 2012. Improving Pronoun Translation for Statistical Machine Translation. In *Proceedings of the Student Research Workshop*, EACL 2012, pages 1–10.

Christian Hardmeier and Marcello Federico. 2010. Modelling Pronominal Anaphora in Statistical Machine Translation. In *Proceedings of the 7th International Workshop on Spoken Language Translation*.

Christian Hardmeier. 2014. *Discourse in Statistical Machine Translation*. Ph.D. thesis, Department of Linguistics and Philology, Uppsala University.

Kerstin Kunz and Ekaterina Lapshinova-Koltunski. 2015. Cross-linguistic analysis of discourse variation across registers. *Nordic Journal of English Studies*, 14(1):258–288.

Ronan Le Nagard and Philipp Koehn. 2010. Aiding Pronoun Translation with Co-Reference Resolution. In *Proceedings of the Joint Fifth Workshop on Statistical Machine Translation and MetricsMATR*, pages 252–261.

Michal Novák, Anna Nedoluzhko, and Zdeněek Žabokrtský. 2013. Translation of "It" in a Deep Syntax Framework. In *Proceedings of the 1st Workshop on Discourse in Machine Translation*, ACL 2013, pages 51–59.

Slav Petrov, Leon Barrett, Romain Thibaux, and Dan Klein. 2006. Learning Accurate, Compact, and Interpretable Tree Annotation. In *Proceedings of the 21st International Conference on Computational Linguistics and the 44th Annual Meeting of the Association for Computational Linguistics*, ACL-44, pages 433–440, Stroudsburg, PA, USA. Association for Computational Linguistics.

Jochen Weiner. 2014. Pronominal Anaphora in Machine Translation. Master's thesis, Karlsruhe Institute of Technology, Karlsruhe, Germany.

Document-Level Machine Translation Evaluation with Gist Consistency and Text Cohesion

Zhengxian Gong Min Zhang Guodong Zhou*
School of Computer Science and Technology, Soochow University, Suzhou, China 215006
{zhxgong, minzhang, gdzhou}@suda.edu.cn

Abstract

Current Statistical Machine Translation (SMT) is significantly affected by Machine Translation (MT) evaluation metric. Nowadays the emergence of document-level MT research increases the demand for corresponding evaluation metric. This paper proposes two superior yet low-cost quantitative objective methods to enhance traditional MT metric by modeling document-level phenomena from the perspectives of gist consistency and text cohesion. The experimental results show the proposed metrics can obtain better correlation with human judgments than traditional metrics on evaluating document-level translation quality.

1 Introduction

Since most of current SMT models impose strong independence assumptions on words and sentences, most of these systems only work at sentence level and cannot employ useful relationships among sentences during decoding. However, a text rather than individual words or fragments of sentences is the basic unit of communication (Al-Amri, 2007). Beaugrande and Dressler (1981) define that text is a communicative occurrence which meets seven standards, such as textuality cohesion, coherence. Text is constituted by sentences, but there exist separate principles of text-construction beyond the rules for making sentences (Fowler, 1991).

Document is the carrier of text in modern computer system. Currently more researching work focus on document-level SMT (Tiedemann, 2010; Xiao et al, 2011; Gong et al, 2011; Ture et al., 2012; Hardmeier et al., 2012; Xiong et al, 2013). However, most of these researches show their improvements by using system-level metrics, such as BLEU (Papineni et al., 2002). Whether improvements in performance at system level are really able to reflect the change of text-level translation quality is still to doubt.

Nowadays, the study of real document-level MT metrics has been drawing more and more attention. Based on Discourse Representation Theory (Kamp and Reyle, 1993), Gimenez et al. (2010) propose to use co-reference and discourse relations to build evaluation metrics. The metrics by extending traditional metrics with lexical cohesion devices show some positive experimental results (Wong and Kit, 2012). Bilingual topic model (Blei et al., 2003) is applied to do MT quality estimation(Raphael et al., 2012; Raphael et al, 2013). Guzman et al. (2014) use two discourse-aware similarity measures based on discourse structure to improve existing MT evaluation metrics.

According to the afore-mentioned definition of text, the most important standard of evaluating translation quality for one document should be to what degree the MT output correctly communicates the main idea of origin text. From this regard, this paper first proposes to measure gist consistency of text via topic model. Topic model is a statistical model which assumes each document can be characterized by a particular set of topics. Currently a variety of probabilistic topic models (Landauer et al., 1998; Hofmann, 1999; Blei et al., 2003) have been used to analyze the content of documents and the meaning of words. Our experimental results show the MT evaluation metrics with robust topic model can effectively capture change of translation quality between reference and MT output at document level.

Furthermore, cohesion and coherence are important standards of textuality. Coherence

*Corresponding author.

Proceedings of the Second Workshop on Discourse in Machine Translation (DiscoMT), pages 33–40,
Lisbon, Portugal, 17 September 2015.

interprets meaning connectedness in the underlying text while cohesion can be formulated quite explicitly on the basis of grammatical and lexical properties (Halliday and Hasan, 1976). This paper describes a simple yet effective cohesion function to measure text cohesion via lexical chain. Our experimental results show that the number of matching lexical chain between reference and MT output can reflect the goodness of translation at document level.

The rest of this paper is organized as follows: Section 2 and 3 respectively describes how to model two kinds of document-level features. Section 4 shows the framework of combing document-level scores with traditional metrics. Section 5 presents the experimental results and Section 6 gives out discussion. Finally, we conclude this paper in Section 7.

2 Gist Consistency Score based on Topic Model

Reeder (2006) proposes to measure MT adequacy at the document level with Latent Semantic Analysis (LSA) (Landauer et al., 1998). However, Reeder only uses a set of complex configuration to show the close correlation between LSA model and human assessments and does not suggest how to use it to design an evaluation metric.

Raphael et al. (2012; 2013) exploit bilingual topic models to do quality estimation (without references) for machine translation. In this study, since each evaluation document has 4 references, we show a simple way to design document-level metrics with monolingual topic model.

2.1 Topic Model

LDA (Blei et al., 2003) is one of the most common topic models which assumes each document is a mixture of various topics and each word is generated with multinomial distribution conditioned on a topic. We use an off-the-shelf LDA tool[1] to train a topic model with 86070 news (happened in 2004 year) documents coming from the Xinhua portion of the Gigaword corpus (LDC2005T12).

A trained LDA model produces two kinds of distributions: the "document-topic" distribution and the "topic-word" distribution. Suppose there are *K* topics, the *k*-th dimension $P(z = k|d)$ means the probability of topic *k* given document d. The whole document-topic distribution over *K* topics for one document d, denoted as $P(Z|d)$, can be represented by a K-dimension vector. In this study, when K set to 120, the trained LDA model can be tuned with the minimal perplexity (Blei et al., 2003).

2.2 Measure of Topic Consistency

After constructing a trained topic model, the "document-topic" distribution of MT output and reference on evaluation dataset (see Section 5.1) can be respectively **inferred**. We use Kullback-Leibler divergence to measure topic consistency between MT output and reference with the basic unit of document. Denote the "document-topic" distribution of one reference (d_r) as $P(Z|d_r)$, and the one of its MT output (d_t) as $Q(Z|d_t)$, the KL divergence of Q from P is defined to be:

$$D_{KL}(P||Q) = \sum_{i=1}^{G} P(z_i|d_r) \times \ln \frac{P(z_i|d_r)}{Q(z_i|d_t)} \quad (1)$$

In theory, G should keep same to the value of the trained LDA model ($K = 120$). However our initial experiment results show the hybrid METEOR has a drop on adequacy on evaluation dataset by using a static G.

To address such problem, we output the number of topics whose document-topic probability is great than 0.01 (called as *valid topic*) for each **reference** document and found the range of this number is [7,31]. Obviously the inferred topic model contains plenty of noise topics and we need measure *valid topic* rather than all topics consistency for each document.

Therefore, before computing topic consistency, we first record the IDs of *valid topics* for one reference, then obtain corresponding "document-topic" probability of evaluation document according to these topic IDs. Thus, in this study, G is dynamically set according to the number of valid topics of each reference.

There are 4 references per document in evaluation data. One machine translated document is scored against each reference independently, and the minimal D_{KL} is used. The score of *topic consistency* for each evaluation document, denoted as S_{topic}, is computed by the following formula:

$$S_{topic} = e^{-D_{KL}} \quad (2)$$

[1] http://www.arbylon.net/projects/

3 Cohesion Score based on Simplified Lexical Chain

Text adequacy is the most important standard for the purpose of successful communication. According to the work of Wong and Kit (2012), cohesion is another important element to organize text. They found: SMT systems tend to use less lexical cohesion devices than those of human translators. Here lexical cohesion devices mainly refer to content words reiterating once or more times in a document. They propose to build document-level MT metrics by integrating cohesion score based on lexical cohesion devices.

However, Carpuat and Simard (2012) draw a different conclusion: MT output tend to have more incorrect repetition than human translation when the MT model is especially trained on smaller corpora. Suppose these incorrect repetition as "false" cohesion, metrics in (Wong and Kit, 2012) will fail to distinguish such "false" cohesion devices.

In our opinion, the lack of Wong's work is completely ignoring text cohesion of references, and they only model the cohesion score of MT output. In this study, we assume the correct cohesion of MT output should be consistent with the one of references. Reference is the equivalent of its source text. The MT output might be cohesive only if source text is cohesive, so the assumption is reliable. In this paper, we implement such assumption via a special structure, simplified lexical chain.

3.1 Simplified Lexical Chain

Differing from lexical chain in these work (Morris and Hirst, 1991; Galley and McKeown, 1993; Xiong et al, 2013) which is the sequence of semantically related words based on special thesaurus, our lexical chain refers to reiterating words including stem-matched words. Furthermore, it only records position information for each content word. Our lexical chain is simpler and might gain broader use because it doesn't require special thesaurus, such as WordNet and HowNet. Thus, we call such lexical chain as simplified lexical chain.

The detailed establishing procedure of simplified lexical chain is described in our another work (Gong and Zhou, 2015). The key of this procedure is to assure that each content word occurring at different sentences one more time is assigned an unique lexical chain. Figure 1 shows a lexical chain $LC1$ for the word "die" (perhaps with different morphology) and it records that "die" occurs at the 1st, 2nd and 3rd sentence. One document often contains several lexical chains, thus a hash table ht is utilized to organize all these chains. For clarity, ht is called as lexical-chain index. In this hash table, keys are content words and values refer to lexical chains.

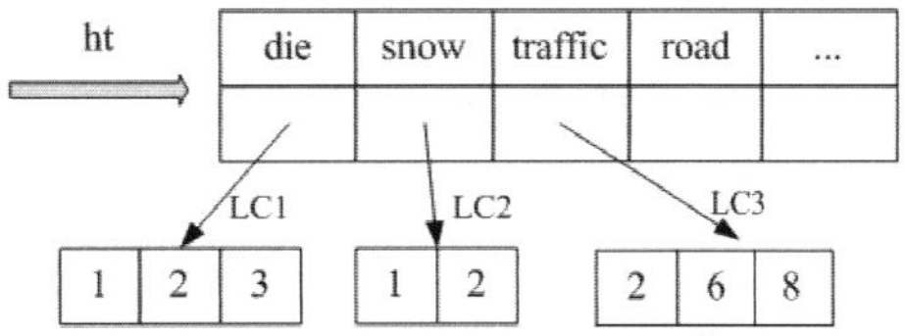

Figure 1: the structure of the lexical-chain index of one document

3.2 Cohesion Score

We constructed lexical-chain index for each document on our evaluation data, including 4 human translations (references) and all MT output on evaluation corpus in advance. Due to high flexibility of natural language utterances, few lexical chains from MT output can completely match the ones from its references. So we design a special function that permits incomplete matching to score text cohesion .

Suppose the lexical-chain index in reference and in MT output as ht_{ref} and ht_{mt} , we can find a pair of matching lexical chain of ht_{ref} and ht_{mt}, denoted as LC_r and LC_t. LC_r contains m elements and LC_t contains n elements, but only m' ($m' <= m$) elements both occur in LC_r and LC_t , then the cohesion score of LC_t can be calculated by the following formula:

$$CS_i = \frac{m'}{m} \tag{3}$$

CS_i only refers to one pair of matching chain. If one chain of MT output cannot be found in its reference, the chain is invalid ("false"). Suppose ht_{mt} contains K lexical chains, we punish such "false" cohesion by averaging K. Given the number of matching chain is L, the final cohesion score assigned to ht_{mt} is calculated as follows:

$$Doc_{cs} = \frac{\sum_{i=1}^{L} CS_i}{K} \tag{4}$$

We choose the best Doc_{cs} for one MT output against 4 references.

4 New Metrics by Combining Traditional Metrics with Document-level Scores

4.1 Traditional MT Evaluation Metrics

For fair comparison and possible integration of our proposed document-level features, this section gives a brief introduction on two widely adopted MT evaluation metrics: BLEU (Papineni et al., 2002) and METEOR (Banerjee and Lavie, 2005).

As the most famous evaluation metric, BLEU is based on n-gram matching. Given a system translation, BLEU first collects all n-grams and count how many of them exist in one or more references (sentence by sentence), and then integrate the precisions of n-grams with different lengths into one score as follows:

$$BLEU = BP \cdot \exp(\frac{1}{4}\sum_{n=1}^{4}\log(P_n)) \ . \quad (5)$$

where p_n is the precision of n-gram and BP is a penalty factor, preventing BLEU from favoring short segments due to the lack of direct consideration of recall. It is obvious that, although BLEU takes all n-grams into consideration, the importance of different n-grams is ignored except their lengths.

METEOR is based on unigram alignment of references and MT output. Each unigram in one system translation is at most mapped to one unigram in the references first and then three successive stages of "exact", "porter stem" and "WN synonymy" are used to create alignment in turn. Once the final alignment is produced, unigram precision (P) and recall (R) are calculated and combined into one F_{mean} score:

$$F_{mean} = \frac{PR}{\alpha P + (1-\alpha)R} \ . \quad (6)$$

Finally, the METEOR score is obtained as follows:

$$score = (1 - pen)F_{mean} \ . \quad (7)$$

Where pen is a penalty factor. METEOR is explicitly designed to improve the correlation with human judgments of MT quality at the sentence level and the performance of METEOR outperforms BLEU at sentence level.

Based on the formula 5 or 7, document-level BLEU/METEOR score can be generated by aggregating sentences in a document rather than simply averaging scores at sentence level.

4.2 The Combining Framework

Gist consistency and text cohesion refer to top-level characteristics of text while traditional MT evaluation metrics, such as document-level BLEU, show the degree to which the n-grams also occur in the MT output. Inspired by the work of Wong and Kit (2012), we construct document-level metric by extending traditional metric with aforementioned two kinds of document-level scores as

$$H = \alpha \times S_{m_{doc}} + \beta \times G_{m_{doc}} \quad (8)$$

where $G_{m_{doc}}$ refers to document-level BLEU or METEOR score (one score per document), $S_{m_{doc}}$ to gist consistency score(S_{topic}) or text cohesion score(Doc_{cs}) proposed in this paper. α and β are weights which are tuned on MTC2 evaluation dataset (see Section 5.1) by a gradient ascending algorithm with the optimum goal of maximum correlation value (Liu and Gildea, 2007).

5 Experiments

5.1 Evaluation Data

Table 1 shows the evaluation data for this study, including Multiple-Translation Chinese Part 2 (LDC2003T17, MTC2 for short) and Multiple-Translation Chinese Part 4 (LDC2006T04, MTC4 for short). The MTC2 consists of 878 source sentences, translated by 4 human translators (references) as well as 3 MT systems. The MTC4 consists of 919 source sentences, translated by 4 human translators (references) as well as 6 MT systems.

Besides, each machine translated sentence on the MTC4 and MTC2 was evaluated by 2 to 3 human judges for their adequacy and fluency on a 5-point scale. To avoid the bias in the distributions of different judges' assessments in the evaluation data, we normalize the scores following Blatz et al. (2003).

It is worth noting that, due to the lack of document-level human assessments on the two evaluation dataset, document-level human assessments are averaged over sentence scores, weighted by sentence length. This method is also adopted by famous MetricsMaTr (the NIST Metrics for Machine Translation Challenge) and approximated in Gimenez et al. (2010) and Wong and Kit (2012).

LDC corpus	LDC2003T17	LDC2006T04
Source language	Chinese	Chinese
Target language	English	English
Number of Systems	3	6
Number of Documents	100	100
Number of Sentences	878	919
Number of References	4	4
Genre	Newswire	Newswire

Table 1: Evaluation Data

5.2 The Performance of Extending Metrics

In this study, Pearson and Kendall coefficients are both used to formulate correlation following the way of MetricsMaTr. It noted, Pearson ranges from -1 to 1 with 1 for total positive correlation, 0 for no correlation and -1 for total negative correlation, while Kendall ranges from 0 to 1 with 0 for no agreement and 1 for complete agreement.

The document-level BLEU and METEOR scores (one score per document) are first obtained via the NIST BLEU script (version 13) and the METEOR toolkit 1.4. The correlation between traditional metrics and human judgements is shown in Table 2.

After introducing gist consistency score into traditional MT metrics, the Kendall correlation between the hybrid BLEU (HBLEU(s_{topic})) and human judgements rise from 42.56% to 48.66% on adequacy on MTC4, and with a similar increase on MTC2. The Kendall correlation of the hybrid METEOR (HMETEOR(s_{topic})) scores also obtain a significant rise (0.8%-1.4%) both on MTC4 and MTC2.

After introducing cohesion score into traditional metrics, the Kendall correlation between the hybrid BLEU (HBLEU) and human judgements rise from 42.56% to 48.00% on Kendall score on MTC4 and with a similar increase on MTC2. Furthermore, differing with the results in Wong's work, our hybrid METEOR (HMETEOR) scores also obtain a moderate rise (0.64%-0.67%) both on MTC4 and MTC2.

It seems gist consistency outperforms text cohesion on evaluating document-level MT output. It is worth noting the α and β is 1.47 and 0.51 on methods of combing gist consistency score with METEOR. The α and β is 1.82 and 0.02 on methods of combing text cohesion score with METEOR. It seems that cohesion score only plays a minor role on improving METEOR in this study. We think the approximated document-level human judgments may be the major reason (see section 5.1).

6 Discussion

6.1 The Impacts of Associating Gist Consistency with Text Cohesion

In this paper, Gist consistency is obtained based on LDA topic model that uses representative term for major topics existed in one document, and the training procedure of LDA actually relies on term repetition. Text cohesion is obtained based on simplified lexical chain which also depends on iterating words. In a sense, both of these measures are based on same kind of information (although measured differently). It would be interesting to see whether BLEU or METEOR with their combination can increase performance or not.

According to the results shown in Table 3, both document-level BLEU and METEOR enhanced with the combination of gist consistency and text cohesion is subordinate to its corresponding metrics only with gist consistency. BLEU with such combination is still superior to its enhanced metrics only with text cohesion while METEOR with such combination has a slight drop compared with its enhanced metrics only with text cohesion.

Metrics	MTC2	MTC4
HBLEU(combination)	0.0736	0.4850
HMETEOR(combination)	0.2083	0.5211

Table 3: The Kendall correlation between human judgments and the proposed metrics with the combination of gist consistency and text cohesion

METEOR uses WordNet to help evaluation, so METEOR can utilize synonym information. In this paper, LDA model utilize an additional large training corpora (see section 2), thus it may contain synonym information in some topics. Furthermore, we only focus on major topics of one document, which may help METEOR highlight some important words in the scope of documents.

In this study, the performance of METEOR with text cohesion has a slight improvement since our lexical chain ignores synonym for the general purpose. However, using different target words to translate the same source word in different context is common. In the future work, we will

Metrics	MTC2		MTC4	
	Pearson	Kendall	Pearson	Kendall
BLEU	0.0994	0.0449	0.5862	0.4256
METEOR	0.3069	0.2037	0.7401	0.5180
HBLEU(s_{topic})	0.1350	0.0741	0.6601	0.4866
HMETEOR(s_{topic})	0.3149	0.2177	0.7481	0.5260
HBLEU(Doc_{cs})	0.1240	0.0698	0.6551	0.4800
HMETEOR(Doc_{cs})	0.3107	0.2103	0.7467	0.5244

Table 2: The correlation between the proposed metrics combining with gist consistency/text cohesion with human judgments

build lexical chain by introducing synonyms.

Furthermore, it noted that one additional weight of formula 8 needs to be tuned with the gradient ascending algorithm, and it might be the another reason for degrading the performance.

6.2 The Characteristic of Text Cohesion based on Simplified Lexical Chain

We output the lexical chains on two evaluation dataset shown in Table 4. On MTC4, the average number of chains extracted from references (2111) is really more than the one of evaluated documents (1999), which is consistent to the observation in Wong's work. But such observation is not true on MTC2. Table 4 also shows each MT system on MTC2 produces more lexical chains (2380) than the average number of its reference (2030).

Genres	Item	Data	
		MTC4	MTC2
Reference	1	2125	2124
	2	2194	2079
	3	2087	2018
	4	2036	1897
	Avg	2111	2030
MT System	1	2488	2333
	2	2066	2469
	3	2029	2337
	4	2001	-
	5	2152	-
	6	1259	-
	Avg	1999	2380

Table 4: The number of lexical chains extracted from human translation and MT output on MTC4 and MTC2 (MTC2 only involves 3 MT systems)

Furthermore, compared with the column of $\sharp chain$ and $\sharp match_{chain}$ shown in Table 5, we observed there are plenty of invalid lexical chains existed in MT output.

Data	System	$\sharp$ chain	$\sharp match_{chain}$
MT System	1	2333	1180
	2	2469	1222
	3	2337	1262
	Avg:	2380	1221

Table 5: The number of lexical chains($\sharp$ chain) extracted from MT output and the number of lexical chain($\sharp match_{chain}$) refers to the chain which have corresponding lexical chain in its references on MTC2

7 Conclusion

We describes two kinds of document-level measures and successfully use them to construct document-level evaluation metrics.

Hybrid metrics based on topic model can produce significant positive impacts when given a robust trained topic model. Since important words will be repeated in one text, lexical chains can not only model text cohesion but also highlight key words. So our proposed metrics can obtain very significant improvement for BLEU and also give might improvement for METEOR. Furthermore, hybrid metrics based on text cohesion has less limitation than topic-based method since it doesn't need additional training data, and it can be easily integrated into existing traditional metrics.

In the future, we will explore how to model more document-level features, such as co-reference matching, and hope our study can bring more inspirations to document-level SMT.

Acknowledgments

This research is supported by the National Natural Science Foundation of China under grant No.61305088 and No.61401295.

References

Al-Amri K.H. 2007. *Text-linguistics for students of translation*. King Saud University.

Alfred V. Aho and Jeffrey D. Ullman. 1972. *The Theory of Parsing, Translation and Compiling*, volume 1. Prentice-Hall, Englewood Cliffs, NJ.

Banerjee Satanjeev and Lavie Alon. 2005. *METEOR: An automatic metric for MT evaluation with improved correlation with human judgments*. In Proceedings of the ACL Workshop on Intrinsic and Extrinsic Evaluation Measures for Machine Translation and/or Summarization, pages: 65-72.

Blatz John, Fitzgerald Erin, Foster George, Gandrabur Simona, Goutte Cyril, Kulesza Alex, Sanchis Alberto and Ueffing Nicola. 2003. *Confidence estimation for machine translation*. In Technical Report Natural Language Engi-neering Workshop Final Report, pages: 97-100.

Blei David M, Ng Andrew Y and Jordan Michael. 2003. *Latent Dirichlet allocation* . Journal of Machine Learning Research, pages: 993-1022.

Carpuat M. and Simard M.. 2012. *The Trouble with SMT Consistency*. Proceedings of the 7th Workshop on Statistical Machine Translation, pages: 442-449.

De Beaugrande R. and Dressler W.U. 1981. *Introduction to text linguistics* , London. New York : Longman.

Fowler Roger. 1991. *Language in the News: Discourse and Ideology in the press*, London: Routledge.

Galley Michel and McKeown Kathleen. 1993. *Improving word sense disambiguation in lexical chaining*. In Proceedings of the 18th international joint conference on Artificial intelligence, IJCAI03, pages: 1486-1488.

Gimenez Jesus, Marquez Lluis, Comelles Elisabet,Castellon Irene and Arranz Victoria. 1993. *Document-level automatic MT evaluation based on discourse representations*. In Proceedings of the Joint 5th Workshop on Statistical Machine Translation and MetricsMATR, pages: 333-338.

Gong Z.X., Zhang M. and Zhou G.D. 2011. *Cache-based document-level statistical machine translation*. In Proceedings of the 2011 Conference on Empirical Methods in Natural Language Processing, pages: 909-919.

Gong Z.X. and Zhou G.D. 2015. *Document-level Machine Translation Evaluation Metrics Enhanced with Simplified Lexical Chain*. In Proceedings of the 4th Conference on Natural Language Processing & Chinese Computing(To be published).

Guzmn Francisco, Joty Shafiq and Mrquez Llułs. 2014. *Using Discourse Structure Improves Machine Translation Evaluation*. In Proceedings of the 52nd Annual Meeting of the Association for Computational Linguistics, pages: 687-698.

Halliday M.A.K and Hasan Ruqayia. 1976. *Cohesion in English*, London: Longman.

Hardmeier Christian, Nivre Joakim and Tiedemann Jörg. 2012. *Document-wide decoding for phrase-based statistical machine translation*. In Proceedings of the 2012 Joint Conference on Empirical Methods in Natural Language Processing and Computational Natural Language Learning, pages: 1179-1190.

Hofmann Thomas. 1999. *Probabilistic Latent Semantic Indexing*. In Proceedings of the Twenty-Second Annual International SIGIR Conference on Research and Development in Information Retrieval, pages: 50-57.

Kamp H. and Reyle U. 1993. *From Discourse to Logic: Introduction to Modeltheoretic Semantics of Natural Language, Formal Logic and Discourse Representation Theory*. Dordrecht C Boston C London: Kluwer Academic Publishers.

Landauer T. K., Foltz P. and Laham D. 1998. *Introduction to Latent Semantic Analysis*. Discourse Processes 25.

Liu D., Gildea D. 2007. *Source-Language Features and Maximum Correlation Training for Ma-chine Translation Evaluation*. In Proceedings of NAACL, pages:41-48.

Morris Jane and Hirst Graeme. 1991. *Lexical cohesion computed by thesaural relations as an indicator of the structure of text*. Computational linguistics, 17(1):21-48.

Papineni Kishore, Roukos Salim, Ward Todd and Zhu WeiJing. 2002. *BLEU: a method for automatic evaluation of machine translation*. In Proceedings of the 40th annual meeting on association for computational linguistics, pages: 311-318.

Raphael Rubino, Jennifer Foster, Joachim Wagner, et al. 2012. *DCU-Symantec Submission for the WMT 2012 Quality Estimation Task*. Proceedings of the 7th Workshop on Statistical Machine Translation, pages: 138-144.

Raphael Rubino, Jos'e G. C. de Souza, Jennifer Foster, Lucia Specia. 2013. *Topic Models for Translation Quality Estimation for Gisting Purposes*. Proceedings of the XIV Machine Translation Summit, pages: 295-302.

Reeder, F. 2006. *Measuring MT Adequacy Using Latent Semantic Analysis*. In Proceedings of the 7th Conference of the Association for Machine Translation of the Americas. Cambridge, Massachusetts, pages: 176-184.

Tiedemann Jörg. 2010. *Context Adaptation in Statistical Machine Translation Using Models with Exponentially Decaying Cache.* In Proceedings of the 2010 Workshop on Domain Adaptation for Natural Language Processing (DANLP), pages: 8-15.

Ture Ferhan, Oard Douglas W and Resnik Philip. 2010. *Encouraging consistent translation choices.* Proceedings of the 2012 Conference of the North American Chapter of the Association for Computational Linguistics: Human Language Technologies, pages: 417-426.

Xiao Tong, Zhu Jingbo , Yao Shujie and Zhang Hao. 2011. *Document-Level Consistency Verification in Machine Translation.* In Proceedings of MT Summit XIII,pages: 131-138.

Xiao Xinyan,Xiong Deyi,Zhang Min, Liu Qun and Lin Shouxun. 2012. *A Topic Similarity Model for Hierarchical Phrase-based Translation.* In Proceedings of the 50th Annual Meeting of the Association for Computational Linguistics, pages: 750-758.

Xiong Deyi, Ding Yang, Zhang Min and Tan Chew Lim. 2013. *Lexical Lexical Chain Based Cohesion Models for Document-Level Statistical Machine Translation.* In Proceedings of the 2013 Conference on Empirical Methods in Natural Language Processing, pages: 1563-1573. Seattle, Washington, USA.

Van Rijsbergen C. 1979. *Information Retrieval.* Butterworths,London, UK.

Wong B.T.M. and Kit C. 2012. *Extending Machine Translation Evaluation Metrics with Lexical Cohesion to Document Level.* In Proceedings of the 2012 Joint Conference on Empirical Methods in Natural Language Processing and Computational Natural Language Learning, pages: 1060-1068.

The Role of Expectedness in the Implicitation and Explicitation of Discourse Relations

Jet Hoek
UiL-OTS, Utrecht University
Trans 10, NL-3512 JK
Utrecht, The Netherlands
j.hoek@uu.nl

Jacqueline Evers-Vermeul
UiL-OTS, Utrecht University
Trans 10, NL-3512 JK
Utrecht, The Netherlands
j.evers@uu.nl

Ted J.M. Sanders
UiL-OTS, Utrecht University
Trans 10, NL-3512 JK
Utrecht, The Netherlands
t.j.m.sanders@uu.nl

Abstract

Translation of discourse connectives varies more in human translations than in machine translations. Building on Murray's (1997) continuity hypothesis and Sanders' (2005) causality-by-default hypothesis we investigate whether expectedness influences the degree of implicitation and explicitation of discourse relations. We manually analyze how source text connectives are translated, and where connectives in target texts come from. We establish whether relations are explicitly signaled in the other language as well, or whether they have to be reconstructed by inference. We demonstrate that the amount of implicitation and explicitation of connectives in translation is influenced by the expectedness of the relation a connective signals. In addition, we show that the types of connectives most often added in translation are also the ones most often deleted.

1 Introduction

Discourse relations that hold between text segments can be explicitly signaled through connectives, but can also remain unmarked. For example, the causal relation in (1a) is explicitly encoded by the connective *because*. In its implicit counterpart in (1b), this causal relation has to be reconstructed by inference.

(1) a. Mike opened his umbrella *because* it was raining.
b. Mike opened his umbrella. It was raining.

In translation, connectives are very volatile items and can be added or removed between source text (ST) and target text (TT) (Halverson, 2004; Zufferey and Cartoni, 2014). Human translators more often leave out or reformulate a connective (up to 18%) than statistical machine translation models (up to 8%) (Meyer and Webber, 2013). In addition, when connectives are left out of machine translation (MT) output, this is not always justified and can result in translations that do not correspond to the original texts (cf. Li et al., 2014; Steele and Specia, 2014).

Specific deletions or additions of connectives in human translations have often been attributed to differences in linguistic resources between the languages in a translation pair (e.g. Becher, 2011; Hansen-Schirra et al., 2007). Other studies, however, have proposed that the deletion or addition of a connective is (also) dependent on the type of discourse relation a connective signals (e.g. Halverson 1996; Hoek and Zufferey, 2015). This study represents a first step in an effort to identify the factors that influence whether a connective can be left out of a translation without changing the interpretation of a fragment, or whether a connective should be translated into a target text by means of a comparable target language connective or another linguistic construction that expresses the same meaning. This knowledge can eventually be used to create MT systems that can translate explicit relations into implicit relations and vice versa in an idiomatic and fluent way that approaches the output of human translators.

Discourse-annotated corpora that include both implicit and explicit relations reveal that certain types of relations are easier to convey implicitly than others (Asr and Demberg, 2012; Das and Taboada, 2013; Versley, 2013). Causal relations, as in (1), for instance, appear more often without a connective or a cue phrase than negative relations, as in (2), or conditional relations, as in (3). The question marks in the b-sentences indicate that it is difficult to arrive at the negative or conditional interpretation, respectively, of the relations in the a-sentences.

(2) a. Ann is happy, *although* she lost the race.
b. ??Ann is happy. She lost the race.

(3) a. *If* he wants to be rich someday, he should get off the couch.
b. ??He wants to be rich someday. He should get off the couch.

Proceedings of the Second Workshop on Discourse in Machine Translation (DiscoMT), pages 41–46,
Lisbon, Portugal, 17 September 2015.

In this paper, we pursue the idea that the types of discourse relations that are often implicit correspond to the types of relations people expect in a discourse. According to the continuity hypothesis (Murray, 1997) and the causality-by-default hypothesis (Sanders, 2005), continuous and causal relations are generally the expected types. These hypotheses are corroborated by processing studies (e.g. Koornneef and Sanders, 2013; Kuperberg et al., 2011; Mak and Sanders, 2013; Sanders and Noordman, 2000) and corpus-based research. Asr and Demberg (2012) for instance demonstrate that the implicit relations in the Penn Discourse Treebank (PDTB, Prasad et al. 2008) are often continuous and/or causal.

If types of discourse relations differ in their degree of expectedness, and thereby in their degree of implicitness in monolingual texts, this should affect translation. In other words: we hypothesize that a discourse relation's potential to remain implicit (because of its expectedness) influences how often that type of relation is implicitated or explicitated in translation. For expected types of relations, which are often implicit in the ST, there are many instances at which translators can choose (either deliberately or subconsciously) to add a connective. Conversely, when an expected relation is explicitly marked in the ST, there will often be the option of leaving out the connective in the TT. What this predicts, then, is that markers of the types of relations that are most often added in translation will also be the ones most often deleted, regardless of language pair or translation direction. In this study, we test these predictions by comparing additions and deletions of connectives in two language pairs (English-Dutch and English-German) from the Europarl Direct corpus[1] (Koehn, 2005; Cartoni et al., 2013), and determining how the (interpretation of the) discourse relation in the ST or TT is conveyed in the other language.

2 Method

We define ***implicitness*** and ***explicitness*** as monolingual concepts that refer to whether the interpretation of, in this case, a discourse relation is explicitly encoded, as in (1a), or if it has to be reconstructed by inference, as in (1b). We use ***implicitation*** and ***explicitation*** to refer to shifts in implicitness or explicitness between ST and TT. In case of implicitation, the TT is more implicit than the ST. In case of explicitation, the TT is more explicit than the ST.

For this study, we compared three types of discourse relations: causal, negative, and conditional relations. Causal relations are among the expected types of relations, while negative and conditional relations are not. We therefore expect more implicitations and explicitations of causal relations than of negative or conditional relations. We selected prototypical connectives signaling these relation types in all three languages in our corpus, see Table 1.

	English	**Dutch**	**German**
Causal	*because*	*omdat*	*weil*
Negative	*although*	*hoewel*	*obwohl*
Conditional	*if*	*als*	*wenn*

Table 1. Connective selection per language and type of relation

We automatically extracted English ST fragments containing *because*, *although*, and *if* from the Europarl Direct corpus, along with their translations in Dutch and German. We also extracted Dutch and German TT fragments containing *omdat*, *hoewel*, and *als*, and *weil*, *obwohl*, and *wenn*, respectively, along with the corresponding English ST fragments. We randomly selected 250 instances of each connective and made sure these were used to mark a discourse relation. In total, we had 3000 ST-TT fragment pairs.

2.1 Annotation

For all connectives we determined how they were translated, or what they were a translation of. In the analysis we used the categories *explicit*, *paraphrase*, *underspecified connective*, *syntax*, and *implicit*.

In *explicit* cases, the connective corresponds to a similar connective or cue phrase in the other language. In the *paraphrase* category the type of relation is still explicitly encoded in the text, but with different linguistic means, as in (4). We coded a fragment as *implicit* if it contained a relation not marked by means of any connective or cue phrase. (5) is an example of implicitation, since the relation is explicitly encoded in the ST, but implicit in the TT. The implicitness is indicated with the Ø symbol.

[1] The Europarl Corpus is a version of the original Europarl corpus that only includes ST fragments that were originally uttered in that language, e.g. all fragments in the EN-DU part of the corpus were originally uttered in English. The corpus is aligned per language pair.

(4) (ep-96-07-03)
TT ***Hoewel*** *"although"* wij wegens de politieke situatie in Italië zelf aanvankelijk twijfels hadden, heeft het voorzitterschap toch opmerkelijke resultaten geboekt.
ST ***Despite*** the initial doubts we had due to the domestic political situation, there were some significant achievements ...
(5) (ep-98-02-20)
ST Insofar as the POSEIMA programme is concerned, we have to admit that you could not think of a more complicated or indirect or inefficient way to aid islands or remote regions, ***because*** in the first place there is no guarantee whatsoever that this money is going to the aid of the people who need it or for whom it was intended.
TT Voor wat betreft het POSEIMA-programma kunnen we alleen maar toegeven dat dit wel de ingewikkeldste, minst directe en meest inefficiënte manier is die je kunt bedenken om hulp te bieden aan eilandregio's en plattelandsgebieden. **Ø** Ten eerste bestaat er geen enkele garantie dat het geld inderdaad bij de mensen terechtkomt die het nodig hebben en voor wie het ook is bedoeld.

In the Dutch TT in (4), the connective *hoewel* "although" expresses a negative relation. The English ST does not contain this negative relation, but uses *despite* plus a noun phrase to explicitly indicate contrast.

In addition, connectives in a ST or TT that were less specific than the corresponding connectives in the other text were considered *underspecified connectives*. In these cases, neither the original nor the translation contains an implicit discourse relation. See for example (6), where the original temporal relation is marked with a more specific causal connective in the German translation. Hence, the translation can be seen as a case of explicitation.

(6) (ep-98-05-27)
TT Wir haben diesen Änderungsantrag im Namen von Herrn Wynn vorgelegt, um die Frage der Personalplanung für den Bürgerbeauftragten noch bis zur ersten Lesung offen zu lassen, ***weil*** *"because"* wir dann den gesamten Personalbedarf genauer einschätzen können.
ST We have tabled this amendment in Mr Wynn's name in order to leave the matter of staffing for the Ombudsman open until the first reading ***when*** one will have a clearer view of the overall need concerning staff.

Furthermore, we distinguish a *syntax* category, in which the syntax of the fragment is dramatically different from the corresponding fragment containing the connective and the relation disappears altogether, as in (7).

(7) (ep-00-03-14)
TT Een aantal Britse leden van het Europees Parlement zijn benaderd door belangengroepen van landbouwers, ***omdat*** *"because"* deze bang zijn dat de verbrandingsrichtlijn ook van toepassing zal zijn op alle verbrandingsinstallaties op boerenbedrijven.
ST A number of United Kingdom MEPs have been contacted by farming interests, ***who*** are very worried that the incineration directive will apply to all on-farm incinerators in the United Kingdom.

In (7) the causal relation signaled by *omdat* "because" in the Dutch TT is absent in the English ST. The second clause in the Dutch causal relation corresponds to a relative clause in the English ST, which does not explicitly signal causality. Instead, it has to be inferred by readers or listeners that the content of the relative clause presents the reason why farming interest groups have been contacting MEPs.

Two trained annotators, the first and second author of this paper, annotated the first 50 fragments for each connective for each language pair and translation direction (6x50 fragments). After establishing that there was a good inter-annotator agreement (κ = 0.84) and discussing the fragments that were disagreed on, one annotator finished the annotation of the remaining fragments.

On the basis of the annotations, we established for each ST-TT fragment pair whether it constituted a case of implicitation or explicitation. The categories *underspecified connective*, *syntax*, and *implicit* were considered to be instances of implicitation if they showed up in the TT equivalents of ST connectives, and instances of explicitation if they showed up in the ST equivalents of TT connectives. The categories *explicit* and *paraphrase* were grouped together as explicit-to-explicit translations. Statistical analysis was thus conducted on two categories instead of five.

2.2 Data analysis

Log-linear analysis was used to estimate the probability of occurrence of implicitations/

explicitations. The null model estimates the average probability. This model was compared to more complex models in which the probability was estimated as a function of our variables and the interactions between them: *relation type* (causal vs. negative vs. conditional), *marking* (implicit in the other language vs. explicit in the other language), *language pair* (EN-DU vs. EN-GE), and *direction* (ST→TT vs. TT→ST).

3 Results

The model in which all variables and several interactions were included was the best model. It retained a main effect of *marking* (χ^2 (1) = 3051.65, p < .001), two-way interactions of *relation type* and *marking* (χ^2 (2) = 82.91, p < .001), and of *marking* and *direction* (χ^2 (1) = 6.23, p = .01), plus a three-way interaction of *language pair*, *marking*, and *direction* (χ^2 (1) = 10.38, p = .001).

The two-way interaction between *relation type* and *marking* indicates that the amount of implicitation and explicitation of connectives in translation is influenced by the type of relation they signal. This relationship is visualized in Figure 1. As we hypothesized, causal relations were more often implicit than negative relations (z = 6.21, p < .001), which in turn showed more implicitation than conditional relations (z = 4.72, p < .001).

Taken together, the three-way interaction between *language pair*, *marking*, and *direction*, and the two-way interaction between *marking* and *direction* indicate the following. The English-German pairs adhere to the two-way interaction: the number of explicitations (explicit in TT, implicit in ST) was higher than the number of implicitations (explicit in ST, implicit in TT). This implies that connectives in German translations stem relatively frequently from an *underspecified connective*, another *syntax* or an *implicit* relation, while English ST connectives are hardly implicitated when translated into German TT.

For English-Dutch, this directional difference does not hold: the number of implications from ST to TT is higher than in German (z = 2.53, p = .01). This can also be derived from Figure 1, which illustrates that for EN-DU the overall number of implicitations is comparable to the overall number of explicitations. Crucially, the three-way interaction does not involve *relation type*, which means that the difference between EN-DU and EN-GE was not affected by the type of relation.

4 Discussion and conclusion

Our results show that the expectedness of discourse relations, as defined on the basis of the continuity hypothesis and the causality-by-default hypothesis, affects translation. Causal connectives, which are expected in discourse, are both more often added and deleted in translation than relations that are not expected, in this case negative and conditional connectives. We also found that negative connectives were more often added and deleted than conditional connectives.

Since this study included only English-Dutch and English-German translations, and Dutch and German are closely related languages, it may be possible that the implicitation and explicitation patterns we found are generalizable only within the language family. However, in an earlier study in which we only looked at the translations of ST connectives we also included English-French and English-Spanish translations (Hoek and Zufferey, 2015). Here we found identical implicitation patterns for French and Spanish (both of which belong to a different language family) as for Dutch and German. This suggests that our results are also generalizable across language families.

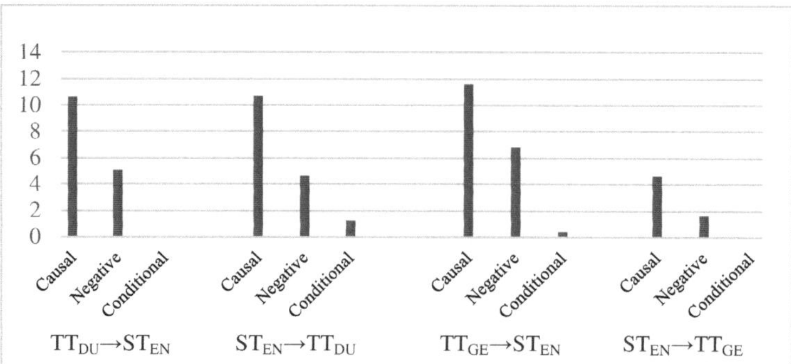

Figure 1. Percentage of implicit translations/originals per type of relation, per language pair

Our finding that negative connectives were more often added and deleted than conditional connectives is not predicted by the continuity hypothesis or the causality-by-default hypothesis, but it seems to be corroborated by corpus studies. Conditional relations hardly ever seem to be implicit in monolingual corpora, while this is less rare for negative relations (e.g. Asr and Demberg, 2012; Das and Taboada, 2013). We will address the difference between negative and conditional relations in further research.

We found more explicitations than implicitations for English-German translations, but not for English-Dutch translations. The observation that translation pairs and translation directions can differ in the overall number of connectives that are added or deleted has also been made in corpus-based studies (e.g. Becher, 2011; Cartoni et al., 2011). This effect did not, however, interact with the relative frequencies of implicitation or explicitation of relation types.

It should be noted the frequency of implicitations (3.6%) that we found was much lower than the frequency reported by Meyer and Webber (2013) (up to 18%). This can probably be attributed to our relatively broad definition of the explicit category *paraphrase*, which for instance included verbs expressing causality (e.g. *make*, *cause*) and the subjunctive in German, since this explicitly encodes conditionality. If we were to include all paraphrases in our implicitations, we would arrive at a higher percentage of 11.2%.

The potential to remain implicit appears to influence how often a relation is implicitated or explicitated in translation. To improve the quality and naturalness of machine translation, it therefore seems crucial to distinguish between deletions and additions of connectives in which the relation in the other language is implicit and those in which the relation is marked by different linguistic means, and to incorporate factors that influence whether a relation can be left implicit or whether it should be explicitly signaled into a machine translation model.

Acknowledgments

We are grateful to the Swiss National Science Foundation (SNSF) for the funding of this work under its Sinergia program, grant n. CRSII2_147653 (MODERN project, see www.idiap.ch/project/modern/).

References

Fatemeh T. Asr and Vera Demberg. 2012. Implicitness of discourse relations. *Proceedings of COLING*. Mumbai, India.

Viktor Becher. 2011. When and why do translators add connectives? *Target*, 23(1):26–47.

Bruno Cartoni, Sandrine Zufferey and Thomas Meyer. 2013. Using the Europarl corpus for linguistics research. *Belgian Journal of Linguistics*, 27:23–42.

Bruno Cartoni, Sandrine Zufferey, Thomas Meyer and Andrei Popescu-Belis. 2011. How comparable are parallel corpora? Measuring the distribution of general vocabulary and connectives. *Proceedings of the 4th Workshop on Building and Using Comparable Corpora*, 78–86. Portland, Oregon.

Debopam Das and Maite Taboada. 2013. Explicit and implicit coherence relations: A corpus study. *Proceedings of the 2013 Annual Conference of the Canadian Linguistic Association.* Victoria, Canada.

Sandra Halverson. 1996. Norwegian-English translation and the role of certain connectives. *Translation and Meaning, part 3: Proceedings of the Maastricht Session of the 2nd International Maastricht-Lodź Duo Colloquium on 'Translation and Meaning'*, 128–139. Maastricht, the Netherlands.

Sandra Halverson. 2004. Connectives as a translation problem. In Harald Kittel, Armin Paul Frank, Norbert Greiner, Theo Hermans, Werner Koller, José Lambert and Fritz Paul. (Eds.), *An International Encyclopedia of Translation Studies*, 562–572. Berlin/New York: Walter de Gruyter.

Silvia Hansen-Schirra, Stella Neuman and Erich Steiner. 2007. Cohesive explicitness and explicitation in an English-German translation corpus. *Languages in Contrast* 7(2):241–265.

Jet Hoek and Sandrine Zufferey. 2015. Factors influencing the implicitation of discourse relations across languages. *Proceedings 11th Joint ACL-ISO Workshop on Interoperable Semantic Annotation (ISA-11)*, 39–45. London, United Kingdom.

Philipp Koehn. 2005. Europarl: A parallel corpus for statistical machine translation. *Proceedings of the 10th Machine Translation Summit*, 79–86. Phuket, Thailand.

Arnout W. Koornneef and Ted J. M. Sanders. 2013. Establishing coherence relations in discourse: The influence of implicit causality and connectives on pronoun resolution. *Language and Cognitive Processes*, 28(8):1169–1206.

Gina R. Kuperberg, Martin Paczynski and Tali Ditman. 2011. Establishing causal coherence across sentences: An ERP study. *Journal of Cognitive Neuroscience*, 23:1230–1246.

Junyi Jessy Li, Marine Carpuat and Ani Nenkova. 2014. Assessing the discourse factors that influence the quality of machine translation. *Proceedings of the 52nd Annual Meeting of the Association for Computational Linguistics,* 283–288. Baltimore, MD, USA.

Willem M. Mak and Ted J. M. Sanders. 2013. The role of causality in discourse processing: Effects of expectation and coherence relations. *Language and Discourse Processes*, 28(9):1414–1437.

Thomas Meyer and Bonnie Webber. 2013. Implicitation of discourse connectives in (machine) translation. *Proceedings of the 1st DiscoMT Workshop at ACL 2013*, 33–42. Sofia, Bulgaria.

John D. Murray. 1997. Connectives and narrative text: The role of continuity. *Memory and Cognition*, 25:227–236.

Rashmi Prasad, Nikhil Dinesh, Alan Lee, Eleni Miltsakaki, Livio Robaldo, Aravind Joshi and Bonnie Webber. 2008. The Penn Discourse Treebank 2.0. *Proceedings of the 6th International Conference on Language Resources and Evaluation* (LREC 2008), 2961–2968. Marrakech, Morocco.

Ted J. M. Sanders. 2005. Coherence, causality and cognitive complexity in discourse. *Proceedings/Actes SEM-05, First International Symposium on the Exploration and Modelling of Meaning,* 105–114.

Ted J. M. Sanders and Leo G. M. Noordman. 2000. The role of coherence relations and their linguistic markers in text processing. *Discourse Processes*, 29:37–60.

David Steele and Lucia Specia. 2014. Divergences in the usage of discourse markers in English and Mandarin Chinese. *Proceedings of the 17th International Conference on Text, Speech and Dialogue*, 189–200. Brno, Czech Republic.

Yannick Versley. 2013. A graph-based approach for implicit discourse relations. *Computational Linguistics in the Netherlands Journal*, 3:148–173.

Sandrine Zufferey and Bruno Cartoni. 2014. A multifactorial analysis of explicitation in translations. *Target*, 26:361–384.

Detecting Document-level Context Triggers to Resolve Translation Ambiguity

Laura Mascarell, Mark Fishel and **Martin Volk**
Institute of Computational Linguistics
University of Zurich
Switzerland
{mascarell,fishel,volk}@cl.uzh.ch

Abstract

Most current machine translation systems translate each sentence independently, ignoring the context from previous sentences. This discourse unawareness can lead to incorrect translation of words or phrases that are ambiguous in the sentence. For example, the German term *Typen* in the phrase *diese Typen* can be translated either into English *types* or *guys*. However, knowing that it co-refers to the compound *Körpertypen* ("body types") in the previous sentence helps to disambiguate the term and translate it into *types*. We propose a method of automatically detecting document-level trigger words (like *Körpertypen*), whose presence helps to disambiguate translations of ambiguous terms. In this preliminary study we analyze the method and its limitations, and outline future work directions.

1 Introduction

Words with ambiguous senses and translations pose a core challenge for machine translation. For example, the English noun *face* is translated into German *Gesicht* ("front of head") or *Wand* ("wall") when talking about mountaineering. Phrase-based Statistical Machine Translation (SMT) systems benefit from using the local context inside the phrases for disambiguation; on the other hand, global sentence-level and document-level context remains largely unmodelled. We focus on cases where the source of disambiguation lies in the sentences preceding the ambiguous term, for example:

> ...on the unclimbed ***East face*** of the Central Tower...
> ...we were swept from the ***face*** by a five-day storm...

Mascarell et al. (2014) and Pu et al. (2015) tackle the issue illustrated in the previous example, and show improvements in correctness, based on the one-translation-per-discourse hypothesis (Carpuat, 2009). Specifically, their method uses the translation of the head of the compound (e.g. *Wand* in *East face*) for the term (e.g. *face*) that co-refers back to it in a later sentence.

Bridging Noun Phrases (NPs) are a similar phenomenon that crosses sentence boundaries:

> The company wrote out ***a new job***.
> ***Two applicants*** were suitable.

Here the bridging NP *two applicants* is ambiguous on its own, as *applicants* can be translated into Spanish as *candidatos* or *solicitantes*. However, in the context of the antecedent of the bridging NP, *a new job*, *applicants* is more appropriately translated into *candidatos*.

In this work we generalize over both these problems (i.e. co-referent compounds and bridging NPs) and disambiguate translations using "trigger words": words whose presence in the preceding sentences indicates a certain context for the ambiguous term in the current sentence. We focus on automatically detecting such trigger words universally without focusing on a single phenomenon like compound co-references or bridging, and analyze the results.

2 Detecting Context Triggers

Ambiguous words with several possible translations have a different translation distribution depending on the sense; for example, the English *driver* in the meaning of the person driving a vehicle will likely be translated into the French *conducteur* or *chauffeur*, and much less likely into *pilote*, which corresponds to the computer device-related meaning. However, when estimated on the whole corpus the likelihoods of the three transla-

Proceedings of the Second Workshop on Discourse in Machine Translation (DiscoMT), pages 47–51,
Lisbon, Portugal, 17 September 2015.

German word:	BILD		LAND		TYP		FLÄCHE	
Translation distributions in different documents:	**doc. #1:**		**doc. #4:**		**doc. #7:**		**doc. #10:**	
	picture:	0.93	country:	0.84	guy:	0.33	surface:	0.93
	frame:	0.04	state:	0.09	jimbo:	0.33	faces:	0.07
	understanding	0.03	arab:	0.07	person:	0.33		
	doc. #2:		**doc. #5:**		**doc. #8:**		**doc. #11:**	
	image:	1.00	country:	1.00	type:	1.00	area:	1.00
	doc. #3:		**doc. #6:**		**doc. #9:**		**doc. #12:**	
	image:	0.73	country:	0.94	guy:	1.00	area:	0.80
	imagery:	0.22	nation:	0.03			space:	0.20
	picture:	0.05	desolate:	0.03				

Table 1: The four ambiguous words selected for our experiments from the WIT3 corpus. The table shows how the translation distribution of each word differ from document to document. Some translations are noise due to wrong word alignments.

tions in $P(\cdot|driver)$ will reflect the frequency of usage and not the particular contexts.

We focus on trigger words that appear in the context of a particular word sense. Identifying them helps to disambiguate the sense of an ambiguous word and translate it correctly. We try to detect trigger words from the preceding context and use them as conditional variables in the translation distributions. This means, for example, that

$$p(tgt = \text{"pilote"}|src = \text{"driver"}, trig = \text{"road"})$$

should be low, while

$$p(tgt = \text{"pilote"}|src = \text{"driver"}, trig = \text{"device"})$$

should be much higher (where src is the source word, tgt – its translation hypothesis and $trig$ – the trigger word).

To identify those trigger words we consider a simplistic method based on translation distribution similarity. The core idea is that the translation distribution of an ambiguous word changes with the presence and absence of a trigger word. That is, non-trigger words (e.g. function words and general vocabulary) lead to similar distributions (i.e. their presence and absence has little effect on the translation choice), whereas relevant triggers result in these two distributions being highly different. To measure this distribution difference we compute the KL-divergence between them. In other words, for each ambiguous term A we are searching for such a trigger word W from the preceding sentences that maximizes

$$D_{KL}(P(\cdot\,|\,A, W)\;||\;P(\cdot\,|\,A, -W)),$$

where $-W$ means the absence of the trigger word W from the preceding sentences.

3 Experiments

In this preliminary evaluation of our method we focus on the specific case of co-references to compounds, where the co-reference is an ambiguous word with several translations. The co-reference is disambiguated using a trigger word from the preceding context (i.e. the compound that the word co-refers to). The idea is that knowing which these compounds are we assess whether our method is able to detect them as relevant triggers.

The data comes from the German-English part of the WIT3 corpus (Cettolo et al., 2012), which is a collection of TED talks in multiple languages. The corpus consists of 194'533 sentences and 3.6 million tokens split into 1'596 talks (i.e. documents). The test set is also a collection of TED talks, consisting of 6'047 sentences and about 100'000 tokens. The talks differ greatly in terms of the covered topics, and therefore, have a high potential for ambiguous translations between them. This topic variety is so high that it is not feasible to tune SMT systems separately to each topic. However, it makes the corpus a feasible target for dynamic adaptation like our method.

For our experiments we first manually select four ambiguous words, and we then obtain the co-referenced compounds by applying the detection method described in (Mascarell et al., 2014). Next, we check whether our method detects these compounds as triggers. The four selected words *Bild*, *Land*, *Typ* and *Fläche* are presented in Table 1; as the table shows their translation distributions indeed differ between different documents.

Top highest distance				Top lowest distance			
Lemma	EN	Score	Freq.	Lemma	EN	Score	Freq.
unterseeboot	submarine	28.8843	1/2	weil	because	0.0053	474/4'231
alvin	alvin	28.8843	3/5	eine	a	0.0061	6257/62'088
gap	gap	28.8843	1/7	leute	people	0.0078	485/4'543
unaufgefordert	unsolicited	28.8843	1/2	"	"	0.0222	1295/15'395

Table 2: Comparison of the lemmas with the highest and lowest KL divergence score in the context of *Land* considering the 4 preceding sentences. The *Freq.* column shows the total number of times the lemma appears in the context of *Land* over the total occurrences of that lemma in the corpus.

Compound	1 sent.		2 sent.		3 sent.		4 sent.	
	pos.	△	pos.	△	pos.	△	pos.	△
Geburtsland	52'133	28.32	53'233	28.32	54'123	28.32	1'430	3.50
Lesterland	19'689	28.32	711	3.50	923	3.50	823	3.50
Entwicklungsland	4'811	24.96	6'744	24.83	8'300	24.93	9'717	24.96
Heimatland	5'483	25.30	94'095	28.33	10'358	28.30	94'084	28.40
Niemandsland	39'698	28.32	854	3.50	1'099	3.50	1'312	3.50

Table 3: Comparison of the resulting KL divergence ranking obtained considering the context of the previous sentences up to 4. The table shows the ranking position of the compounds co-referenced by *Land* in the corpus, and the difference between their distance score and the word with the highest distance.

4 Results and Analysis

We assess whether our method detects as triggers the compounds that the selected words (see Table 1) co-refer to. We do not try to detect the compounds directly because we aim at generalizing and applying our method to other phenomena, such as bridging. Since all selected words have a similar outcome, we focus on the results of *Land*.

We first analyze which are the detected triggers by our method for the word *Land*, considering the 4 previous sentences (see Table 2). Note that to detect the triggers, our method computes the distance between the translation distribution of the word *Land* when the trigger candidate appears in the context and when it does not. Therefore, the words with the highest distance score are the relevant triggers, while the words with the lowest are mostly frequent non-content words that do not give any information of the correct translation of *Land*. We also observe that none of the compounds are in the list of trigger words, but other non-related words. The reason is that these occur together with the ambiguous word (*Land*) only once, causing the distribution to contain only one translation with 1.0 probability. This distribution is then very different from the one without that infrequent faux-trigger over the rest of the document, which includes several translation variants.

The position of the compounds in the resulting KL divergence ranking is shown in Table 3, considering the context of the previous sentences up to 4. Table 3 also shows the difference between the compound score and the word with the highest distance (i.e. most relevant trigger detected).

To get a better overview, Figure 1 illustrates where the listed compounds (see Table 3) are positioned over the whole ranking in the context of the previous sentences up to 4. We observe that some of these compounds appear in the first quartile of the ranking. However, there are compounds in the bottom half of the graph, that is they are not detected as relevant trigger words.

5 Outlook for future research extensions

We observe in the analysis (see section 4) that our method is sensitive to detect non-related infrequent words as potential triggers. To solve this problem, we want to steer the search to semantically related words, instead of only filtering out infrequent words. The reason is that trigger words that only appear in the context of an ambiguous term would be detected as infrequent, and therefore, incorrectly discarded. We are then planning to combine the distribution difference (measured with the KL divergence or other metrics) with a measure of similarity between the trigger candidate and the ambiguous word. Their simi-

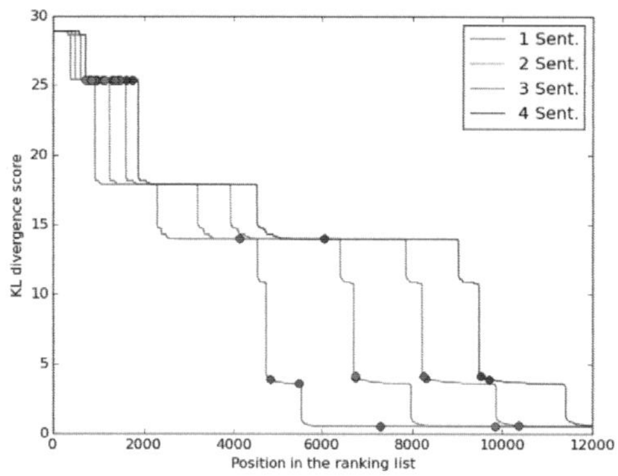

Figure 1: Comparison of the KL divergence rankings considering up to 4 previous sentences. The position of the compounds listed in table 3 are pointed out among all trigger candidates.

larity can be measured using a vector representation (Mikolov et al., 2013), for example with the *word2vec* tool[1].

Since our method suffers from data sparsity, only trigger words that appear in the training data are taken into account. Using *word2vec* we can compare the vector representation of the detected trigger words and the trigger candidates in the test set. We would then also consider trigger words that do not appear in the training data, but have the same vector representation.

Finally, the goal of our method is to generalize the detection of trigger words. Thus, we want to extend our study testing whether our method detects the antecedent of bridging NPs as a trigger word, and other discourse-oriented phenomena.

6 Related Work

Several approaches focus on improving lexical choice in SMT by enforcing consistency at document level. These are based on the one-translation-per-discourse hypothesis (Carpuat, 2009), which shows that more than one translation of the same term in the document leads to incorrect translations. Mascarell et al. (2014) and Pu et al. (2015) take advantage of compounds, which have more context than single-root words, and use the translation of the head of the compound for later occurrences of the single co-referring head noun in isolation. Using an enforcing and post-editing method, they show improvement of translation correctness of co-referring terms in German-French and Chinese-English. Other approaches (see (Tiedemann, 2010) and (Gong et al., 2011)) use a cache-model for the same purpose. Xiao et al. (2011) enforce the translation of ambiguous words to be consistent across the document by applying a three-steps procedure.

The term "trigger" is first introduced by Rosenfeld (1994). The approach to adaptive language modeling uses a maximum entropy model, showing perplexity improvements over the conventional trigram model.

A recently popular approach is to include topic modeling into the SMT pipeline and to use topic distributions to disambiguate phrase translations (see e.g. (Hasler et al., 2014)). Xiong et al. (2014) present a sense-based translation model that integrates word senses using maximum entropy classifiers. Meng et al. (2014) propose three term translation models to disambiguate, enforce consistency and guarantee integrity. Finally, Xiong et al. (2013) introduce a method that translates the coherence chain of the source, and uses it to produce a coherent translation. This topic modeling line of research can be combined with our own by including preceding sentences or their parts into the topic model training process.

7 Conclusions

We present a method that crosses sentence boundaries to automatically detect the words that help to correctly translate terms with several senses. We call them trigger words, and they appear in the context of a particular word sense. To detect them we compute the distance between the translation distributions of the ambiguous word with and without the presence of the trigger candidate. Higher distances suggest a likely trigger for a particular word sense.

There are two main issues that need to be solved. First, infrequent non-related trigger candidates that appear in the context of the word obtain a high distance score, and therefore, they are detected as potential triggers. Second, only the triggers detected in the training data can be used in the test set. To solve these issues, we are planning to use word vector representations to include the measurement of semantic relatedness between the ambiguous word and its triggers.

[1] https://code.google.com/p/word2vec/

References

Marine Carpuat. 2009. One translation per discourse. In *Proceedings of the Workshop on Semantic Evaluations: Recent Achievements and Future Directions*, pages 19–27, Boulder, Colorado.

Mauro Cettolo, Christian Girardi, and Marcello Federico. 2012. Wit^3: Web inventory of transcribed and translated talks. In *Proceedings of the 16th Conference of the European Association for Machine Translation*, pages 261–268, Trento, Italy.

Zhengxian Gong, Min Zhang, and Guodong Zhou. 2011. Cache-based document-level Statistical Machine Translation. In *Proceedings of the 2011 Conference on Empirical Methods in Natural Language Processing*, pages 909–919, Edinburgh, UK.

Eva Hasler, Barry Haddow, and Philipp Koehn. 2014. Dynamic topic adaptation for smt using distributional profiles. In *Proceedings of the 9th Workshop on Statistical Machine Translation*, pages 445–456, Baltimore, MD, USA.

Laura Mascarell, Mark Fishel, Natalia Korchagina, and Martin Volk. 2014. Enforcing consistent translation of german compound coreferences. In *Proceedings of the 12th Konvens Conference*, pages 58–65, Hildesheim, Germany.

Fandong Meng, Deyi Xiong, Wenbin Jiang, and Qun Liu. 2014. Modeling term translation for document-informed machine translation. In *Proceedings of the 2014 Conference on Empirical Methods in Natural Language Processing*, pages 546–556, Doha, Qatar.

Tomas Mikolov, Kai Chen, Greg Corrado, and Jeffrey Dean. 2013. Efficient estimation of word representations in vector space. In *Proceedings of Workshop at the International Conference on Learning Representations*, Scottsdale, Arizona, USA.

Xiao Pu, Laura Mascarell, Andrei Popescu-Belis, Mark Fishel, Ngoc-Quang Luong, and Martin Volk. 2015. Leveraging compounds to improve noun phrase translation from chinese and german. In *Proceedings of the ACL-IJCNLP 2015 Student Research Workshop*, pages 8–15, Beijing, China.

Ronald Rosenfeld. 1994. A hybrid approach to adaptive statistical language modeling. In *Proceedings of the Workshop on Human Language Technology*, pages 76–81, Stroudsburg, PA, USA.

Jörg Tiedemann. 2010. Context adaptation in Statistical Machine Translation using models with exponentially decaying cache. In *Proceedings of the 2010 Workshop on Domain Adaptation for Natural Language Processing*, pages 8–15, Uppsala, Sweden.

Tong Xiao, Jingbo Zhu, Shujie Yao, and Hao Zhang. 2011. Document-level consistency verification in Machine Translation. In *Proceedings of the 13th Machine Translation Summit*, pages 131–138, Xiamen, China.

Deyi Xiong and Min Zhang. 2013. A topic-based coherence model for statistical machine translation. In *Proceedings of the 27th AAAI Conference on Artificial Intelligence*, Bellevue, Washington, USA.

Deyi Xiong and Min Zhang. 2014. A sense-based translation model for statistical machine translation. In *Proceedings of the 52nd Annual Meeting of the Association for Computational Linguistics*, pages 1459–1469, Baltimore, Maryland.

A Proposal for a Coherence Corpus in Machine Translation

Karin Sim Smith[§], **Wilker Aziz**[†] and **Lucia Specia**[§]
§Department of Computer Science, University of Sheffield, UK
{kmsimsmith1,l.specia}@sheffield.ac.uk

†Institute for Logic, Language and Computation
University of Amsterdam, The Netherlands
w.aziz@uva.nl

Abstract

Coherence in Machine Translation (MT) has received little attention to date. One of the main issues we face in work in this area is the lack of labelled data. While coherent (human authored) texts are abundant and incoherent texts could be taken from MT output, the latter also contains other errors which are not specifically related to coherence. This makes it difficult to identify and quantify issues of coherence in those texts. We introduce an initiative to create a corpus consisting of data artificially manipulated to contain errors of coherence common in MT output. Such a corpus could then be used as a benchmark for coherence models in MT, and potentially as training data for coherence models in supervised settings.

1 Introduction

Discourse information has only recently started to attract attention in MT, particularly in Statistical Machine Translation (SMT), the focus of this paper. Most decoders work on a sentence by sentence basis, isolated from context, due to both modelling and computational complexity. An exception are approaches to multi-pass decoding, such as Docent (Hardmeier et al., 2013a). Our work focuses on an issue which has not yet been much explored in MT, that of coherence.

Coherence is undeniably a cognitive process, and we will limit our remit to the extent that this process is guided by linguistic elements discernible in the discourse. While it does include cohesion, it is wider in terms of describing how a text becomes semantically meaningful overall, and additionally spans the entire document. We are interested in capturing aspects of coherence as defined by Grosz and Sidner (1986), based on the attentional state, intentional structure and linguistic structure of discourse. As a result, we believe that a coherent discourse should have a context and a focus, be characterised by appropriate coherence relations, and structured in a logical manner.

Previous computational models for assessing coherence in a monolingual context have covered entity transitions (Barzilay and Lapata, 2008; Elsner and Charniak, 2011; Burstein et al., 2010; Guinaudeau and Strube, 2013), syntactic patterns (Louis and Nenkova, 2012), discourse relations (Lin et al., 2011), distributed sentence representations (Li and Hovy, 2014) and lexical chains (Somasundaran et al., 2014). For evaluation, these studies in coherence have typically used automatically summarized texts, or texts with sentences artificially shuffled as their 'incoherent' data. The latter is an example of artificially created labelled data, distorting the ordered logic of the text and thus affecting some aspects of coherence. However, it is inadequate for our task, as MT preserves the sentence ordering, but suffers from other aspects of incoherence. Moreover, while the MT output can potentially be considered 'incoherent', it contains a multitude of problems, which are not all due to lack of coherence.

For the evaluation of coherence models in the MT context, as well as for supervised learning of coherence models it is necessary to have data annotated with issues of incoherence. In particular, we are interested in coherence issues which are deemed to occur specifically in MT output. The purpose of this initiative is to ensure that we can assess coherence models by isolating other issues that are not related to coherence.

In the remainder of this paper, we start by presenting previous work (Section 2). We then describe how problems related to lack of coherence are manifested in MT output (Section 3). In Section 4 we detail how we plan to manipulate the data in systematic ways to create a corpus of artificially generated incoherent data.

Proceedings of the Second Workshop on Discourse in Machine Translation (DiscoMT), pages 52–58,
Lisbon, Portugal, 17 September 2015.

2 Existing work

There has been previous work in the area of lexical cohesion in MT (Wong and Kit, 2012; Xiong et al., 2013a; Xiong et al., 2013b; Tiedemann, 2010; Hardmeier, 2012; Carpuat and Simard, 2012). Lexical cohesion is part of coherence, as it looks at the linguistic elements which hold a text together. However, there has been very little work in the wider area of coherence as a whole.

Besides lexical cohesion, another discourse related phenomenon that has been addressed in MT is reference resolution. As detailed in greater depth by Hardmeier (2012), the results for earlier attempts to address this issue were not very successful (Hardmeier and Federico, 2010; Le Nagard and Koehn, 2010). More recent work includes that of Guillou (2012), which highlights the differences of coreference depending on the language pair. Since then Hardmeier et al. (2013b) have used a new approach for anaphora resolution via neural networks which achieves comparable results to a standard anaphora resolutions system, but without annotated data. Recently work has begun on negation in MT, particularly by Wetzel and Bond (2012; Fancellu and Webber (2014). There is also work focusing on evaluation against reference translations (Guzmán et al., 2014) based on the comparison between discourse trees in MT versus reference. This information was found to improve evaluation of MT output.

Drawing from research on topic modelling (Eidelman et al., 2012), where lexical probabilities conditioned on topics are computed, Xiong and Zhang (2013) attempt to improve coherence based using topic information. They determine the topic of the source sentence and project it onto the target as a feature to ensure the decoder selects the appropriate words. They observed slight improvements in terms of general standard metrics, indicating perhaps that these metrics fail to account for discourse improvements.

As far as we aware, no attempts have been made to create a corpus exhibiting incoherence, other than by shuffling ordered sentences. There has been work in other areas to introduce errors in correct texts. For example, Felice and Yuan (2014) and Brockett et al. (2006) inject grammatical errors common to non-native speakers of English in good quality texts. Felice and Yuan (2014) use existing corrected corpora to derive the error distribution, while Brockett et al. (2006) adopt a deterministic approach based on hand-crafted rules. Logacheva and Specia (2015) inject various types of errors to generate negative data for quality estimation purposes, but these are at the word level, and the process was guided by post-editing data. They derived an error distribution of MT output by inspecting post editing data. We do not have a similar way of inducing a distribution of errors for coherence. A large amount of post editings of entire documents would be needed, and it still be difficult to isolate which of the edits relate to coherence errors.

3 Issues of incoherence in MT systems

Current MT approaches suffer from a lack of linguistic information at various stages (modelling, decoding, pruning) causing the lack of coherence in the output. Below we describe a number of issues that are generally viewed as coherence issues which MT approaches deal poorly with and which have also been the subject of previous work. The examples given have been identified in error analysis done by ourselves in either of the following corpora:

- the **newstest** data (source and output) from the WMT corpus,[1] focusing on French and German source, and English as output.
- the **LIG** corpus (Potet et al., 2012) of French-English translations: 361 parallel documents comprising source, reference translation, machine translated output and post-edited output, drawn from various WMT editions.

The following are issues of incoherence which have been identified by ourselves (below) and others (Section 2) as particularly common in MT systems.

Lexical cohesion MT has been shown to be consistent in its use of terminology (Carpuat and Simard, 2012), which can be an advantage for narrow texts domains with significant training data. However, MT systems may output direct translations of source text items that may be inappropriate in the target context. Moreover, while a specific target text word may correctly translate a source text word in one context, it may require a totally different word in another context. In our data *'boucher'* occur

[1] `http://www.statmt.org/wmt13/`

more often as a French noun, corresponding to *'butcher'*. This increases the probability of the translation equivalence *'butcher'*, yet in the translated text it is used as a noun indicating to *'block'* (for example, *'road block'*).

src: *'Cette anne, c'était* ***au tour de*** *l'Afrique de nommer le président et elle a nommé la Libye.'*

mt: *'This year, it was* ***at the tour of*** *Africa to appoint the president and has appointed Libya.'*

ref: *'This year it was Africa****'s turn*** *to nominate the chairman, and they nominated Libya.'*

Here the wrong meaning of *tour* was used, and renders the sentence incoherent. As Wong and Kit (2012) note, the lexical cohesion devices have to not only be recognised, but used appropriately. And this may differ from the source text to the target text.

Referencing Anaphora resolution is a very challenging issue in current MT approaches (Michal, 2011; Le Nagard and Koehn, 2010; Hardmeier and Federico, 2010; Hardmeier et al., 2013b; Guillou, 2012). This is again due to the fact that intersentential references are lost in most decoders as they translate one sentence at a time. Reference resolution is affected in several ways. The context of the preceding sentences is absent, meaning that the reference is undetermined. Even once it is correctly resolved (by additional pre-training or a second-pass), reference resolution is directly impacted by linguistic differences, for example, the target language may have multiple genders for nouns while the source only has one. The result is that references can be missing or wrong.

src: *'L'extrême droite européenne est caractérisée par* ***son*** *racisme...'*

mt: *'The extreme right is characterised by* ***his*** *racism...'*

ref: *'A common feature of Europe's extreme right is its racism...'* (Potet et al., 2012).

Here the pronoun *'son'*, referring to the racism of the extreme right, is wrongly rendered as *'his'*.

Discourse connectives Discourse connectives are vital for the correct understanding of discourse. Yet in MT systems these can be incorrect or missing (Meyer and Poláková, 2013; Meyer and Popescu-Belis, 2012; Meyer et al., 2011; Steele, 2015). In particular, where discourse connectives are ambiguous, e.g. those which can be temporal or causal in nature, the MT system may choose the wrong connective translation, which distorts the meaning of the text. It is also possible that the discourse connective is implicit in the source, and thus need to be inferred. While a human translator can detect this, an MT system cannot.

src: *'Die Rechtsanwlte der Republikaner haben in 10 Jahren in den USA* ***übrigens*** *nur 300 Flle von Wahlbetrug verzeichnet.'*

mt: *'The Republican lawyers have listed over 10 years in the United States, only 300 cases of electoral fraud.'*

ref: ***Indeed****, Republican lawyers identified only 300 cases of electoral fraud in the United States in a decade.*

The discourse marker is missing altogether in the MT output above (in addition to the ordering error). While small, cue words guide the reader and help create the logic in the text. Here the discourse marker was for emphasis, illustrating the writer's claim.

Syntax structure Different languages have different syntactic structures. In MT system the syntax of the target language may get distorted, often too close to the syntax of the source language, leading to an incoherent sentence formation.

src: *'Ce ne sera pas le cas, comme le démontre clairement l'histoire raciale de l'Amérique.'*

mt: *'This is not the case, as clearly demonstrates the history of race in America.'*

ref: *It will not, as America's racial history clearly shows.* (Potet et al., 2012)

Here the natural logic of the sentence is distorted, with the subject coming after the verb, directly affecting the coherence.

Clauses ordering Particularly in hierarchical or tree-based MT systems, the order of clauses within sentences may have become reversed, or may be unnatural for the target language.

src: *'Das Opfer war später an den Folgen der schweren Verletzungen gestorben.'*

mt: *'The victim was later at the consequences of the serious injuries died.'*

ref: *'The victim later died as a result of the serious injuries.'* (Bojar et al., 2014).

This can affect the understanding of the sentence, the overall logic of it in the context of the surrounding sentences, or simply require a reread which itself is indicative of impaired coherence.

src: *'Bereits im Jahr 1925 wurde in Polen eine Eisenbahn-Draisine gebaut, für die ein Raketenantrieb geplant war. Der Autor des Entwurfs und die Details dieses Vorhabens blieben leider unbekannt.'*
mt: *'Already in 1925 a railway trolley was built in Poland, for which a rocket was planned. The author of the design and the details of the project remained unfortunately unknown.'*
ref: *In 1925, Poland had already built a handcar which was supposed to be fitted with a rocket engine. Unfortunately, both the project's designer, and the project's details, are unknown.* (Bojar et al., 2013)

The reference translation has a clausal pattern which is more cohesive to the English reader.

Negation MT systems often miss the focus of the negation. This results in incorrectly transferred negations that affect coherence (Wetzel and Bond, 2012; Fancellu and Webber, 2014).

src: *'**Aucun** dirigeant serbe **n**'acceptera l'indépendance du Kosovo'*
mt: *'**No** leader of Serbia will **not** accept the independence of Kosovo..'*
ref: *'No leader of Serbia will accept the independence of Kosovo'.*(Potet et al., 2012)

In this case the negation is distorted, influenced by the structure of the source text.

4 Artificially generating coherence errors

Significant work has already been done in the areas of coreference resolution (Michal, 2011; Le Nagard and Koehn, 2010; Hardmeier and Federico, 2010; Hardmeier et al., 2013b; Guillou, 2012) and negation (Wetzel and Bond, 2012; Fancellu and Webber, 2015; Fancellu and Webber, 2014) in MT. In our corpus we will focus on less studied issues and limit ourselves to targeting coherence more specifically than cohesion.

The proposed framework will take as input well-formed documents that are determined 'coherent' (i.e. grammatically correct and coherent) and then artificially distort them in ways (detailed below) that directly affect coherence in the manner that an MT system would. The resulting texts will make a corpus of 'incoherent' texts for assessing the ability of models to discriminate between coherent and incoherent texts.

This will be done in a flexible manner, such that the incoherent documents can be created for a variety of (coherent) input texts. Moreover they can be created for specific types of errors. The quality of MT output varies greatly from one language pair and MT system to another. For example, the output from a French-English MT system trained in very large collections is superior to that of, for example, an English-Finnish system trained on smaller quantities of data (Koehn and Monz, 2005; Bojar et al., 2015).The errors encountered also vary, depending on the language pair, in particular for aspects such as discourse markers and syntax. Some of these error patterns are more relevant for particular language pairs, e.g. negation for French-English, which is otherwise a well-performing language pair.

We propose to inject errors programmatically in a systematic manner, as detailed below.

4.1 Error distribution

While ideally we would establish the distribution of errors from their occurrences in MT output, determining an appropriate error distribution based on observations is very problematic. The distributions would be specific to given language pairs and MT systems. More important, detecting coherence automatically to count errors is difficult: if we could do that, than we would be able to directly solve the problem we are attempting to, i.e. measure coherence. This is exactly why we need this corpus. Additionally, manual inspection and annotation for coherence is very hard to formalise as a task, time consuming and costly. Therefore, the distribution of errors in our corpus will be based on linguistic insights, and on findings from previous work, where available. Where this is not the case, for instance for distorting discourse patterns, versions of the corpus with different proportions of errors will be created. We will inject errors systematically and incrementally to vary the degree and location of the errors.

The errors will be introduced systematically via pattern-matching, and as highlighted by Brockett et al. (2006), may not be distributed in a natural way.

4.2 Error Injection

We will inject errors of the types below via the four basic edit operations, as appropriate for each type of error: replace, delete, add, shift.

Sentence level discourse structure We will inject errors related to discourse elements, in terms of cue words, and their organisation. A comparison of the discourse connectives in the MT and the Human Translation (HT) will be established, and where these differ, a syntactic check is made automatically (Pitler and Nenkova,) to establish if the connective is a synonym or incorrect. We can also refer to the discourse connectives in the original source text, and automatically check, for example, if the correct sense of the connective has been transferred. These can be identified from a list compiled from appropriate resources (e.g. DiMLex for German, LexConn for French)(Stede and Umbach, 1998; Roze and Danlos, 2012) and a list of problematic ones derived e.g. from work by (Meyer and Popescu-Belis, 2012; Meyer and Poláková, 2013) for French.

We can parse the discourse tree structure and extract grammatical information using the Stanford parser[2] and POS tagger[3], before distorting the parse tree by swapping nodes at the relevant level.

Lexical cohesion We propose replacing entities with alternatives (which will directly affect lexical coherence), using phrase tables from an MT system to generate likely entity variations. This has to be tailored to ensure that the result reflects realistic error levels, so need to verify correct parameter to gauge the amount of substitutions. We can also investigate pre-trained word embeddings, such as word2vec representations (Mikolov et al., 2013), and using word intrusion detection (Chang et al., 2009).

Clausal patterns Coherent syntax patterns can be derived from coherent text, for example using patters established in (Louis and Nenkova, 2012). We can determine the clausal patterns from training data, establishing frequent patterns which are indicative of specific coherence relations. Then the order of sibling nodes in the syntax tree can be modified (e.g. reversed) at the appropriate level in order to alter the order of clauses. The exact level of the distortion will be determined according to pre-defined criteria – e.g. every 8th clause, to depth 5 in the parse tree or, where possible, derived from the MT output.

[2]http://nlp.stanford.edu/software/lex-parser.shtml

[3]http://nlp.stanford.edu/software/tagger.shtml

5 Conclusion

We have introduced our initiative for artificially generating a corpus with coherence errors from well-formed data that specifically simulate coherence issues in MT.

Other possible direction could be to use an n-best list, taking sentences from different positions in that list for each source sentence to form a possibly incoherent document. Similarly, we could extract sentences from multiple MT systems for the same text, alternating their origin and concatenating to form one single document. In both cases, a difficulty that remains is that of isolating coherence issues from other errors and from stylistic issues, as well as quantifying the degree of incoherence in the generated texts.

References

Regina Barzilay and Mirella Lapata. 2008. Modeling local coherence: An entity-based approach. *Comput. Linguist.*, 34(1):1–34.

Ondřej Bojar, Christian Buck, Chris Callison-Burch, Christian Federmann, Barry Haddow, Philipp Koehn, Christof Monz, Matt Post, Radu Soricut, and Lucia Specia. 2013. Findings of the 2013 Workshop on Statistical Machine Translation. In *Proceedings of the Eighth Workshop on Statistical Machine Translation*, Sofia, Bulgaria.

Ondrej Bojar, Christian Buck, Christian Federmann, Barry Haddow, Philipp Koehn, Johannes Leveling, Christof Monz, Pavel Pecina, Matt Post, Herve Saint-Amand, Radu Soricut, Lucia Specia, and Aleš Tamchyna. 2014. Findings of the 2014 workshop on statistical machine translation. In *Proceedings of WMT*, pages 12–58, Baltimore, Maryland.

Ondrej Bojar, Rajan Chatterjee, Christian Federmann, Barry Haddow, Chris Hokamp, Matthias Huck, Varvara Logacheva, , Philipp Koehn, , Christof Monz, Matteo Negri, Pavel Pecina, Matt Post, Carolina Scarton, Lucia Specia, and Marco Turchi. 2015. Findings of the 2015 Workshop on Statistical Machine Translation. In *Proceedings of the 10th Workshop on Statistical Machine Translation*, WMT, Lisbon, Portugal.

Chris Brockett, William B Dolan, and Michael Gamon. 2006. Correcting esl errors using phrasal smt techniques. In *Proceedings of the 21st International Conference on Computational Linguistics and the 44th annual meeting of the Association for Computational Linguistics*, pages 249–256.

Jill Burstein, Joel R. Tetreault, and Slava Andreyev. 2010. Using entity-based features to model coherence in student essays. In *Proceedings of the Con-*

ference of the North American Chapter of the Association for Computational Linguistics, pages 681–684.

Marine Carpuat and Michel Simard. 2012. The trouble with smt consistency. In *Proceedings of WMT*, pages 442–449, Montreal, Canada.

Jonathan Chang, Sean Gerrish, Chong Wang, Jordan L Boyd-Graber, and David M Blei. 2009. Reading tea leaves: How humans interpret topic models. In *Advances in neural information processing systems*, pages 288–296.

Vladimir Eidelman, Jordan Boyd-Graber, and Philip Resnik. 2012. Topic models for dynamic translation model adaptation. In *Proceedings of the 50th Annual Meeting of the Association for Computational Linguistics*, ACL, pages 115–119.

Micha Elsner and Eugene Charniak. 2011. Extending the entity grid with entity-specific features. In *Proceedings of ACL*, pages 125–129.

Federico Fancellu and Bonnie L. Webber. 2014. Applying the semantics of negation to SMT through n-best list re-ranking. In *Proceedings of the 14th Conference of the European Chapter of the Association for Computational Linguistics*, EACL, pages 598–606, Gothenburg, Sweden.

Federico Fancellu and Bonnie Webber. 2015. Translating negation: A manual error analysis. In *Proceedings of the Second Workshop on Extra-Propositional Aspects of Meaning in Computational Semantics (ExProM 2015)*, pages 2–11, Denver, Colorado, June. Association for Computational Linguistics.

Mariano Felice and Zheng Yuan. 2014. Generating artificial errors for grammatical error correction. In *Proceedings of the Student Research Workshop at the 14th Conference of the European Chapter of the Association for Computational Linguistics*, Gothenburg, Sweden, April.

Barbara J. Grosz and Candace L. Sidner. 1986. Attention, intentions, and the structure of discourse. *Comput. Linguist.*, 12(3):175–204, July.

Liane Guillou. 2012. Improving pronoun translation for statistical machine translation. In *Proceedings of the Student Research Workshop at the 13th Conference of the European Chapter of the Association for Computational Linguistics*, EACL '12, pages 1–10, Stroudsburg, PA, USA. Association for Computational Linguistics.

Camille Guinaudeau and Michael Strube. 2013. Graph-based local coherence modeling. In *Proceedings of ACL*, pages 93–103.

Francisco Guzmán, Shafiq Joty, Lluís Màrquez, and Preslav Nakov. 2014. Using discourse structure improves machine translation evaluation. In *Proceedings of the 52nd Annual Meeting of the Association for Computational Linguistics, ACL 2014, June 22-27, 2014, Baltimore, MD, USA, Volume 1: Long Papers*, pages 687–698. The Association for Computer Linguistics.

Christian Hardmeier and Marcello Federico. 2010. Modelling pronominal anaphora in statistical machine translation. In *IWSLT*, pages 283–289.

Christian Hardmeier, Sara Stymne, Jörg Tiedemann, and Joakim Nivre. 2013a. Docent: A document-level decoder for phrase-based statistical machine translation. In *Proceedings of the 51st Annual Meeting of the Association for Computational Linguistics*, pages 193–198, Sofia, Bulgaria.

Christian Hardmeier, Jörg Tiedemann, and Joakim Nivre. 2013b. Latent anaphora resolution for cross-lingual pronoun prediction. In *Proceedings of the 2013 Conference on Empirical Methods in Natural Language Processing*, pages 380–391, Seattle, Washington.

Christian Hardmeier. 2012. Discourse in statistical machine translation. *Discours 11-2012*, (11).

Philipp Koehn and Christof Monz. 2005. Shared task: Statistical machine translation between european languages. In *Proceedings of the ACL Workshop on Building and Using Parallel Texts*, pages 119–124.

Ronan Le Nagard and Philipp Koehn. 2010. Aiding pronoun translation with co-reference resolution. In *Proceedings of the Joint Fifth Workshop on Statistical Machine Translation and MetricsMATR*, pages 252–261, Uppsala, Sweden.

Jiwei Li and Eduard H. Hovy. 2014. A model of coherence based on distributed sentence representation. In *Proceedings of the 2014 Conference on Empirical Methods in Natural Language Processing*, pages 2039–2048, Doha, Qatar.

Ziheng Lin, Hwee Tou Ng, and Min-Yen Kan. 2011. Automatically evaluating text coherence using discourse relations. In *Proceedings of ACL*, pages 997–1006.

Varvara Logacheva and Lucia Specia. 2015. The role of artificially generated negative data for quality estimation of machine translation. In *Proceedings of the 18th Annual Conference of the European Association for Machine Translation*, pages 51–58, Antalya, Turkey.

Annie Louis and Ani Nenkova. 2012. A coherence model based on syntactic patterns. In *Proceedings of EMNLP-CoNLL*, pages 1157–1168, Jeju Island, Korea.

Thomas Meyer and Lucie Poláková. 2013. Machine Translation with Many Manually Labeled Discourse Connectives. In *Proceedings of the 1st DiscoMT Workshop at ACL 2013*, Sofia, Bulgaria.

Thomas Meyer and Andrei Popescu-Belis. 2012. Using sense-labeled discourse connectives for statistical machine translation. In *Proceedings of the Joint Workshop on Exploiting Synergies Between Information Retrieval and Machine Translation (ESIRMT) and Hybrid Approaches to Machine Translation (HyTra)*, pages 129–138, Avignon, France.

Thomas Meyer, Andrei Popescu-Belis, Sandrine Zufferey, and Bruno Cartoni. 2011. Multilingual annotation and disambiguation of discourse connectives for machine translation. In *SIGDIAL Conference*, pages 194–203. The Association for Computer Linguistics.

Novák Michal. 2011. Utilization of anaphora in machine translation. In *WDS Week of Doctoral Students*, June.

Tomas Mikolov, Kai Chen, Greg Corrado, and Jeffrey Dean. 2013. Efficient estimation of word representations in vector space. *CoRR*, abs/1301.3781.

Emily Pitler and Ani Nenkova. Using syntax to disambiguate explicit discourse connectives in text. In *Proceedings of the 47th Annual Meeting of the Association for Computational Linguistics and the 4th International Joint Conference on Natural Language Processing of the AFNLP*, Singapore.

Marion Potet, Emmanuelle Esperança-rodier, Laurent Besacier, and Hervé Blanchon. 2012. Collection of a large database of french-english smt output corrections.

Charlotte Roze and Laurence Danlos. 2012. Lexconn: a french lexicon of discourse connectives. *Discours*.

Swapna Somasundaran, Jill Burstein, and Martin Chodorow. 2014. Lexical chaining for measuring discourse coherence quality in test-taker essays. In *Proceedings of COLING*.

Manfred Stede and Carla Umbach. 1998. Dimlex: A lexicon of discourse markers for text generation and understanding. In *Proceedings of the 36th Annual Meeting of the Association for Computational Linguistics and 17th International Conference on Computational Linguistics*, ACL, pages 1238–1242, Montreal, Quebec.

David Steele. 2015. Improving the translation of discourse markers for chinese into english. In *Proceedings of the Conference of the North American Chapter of the Association for Computational Linguistics*, NAACL, pages 110–117, Denver, Colorado.

Jörg Tiedemann. 2010. Context adaptation in statistical machine translation using models with exponentially decaying cache. In *Proceedings of the 2010 Workshop on Domain Adaptation for Natural Language Processing*, pages 8–15, Uppsala, Sweden.

Dominikus Wetzel and Francis Bond. 2012. Enriching parallel corpora for statistical machine translation with semantic negation rephrasing. In *Proceedings of the Sixth Workshop on Syntax, Semantics and Structure in Statistical Translation*, SSST-6, pages 20–29, Jeju, Republic of Korea.

Billy Tak-Ming Wong and Chunyu Kit. 2012. Extending machine translation evaluation metrics with lexical cohesion to document level. In *Proceedings of EMNLP-CoNLL*, pages 1060–1068.

Deyi Xiong and Min Zhang. 2013. A topic-based coherence model for statistical machine translation. In *Proceedings of AAAI*, pages 977–983.

Deyi Xiong, Guosheng Ben, Min Zhang, Yajuan Lv, and Qun Liu. 2013a. Modeling lexical cohesion for document-level machine translation. In *Proceedings of IJCAI*.

Deyi Xiong, Yang Ding, Min Zhang, and Chew Lim Tan. 2013b. Lexical chain based cohesion models for document-level statistical machine translation. In *Proceedings of EMNLP*, pages 1563–1573.

Part-of-Speech Driven Cross-Lingual Pronoun Prediction with Feed-Forward Neural Networks

Jimmy Callin, Christian Hardmeier, Jörg Tiedemann
Department of Linguistics and Philology
Uppsala University, Sweden
jimmy.callin.3439@student.uu.se
{christian.hardmeier, jorg.tiedemann}@lingfil.uu.se

Abstract

For some language pairs, pronoun translation is a discourse-driven task which requires information that lies beyond its local context. This motivates the task of predicting the correct pronoun given a source sentence and a target translation, where the translated pronouns have been replaced with placeholders. For cross-lingual pronoun prediction, we suggest a neural network-based model using preceding nouns and determiners as features for suggesting antecedent candidates. Our model scores on par with similar models while having a simpler architecture.

1 Introduction

Most modern statistical machine translation (SMT) systems use context for translation; the meaning of a word is more often than not ambiguous, and can only be decoded through its usage. That said, context use in modern SMT still mostly assumes that sentences are independent of one another, and dependencies between sentences are simply ignored. While today's popular SMT systems could use features from previous sentences in the source text, translated sentences within a document have up to this point rarely been included.

Hardmeier and Frederico (2010) argue that SMT research has become mature enough to stop assuming sentence independence, and start to incorporate features beyond the sentence boundary. Languages with gender-marked pronouns introduce certain difficulties, since the choice of pronoun is determined by the gender of its antecedent. Picking the wrong third-person pronoun might seem like a relatively minor error, especially if present in an otherwise comprehensible translation, but could potentially produce misunderstandings. Take the following English sentences:

- The monkey ate the banana because *it* was hungry.
- The monkey ate the banana because *it* was ripe.
- The monkey ate the banana because *it* was tea-time.

It in each of these three cases reference something different, either the monkey, the banana, or the abstract notion of time. If we were to translate these sentences to German, we would have to consciously make decisions whether *it* should be in masculine (*er*, referring to the monkey), feminine (*sie*, referring to the banana), or neuter (*es*, referring to the time) (Mitkov et al., 1995). While these examples use a local dependency, the antecedent of *it* could just as easily have been one or several sentences away which would have made necessary translation features out of reach for sentence based SMT decoders.

2 Related work

Most of the work in anaphora resolution for machine translation has been done in the paradigm of rule-based MT, while the topic has gained little interest within SMT (Hardmeier and Federico, 2010; Mitkov, 1999). One of the first examples of using discourse analysis for pronoun translation in SMT was done by Nagard and Koehn (2010), who use co-reference resolution to predict the antecedents in the source language as features in a standard SMT system. While they saw score improvements in pronoun prediction, they claim the bad performance of the co-reference resolution seriously impacted the results negatively. They performed this as a post-processing step, which seems to be primarily for practical reasons since most popular SMT frameworks such as Moses (Koehn et al., 2007) do not provide previous target translations for use as features. Guillou et al. (2012)

Proceedings of the Second Workshop on Discourse in Machine Translation (DiscoMT), pages 59–64,
Lisbon, Portugal, 17 September 2015.

tried a similar approach for English-Czech translation with little improvement even after factoring out major sources of error. They singled out one possible reason for this, which is how a reasonable translation alternative of a pronoun's antecedent could affect the predicted pronoun, including the possibility of simply canceling out pronouns. E.g, *the u.s. , claiming some success in its trade* could be paraphrased as *the u.s. , claiming some success in trade diplomacy* without any loss in translation quality, while still affecting the score negatively. This demonstrates there is necessary linguistic information in the target translation that is not available in the source. Hardmeier and Frederico (2010) extended the phrase-based Moses decoder with a word dependency model based on existing co-reference resolution systems, by parsing the output of the decoder and catching its previous translations. Unfortunately they only produced minor improvements for English-German.

In light of this, there have been attempts at considering pronoun translation a classification task separate from traditional machine translation. This could potentially lead to further insights into the nature of anaphora resolution. In this fashion a pronoun translation module could be treated as just another part of translation by discourse oriented machine translation systems, or as a post-processing step similarly to Guillou et al. (2012). Hardmeier et al. (2013b) introduced this task and presented a feed-forward neural network model using features from an external anaphora resolution system, BART (Broscheit et al., 2010), to infer the pronoun's antecedent candidates and use the aligned words in the target translation as input. This model was later integrated into their document-level decoder Docent (Hardmeier et al., 2013a; Hardmeier, 2014, chapter 9).

3 Task setup

The goal of cross-lingual pronoun prediction is to accurately predict the correct missing pronoun in translated text. The pronouns in focus are *it* and *they*, where the word aligned phrases in the translation have been replaced by placeholders. The word alignment is included, and was automatically produced by GIZA++ (Och, 2003). We are also aware of document boundaries within the corpus. The corpus is a set of three different English-French parallel corpora gathered from three separate domains: transcribed TED talks, Europarl (Koehn, 2005) with transcribed proceedings from the European parliament, and a set of news texts. Test data is a collection of transcribed TED talks, in total 12 documents containing 2093 sentences with a total of 1105 classification problems, with a similar development set. Further details of the task setup, including final performance results, are available in Hardmeier et. al. (2015).

4 Method

Inspired by the neural network architecture set up in Hardmeier et al. (2013b), we similarly propose a feed-forward neural network with a layer of word embeddings as well as an additional hidden layer for learning abstract feature representations. The final architecture as shown in fig. 1 uses both source context and translation context around the missing pronoun, by encoding a number of word embeddings n words to the left and m words to the right (hereby referred to as having a context window size of $n+m$).

The main difference in our model lies in avoiding using an external anaphora resolution system to collect antecedent features. Rather, to simplify the model we simply look at the four closest previous nouns and determiners in English, and use the corresponding aligned French nouns and articles in the model, as illustrated in fig. 2. Wherever the alignments map to more than one word, only the left-most word in the phrase is used. We encode these nouns and articles as embeddings in the first input layer. This way, the order of each word is embedded, which should approximate the distance from the missing pronoun. Additionally, we allow ourselves to look at the French context of the missing pronoun. While the automatically translated context might be too unreliable, French usage should be a better indicator for some of the classes, e.g. *ce* which is highly dependent on being precedent of *est*. See fig. 3 for an example of context in source and translation as features.

Similarly to the original model in Hardmeier et al. (2013b), the neural network is trained using stochastic gradient descent with mini-batches and L2 regularization. Cross-entropy is used as a cost function, with a softmax output layer. Furthermore the dimensionality of the embeddings is increased from 20 to 50, since we saw minor improvements of the scores on the development set with the increase. To reduce training time and speed up convergence, we use $\tanh$ as activa-

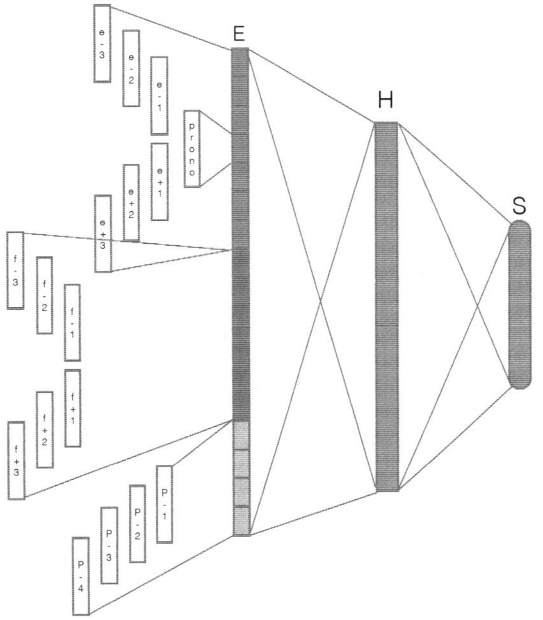

Figure 1: Neural network architecture. Blue embeddings (E) signifies source context, red target context, and yellow the preceding POS tags. The shown number of features is not equivalent with what is used in the final model.

tion function between the hidden layers (LeCun et al., 2012), in contrast to the sigmoid function used in Hardmeier's model. To avoid overfitting, early stopping is introduced where the training stops if no improvements have been found within a certain number of iterations. This usually results in a training time of 130 epochs, when run on TED data. The model uses a layer-wise uniform random weight initialization as proposed by Glorot and Bengio (2010), where they show that neural network models using $\tanh$ as activation function generally perform better with a uniformally distributed random initialization within the interval $[-\frac{\sqrt{6}}{\sqrt{\text{fan}_{in}+\text{fan}_{out}}}, \frac{\sqrt{6}}{\sqrt{\text{fan}_{in}+\text{fan}_{out}}}]$, where fan_{in} and fan_{out} are number of inputs and number of hidden units respectively.

Since the model uses a fixed context window size for English and French, as well as a fixed number of preceding nouns and articles, we need to find out optimal parameter settings. We observe that a parameter setting of 4+4 context window for English and French, with 3 preceding nouns and articles each perform well. Figure 4 showcases how window size and number of preceding POS tags affect the performance outcome on the development set. We also look into asymmetric window sizes, but notice no improvements (fig. 5).

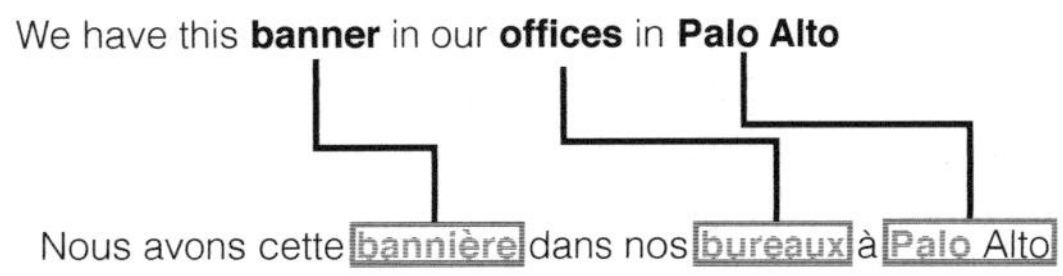

Figure 2: An English POS tagger is used to find nouns and articles in preceding utterances, while the word alignments determine which French words are to be used as features.

Feature ablation as presented in table 1 shows that while all feature classes are required for retrieving top score, POS features are generally the feature class that contributes the least to improved results. It is curious to notice that *elle* even performs better without the POS features, while *elles* receives a sufficient bump with them. Furthermore, the results indicate that target features is the most informative of the tested feature classes.

The neural network is implemented in Theano (Bergstra et al., 2010), and is publicly available on Github.[1]

[1] `http://github.com/jimmycallin/whatelles`

<S> <S> <S> it expresses our view of how we...

<S> <S> <S> __ exprime notre manière d' aborder ...

Figure 3: Example of context used in the classification model, color coded according to their position in the neural network as illustrated in fig. 1.

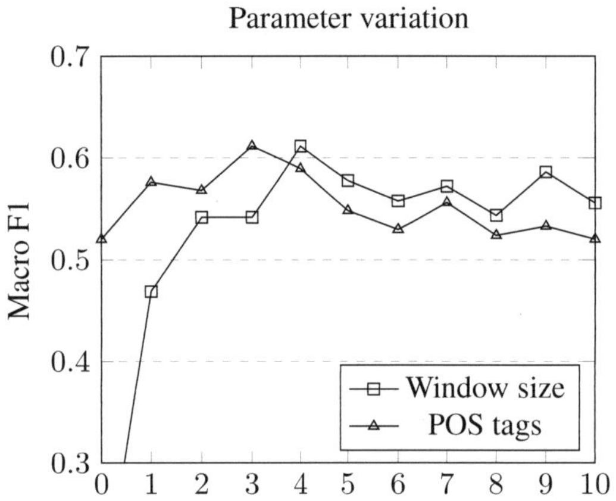

Figure 4: Parameter variation of window size and number of preceding POS tags. Window size is varied in a symmetrical fashion of n+n. When varying window size, 3 preceding POS tags are used. When varying number of POS tags, a window size of 4+4 is used.

5 Results

The results from the shared task are presented in table 2 and table 3. The best performing classes are *ce*, *ils*, and *other*, all reaching F1 scores over 80 percent. The less commonly occurring classes *elle* and *elles* perform significantly worse, especially recall-wise. The overall macro F1 score ends up being 55.3%.

6 Discussion

Results indicate that the model performs on par with previously suggested models (Hardmeier et al., 2013b), while having a simpler architecture. Classes highly dependent on local context, such as *ce*, perform especially well, which is likely due to *est* being a good indicator of its presence. This is supported by the large performance gains from 4+0 to 4+1 in fig. 5, since *est* usually follows *ce*. Singular and plural classes rarely get confused, due to them being predicated on the English pronoun which marks *it* or *they*. The classes of feminine gender do not perform as well, especially recall-wise, but this was to be expected

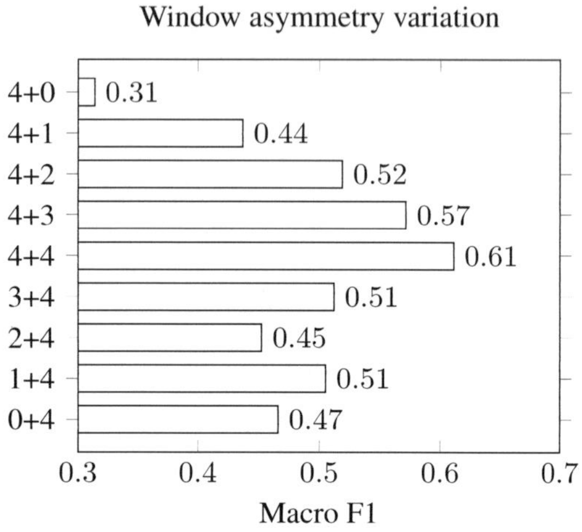

Figure 5: Parameter variation of window size asymmetry, where each label corresponds to *n+n*, where *n* is the context size in each direction.

since the only information from which to infer its antecedent is ordered distance from the pronoun in focus. It is apparent that the model has a bias towards making majority class predictions, especially given the low number of wrong predictions on the *elle* and *elles* classes relative to *il* and *ils*. The high recall of *ils* is explained by this phenomenon as well. An additional hypothesis is that there is simply too little data to realistically create usable embeddings, except for a few reoccurring circumstances.

A somewhat interesting example of what POS tags might cause is:

... which is the history of who invented games ... and they would be so immersed in playing the dice games ...

... l' histoire de qui a inventé le jeu et pourquoi ... __ seraient si concentrés sur leur jeu de dés ...

This is one of the few instances where *ils* has been misclassified as *elles*. Since this classification only happens when using at least three preceding POS tags, it is likely there is something happening with the antecedent candidates. The third determiner is *the (history)*, and points to *histoire* which is a noun of feminine gender. It is likely the classifier has learned this connection and has put too much weight into it.

The extra number of features as well as the increase in embedding dimensionality makes the training and prediction slightly slower, but since the training still is done in less than an hour, and testing does not take longer than a few seconds,

	POS	Source	Target	None
ce	**0.9236**	0.8629	0.6405	0.8822
cela	0.6179	**0.6324**	0.4156	0.6260
elle	0.2963	0.3019	0.0930	**0.3571**
elles	**0.2500**	0.2069	0.1667	0.2222
il	0.5366	0.4426	0.3651	**0.5620**
ils	0.8364	0.8345	0.7050	**0.8754**
OTHER	**0.8976**	0.8769	0.6969	0.8847
Macro	0.5526	0.5128	0.3569	**0.6299**
Micro	0.7871	0.7510	0.5797	**0.8019**

Table 1: F1-score for each label in a feature ablation test, where the specified feature classes were *removed* in training and testing on the development set. The *None* column has *no* removed features. Micro score is the overall classification score, while macro is the average over each class.

	Precision	Recall	F1
ce	0.8291	0.8967	0.8616
cela	0.7143	0.6202	0.6639
elle	0.5000	0.2651	0.3465
elles	0.6296	0.3333	0.4359
il	0.5161	0.6154	0.5614
ils	0.7487	0.9312	0.8301
other	0.8450	0.8579	0.8514
Macro	0.5816	0.5495	0.5530
Micro	0.7213	0.7213	0.7213

Table 2: Precision, recall, and F1-score for all classes. Micro score is the overall classification score, while macro is the average over each class. The latter scoring method is used for increasing the importance of classes with fewer instances.

	ce	cela	elle	elles	il	ils	other	sum
ce	165	3	0	1	8	1	6	184
cela	5	80	4	1	21	0	18	129
elle	7	10	22	2	22	2	18	83
elles	0	0	0	18	0	31	3	51
il	11	7	9	0	64	1	12	104
ils	1	0	0	5	0	149	5	160
other	10	12	9	1	9	15	338	394
sum	199	112	44	27	124	199	400	

Table 3: Confusion matrix of class predictions. Row signifies actual class according to gold standard, while column represents predicted class according to the classifier.

it is still good enough for general usage. Furthermore, the implementation is made in such a way that further performance increases are to be expected if you run it on CUDA compatible GPU with minor changes.

While three separate training data collections were available, we only found interesting results when using data from the same domain as the test data, i.e. transcribed TED talks. To overcome the skewed class distribution, attempts were made at oversampling the less frequent classes from Europarl, but unfortunately this only led to performance loss on the development set. The model does not seem to generalize well from other types of training data such as Europarl or news text, despite Europarl being transcribed speech as well. This is an obvious shortcoming of the model.

We tried several alterations in parameter settings for context window and POS tags, and found no significant improvements beyond the final parameter settings when run on the development set, as seen in fig. 4. Figure 5 makes it clear that a symmetric window size is beneficial, while we are not as sure of why this is the case. Right context seems to be more important than left context, which could be due to the fact that pronouns in their role as subjects largely appears early in sentences, making left context nothing but sentence start markers.

In future work, it would be interesting to look into how much source context actually contributes to the classification, given a target context. Preliminary results of the feature ablation test in table 1 indicate that we indeed capture information for at least some of the classes with the use of source features, while it is not quite clear why this is the case. While the English context is nice to have, since you cannot be entirely certain of the translation quality in the target language, intuitively all necessary linguistic information for inferring the correct pronoun should be available in the target translation. After all, the gender of a pronoun is not dependent on whatever source language you translate from, as long as you have found its antecedent. If the source text still were found useful, all English word embeddings could be pretrained on a large number of translation examples and through this process learn the most probable cross-linguistic gender. In the same manner, gender aware French word embeddings would hypothetically increase the score as well.

7 Conclusion

In this work, we develop a cross-lingual pronoun prediction classifier based on a feed-forward neural network. The model is heavily inspired by Hardmeier et al. (2013b), while trying to simplify the architecture by using preceding nouns and determiners for coreference resolution rather than using features from an anaphora extractor such as BART, as in the original paper.

We find out that the model indeed performs on par with similar models, while being easier to train. There are some expected drops in performance for the less common classes heavily dependent on finding their antecedent. We discuss probable causes for this, as well as possible solutions using pretrained embeddings on larger amounts of data.

References

[Bergstra et al.2010] James Bergstra, Olivier Breuleux, Frédéric Bastien, Pascal Lamblin, Razvan Pascanu, Guillaume Desjardins, Joseph Turian, David Warde-Farley, and Yoshua Bengio. 2010. Theano: a cpu and gpu math expression compiler. In *Proceedings of the Python for Scientific Computing Conference (SciPy)*.

[Broscheit et al.2010] Samuel Broscheit, Massimo Poesio, Simone Paolo Ponzetto, Kepa Joseba Rodriguez, Lorenza Romano, Olga Uryupina, Yannick Versley, and Roberto Zanoli. 2010. Bart: A multilingual anaphora resolution system. In *Proceedings of the 5th International Workshop on Semantic Evaluation*, pages 104–107. Association for Computational Linguistics.

[Glorot and Bengio2010] Xavier Glorot and Yoshua Bengio. 2010. Understanding the difficulty of training deep feedforward neural networks. In *International conference on artificial intelligence and statistics*, pages 249–256.

[Guillou2012] Liane Guillou. 2012. Improving pronoun translation for statistical machine translation. In *Proceedings of the Student Research Workshop at the 13th Conference of the European Chapter of the Association for Computational Linguistics*, EACL '12, pages 1–10. Association for Computational Linguistics.

[Hardmeier and Federico2010] Christian Hardmeier and Marcello Federico. 2010. Modelling pronominal anaphora in statistical machine translation. In *Proceedings of the 7th International Workshop on Spoken Language Translation*, pages 283–289.

[Hardmeier et al.2013a] Christian Hardmeier, Sara Stymne, Jörg Tiedemann, and Joakim Nivre. 2013a. Docent: A document-level decoder for phrase-based statistical machine translation. In *ACL 2013 (51st Annual Meeting of the Association for Computational Linguistics)*, pages 193–198. Association for Computational Linguistics.

[Hardmeier et al.2013b] Christian Hardmeier, Jörg Tiedemann, and Joakim Nivre. 2013b. Latent anaphora resolution for cross-lingual pronoun prediction. In *Proceedings of the 2013 Conference on Empirical Methods in Natural Language Processing*, pages 380–391.

[Hardmeier et al.2015] Christian Hardmeier, Preslav Nakov, Sara Stymne, Jörg Tiedemann, Yannick Versley, and Mauro Cettolo. 2015. Pronoun-focused MT and cross-lingual pronoun prediction: Findings of the 2015 DiscoMT shared task on pronoun translation. In *Proceedings of the Second Workshop on Discourse in Machine Translation*, Lisbon, Portugal.

[Hardmeier2014] Christian Hardmeier. 2014. *Discourse in Statistical Machine Translation*. Phd thesis, Uppsala University, Department of Linguistics and Philology.

[Koehn et al.2007] Philipp Koehn, Hieu Hoang, Alexandra Birch, Chris Callison-Burch, Marcello Federico, Nicola Bertoldi, Brooke Cowan, Wade Shen, Christine Moran, Richard Zens, et al. 2007. Moses: Open source toolkit for statistical machine translation. In *Proceedings of the 45th annual meeting of the ACL on interactive poster and demonstration sessions*, pages 177–180. Association for Computational Linguistics.

[Koehn2005] Philipp Koehn. 2005. Europarl: A parallel corpus for statistical machine translation. In *MT summit*, volume 5, pages 79–86.

[Le Nagard and Koehn2010] Ronan Le Nagard and Philipp Koehn. 2010. Aiding pronoun translation with co-reference resolution. In *Proceedings of the Joint Fifth Workshop on Statistical Machine Translation and MetricsMATR*, WMT '10, pages 252–261. Association for Computational Linguistics.

[LeCun et al.2012] Yann A. LeCun, Léon Bottou, Genevieve B. Orr, and Klaus-Robert Müller. 2012. Efficient backprop. In *Neural networks: Tricks of the trade*, pages 9–48. Springer.

[Mitkov et al.1995] Ruslan Mitkov, Sung-kwon Choi R, and All Sharp. 1995. Anaphora resolution in machine translation. In *Proceedings of the Sixth International Conference on Theoretical and Methodological Issues in Machine Translation*, pages 5–7.

[Mitkov1999] Ruslan Mitkov. 1999. Introduction: Special issue on anaphora resolution in machine translation and multilingual nlp. *Machine translation*, 14(3):159–161.

[Och2003] Franz Josef Och. 2003. *Giza++ software*. Internal report, RWTH Aachen University.

Automatic Post-Editing for the DiscoMT Pronoun Translation Task

Liane Guillou
School of Informatics
University of Edinburgh
Scotland, United Kingdom
L.K.Guillou@sms.ed.ac.uk

Abstract

This paper describes an automated post-editing submission to the DiscoMT 2015 shared task on pronoun translation. Post-editing is achieved by applying pronoun-specific rules to the output of an English-to-French phrase-based SMT system.

1 Introduction

The shared task (Hardmeier et al., 2015) focusses on the translation of the English pronouns "it" and "they" into French. While they both serve multiple functions in English, the most significant is as *anaphoric* pronouns, referring back to an entity previously mentioned in the discourse, known as the *antecedent*.

When translated into French, anaphoric pronouns must agree with their antecedent in terms of both number and grammatical gender. Therefore, selecting the correct pronoun in French relies on knowing the number and gender of the antecedent. This presents a problem for current state-of-the-art Statistical Machine Translation (SMT) systems which translate sentences in isolation.

Inter-sentential anaphoric pronouns, i.e. those that occur in a different sentence to their antecedent, will be translated with no knowledge of their antecedent. Pronoun-antecedent agreement therefore cannot be guaranteed. Even *intra-sentential* pronouns, i.e. those that occur in the same sentence as their antecedent, may lack sufficient local context to ensure agreement.

The English pronoun "it" may also be used as a pleonastic or event pronoun. *Pleonastic* pronouns such as the "it" in "**it** is raining" or the "il" in "**il** pleut" do not refer to anything but are required by syntax to fill the subject-position slot. *Event* pronouns may refer to a verb, verb phrase or even an entire clause or sentence. The pronoun "they" may also serve as a *generic* pronoun, as in "**They** say it always rains in Scotland" – here "they" does not refer to a specific person or group. For each pronoun type, translations into French must meet different requirements.

This paper presents an automatic post-editing approach which applies two pronoun-specific rules to the output of an English-to-French phrase-based SMT system. One rule handles anaphoric pronouns and the other handles non-anaphoric (i.e. event and pleonastic) pronouns.

The advantage of a post-editing approach is that the translations of both pronouns and their antecedents (for anaphoric pronouns) are already known. There is therefore no need to keep track of this information within the decoder. Instead, the problem becomes one of identifying incorrectly translated pronouns and amending them based on information extracted from the source-language text. The aim is to leverage knowledge about the target-language and through this maximise the number of changes that will improve the pronoun translations, whilst also attempting to minimise those that may have a detrimental effect.

The post-editing rules make use of information automatically obtained from the source-language text. The risk of doing this is that inaccurate information could lead to incorrect translations. As post-editing takes place after translation, the decoder and language model can no longer be relied upon to recover from bad decisions. However, due to the simplicity of the approach and encouraging results from Weiner (2014) for the English-German pair, post-editing is worth exploring.

2 Post-editing Overview

Using the ParCor corpus (Guillou et al., 2014) annotations as a model, automated tools are applied to the full text of each (sentence-split) source-language document in the dataset to extract the following information: anaphoric vs. non-anaphoric pronouns, subject vs. object position and the an-

Proceedings of the Second Workshop on Discourse in Machine Translation (DiscoMT), pages 65–71,
Lisbon, Portugal, 17 September 2015.

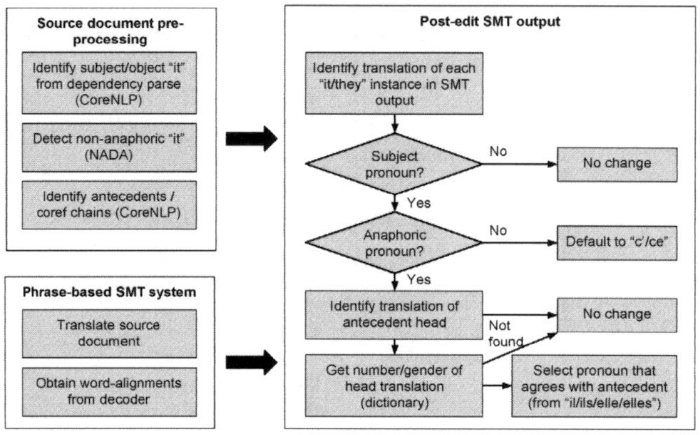

Figure 1: The post-editing process

Data	Description	Parallel Sentences	Monolingual Sentences
Training	TED, Europarl, News Commentary	2,372,666	
Tuning	dev2010 + tst2011	1,705	
Development test	tst2010	1,664	
Development test	tst2012	1,124	
Language model	TED, Europarl, News Commentary and News		33,869,133

Table 1: Baseline training, tuning and development data.

tecedent of each anaphoric pronoun. This information is then leveraged by two post-editing rules; one for anaphoric pronouns and one for non-anaphoric pronouns. These rules are automatically applied to the 1-best output of the baseline SMT system described in Section 3. The process for extracting source-language information and application of the post-editing rules is outlined in Figure 1 and described in Sections 4 and 5.

3 Baseline Machine Translation System

The baseline system used to produce the SMT output is of a similar design to that provided as part of the shared task resources. It is a phrase-based system built using the Moses toolkit (Koehn et al., 2007) and trained/tuned using only the pre-processed (tokenised, lower-cased) parallel data provided for the shared task. Training, tuning and (development) test data are described in Table 1.

Word alignments are computed using Giza++ with *grow-diag-final-and* symmetrization, and with sentences restricted to 80 tokens or fewer (as Giza++ produces more robust alignments for shorter sentences). The maximum phrase length is set to 7. As memory and disk space are not a concern, sig-test filtering which prunes unlikely phrase pairs from the phrase table, is not used in training the baseline system. Tuning is performed using MERT (Och, 2003) with an N-best list of 200, and using the dev2010+tst2011 data.

The language model is a 5-gram KenLM (Heafield, 2011) model, trained using lmplz, with modified Kneser-Ney smoothing and no pruning. The memory optimisations that were made for the shared task baseline[1] are not replicated as they are not required. The language model uses the *probing data structure*; the fastest and default data structure for KenLM, it makes use of a hash table to store the language model n-grams.

By restricting the training data to sentences of 80 or fewer tokens, the baseline SMT system is trained on 27,481 fewer parallel sentences than the shared task baseline. There are no other differences in the data used; for tuning, development-testing or language model construction.

The baseline SMT system scores nearly one BLEU point higher than the shared task baseline for the IWSLT 2010 (34.57 vs. 33.86) and 2012 (41.07 vs. 40.06) test sets. BLEU scores were calculated using the case-insensitive, multi-bleu perl script provided in the Moses toolkit.

The decoder is set to output word alignments, which are used later for automatic post-editing.

[1]Provided as part of the shared task resources

4 Extracting Source-language Information

Guided by the ParCor annotation scheme, the following is extracted from the source-language text:

- Position: subject or object ("it" only)
- Function: anaphoric or non-anaphoric (i.e. pleonastic / event, for "it" only)
- Antecedent: for anaphoric pronouns only

The first step is to identify whether the pronoun appears in subject or object position. The pronoun "it" may be used in either position, unlike "they" which is always a subject-position pronoun. When translating into French it is necessary to ensure that each instance of "it" is correctly translated, with different French pronouns used depending on the position that the pronoun fills. Instances of "it" are categorised as being either subject- or object-position pronouns using the dependency parser provided as part of the Stanford CoreNLP tool[2]. Subject-position pronouns are those that participate in an *nsubj* or *nsubjpass* dependency relation.

The next step is to determine the function of each instance of "it". NADA (Bergsma and Yarowsky, 2011) is used as it considers the entire sentence, unlike the pleonastic sieve in the Stanford coreference resolution system (Lee et al., 2011), which uses only fixed expressions to identify pleonastic "it". Instances of "it" with a NADA probability below a specified threshold are treated as non-anaphoric, and those above, as anaphoric. Here, a non-anaphoric pronoun is either an event or pleonastic pronoun; a finer distinction cannot be made using currently available tools. The NADA threshold is set to 0.41 (see Section 6).

For instances of "it" identified as anaphoric, and all instances of "they", the pronoun's nearest non-pronominal antecedent is extracted using the coreference resolution system (Raghunathan et al., 2010; Lee et al., 2011) provided in the Stanford CoreNLP tool[3]. To avoid falsely identifying coreference chains across document boundaries, the source-language text is split into documents prior to coreference resolution. Full coreference chains are retained in case the nearest antecedent is not translated by the baseline SMT system.

NADA and CoreNLP were run on tokenised, but not lower-cased data, in order to ensure parser accuracy. The tokenisation and sentence segmentation is the same as that used in the pre-processed data distributed for the shared task. The CoreNLP tool was run with the following annotators: *tokenize*, *ssplit*, *pos*, *lemma*, *ner*, *parse* and *dcoref*. The following parameters were set to true: *tokenize.whitespace* and *ssplit.eolonly*.

[2]Stanford CoreNLP version 3.3.1 `http://nlp.stanford.edu/software/corenlp.shtml`

[3]Considers pronoun-antecedent distances ≤ 3 sentences

5 Automatic Post-Editing Rules

Automatic post-editing is applied to the 1-best output of the baseline SMT system described in Section 3. The process makes use of information extracted from the source-language text (Section 4) and the word alignments output by the decoder.

For each source-language pronoun, one of two post-editing rules is applied, depending on whether the pronoun is identified as anaphoric or non-anaphoric. The rules are outlined in Figure 1 and described in detail in the following sections.

5.1 Anaphoric Rule

This rule is applied to all instances of "they" and subject-position "it" that are identified as anaphoric, both inter- and intra-sentential. *Cataphoric* pronouns, where the pronoun appears before its antecedent, are very rare (Guillou et al., 2014) and are ignored for the sake of simplicity. Instances of object-position "it" are excluded as the focus of the shared task is on subject-position pronouns only. Target-language pronoun forms are predicted using the projected translation of the head of the nearest non-pronominal antecedent.

On the source-language side:

1. Identify the nearest non-pronominal antecedent
2. Identify the antecedent head word (provided by CoreNLP for each antecedent)
3. Using word alignments output by the decoder, project source-language pronoun and antecedent head positions to the SMT output

On the target-language side (SMT output):

4. If no antecedent can be found for the pronoun, do not attempt to amend its translation. (It may be non-anaphoric but not detected by NADA)
5. For all other pronouns, use the word alignments to identify the translations of the pronoun and antecedent head
6. Extract the number and gender of the antecedent head translation via a dictionary of

French nouns extracted from the Lefff (Sagot, 2010) and augmented by entries from dict.cc[4]

7. If the antecedent head word is aligned to multiple words in the translation select the right-most noun (should be the head in most cases)
8. If the antecedent head translation **is a noun**[5]:
   (a) Predict "elle" for feminine, singular; "il" for masculine, singular
   (b) Predict "elles" for feminine, plural; "ils" for masculine, plural
   (c) If the antecedent is split-reference of the format **N and N**, split it into two nouns. If both are feminine, predict "elles", otherwise predict "ils"
9. If the antecedent head translation **is not a noun** (i.e. not in the dictionary) or is not translated:
   (a) Traverse further back through the coreference chain and repeat from *step 5*
   (b) If the antecedent head is not translated, apply a default value. If the source-language pronoun is translated as a pronoun, but not "il/elle" (for "it") or "ils/elles" (for "they"), predict "il" for "it" and "ils" for "they". If the pronoun is not translated, do nothing as the SMT system may have correctly learned to drop a pronoun
10. If the pronoun in the SMT output and the predicted translation disagree, the post-editing rule replaces the translation in the SMT output with the predicted value

This method allows for the prediction of a plural pronoun for cases where an English singular noun is translated into French using a plural noun. For example, "vacation" is singular in English but may be translated as "vacances" (plural) in French.

5.2 Non-Anaphoric Rule

This rule is applied to instances of subject-position "it" that are identified as non-anaphoric, i.e. those with a NADA probability below the specified threshold. It does not apply to instances of "they".

The first step is to identify the translation of the pronoun (using the word alignments). The translation that should appear in the post-edited SMT output is then predicted.

[4] `www.dict.cc`

[5] If the word is hyphenated and not in the dictionary, look up the right-most part, which should be the head

1) Translation is an event/pleonastic pronoun: As NADA does not appear to distinguish event and pleonastic pronouns (i.e. both are considered equally non-anaphoric; see Section 6) it is not straightforward to predict a correct translation for non-anaphoric "it". The French pronoun "ce" may function as both an event and a pleonastic pronoun, but "il" is used only as a pleonastic pronoun. All instances of "it" translated as "ce/c'/il" are left as they are in the SMT output. Changing them may do more harm than good and would be performed in an uninformed manner. The hope is that these pronouns, or at least the pleonastic ones, may be correctly translated using local context.

2) Translation is another pronoun: If an instance of "it" is translated as a pronoun outwith the set "ce/c'/il", it will be corrected to the default "ce" (or "c' " if the next word in the SMT output starts with a vowel or silent "h"). The French pronouns "ce/c'/cela/ça" may be used as neutral pronouns, referring to *events*/actions/states or general classes of people/things, and "il/ce/c'/cela/ça" may be used as impersonal pronouns, marking the subject position but not referring to an entity in the text, i.e. *pleonastically* (Hawkins et al., 2001). "ce/c'/cela/ça" may all be used as either pleonastic or event pronouns. "ce" is selected as the default as it occurs most frequently in the training data, suggesting common usage. There are some cases in which only "il" should be used as the impersonal pronoun, such as expressions of time. These are not easy to detect and are therefore ignored.

3) Translation is not a pronoun: If an instance of "it" is translated using something other than a pronoun, it is not amended. This may also indicate that the pronoun has been dropped.

4) No translation: There is no provision for handling cases where a pleonastic or event pronoun may in fact be required but was dropped in the SMT output. I am not aware of any tools that can separate pleonastic and event instances of "it" for English and inserting a pronoun might not be the correct thing to do in all cases.

If the pronoun in the SMT output and the predicted translation disagree, the post-editing rule replaces the translation in the SMT output with the predicted value.

6 Setting the NADA Threshold

NADA returns a probability between 0 and 1, and the decision as to whether an instance of "it" is anaphoric can be made by thresholding this probability. The NADA documentation suggests a general threshold value of 0.5; for probabilities over this value the pronoun is said to be referential (i.e. anaphoric) and for those below this value, that it is non-referential. However, different threshold values may be appropriate for different genres[6].

The TED-specific NADA threshold was set using the manual ParCor (Guillou et al., 2014) annotations over the TED Talks portion of the corpus. NADA was run over the English TED Talks in ParCor and the probabilities it assigned for each instance of "it" were compared with the pronoun type labels (i.e. anaphoric/pleonastic/event).

There are 61 instances of "it" marked as pleonastic in the ParCor annotations. Looking at *all* 133 instances of "it" in the ParCor TED Talks for which their NADA probabilities fall below 0.5, there are a mixture of pleonastic, event, and "anaphoric with no explicit antecedent" pronouns. These could acceptably be treated as non-referential. However, there are also a number of anaphoric pronouns that fall into this range and it would be unacceptable to treat these as non-referential. Setting the threshold is therefore a trade-off between precision and recall. Whatever threshold is set, there will be both false positives and false negatives. At a threshold of ≤ 0.41, 37 (60.66%) of pronouns marked as pleonastic in ParCor are correctly identified and 24 (39.34%) are not. 37 pronouns marked in ParCor as event pronouns and 35 anaphoric pronouns (of which 4 have no explicit antecedent) are also (incorrectly) identified as non-referential.

7 Post-Editing Statistics

The shared task test set contains 307 instances of "they" and 809 instances of "it". Automated pre-processing of the source-language texts identifies 581 instances of "it" as subject-position pronouns and 228 as object-position pronouns (for which no change will be made). Of the 888 instances of "it" and "they" identified as subject-position pronouns, the translation of 316 are changed in the SMT output by the post-editing rules. 303 changes are applied to pronouns identified as anaphoric (36 "they" and 267 "it") and 13 to pronouns identified as non-anaphoric. The pronoun changes are summarised in Table 2. 10 pronouns were not translated by the baseline SMT system, and as such, were not considered for amendment.

Pronoun type	Form	Before	After	Count
Non-anaphoric	it	ç	ce/c'	7
Non-anaphoric	it	cela	ce/c'	3
Non-anaphoric	it	elle	ce/c'	1
Non-anaphoric	it	le	ce/c'	1
Non-anaphoric	it	on	ce/c'	1
Anaphoric	it	il	ils	3
Anaphoric	it	il	elle	51
Anaphoric	it	il	elles	3
Anaphoric	it	elle	il	17
Anaphoric	it	elle	ils	1
Anaphoric	it	le/l'	il	3
Anaphoric	it	on	il	1
Anaphoric	it	ç	il	10
Anaphoric	it	ç	ils	2
Anaphoric	it	ç	elle	5
Anaphoric	it	cela	il	6
Anaphoric	it	cela	elle	3
Anaphoric	it	cela	elles	1
Anaphoric	it	ce/c'	il	84
Anaphoric	it	ce/c'	ils	5
Anaphoric	it	ce/c'	elle	68
Anaphoric	it	ce/c'	elles	4
Anaphoric	they	ils	elles	32
Anaphoric	they	elles	ils	4
Total				316

Table 2: Automated post-editing changes

The most frequent changes are "c'/ce" → "il" (84), "c'/ce" → "elle" (68), "il" → "elle" (51), and "ils" → "elles" (32). The change "c'/ce" → "il/elle" takes place due to the decision to use gendered translations of all instances of "it" identified as anaphoric (even if "c'/ce" might also have been an acceptable translation). Biases in the training data may account for some of the other changes. For example, the change "ils" → "elles" may result from the common alignment of "they" to "ils" which arises due to the rule in French that "ils" is used unless all of the antecedents are feminine (in which case "elles" is used). This may result in more masculine pronouns requiring replacement with a feminine pronoun than vice versa.

The changes "il" → "elle" and "ils" → "elles" are made to conform with the gender of the translation of the antecedent head of an anaphoric pronoun. The post-editing rules also allow for changes from singular to plural (and vice versa) and from one number and gender to another. For example in translating "it" → "vacation" the anaphoric rule would allow for an instance of "il" (masc. sg.) in the SMT output to be changed to "elles" → "vacances" (fem. pl.).

[6]TED Talks are considered out-of-domain. NADA was trained using the Penn Treebank and Google N-Grams corpus

8 Results

The official shared task results report a BLEU score of 36.91 for the post-edited SMT output. This score is lower than the official baseline system (37.18), comparable with the UU-Tiedemann system (36.92), and higher than the other competing systems. However, the post-editing system outperformed only two of the five competing systems in terms of the *accuracy* measures, suggesting that BLEU is a poor measure of pronoun translation performance. The *accuracy with OTHER* measure reveals that the post-edited SMT output contains correct translations for only 114/210 pronoun instances, according to human judgements.

There is a small decrease of 0.36 BLEU between the baseline system used to provide SMT output and the post-edited version for the test set (38.83 vs. 38.47 respectively, as calculated using case-insensitive multi-bleu[7]).

An examination of the human judgements from the shared task manual evaluation reveals that the post-editing process makes many mistakes. 34 instances were worsened by post-editing and only 9 improved. The remaining instances were neither better nor worse following post-editing. Translation accuracy differs for "it" and "they". For "it" 32 instances are judged to be correct vs. 60 incorrect. The opposite is observed for "they", with 47 instances judged to be correct vs. 14 incorrect. (Instances marked as "other" or "bad translation" cannot be commented upon further and are excluded from the counts). The poor translation of "it" could be due to the method used to identify anaphoric and non-anaphoric instances (no such method was used for "they"), differences in coreference resolution accuracy for "it" and "they", or something else entirely.

9 Limitations of Post-Editing

Although specific failures in the baseline SMT system, the external tools and the post-editing rules await detailed analysis, the following possible problems with the external tools should at least be considered: incorrect identification of subject-position "it", of non-anaphoric pronouns and of antecedents. These problems may arise from a mismatch between the TED Talks domain, and the domain of the data that the tools were trained on.

As the post-editing rules affect only pronouns, agreement issues may occur. For example, if the baseline SMT system outputs "ils sont partis" ("they[masc] have left") and the post-editing rules amend "ils" to "elles", the verb "partis" should also be amended: "elles sont *parties*" ("they[fem] have left"). Agreement issues could be addressed within a dependency-parser-based post-editing framework such as the Depfix system for Czech (Mareček et al., 2011; Rosa, 2014).

Another limitation is the lack of an available tool for detecting event pronouns. Whilst NADA appears to detect some of these, it is an accidental consequence of its inability to distinguish a pleonastic ("il/ce") from an event pronoun ("ce"). NADA was also shown to perform poorly for TED data (see Section 6).

While post-editing rules could potentially be written to insert a pronoun in the SMT output where one is syntactically required in the the target language, or to delete a pronoun for syntactic or stylistic reasons, this was not done in the current system.

The approach may also be difficult to extend to other languages which are less well provisioned in terms of parsers and coreference resolution systems or for which baseline SMT quality is poor.

10 Summary and Future Work

The post-editing approach makes use of two pronoun-specific rules applied to the output of a baseline English-to-French phrase-based SMT system. One rule handles anaphoric pronouns, the other handles non-anaphoric pronouns.

Before extending this work to develop new rules or applying the technique to other language pairs, it is important to first understand where the post-editing method performs well and where it performs poorly. A detailed analysis of the post-edits as compared with the human judgements from the manual evaluation would be a logical first step. Limitations of both the external tools and the post-editing rules should be assessed.

Acknowledgements

Thanks to Professor Bonnie Webber and the three anonymous reviewers for their feedback. This project has received funding from the European Union's Horizon 2020 research and innovation programme under grant agreement n° 645452 (QT21).

[7]The official shared task BLEU scores appear to have been calculated using a different method

References

Shane Bergsma and David Yarowsky. 2011. NADA: A Robust System for Non-Referential Pronoun Detection. In *Proceedings of DAARC 2011*, pages 12–23.

Liane Guillou, Christian Hardmeier, Aaron Smith, Jörg Tiedemann, and Bonnie Webber. 2014. ParCor 1.0: A Parallel Pronoun-Coreference Corpus to Support Statistical MT. In *Proceedings of the Ninth International Conference on Language Resources and Evaluation (LREC'14)*, Reykjavik, Iceland. European Language Resources Association (ELRA).

Christian Hardmeier, Preslav Nakov, Sara Stymne, Jörg Tiedemann, Yannick Versley, and Mauro Cettolo. 2015. Pronoun-focused MT and cross-lingual pronoun prediction: Findings of the 2015 DiscoMT shared task on pronoun translation. In *Proceedings of the Second Workshop on Discourse in Machine Translation*, Lisbon, Portugal.

Roger Hawkins, Richard Towell, and Marie-Noëlle Lamy. 2001. *French Grammar and Usage*. Hodder Arnold, 2 edition.

Kenneth Heafield. 2011. KenLM: Faster and smaller language model queries. In *Proceedings of the Sixth Workshop on Statistical Machine Translation.*

Philipp Koehn, Hieu Hoang, Alexandra Birch, Chris Callison-Burch, Marcello Federico, Nicola Bertoldi, Brooke Cowan, Wade Shen, Christine Moran, Richard Zens, Chris Dyer, Ondřej Bojar, Alexandra Constantin, and Evan Herbst. 2007. Moses: Open Source Toolkit for Statistical Machine Translation. In *Proceedings of the 45th Annual Meeting of the ACL on Interactive Poster and Demonstration Sessions*, ACL '07, pages 177–180, Stroudsburg, PA, USA. Association for Computational Linguistics.

Heeyoung Lee, Yves Peirsman, Angel Chang, Nathanael Chambers, Mihai Surdeanu, and Dan Jurafsky. 2011. Stanford's Multi-pass Sieve Coreference Resolution System at the CoNLL-2011 Shared Task. In *Proceedings of the Fifteenth Conference on Computational Natural Language Learning: Shared Task*, CONLL Shared Task '11, pages 28–34, Stroudsburg, PA, USA. Association for Computational Linguistics.

David Mareček, Rudolf Rosa, Petra Galuščáková, and Ondřej Bojar. 2011. Two-step Translation with Grammatical Post-processing. In *Proceedings of the Sixth Workshop on Statistical Machine Translation*, WMT '11, pages 426–432, Stroudsburg, PA, USA. Association for Computational Linguistics.

Franz Josef Och. 2003. Minimum Error Rate Training in Statistical Machine Translation. In *Proceedings of the 41st Annual Meeting on Association for Computational Linguistics - Volume 1*, ACL '03, pages 160–167, Stroudsburg, PA, USA. Association for Computational Linguistics.

Karthik Raghunathan, Heeyoung Lee, Sudarshan Rangarajan, Nathanael Chambers, Mihai Surdeanu, Dan Jurafsky, and Christopher Manning. 2010. A Multi-pass Sieve for Coreference Resolution. In *Proceedings of the 2010 Conference on Empirical Methods in Natural Language Processing*, EMNLP '10, pages 492–501, Stroudsburg, PA, USA. Association for Computational Linguistics.

Rudolf Rosa. 2014. Depfix, a Tool for Automatic Rule-based Post-editing of SMT. *The Prague Bulletin of Mathematical Linguistics*, 102:47–56.

Benoît Sagot. 2010. The Lefff, a Freely Available and Large-coverage Morphological and Syntactic Lexicon for French. In *7th International Conference on Language Resources and Evaluation (LREC 2010)*, Valletta, Malta.

Jochen Weiner. 2014. Pronominal anaphora in machine translation. Master's thesis, Karlsruhe Institute of Technology, Karlsruhe, Germany.

A Document-Level SMT System with Integrated Pronoun Prediction

Christian Hardmeier
Uppsala University
Department of Linguistics and Philology
Box 635, 751 26 Uppsala, Sweden
`first.last@lingfil.uu.se`

Abstract

This paper describes one of Uppsala University's submissions to the pronoun-focused machine translation (MT) shared task at DiscoMT 2015. The system is based on phrase-based statistical MT implemented with the document-level decoder Docent. It includes a neural network for pronoun prediction trained with latent anaphora resolution. At translation time, coreference information is obtained from the Stanford CoreNLP system.

1 Introduction

One of Uppsala University's submissions to the pronoun-focused translation task at DiscoMT 2015 is a document-level phrase-based statistical machine translation (SMT) system integrating a neural network classifier for pronoun prediction. The system unites various contributions to discourse-level machine translation that we made during the last few years: The translation system uses our document-level decoder for phrase-based SMT, Docent (Hardmeier et al., 2012; Hardmeier et al., 2013a). The pronoun prediction network was first described by Hardmeier et al. (2013b), and its integration into the decoder by Hardmeier (2014, Chapter 9). In comparison to previous work, the size of the parallel training corpus has been reduced to be more consistent with the official data sets of the shared task. However, for practical reasons, we still use previously trained models that do not match the constraints of the official data sets exactly. Also, while the latent anaphora resolution approach of Hardmeier et al. (2013b) is used for training, allowing us to train our system without running anaphora resolution over the entire training corpus, we rely on coreference annotations generated with the Stanford CoreNLP toolkit (Lee et al., 2013) at test time, as we believe them to be more reliable.

2 MT setup

Owing to time constraints, the setup of our MT system is different from the official baseline provided by the shared task organisers. The system we use is a standard phrase-based SMT system with a phrase table trained on the TED, Europarl (v7) and News commentary (v9) corpora. The system has 3 language models (LMs). The main LM is a 6-gram model with modified Kneser-Ney smoothing (Chen and Goodman, 1998), trained with KenLM (Heafield, 2011) on the TED, News commentary and News crawl corpora provided for the WMT 2014 shared task (Bojar et al., 2014) and the French Gigaword corpus, LDC2011T10. Additionally, we include a 4-gram bilingual LM (Niehues et al., 2011) and a 9-gram LM over Brown clusters (Brown et al., 1992). Both of these are trained with SRILM (Stolcke et al., 2011) using Witten-Bell smoothing (Witten and Bell, 1991) over a corpus consisting of TED, Europarl, News commentary and United Nations data. Unlike the official baseline, we do not use any lowercasing, recasing or truecasing steps in our training procedure. Instead, all our models are trained directly on the original text in the form in which it occurs in the corpus data. The phrase table is trained with the Moses toolkit (Koehn et al., 2007), and the feature weights of all the models except for the pronoun prediction classifier are optimised towards the BLEU score (Papineni et al., 2002) with the MERT algorithm (Och, 2003) as implemented in Moses.

To increase the effect of the pronoun prediction model, our system uses pronoun placeholders for the pronouns *il*, *elle*, *ils* and *elles* (Hardmeier, 2014, Chapter 9). In the phrase table and the main LM, these pronouns are substituted by four placeholders, LCPRONOUN-SG and UCPRONOUN-SG for upper- and lowercase *il* or *elle* and LCPRONOUN-PL and UCPRONOUN-PL for upper- and lowercase *ils* and

Proceedings of the Second Workshop on Discourse in Machine Translation (DiscoMT), pages 72–77,
Lisbon, Portugal, 17 September 2015.

elles, respectively. This means that the translation probabilities and the main LM do not offer the system any help to select between the masculine and the feminine forms of the pronouns. The same is true of the Brown cluster LM, since the clustering algorithm automatically assigned the feminine and masculine pronouns to the same clusters. In the bilingual LM, no substitution was made, so this LM still contains information about pronoun choice.

At decoding time, we first run a pass of dynamic-programming beam search decoding with Moses, using only sentence-level models, to initialise the state of our document-level decoder, Docent. Then we add the pronoun prediction model and continue decoding with Docent for 2^{25} iterations. In Docent, we use the simulated annealing search algorithm with a geometric decay cooling schedule, starting at a temperature of 1 and reducing the temperature by a decay factor of 0.99999 at each accepted step. In addition to the *change-phrase-translation*, *swap-phrases* and *resegment* operations described by Hardmeier et al. (2012), we include a *crossover* operation that generates a new state by randomly picking complete sentences either from the current decoder state or from the best state encountered so far, and a *restore-best* operation that unconditionally jumps back to the best state encountered. The last two operations are necessary because simulated annealing accepts state changes with a certain probability even if they decrease the score, and after a sequence of accepted changes to the worse the decoder may get lost in unpromising regions of the search space.

3 The Pronoun Prediction Network

We model pronoun prediction with the feed-forward neural network classifier introduced by Hardmeier et al. (2013b). Its overall structure is shown in figure 1. To create input data for the network, we first generate a set of antecedent candidates for a given pronoun by running the preprocessing pipeline of the coreference resolution system BART (Versley et al., 2008). Each training example for our network can have an arbitrary number of antecedent candidates. Next, we prepare three types of features. *Anaphor context features* describe the source language (SL) pronoun (**P**) and its immediate context consisting of three words to its left (**L1** to **L3**) and three words to its right (**R1** to **R3**), encoded as one-hot vectors. *Antecedent features* (**A**) describe an antecedent candidate. Candidates are represented by the TL words aligned to the syntactic head of the source language markable noun phrase as identified by the Collins head finder (Collins, 1999), again represented as one-hot vectors. These vectors cannot be fed into the network directly because their number depends on the number of antecedent candidates and on the number of TL words aligned to the head word of each antecedent. Instead, they are averaged to yield a single vector per antecedent candidate. Finally, *anaphoric link vectors* (**T**) describe the relationship between an anaphor and a particular antecedent candidate. These vectors are generated by the feature extraction machinery in BART and include a standard set of features for coreference resolution (Soon et al., 2001; Uryupina, 2006) borrowed wholesale from a working coreference system.

In the forward propagation pass, the input word representations are mapped to a low-dimensional representation in an embedding layer (**E**). In this layer, the embedding weights for all the SL vectors (the pronoun and its 6 context words) are tied, so if two words are the same, they are mapped to the same lower-dimensional embedding regardless of their position relative to the pronoun. To process the information contained in the antecedents, the network first computes the link probability for each antecedent candidate. The anaphoric link features (**T**) are mapped to a hidden layer with logistic sigmoid units (**U**). The activations of the hidden units are then mapped to a single value, which functions as an element in an internal softmax layer over all antecedent candidates (**V**). This softmax layer assigns a probability $p_1 \dots p_n$ to each antecedent candidate. The antecedent feature vectors **A** are projected to lower-dimensional embeddings, weighted with their corresponding link probabilities and summed. The weighted sum is then concatenated with the source language embeddings in the **E** layer. The embedding of the antecedent word vectors is independent from that of the SL features since they refer to a different vocabulary.

In the next step, the entire **E** layer is mapped to another hidden layer (**H**), which is in turn connected to a binary output layer predicting the classes *il* and *elle* for the singular classifier and *ils* and *elles* for the plural classifier, respectively. The non-linearity of both hidden layers is the logistic sigmoid function. The dimensionality of the source and target language word embeddings is 50 in our setup, resulting in a total embedding layer

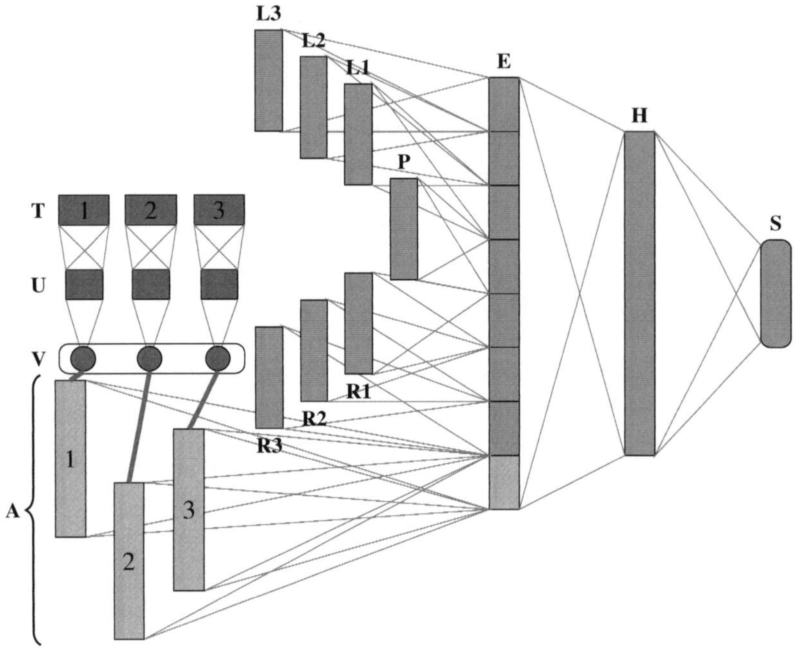

Figure 1: Neural network with latent anaphora resolution

size of 400, and the size of the last hidden layer is set to 150. The network was regularised with an ℓ_2 penalty that was set using grid search over a held-out development set. The network is trained with the RMSPROP algorithm with cross-entropy as the training objective. The gradients are computed using backpropagation. Note that the number of weights in the network is the same for all training examples even though the number of antecedent candidates varies because all weights related to antecedent word features and anaphoric link features are shared between all antecedent candidates. The model is trained on the entirety of the TED corpus enriched with examples from the 10^9 corpus. We reserve a random sample of 10 % of the TED part of the training data as a validation set. Training is run for 300 epochs, and the model used for testing is the one that achieves the best classification accuracy on the validation set.

As earlier experiments suggested that the latent anaphora resolution method integrated in the pronoun prediction network, though useful for training, may not be sufficient for good performance at test time, we decided to use annotations created with an external coreference resolution system when translating the test set. Coreference links were generated with the Stanford CoreNLP software[1] (Lee et al., 2013). The output of the anaphora resolver is deterministic and clusters the mention in the document into a number of coreference sets. We transform these clusters into links by selecting, for each anaphoric pronoun, the closest preceding mention in the same coreference set that is realised as a full noun phrase (rather than another pronoun), if such a mention exists, or the closest mention in the same set otherwise. This leaves us with (at most) a single antecedent per pronoun, so the **V** layer of the neural network is trivially reduced to a single element with probability one, and the **T** and **U** layers are not used at all at test time.

4 Results and Discussion

When considering the outcome of the shared task, we first notice that the performance of our system in terms of BLEU scores (Papineni et al., 2002), with a score of 32.6 %, is several points below that of the systems based on the officially provided baseline, which range around 37 %.[2] It seems likely that this difference, which is confirmed by other automatic

[1]We are grateful to Liane Guillou for providing us with ready-made CoreNLP annotations of the DiscoMT test set.

[2]For a presentation and discussion of the complete shared task methodology and results, we refer the reader to the shared task overview paper (Hardmeier et al., 2015).

	This system					Baseline
	Precision		R_{max}		F_{max}	F_{max}
ce	29/ 35	(0.829)	32/ 45	(0.711)	0.765	0.832
ça/cela	9/ 10	(0.900)	22/ 60	(0.367)	0.521	0.631
elle	3/ 9	(0.333)	3/ 20	(0.150)	0.207	0.452
elles	3/ 3	(1.000)	4/ 15	(0.267)	0.421	0.436
il	7/ 43	(0.163)	11/ 19	(0.579)	0.254	0.522
ils	45/ 54	(0.833)	45/ 48	(0.938)	0.882	0.900
on	0/ 0	(n/a)	0/ 0	(n/a)	n/a	n/a
Micro-average	96/154	(0.623)	96/177	(0.542)	0.580	0.699

Accuracy with OTHER: 122/210 = 0.581 (Baseline: 0.676)
Accuracy without OTHER: 96/183 = 0.525 (Baseline: 0.630)
6 bad translations (Baseline: 9)

Table 1: Manual evaluation results for the UU-HARDMEIER system

metrics, is mainly due to differences in the underlying SMT baseline, and the result suggests that we should reconsider the baseline to be used in future experiments. At the same time, it is worth pointing out that the SMT system described in our earlier work (Hardmeier, 2014) used a considerably larger phrase table than our DiscoMT system. It included, in addition to the News commentary and the Europarl corpora, a large amount of data from the Common crawl, United Nations and 10^9 corpora from the WMT shared tasks, and we expect that a system with the full phrase table would reach a higher performance than the one presented here.

The results of our system in the official manual evaluation are shown in Table 1. In the manual evaluation, 210 instances of the English pronouns *it* and *they* were annotated with correct pronouns in the context of the MT output. The table displays the class-specific evaluation metrics for each of the pronoun types in the human evaluation, two accuracy scores including and excluding the OTHER label and the number of examples labelled BAD TRANSLATION by the human annotators. The primary metric of the shared task evaluation is the "Accuracy with OTHER" score, which corresponds to the total proportion of matching examples in the annotated sample. The "Accuracy without OTHER" score is computed over the subset of the examples not annotated with OTHER only. The class-specific scores include a standard precision score in combination with a modified recall score named R_{max} that accounts for the fact that every example potentially has multiple correct annotations, as well as an F_{max} score defined as the harmonic mean of these two quantities. A more detailed description of and rationale for the scores can be found in the shared task overview paper (Hardmeier et al., 2015). For comparison, the table also includes the scores of the official baseline system, which happens to be the top-ranked system in the evaluation.

In terms of pronoun translation accuracy, our model ends up in the middle field of the participants with rank 4 out of 7 (including the baseline). The class-specific scores are consistently below the baseline, in particular for the singular pronouns *il* and *elle*. The masculine pronoun *il* seems to suffer from serious overgeneration, which leads to a very low precision score. The instances of *elle* that the system generated, by contrast, are both too few and mostly wrong. On the whole, the results are rather disappointing, especially since our earlier results with this model (Hardmeier, 2014) had resulted in slightly positive findings. In those experiments, however, we had used oracle annotations of pronoun coreference instead of the automatic CoreNLP annotations used here, and even in that setting, the improvement was very modest.

The results of the shared task suggest that in both the pronoun prediction and the pronoun-focused translation task, it is very hard to beat the baseline systems. In both baseline systems, the *n*-gram model is the only context-sensitive source of information for pronoun choice, and it seems that it is surprisingly difficult to improve pronoun prediction or translation by exploiting additional information despite the obvious and well-known shortcomings of the *n*-gram approach. Future work must show whether this is due to the *n*-gram model's extraordinary capacity for making guesses about remote context by analysing local context, as certain findings suggest (Hardmeier, 2014, 137–138), or just to the fact that our incomplete understanding of the problem leads us to design bad predictors that are easily beaten by a somewhat sophisticated baseline. By using placeholders in the phrase table and the main LM, we explicitly disable the n-gram model for pronoun prediction in our system. It seems likely that this, in conjunction with the fact that our prediction model does not appear to deliver the performance required for improved pronoun translation, is one of the reasons contributing to the lower scores we achieve.

Acknowledgements

This work was supported by the Swedish Research Council under project 2012-916 *Discourse-Oriented Statistical Machine Translation*. The experiments were run on the Abel cluster, owned by the University of Oslo and the Norwegian metacenter for High Performance Computing (NOTUR), and operated by the Department for Research Computing at USIT, the University of Oslo IT-department.

References

Ondrej Bojar, Christian Buck, Christian Federmann, Barry Haddow, Philipp Koehn, Johannes Leveling, Christof Monz, Pavel Pecina, Matt Post, Herve Saint-Amand, Radu Soricut, Lucia Specia, and Aleš Tamchyna. 2014. Findings of the 2014 workshop on statistical machine translation. In *Proceedings of the Ninth Workshop on Statistical Machine Translation*, pages 12–58, Baltimore (Maryland, USA).

Peter F. Brown, Peter V. deSouza, Robert L. Mercer, Vincent J. Della Pietra, and Jenifer C. Lai. 1992. Class-based n-gram models of natural language. *Computational linguistics*, 18(4):467–479.

Stanley F. Chen and Joshua Goodman. 1998. An empirical study of smoothing techniques for language modeling. Technical report, Computer Science Group, Harvard University, Cambridge (Mass.).

Michael Collins. 1999. *Head-Driven Statistical Models for Natural Language Parsing*. Ph.D. thesis, University of Pennsylvania.

Christian Hardmeier, Joakim Nivre, and Jörg Tiedemann. 2012. Document-wide decoding for phrase-based statistical machine translation. In *Proceedings of the 2012 Joint Conference on Empirical Methods in Natural Language Processing and Computational Natural Language Learning*, pages 1179–1190, Jeju Island (Korea).

Christian Hardmeier, Sara Stymne, Jörg Tiedemann, and Joakim Nivre. 2013a. Docent: A document-level decoder for phrase-based statistical machine translation. In *Proceedings of the 51st Annual Meeting of the Association for Computational Linguistics: System Demonstrations*, pages 193–198, Sofia (Bulgaria).

Christian Hardmeier, Jörg Tiedemann, and Joakim Nivre. 2013b. Latent anaphora resolution for cross-lingual pronoun prediction. In *Proceedings of the 2013 Conference on Empirical Methods in Natural Language Processing*, pages 380–391, Seattle (Washington, USA).

Christian Hardmeier, Preslav Nakov, Sara Stymne, Jörg Tiedemann, Yannick Versley, and Mauro Cettolo. 2015. Pronoun-focused MT and cross-lingual pronoun prediction: Findings of the 2015 DiscoMT shared task on pronoun translation. In *Proceedings of the Second Workshop on Discourse in Machine Translation*, Lisbon (Portugal).

Christian Hardmeier. 2014. *Discourse in Statistical Machine Translation*, volume 15 of *Studia Linguistica Upsaliensia*. Acta Universitatis Upsaliensis, Uppsala.

Kenneth Heafield. 2011. KenLM: faster and smaller language model queries. In *Proceedings of the Sixth Workshop on Statistical Machine Translation*, pages 187–197, Edinburgh (Scotland, UK).

Philipp Koehn, Hieu Hoang, Alexandra Birch, et al. 2007. Moses: Open source toolkit for Statistical Machine Translation. In *Annual Meeting of the Association for Computational Linguistics: Demonstration session*, pages 177–180, Prague (Czech Republic).

Heeyoung Lee, Angel Chang, Yves Peirsman, Nathanael Chambers, Mihai Surdeanu, and Dan Jurafsky. 2013. Deterministic coreference resolution based on entity-centric, precision-ranked rules. *Computational linguistics*, 39(4):885–916.

Jan Niehues, Teresa Herrmann, Stephan Vogel, and Alex Waibel. 2011. Wider context by using bilingual language models in machine translation. In *Proceedings of the Sixth Workshop on Statistical Machine Translation*, pages 198–206, Edinburgh (Scotland, UK).

Franz Josef Och. 2003. Minimum error rate training in Statistical Machine Translation. In *Proceedings of the 41st Annual Meeting of the Association for Computational Linguistics*, pages 160–167, Sapporo (Japan).

Kishore Papineni, Salim Roukos, Todd Ward, and Wei-Jing Zhu. 2002. BLEU: A method for automatic evaluation of machine translation. In *Proceedings of the 40th Annual Meeting of the Association for Computational Linguistics*, pages 311–318, Philadelphia (Pennsylvania, USA).

Wee Meng Soon, Hwee Tou Ng, and Daniel Chung Yong Lim. 2001. A machine learning approach to coreference resolution of noun phrases. *Computational linguistics*, 27(4):521–544.

Andreas Stolcke, Jing Zheng, Wen Wang, and Victor Abrash. 2011. SRILM at sixteen: Update and outlook. In *Proceedings of the IEEE Automatic Speech Recognition and Understanding Workshop*, Waikoloa (Hawaii, USA).

Olga Uryupina. 2006. Coreference resolution with and without linguistic knowledge. In *Proceedings of the Fifth Language Resources and Evaluation Conference (LREC-2006)*, pages 893–898, Genoa (Italy).

Yannick Versley, Simone Paolo Ponzetto, Massimo Poesio, Vladimir Eidelman, Alan Jern, Jason Smith, Xiaofeng Yang, and Alessandro Moschitti. 2008. BART: A modular toolkit for coreference resolution. In *Proceedings of the ACL-08: HLT Demo Session*, pages 9–12, Columbus (Ohio, USA).

Ian H. Witten and Timothy C. Bell. 1991. The zero-frequency problem: Estimating the probabilities of novel events in adaptive text compression. *IEEE Transactions on Information Theory*, 37(4):1085–1094.

Predicting Pronoun Translation Using Syntactic, Morphological and Contextual Features from Parallel Data

Sharid Loáiciga
Département de Linguistique
Centre Universitaire d'Informatique
Université de Genève
sharid.loaiciga@unige.ch

Abstract

We describe the systems submitted to the shared task on pronoun prediction organized within the Second DiscoMT Workshop. The systems are trained on linguistically motivated features extracted from both sides of an English-French parallel corpus and their parses. We have used a parser that integrates morphological disambiguation and which handles the REPLACE_XX placeholders explicitly. In particular, we compare the relevance of three groups of features: a) syntactic (from the English parse), b) morphological (from the French morphological analysis) and c) contextual (from the French sentence) for French pronoun prediction. A discussion on the role of these sets of features for each pronoun class is included.

1 Introduction

In this paper we describe the Geneva 1 and Geneva 2 systems submitted for the shared task on pronoun prediction organized in conjunction with the EMNLP 2015 Second Workshop on Discourse in Machine Translation (MT) (Hardmeier et al., 2015). Additionally, two contrastive systems are included.

Pronouns are economical, short and independent words which can stand in the place of a more cumbersome word, and thus they lack some informativity. Their main purpose is to avoid unnecessary repetition of concepts (De Beaugrande and Dressler, 1981). Because they "cannot be interpreted without considering the discourse context", some of them are considered *anaphora* (Stede, 2012, 41). In other words, they *corefer* with other element to find their meaning.

The task of finding the referent or *the antecedent* for each anaphor is known as *Anaphora Resolution* (AR). Research on this problem has been active for some time now (Mitkov, 2001; Mitkov, 2002; Strube, 2007; Stoyanov et al., 2009; Ng, 2010). However, the independent development of MT, and Statistical Machine Translation (SMT) especially, has encountered a new dimension of the same problem: inaccurate pronoun translation. Indeed, inaccurate pronoun translation is the result of non-existent AR when passing from the source to the target language. However, plugging a AR system into the MT system has not proved to be a suitable solution to the problem (Hardmeier and Federico, 2010; Le Nagard and Koehn, 2010; Guillou, 2012). AR systems rely on a heavy preprocessing of the text, with several sub-tasks which are themselves imperfect and hard. Besides, their quality is not good enough yet to have a serious impact in MT output quality. Last, most of them exist only for English (Mitkov and Barbu, 2002; Stede, 2012).

The systems described in this paper are not developed nor intended as AR systems. Therefore, they do not explicitly search the antecedent of pronouns, but their purpose is to predict directly a pronoun translation using a classifier fed with features extracted from parallel data. They represent an alternative to the use of an AR system for helping MT. Unlike SMT systems, these classifiers have access to both source and target language data (excepting the target pronoun) during training and testing time. This data can be analyzed in order to create features which encode different types of information. Other than *generating* a possible translation, a pronoun predictor *chooses* a translation among a list of several classes.

2 Related Work

The idea of using word-aligned parallel data for AR was first introduced by Mitkov and Barbu (2002) to tackle difficult cases for common English AR systems. As an illustration, one of

Proceedings of the Second Workshop on Discourse in Machine Translation (DiscoMT), pages 78–85,
Lisbon, Portugal, 17 September 2015.

their examples is repeated here:

(1) a. *en* John removes the cassette from the videoplayer and disconnects **it**.
 b. *fr* Jean éjecte la cassette du magnétoscope et **le** débranche.

In (1a), the pronoun *it* has both *cassette* and *videoplayer* as potential antecedents. However, the first is more prominent (a direct object), while the actual antecedent is a prepositional phrase, a syntactic type heavily penalized by most AR systems. This case can be disambiguated by looking at its gender-marked translation (1b). Since both *magnétoscope* and *le* are masculine in French, they can be matched safely as coreferring, excluding *cassette* which is feminine.

Pronoun prediction is based on the parallel data used for building SMT systems and follows Mitkov and Barbu's intuition of disambiguating pronouns based on their translation.

Building a predictor of target-language translations is a strategy introduced by Popescu-Belis et al. (2012). Using English-French parallel data, the authors manually gathered a corpus of 400 instances of *it* and their translation and used it as training data. Features include the gender of the previous ten NPs, and positional and grammatical information about the pronoun. Accuracy is reported to be around 60%.

Hardmeier, Tiedemann, and Nivre (2013) run classifiers for the same task using all the parallel data from SMT training. Their features come from the context of the pronoun in the source language (three words before and after) and from the potential antecedents (determined using a AR toolkit in the target language). In experiments with a Maximum Entropy classifier, a performance of 0.54 precision, 0.06 recall is obtained. A second set of experiments, where the AR results are dropped and a neural network classifier is used, they report precision of 0.565 and recall of 0.116. It is argued that performance is particularly good with low-frequency classes such as the feminine pronoun *elles*. In a later stage of this work, the neural network classifier is combined with a SMT system built using the Docent decoder (Hardmeier, 2014). Similarly, Weiner (2014) uses Discriminative Word Lexicon (DWL)[1] with an AR algorithm on the English side of a parallel and their correspondent word-aligned German token.

Finally, Novák (2011), Novák et al. (2013) model pronoun prediction for Czech. Features are extracted exclusively from the source text (English) following the Czech grammar rules that disambiguate the possible translations of *it*. Accuracy is around 70%.

3 Pronoun Mapping Between English and French

The shared task consisted in predicting the French translations of the English third-person subject pronouns *it* and *they* (Hardmeier et al., 2015). The nine classes shown in Table 1 were defined. They are presented along with their possible translations. These correspondences were determined using the word alignments provided with the training data and corrected by hand[2]. The important imbalance in the distribution of the classes, concerning the OTHER class in particular, is to be noted. A manual review of the data uncovered that this class includes translations as lexical NPs (2), other pronouns (3) and nothing at all as in the case of paraphrases (4). Object pronouns are included as well (4), (5). This is likely a source of errors, since they are homographic to subject pronouns in English.

(2) a. Certainly **it** is perceived de facto to be impossible.
 b. **La chose** est certainement perçue de facto comme étant impossible.

(3) a. It was not able to do very much but **it** was repeatedly abused by Members of this House [...].
 b. Elle ne permettait pas de faire grand-chose mais les députés de cette Assemblée **en** abusaient constamment [...].

(4) a. I believe **it** to be of vital importance that where Member States allow regions and local authorities to raise taxes, **they** should continue to be able to do so and not be subject to across-the-board regulation by Europe.
 b. Je voudrais dire que j'estime indispensable que les États membres puissent continuer d'autoriser les régions et les communes à percevoir des taxes et que ce domaine ne soit pas uniformément réglé par l'Europe.

[1]DWL models aim at improving the general word choice in the target language (Mauser et al., 2009).

[2]Specifically, 446 instances of pronouns aligned to random words were corrected by hand.

French	it #	it %	they #	they %
ça	79	0.43	1	0.02
cela	585	3.19	22	0.33
elle	2,392	13.03	93	1.40
il	5,332	29.04	275	4.14
ce	1,919	10.45	128	1.93
elles	101	0.55	911	13.72
ils	158	0.86	3,263	49.13
on	360	1.96	97	1.46
OTHER	7,432	40.48	1,852	27.88
Total	18,358	100.00	6,642	100.00

Table 1: Distribution of the French translations of English pronouns *it* and *they* in the training data described in Section 4.1.

(5) a. We have that opportunity right now. Let us grasp **it**.
b. Cette chance se présente aujourd'hui, et nous devons **la** saisir !

Examples (2) to (5) are taken from the Europarl section of the data. Table 1 also shows why the problem of pronoun translation is hard: there is no 1-1 correspondence between any English and French pronoun.

Moreover, even if only pronoun-to-pronoun translations are considered, there is no equal distribution of the genders in French. Because all impersonal uses of the pronoun *it* are translated into French *il*, the balance of learning algorithms such as language models is often tilted in favor of the masculine translation. Something similar happens with *they*. In principle, this pronoun can be translated either as *ils* or *elles*; nevertheless, all the members of the group it refers to must be feminine in order to use the feminine *elles*, making this translation much rarer.

4 Cross-lingual Pronoun Prediction

4.1 Data and Tools

Both sides of the parallel data provided for the shared task are parsed using the Fips parser (Wehrli, 2007). This is a rule-based parser which produces an information-rich phrase-structure representation with predicate-argument labels. Besides, it can also be used as a tagger, generating a POS-tag (containing disambiguated morphological information) and a grammatical function for each word of a given sentence. We relied on this tagger output for extracting most of our features. An example of the output is given in Figure 1.

And	CONJ-COO	and	
it	PRO-PER-3-SIN	it	SU
's	VERB-IND-PRE-3-SIN	be	
a	DET-SIN-NEU	a	FO
very	ADV-INT	very	
easy	ADJ	easy	
question	NOUN-SIN-NEU	question	
.	PUNC-POINT		

Figure 1: Example of the tagger output of the Fips parser for the sentence *"And it's a very easy question"*. The first column contains the words in the sentence, the second the POS-tags and morphological analysis, the third consists of the lemmas and the fourth of the predicate-argument labels.

For the French side, a unique placeholder is inserted in the place of each REPLACE_XX. This ensures coherent syntactic analysis by the parser, since projections are based on the lexical properties of the heads. The placeholder was inserted in the lexicon as a token with all possible morphological features: both masculine and feminine gender, singular and plural number and the three possible persons. Due to its rule-based nature, the parser unifies only the compatible feature values on each sentence. Consequently, the placeholder allowed us to retrieve some information from the unification process with the verb.

The final training data consists of 25,000 examples composed from a subset of the shared-task data. It includes 747 instances from the TED talks, 14,561 from News Commentary and 9,691 from EuroParl. All systems are built using the Stanford Maximum Entropy package (Manning and Klein, 2003).

4.2 Features

We use three types of features roughly following the categorization of Friedrich and Palmer (2014). Most of them rely on the predicate-argument structure of the English side and morphological analysis of the French side. The rationale for this choice is to simulate an MT scenario (where target sentences are not available) in which one could parse the source language to find the argument of interest and may use a dictionary for getting the target-language correspondent morphology. The possible values of all features are listed in Table 2. For each training example, we extracted the following information:

Syntactic Features These features refer to the arguments present in the English sentence (fourth column in Figure 1). Once an argument is identified in the English sentence, the gender and number of the word-aligned French token (most often the head) is retrieved. In the case of the sentential objects, only the values YES or NO are assigned.[3]

1. Current sentence subject
2. Current sentence object
3. Current sentence predicative object
4. Current sentence sentential object
5. Previous sentence subject
6. Previous sentence object
7. Previous sentence predicative object
8. Previous sentence sentential object

Morphological Features This information concerns the POS and morphological tags (second column in Figure 1) of the words in the immediate context of each pronoun to predict.

9. Gender and number of all adjectives
10. Previous word POS-tag
11. Following word POS-tag
12. Voice of following verb
13. Person and number of following verb

To obtain the value for feature 9, all adjectives in the previous and the current sentence are identified and the gender and number of their French word-aligned token is searched. Then French gender and number information is aggregated and the most frequent one is selected.

Context Features This last set of features refers to the preceding or following tokens of each French pronoun to predict. For these, sentence boundaries are ignored. If the previous word happened to be the full stop of the previous sentence, a full stop is then taken as the value for previous word token.

14. Previous lemma
15. Following lemma
16. Previous word token
17. Following word token
18. Second following word token

4.3 System 1

Features 1 and 5 refer to subjects, which are likely to be pronouns aligned with REPLACE_XX items on the French side. In order to simulate the use of an unmodified parser, we dropped the morphological features obtained by unification for the REPLACE_XX items and inserted the special feature value PRON instead. Table 3 contains the obtained results.

Features	Values
1,2,3,5,6,7,9	{SIN-FEM, SIN-MAS, PLU-FEM, PLU-MAS, INN-FEM, INN-MAS}
4,8	{YES, NO}
10,11	{NOUN,VERB,ADV,PRO,CONJ, PUNC,DET,ADJ,PREP}
12	{ACTIVE, PASSIVE}
13	{1-SIN, 1-PLU, 2-SIN, 2-PLU, 3-SIN, 3-PLU}
14,15	e.g. {*le,avoir,venir,être,rester,...*}
16,17,18	e.g. {*la,ont,viennent,sont,restent,...*}

Table 2: Possible values for each of the features. INN stands for *unknown number*.

4.4 System 2

For this second experiment, we use the unified values for REPLACE_XX subjects (features 1 and 5). Additionally, the vast OTHER class was split in two classes in order to reduce the imbalance: i) translations by a pronoun not considered among the classes or by a lexical NP, and ii) translations without any pronoun in French. The labels for the latter were taken from the annotation furnished with the training data. After classification, the two subclasses were merged again. The obtained results are presented in Table 3.

4.5 Discussion

From the results of System 1 and System 2, it can be noted that the absence of syntactic features (columns **M+C** in Table 3) seems to have a rather small impact in the final results. The syntactic features are motivated in the salience hierarchies established within linguistic theories of salience and AR. In these theories, a syntactically salient argument such as the subject, is more likely to be the antecedent of a pronoun. Our results show, however, that this particular set of features does not contribute much knowledge to the model, and in some cases it only adds noise, as shown by an increase in the scores of columns **M+C**.

Morphology features, on their part, influence the pronouns with feminine and masculine forms, i.e. *il, elle, ils, elles*. However, results are ambiguous: for System 1 there is a positive effect, but for

[3]Sentential objects are sentences acting as complements of the verb and very often with a conjunction or preposition as their head; therefore, we did not look for gender and number.

	System 1				System 2			
Prediction	**S+M**	**S+C**	**M+C**	**S+M+C**	**S+M**	**S+C**	**M+C**	**S+M+C**
ce	21.19	61.02	62.03	61.06	23.20	65.95	62.43	64.66
cela	0	17.91	9.68	14.71	0	20.59*	9.38	19.67
elle	14.68	33.55	36.73	35.29	25.40	38.93*	36.92	36.48
elles	33.33	27.03	20.25	31.33	32.50	36.11*	20.25	32.10
il	29.51	44.22	37.91	44.23	27.13	50.19	38.22	47.52
ils	70.34	70.80	75.07	75.88	68.97	69.16	75.00	76.13*
on	0	32.35	24.62	30.99	10.42	31.58	26.23	34.00
ça	0	5.66	5.61	9.17	0	9.35	5.61	7.48
OTHER	72.60	74.73	76.45	75.87	71.61	73.09	76.29	75.69

Table 3: Comparison of F1 scores (%) obtained in the test set with different groups of features. F1 scores were computed using the shared-task scorer. S+M+C correspond to results submitted to the shared-task. *Best results throughout all the systems presented here.

System 2 there is a negative effect columns **S+C** in Table 3). Pronoun *on* is affected in the same way, although we observed that many occurrences referred to a passive construction in English such as (6).

(6) a. *en* ..., if they're given the right work
b. *fr.*...si l'<u>on</u> leur confie la bonne mission.

Systems 1 and 2 additionally show that context features are highly important. When they are removed from the model (columns **S+M**), an important drop in the performance is observed. They are particularly determinant for the *ça* and *cela* classes. We had the hypothesis that these pronouns were determined instead by sentential objects, either from the current or the previous sentence.

Looking at the features individually (Table 4), it can be noted that for both systems the morphology information of the following verb (feature 13) is the most important parameter, which makes sense since the task deals mostly with subject pronouns. The other top-ranking features are the following word POS-tag (18), the following lemma (17) and the previous predicative object (10).

The hierarchy in Table 4 reveals further understanding about the context features as well. Features concerning lemmas (15 and 14) have almost as much weight as features concerning raw tokens (16, 17, 18), especially the following lemma. Their influence depends on the pronoun to predict: while raw tokens are determining for pronouns *ce, ça* and *on*, lemmas are determining for pronouns *il, elle, ils* and *elles*.

Furthermore, as depicted in Figure 2, results from System 2 are better[4] than those of System 1 for all the classes. This evidences misclassification due to the big OTHER class, in particular of the less frequent classes. Our two-way distinction is straightforward using the provided data, but we suspect that a finer distinction could further improve results. One could for instance use parsing to distinguish between subject pronouns and object pronouns (such as examples (4), (5)).

System	**Feature number**
System 1	13,18,10,17,15,16,14,12,11, 8,2,3,5,9,6,7,1,4
System 2	13,18,17,10,15,16,14,11,12 1,4,8,2,9,5,3,6,7

Table 4: Features of the model ordered from the most to the least informative.

The distance between a pronoun and its antecedent is implicitly handled by a language model within a limited window when computing n-gram probabilities. In an attempt to model the notion of distance between the pronoun and each of the arguments in the sentence, we did some tests with the position of each argument as a feature (these were numerical features, then treated as real values). This did not change anything to the model, therefore we dropped it early on.

4.6 System 2b and System 2c

Knowing that the test set is composed of TED data, we build an in-domain classifier, System 2b, using only the TED and IWSLT14 corpus for training. Otherwise, it is identical to System 2 (i.e.

[4] τ = -12.1579, df = 1104, p-value < 2.2e-16

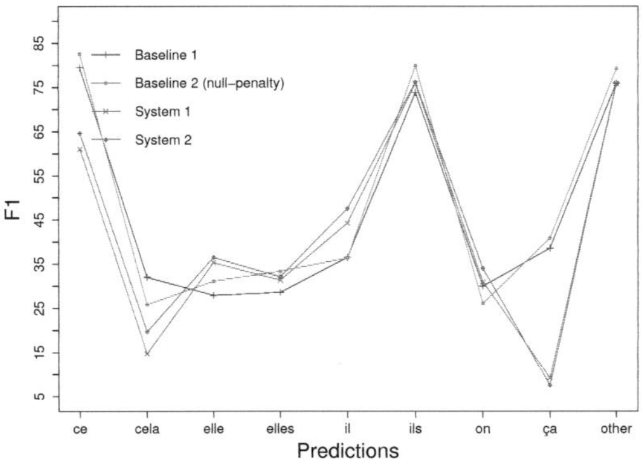

Figure 2: Comparison of fine-grained F-scores of the submitted systems and the task baselines.

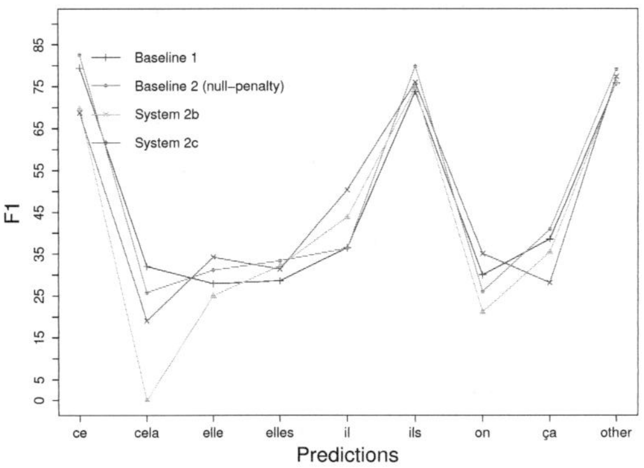

Figure 3: Comparison of fine-grained F-scores of System 2b, System 2c and the task baselines.

with splitting of the OTHER class). Since the training data is much smaller, with only 6,543 training examples, we expect results to be lower than in previous experiments. Results are presented in Table 5.

Results for this system show that context features benefit from the similarity between training and testing data. However, this is not true for pronouns which are determined morphologically as shown by the results of System 1.

Last, the initial training data (25,000 examples from TED, News Commentary and EuroParl) is combined with the 5,796 examples from the IWSLT14 corpus for building System 2c. Results are presented in Table 5. In comparison to System 1 or System 2, the additional training data improves the classification of pronouns *ça* and *ce* (due to the same-domain effect), and additionally,

	Features S+M+C	
Prediction	**System 2b**	**System 2c**
ce	69.71*	68.70
cela	0	19.05
elle	25.00	34.21
elles	32.10	31.33
il	43.80	50.39*
ils	74.71	76.02
on	21.21	35.05*
ça	35.43*	28.12
OTHER	75.93	77.36*

Table 5: Comparison of F1 scores (%) obtained in the test set using the shared-task scorer. *Best results throughout all the systems presented here.

it has a small improvement on the pronouns *il* and *on*. Figure 3 presents a comparison of these two systems with the shared-task baselines.

5 Conclusions and Future Work

The selection of features in our experiments showed that the role of syntax is rather small in determining the translation of the English pronouns *it* and *they*. Morphological features on the other hand, had an effect on the prediction of gender-determined pronouns, i.e. feminine and masculine in the case of French. However, we think that more experiments are necessary in order to fully exploit their potential, for instance, with languages with more than two genders. Last, context features proved to be of particular importance to all the classes, above all when the training and testing data are similar. This stress the relevance of the language model for the translation of pronouns and explains the high performance of the baseline as well.

Moreover, our experiments show undoubtedly that splitting the OTHER class improves performance. We think that this a clear step to take in our future work.

Finally, we think that if the notion of *animacy* could be formalized and used as feature, some of the classes would benefit. For instance, it could help to distinguish between human or non-human antecedents, a determining factor for distinguishing between and *it* translated either as *ce* or *il/elle* (Moore et al., 2013). In all the cases, there is plenty of room for improvement.

References

Robert De Beaugrande and Wolfgang Dressler. 1981. *Introduction to Text Linguistics*. Longman Linguistics Library, Essex.

Annemarie Friedrich and Alexis Palmer. 2014. Automatic prediction of aspectual class of verbs in context. In *Proceedings of the 52nd Annual Meeting of the Association for Computational Linguistics (Volume 2: Short Papers)*, pages 517–523, Baltimore, Maryland. Association for Computational Linguistics.

Liane Guillou. 2012. Improving pronoun translation for statistical machine translation. In *Proceedings of the Student Research Workshop at the 13th Conference of the European Chapter of the Association for Computational Linguistics*, pages 1–10, Avignon, France, April. Association for Computational Linguistics.

Christian Hardmeier and Marcello Federico. 2010. Modelling pronominal anaphora in statistical machine translation. In *Proceedings of the 7th International Workshop on Spoken Language Translation*, pages 283–289.

Christian Hardmeier, Jörg Tiedemann, and Joakim Nivre. 2013. Latent anaphora resolution for cross-lingual pronoun prediction. In *Proceedings of the 2013 Conference on Empirical Methods in Natural Language Processing*, EMNLP, pages 380–391, Seattle, Washington. Association for Computational Linguistics.

Christian Hardmeier, Preslav Nakov, Sara Stymne, Jörg Tiedemann, Yannick Versley, and Mauro Cettolo. 2015. Pronoun-focused MT and cross-lingual pronoun prediction: Findings of the 2015 DiscoMT shared task on pronoun translation. In *Proceedings of the Second Workshop on Discourse in Machine Translation*, DiscoMT 2015, Lisbon, Portugal.

Christian Hardmeier. 2014. *Discourse in Statistical Machine Translation*. Ph.D. thesis, Department of Linguistics and Philology, Uppsala University.

Ronan Le Nagard and Philipp Koehn. 2010. Aiding pronoun translation with Co-Reference Resolution. In *Proceedings of the Joint 5th Workshop on Statistical Machine Translation*, pages 258–267, Uppsala, Sweden.

Christopher Manning and Dan Klein. 2003. Optimization, MaxEnt models, and conditional estimation without magic. In *Tutorial at HLT-NAACL and 41st ACL conferences*, Edmonton, Canada and Sapporo, Japan.

Arne Mauser, Saša Hasan, and Hermann Ney. 2009. Extending statistical machine translation with discriminative and trigger-based lexicon models. In *Proceedings of the 2009 Conference on Empirical Methods in Natural Language Processing: Volume 1 - Volume 1*, EMNLP'09, pages 210–218, Stroudsburg, PA. Association for Computational Linguistics.

Ruslan Mitkov and Catalina Barbu. 2002. Using bilingual corpora to improve pronoun resolution. *Languages in Contrast*, 4(2):201–211.

Ruslan Mitkov. 2001. Outstanding issues in anaphora resolution. In Alexander Gelbukh, editor, *Computational Linguistics and Intelligent Text Processing*, volume 2004, pages 110–125. Springer Berlin Heidelberg.

Ruslan Mitkov. 2002. *Anaphora Resolution*. Pearson Education Limited, Harlow.

Joshua Moore, Christopher J.C. Burges, Erin Renshaw, and Wen-tau Yih. 2013. Animacy detection with voting models. In *Proceedings of the 2013 Conference on Empirical Methods in Natural Language Processing*, pages 55–60, Seattle, Washington, USA, October. Association for Computational Linguistics.

Vincent Ng. 2010. Supervised noun phrase coreference research: The first fifteen years. In *Proceedings of the 48th Annual Meeting of the Association for Computational Linguistics*, pages 1396–1411.

Michal Novák, Anna Nedoluzhko, and Zdeněk Žabokrtský. 2013. Translation of "It" in a deep syntax framework. In *Proceedings of the Workshop on Discourse in Machine Translation*, pages 51–59, Sofia, Bulgaria. Association for Computational Linguistics.

Michal Novák. 2011. Utilization of anaphora in machine translation. In *Proceedings of the 20th Annual Conference of Doctoral Students–Contributed Papers: Part I*, WDS11, pages 155 — 160, Prague. Matfyzpress.

Andrei Popescu-Belis, Thomas Meyer, Jeevanthi Liyanapathirana, Bruno Cartoni, and Sandrine Zufferey. 2012. Discourse-level annotation over europarl for machine translation: Connectives and pronouns. In *Proceedings of the 8th International Conference on Language Resources and Evaluation*, LREC'12, Istanbul, Turkey. European Language Resources Association (ELRA).

Manfred Stede. 2012. *Disourse Processing*. Morgan and Claypool Publishers, Toronto.

Veselin Stoyanov, Claire Cardie, Nathan Gilbert, Ellen Riloff, David Buttler, and David Hysom. 2009. Conundrums in noun phrase coreference resolution: Making sense of the state-of-the-art. In *Proceedings of the Joint Conference of the 47th Annual Meeting of the Association for Computational Linguistics and the 4th International Joint Conference on Natural Language Processing of the Asian Federation of Natural Language Processing*, ACL-IJCNLP 2009.

Michael Strube. 2007. Corpus-based and machine learning approaches to coreference resolution. In Monika Schwarz-Friesel, Manfred Consten, and Mareile Knees, editors, *Anaphors in Text. Cognitive, Formal and Applied Approaches to Anaphoric Reference*, pages 207–222. John Benjamins Publishing Company, Amsterdam.

Eric Wehrli. 2007. Fips, a "Deep" linguistic multilingual parser. In *Proceedings of the Workshop on Deep Linguistic Processing*, pages 120–127. Association for Computational Linguistics.

Jochen Stefan Weiner. 2014. Pronominal anaphora in machine translation. Master of science, Karlsruhe Institute of Technology.

Rule-Based Pronominal Anaphora Treatment for Machine Translation

Sharid Loáiciga
Département de Linguistique
Centre Universitaire d'Informatique
Université de Genève
sharid.loaiciga@unige.ch

Éric Wehrli
Département de Linguistique
Centre Universitaire d'Informatique
Université de Genève
eric.wehrli@unige.ch

Abstract

In this paper we describe the rule-based MT system Its-2 developed at the University of Geneva and submitted for the shared task on pronoun translation organized within the Second DiscoMT Workshop. For improving pronoun translation, an Anaphora Resolution (AR) step based on Chomsky's Binding Theory and Hobbs' algorithm has been implemented. Since this strategy is currently restricted to 3rd person personal pronouns (i.e. *they, it* translated as *elle, elles, il, ils* only), absolute performance is affected. However, qualitative differences between the submitted system and a baseline without the AR procedure can be observed.

1 Introduction

In this paper we describe the system submitted for the shared task on pronoun translation organized in conjunction with the EMNLP 2015 Second Workshop on Discourse in Machine Translation (Hardmeier et al., 2015). We present the rule-based Machine Translation (MT) system Its-2 developed at the University of Geneva. A demo can be found here: `http://latlapps.unige.ch/Translate?`

The interest for the pronoun translation task is at the heart of a line of research concerned with discourse phenomena and MT. Now, it is widely acknowledged that many remaining problems within MT can improve only if discourse knowledge, i.e., processing of phenomena beyond the sentence level, is taken into account (Webber and Joshi, 2012; Hardmeier, 2012; Joty et al., 2014).

The problem of pronoun translation has its roots in the nature of *anaphors*. These are words empty of semantic content themselves, such as third person referential pronouns, which refer back to other words with semantic content to find their meaning. We know which element a pronoun refers to (its *antecedent*), in part because it agrees in gender or number. For example, in (1a), we are able to link *they* (pronoun) with *bikes* (antecedent) because they agree in number. This linking, or resolution, seems trivial for a human, but is not straightforward for a machine, especially if the antecedent and the anaphor are not in the same sentence and the text in question contains several sentences with several potential antecedents. Developing automatic Anaphora Resolution (AR) systems is a research domain on its own and has been active for decades (Mitkov, 2001; Mitkov, 2002; Strube, 2007; Stoyanov et al., 2009; Ng, 2010).

(1) a. Paul left two bikes in front of the house. When he came back, they were no longer there.

1.1 The Problem of Pronoun Translation for English-French

If sentence (1) is to be translated into French, one has the choice (mainly) between *ils* and *elles* for translating the pronoun *they*. This choice is no longer dependent on the English antecedent *bikes*, but on its translation in French either as the masculine noun *vélos* (2a) or as the feminine noun *bicyclettes* (2b).

(2) a. Paul a laissé les deux vélos devant la maison. Lorsqu'il est revenu, ils n'étaient plus là.

b. Paul a laissé les deux bicyclettes devant la maison. Lorsqu'il est revenu, elles n'étaient plus là.

The focus of the shared task is on the English third person pronouns *it* and *they*. As observed in corpus, these pronouns are not always translated as pronouns, but can correspond to a content noun phrase (NP) or to nothing at all. This is the case

Proceedings of the Second Workshop on Discourse in Machine Translation (DiscoMT), pages 86–93,
Lisbon, Portugal, 17 September 2015.

French	it #	it %	they #	they %
ça	79	0.43	1	0.02
cela	585	3.19	22	0.33
elle	2,392	13.03	93	1.40
il	5,332	29.04	275	4.14
ce	1,919	10.45	128	1.93
elles	101	0.55	911	13.72
ils	158	0.86	3,263	49.13
on	360	1.96	97	1.46
NONE	2,895	15.77	515	7.75
OTHER	4,537	24.71	1,337	20.13
Total	18,358	100.00	6,642	100.00

Table 1: Distribution of the French Translations of English pronouns *it* and *they*.

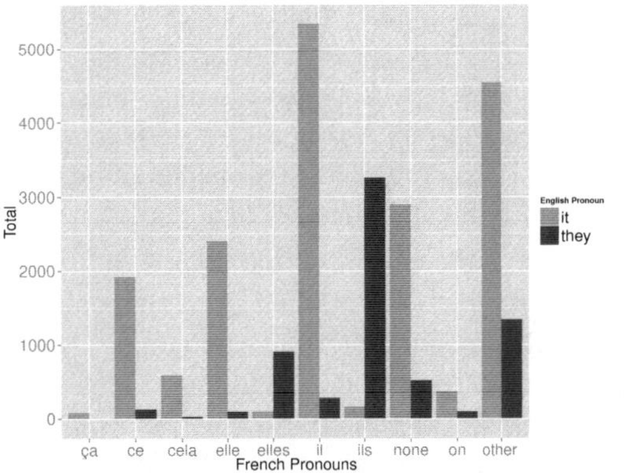

Figure 1: Distribution of the French translations of English pronouns *it* and *they*.

in example (3) where the English pronoun *they* in (3a) corresponds to a content NP in French (3b).

(3) a. To conclude, I would just like to say something on the principle of subsidiarity. I believe it to be of vital importance that where Member States allow regions and local authorities to raise taxes, **they** should continue to be able to do so and not be subject to across-the-board regulation by Europe.

b. Enfin, concernant le principe de subsidiarité, je voudrais dire que j'estime indispensable que **les États membres** puissent continuer d'autoriser les régions et les communes à percevoir des taxes et que ce domaine ne soit pas uniformément réglé par l'Europe .

Moreover, even in cases where a pronoun is translated as a pronoun, the mapping is not one-to-one. To illustrate this, we composed a sample of 25,000 *it* and *they* taken from the Workshop data (instances from the Europarl, TED and News Commentary files are included) (Hardmeier et al., 2015). The translation distribution of these two pronouns is presented in Table 1 and Figure 1.[1]

Table 1 shows that each of these pronouns can be translated with at least 7 other pronouns in different proportions. This emphasizes the fact that agreement must be checked in the target language.

[1]These correspondences were determined using the automatic word alignments provided with the training data for the prediction track of the shared task and they were corrected by hand. Specifically, 446 instances of pronouns aligned to random words were corrected.

The OTHER category stands for cases such as example (3), where the translation corresponds to something which is not a pronoun. This category amounts to ≈20-25% of the translations. NONE, on the other hand, corresponds to English pronouns which were not translated at all in French (4).[2] Similar proportions were reported by Weiner (2014) for the translation from English to German.

(4) a. Mr President, enlargement is essential. **It** is genuinely important for the future of the European Union, [...].

b. Monsieur le Président, l'élargissement est indispensable et réellement important pour l'avenir de l'Union européenne, [...].

2 Related Work

The AR problem has been vastly addressed since the 1980s using rule-based methods first, and corpus-based methods more recently. Two algorithms are particularly important both for their foundational character and their pertinence with the system described here: Hobbs' (1978) algorithm and Lappin & Leass' (1994) Resolution of Anaphora Procedure (RAP).

Hobbs' algorithm deals with third person pronouns only (*he, she, it, they*). It traverses the parse trees of the sentences looking for NPs of the same gender and number as the anaphor to resolve. The potential antecedents are prioritized according to their grammatical function, in a way that a subject

[2]Ultimately, these translations are choices of the human translator at the origin of the texts. However, in many of the NONE/OTHER cases, a pronoun would be appropriate as well.

is preferred to a direct object which is also preferred to an indirect object. While reporting accuracy of 88.3%, Hobbs' algorithm has been criticized because of its assumption of perfect syntactic analysis, since results are computed using parse trees built manually.

The RAP algorithm, on the other hand, treats third person pronouns, reflexives, reciprocals and pleonastic pronouns. RAP is based on a series of agreement filters, a binding algorithm which prioritizes arguments according to their function –like Hobbs' algorithm– and salience weighting, a concept of centering theory. It builds on parse trees and identifies referents by analyzing each noun phrase. Each referent has an associated salience value according to a predefined scale, which is updated with every sentence, when the value reaches zero, the potential referent is removed from the list. The authors report 86% accuracy, however this figure is computed using perfect syntactic analysis as well.

A third system is particularly important in the development of AR. We refer to Soon, H. T. Ng, and Lim (2001) one of the first corpus-based successful systems. Rather than finding antecedents for pronouns, their interest is coreference resolution (CR), i.e., finding all NPs in a text which refer to the same world entity. The system uses a pairwise classification paradigm based on a set of features encoding distance, morphological and semantic agreement, definiteness and type of NPs. It achieves a recall of 58.6% and a precision of 67.3% on the MUC-6 corpus (Grishman and Sundheim, 1995).

The question of pronoun translation, on the other hand, has caught the attention of researchers working on Statistical Machine Translation (SMT) for a few years now, resulting in more or less regular publications on the subject since 2010. The most straightforward methods have already been explored, although with limited performance. The first attempts to improve pronoun MT relied on external AR systems difficult to reconcile with SMT systems themselves, an approach which introduces many errors (Le Nagard and Koehn, 2010; Hardmeier and Federico, 2010; Guillou, 2011; Guillou, 2012).

The latest solution has taken the form of a pronoun predictor, an algorithm able to predict a pronoun in the target language using source language information and easily embeddable with a SMT system. Such a predictor, however, is hard to train and results are yet unsatisfactory (Popescu-Belis et al., 2012; Hardmeier et al., 2013; Hardmeier et al., 2014). An automatic post-processing approach has also been reported by Weiner (2014). This method consists in automatically correcting the MT output based on the anaphora-pronoun pairs collected from the source text using a AR system.

Finally, using the coreference annotation of the Prague Dependency Treebank (PDT) (Kučová and Hajičová, 2005; Nedoluzhko et al., 2013), Novák (2011; 2013) focuses on the translation of *it* using a classic transfer system. During the parsing stage, each English *it* pronoun is assigned a label for its interpretation. These labels are then used for generating the correct translation in English.

3 Its-2

Its-2 (Wehrli et al., 2009; Wehrli and Nerima, 2009) is a rule-based translation system based on the Fips parser (Wehrli, 2007). The translation process follows the three classic steps: analysis, transfer and generation. Start with the analysis module. For a given source language sentence, the parser produces an information-rich phrase-structure representation, along with predicate-argument labels. The grammar implemented in the Fips parser is heavily influenced by Chomsky's minimalism program and earlier work (Chomsky, 1995), but also includes concepts from other theories such as LFG (Bresnan, 2001) and Simpler Syntax (Culicover and Jackendoff, 2005). The syntactic structures built by the parser follow the general X-bar schema shown in (5), which yields relatively flat structures, without intermediate nodes.

(5) $[_{XP}$ L X R$]$

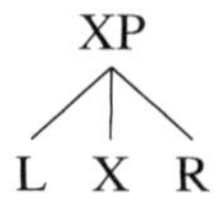

Each constituent XP is composed of a head, X, along with a (possibly empty) list of left sub-constituents (L) and a (possibly empty) list of right sub-constituents (R), where X stands for the usual lexical categories – N(oun), V(erb), A(djective), Adv(erb), P(reposition), C(onjunction), etc., to which we add T(ense) and F(unctional). The T category stands for tensed phrases, corresponding, roughly, to the traditional S category of standard generative linguistics. As for F, it is used to represent secondary predicates, as in the so-called small clause constructions.

The transfer module maps this source language abstract representation to an equivalent target language representation. The mapping is achieved by a recursive traversal of the source-language structure, starting with the head of a constituent, and then its right and left subconstituents. Lexical transfer occurs at the head level and yields a target language equivalent term of the same or different category, which becomes the new current head. The target language structure is then projected on the basis of the head. In this way, the final output is generated according to the lexical features of the target language. Argument constituents, on the other hand, are determined by the subcategorization properties of the target language predicate. The necessary information is available in the lexical database. Transformational rules, in the traditional Chomskyan sense, can apply to generate specific structures such as passive or *wh*-constructions (interrogative, relative, *tough*-movement[3]). In addition, the transfer procedure can be augmented with language-pair specific transfer rules, for instance to modify the constituent order.

Currently, the Its-2 system is available for ten language pairs between English, French, German, Italian and Spanish. For each language pair, there is a bilingual, bidirectional dictionary implemented as a relational table containing the associations between the lexical items of source and target languages. Other specifications such as translation context, semantic descriptors and argument matching for predicates are also contained in the table.

In the Its-2 system, pronouns are handled like other lexical heads, that is, they are transferred and translated as heads of phrases, using the bilingual dictionary. This strategy, which works fine for non-anaphoric pronouns, is clearly insufficient for anaphoric pronouns, for which knowledge of antecedent is mandatory. The following section describes our preliminary attempt to implement an anaphora resolution component in the Its-2 system, as part of the Fips parser. For the time being, this AR component only deals with 3rd person personal pronouns such as (*he, she, it, her, him*, etc.). The basic idea underlying our implementation is that the proper form of a target-language pronoun depends on the gender and number features of its (target-language) antecedent. Since we do not perform AR on the target language, this information can be retrieved through the links connecting the source-language pronoun, its antecedent and the target-language correspondence of the antecedent. To illustrate this process, consider the following example:

(6) a. *en* Paul bought an ice-cream and will eat **it** later.
    b. *fr* Paul a acheté une glace et **la** mangera plus tard.

The pronoun *it* in the source language should be translated as a feminine (clitic) pronoun **la** in the French sentence, because *ice-cream*, the antecedent of *it*, is translated as *glace*, a feminine noun.

4 Binding Theory AR

As indicated above, our AR procedure is part of the Fips parser and currently only deals with 3rd person personal pronouns. It is highly influenced by Chomsky's Binding Theory (1981), which is not an AR method *per se*, but rather a set of constraints useful to exclude otherwise potential antecedents. These constraints follow two principles: **Principle A** states that reflexive and reciprocal pronouns find their antecedents within their governing category (the smallest clause that includes them); **Principle B** states that 3rd person personal pronouns find their antecedents outside of the clause that includes them (Reinhart, 1983; Büring, 2005).[4]

Our strategy for anaphora resolution recalls in several ways the one used by Hobbs (1978) or Lappin & Leass (Lappin and Leass, 1994), adapted to the specific structures of the Fips parser.

The algorithm comprises three steps:

1. **impersonal pronouns**
   The impersonal pronoun *it* in English – *il* in French – has no antecedent and should be excluded from further consideration by the AR procedure. The identification of impersonal pronouns is achieved on the basis of lexical

[3] *tough*-movement refers to subjects of a main verb which are also the object of an embedded infinitive verb. In *This book is easy to read*, for instance, *this book* is both the subject of the main verb and the logical object of the verb *to read*.

[4] Notice that Binding Theory includes a third principle, Principle C, which states that referring expressions (lexical noun phrases) cannot be bound. This principle is not relevant in this work.

information (verbs lexically marked as impersonal, for instance meteorological verbs such as *to rain* or *to snow*), as well as syntactic information. For instance, adjectives which can take so-called sentential subjects occur with an impersonal subject when the sentence is extraposed as in:

(7) a. *It* was obvious that Paul had lied.
b. *It* is easy to see that.

Similarly, impersonal subject pronouns can be found in passive structures with sentential complements:

(8) *It* was suggested that Paul would do the job.

2. **reflexive or reciprocal pronouns**
We assume a simplified interpretation of **Principle A** in which this type of pronoun always refers to the subject of the sentence that contains it. In cases of embedded infinitive sentences, we assume the presence of an abstract subject pronoun (PRO, unrealized lexically) whose antecedent is determined by the *control theory* and ultimately by lexical information. For example, in the sentence *Paul*$_i$ *promised Mary [PRO to take care of himself*$_i$*]*, *himself* refers to the subject pronoun PRO, which in turn refers to the noun phrase *Paul*.

3. **referential non-reflexive/reciprocal pronouns**
Such pronouns, currently restricted to the non-impersonal *it*, along with *he, him, she, her, they, them*, etc., undergo our simplified interpretation of Principle B, which means that they must have an antecedent outside of the clause that contains them. We further restrict possible antecedents to arguments, excluding adjuncts noun phrases. The search for antecedents considers all preceding clauses within the sentence as well as within the previous sentence and makes an ordered list of the noun phrases which agree in number and gender with the pronoun.[5] The order is determined by proximity, as well as by the grammatical function of the antecedent (subject, then grammatical object, then prepositional complements, etc.).

[5]The *n* preceding sentences for finding an antecedent is a variable number (Klappholtz and Lockman, 1975). However, the large majority of the works in the field use an *n* value between 1 and 5. Here we follow Hobbs' estimation of $n \leq 1$ for 90% of the cases.

In summary, our AR procedure is based on a simplified interpretation of the principles A and B of the Binding Theory. After attempting to eliminate impersonal pronouns, the procedure uses principles A and B, respectively to handle reflexive/reciprocal pronouns and other 3rd personal referential pronouns. Our simplified interpretation of those principles state that reflexive/reciprocal pronouns can only refer to the subject of their clause, while other pronouns can refer to noun phrases outside of their immediate clause. When several noun phrases meet those conditions, priority is given to grammatical function and locality.

5 Results and Discussion

The translation of the test set using the AR component does not have an impact on the BLEU scores (Papineni et al., 2002) (as expected). When measuring only the translations of pronouns, however, the AR component shows a positive effect when compared to a baseline without it, as shown in Table 2. Since these results are computed using exact word-level alignment matching between the candidate translation and an unique reference (Hardmeier et al., 2015), they are only indicative.

	BLEU		Precision	Recall
w/ AR	22.43	it	0.1174	0.1173
		they	0.3631	0.3481
w/o AR	22.44	it	0.0917	0.0919
		they	0.2710	0.2566

Table 2: Contrastive results obtained from the test set. Precision and recall scores were computed using the automatic scorer by Hardmeier and Federico (2010).

For the sake of completeness, a manual evaluation of two documents from the testset, amounting to 405 sentences or 203 pronouns, was completed. Two translations with and without the AR component were evaluated. The results are given in Table 3.

It can be seen that the reflexive/reciprocal pronouns did not change between the two outputs. Besides, all observed errors were due to incorrect antecedent identification, leading to incorrect pronoun generation. One such a case is (9), where the

EN Pronoun	Improved	Unchanged	Degraded
him	0	17	0
it	18	86	6
them	0	21	0
themselves	0	1	0
they	2	47	5
Total	20	172	11

Table 3: Results obtained from the manual evaluation of 203 pronouns from the test set.

algorithm turns a correctly translated pronoun by the baseline into an incorrect one. In this example, the word procedures, which is feminine in French, is identified as antecedent, causing then the generation of *elles* instead of *ils*.

(9) a. SRC And he spent all this time stuck in the hospital while he was having those procedures, as a result of which he now can walk. And while he was there, **they** sent tutors around to help him with his school work.

b. W/O AR Et il a passé tout ce temps englué dans l'hôpital tandis qu'il avait ces procédures, comme un résultat de lequel maintenant il peut marcher. Et tandis qu'il était là-bas, **ils** ont envoyé des professeurs autour pour l'aider avec son école à travailler.

c. W/ AR Et il a passé tout ce temps englué dans l'hôpital tandis qu'il avait ces procédures, comme un résultat de lequel maintenant il peut marcher. Et tandis qu'il était là-bas, **elles** ont envoyé des professeurs autour pour l'aider avec son école à travailler

In almost the double of cases, however, the AR works in favor of a better pronoun translation. This is the case in example (10). Here the word *acceptance* is correctly identified as the antecedent. This translates as the feminine **acceptation** in French, therefore, the pronoun *it* is translated as *elle*.

(10) a. SRC But acceptance is something that takes time. It always takes time .

b. W/O AR Mais l'acceptation est quelque chose qui prend le temps. **Il** prend toujours le temps.

c. W/ AR Mais **l'acceptation** est quelque chose qui prend le temps. **Elle** prend toujours le temps.

Despite our own evaluation, the official manual evaluation results of the task produced an accuracy of 0.419 without translations as OTHER and 0.339 with OTHER. These results were rather low when compared with the other submitted systems, but they are not discouraging. These scores are rather due to the fact that our system does not generate *ça, cela, ce* or *on* as possible translations of *it, they*. This is the case of example (11), where a translation of *it* as *ça* or *cela* would have been preferable. Yet, there is an effect of the AR component, visible in the generation of pronoun *elle*.

(11) a. SRC And when I was an adolescent, I thought that I'm gay, and so I probably can't have a family. And when she said it, **it** made me anxious.

b. W/O AR Et quand j'étais un adolescent, j'ai pensé que je suis gai, probablement et ainsi je ne peux pas avoir une famille. Et quand elle l'a dit **il** m'a rendu anxieux.

c. W/ AR Et quand j'étais un adolescent, j'ai pensé que je suis gai, probablement et ainsi je ne peux pas avoir une famille. Et quand elle l'a dite **elle** m'a rendu anxieux .

The manual evaluation also revealed that refining our rules to translate cases such as (7) and (8) as *ce* instead of *il* would be a good start for tackling this problem.

6 Conclusion and Future Work

We have presented an implementation of an AR component within the transfer-based system Its-2. The AR strategy, which applies during parsing, is based on the principles of Chomsky's Binding Theory. Currently, this strategy is restricted to 3rd person personal pronouns *they, he, she, it, her, him* and does not consider translations as demonstrative pronouns *ça, cela* or *ce*. However, given recent evidence from different corpora, rules to include these translation options will be developed in the future.

References

Joan Bresnan. 2001. *Lexical Functional Grammar*. Blackwell Publishers, Oxford.

Daniel Büring. 2005. *Binding Theory*. Cambridge University Press.

Noam Chomsky. 1981. *Lectures on Government and Binding: The Pisa Lectures*. Mouton de Gruyter.

Noam Chomsky. 1995. *The Minimalist Program*. MIT Press, Cambridge, Massachusetts.

Peter Culicover and Ray Jackendoff. 2005. *Simpler Syntax*. Oxford Univesity Press, New York.

Ralph Grishman and Beth Sundheim. 1995. Design of the muc-6 evaluation. *ACL Anthology: A Digital Archive of Research Papers in Computational Linguistics*.

Liane Guillou. 2011. Improving pronoun translation for statistical machine translation. Master of science, University of Edinburgh.

Liane Guillou. 2012. Improving pronoun translation for statistical machine translation. In *Proceedings of the Student Research Workshop at the 13th Conference of the European Chapter of the Association for Computational Linguistics*, pages 1–10, Avignon, France, April. Association for Computational Linguistics.

Christian Hardmeier and Marcello Federico. 2010. Modelling pronominal anaphora in statistical machine translation. In *Proceedings of the 7th International Workshop on Spoken Language Translation*, pages 283–289.

Christian Hardmeier, Jörg Tiedemann, and Joakim Nivre. 2013. Latent anaphora resolution for cross-lingual pronoun prediction. In *Proceedings of the 2013 Conference on Empirical Methods in Natural Language Processing*, EMNLP, pages 380–391, Seattle, Washington. Association for Computational Linguistics.

Christian Hardmeier, Sara Stymne, Jörg Tiedemann, Aaron Smith, and Joakim Nivre. 2014. Anaphora models and reordering for phrase-based SMT. In *Proceedings of the Ninth Workshop on Statistical Machine Translation*, pages 122–129, Baltimore, Maryland, USA, June. Association for Computational Linguistics.

Christian Hardmeier, Preslav Nakov, Sara Stymne, Jörg Tiedemann, Yannick Versley, and Mauro Cettolo. 2015. Pronoun-focused MT and cross-lingual pronoun prediction: Findings of the 2015 DiscoMT shared task on pronoun translation. In *Proceedings of the Second Workshop on Discourse in Machine Translation*, DiscoMT 2015, Lisbon, Portugal.

Christian Hardmeier. 2012. Discourse in statistical machine translation: A survey and a case study. *Discours*, 1(11):5–38.

Jerry Hobbs. 1978. Resolving Pronoun References. *Lingua*, 1(44):311–338.

Shafiq Joty, Francisco Guzmán, Lluís Màrquez, and Preslav Nakov. 2014. DiscoTK: Using Discourse Structure for Machine Translation Evaluation. In *Proceedings of the Ninth Workshop on Statistical Machine Translation*, WMT, pages 402–408, Baltimore, Maryland. Association for Computational Linguistics.

David Klappholtz and Abe Lockman. 1975. Contextual reference resolution. In *Proceedings of the 13th Annual Meeting of the Association for Computational Linguistics*, ACL 75, pages 4–25, Minnesota.

Lucie Kučová and Eva Hajičová. 2005. Coreferential Relations in the Prague Dependency Treebank. In *Proceedings of the 5th International Conference on Discourse Anaphora and Anaphor Resolution 2004*, pages 97–102, San Miguel, Azores.

Shalom Lappin and Herbert J. Leass. 1994. An Algorithm for Pronominal Anaphora Resolution. *Computational Linguistics*, 20(4):535–561.

Ronan Le Nagard and Philipp Koehn. 2010. Aiding pronoun translation with Co-Reference Resolution. In *Proceedings of the Joint 5th Workshop on Statistical Machine Translation*, pages 258–267, Uppsala, Sweden.

Ruslan Mitkov. 2001. Outstanding issues in anaphora resolution. In Alexander Gelbukh, editor, *Computational Linguistics and Intelligent Text Processing*, volume 2004, pages 110–125. Springer Berlin Heidelberg.

Ruslan Mitkov. 2002. *Anaphora Resolution*. Pearson Education Limited, Harlow.

Anna Nedoluzhko, Jiří Mírovský, and Michal Novák. 2013. A coreferentially annotated corpus and anaphora resolution for Czech. In *Computational Linguistics and Intellectual Technologies*, pages 467–475, Moskva, Russia. ABBYY.

Vincent Ng. 2010. Supervised noun phrase coreference research: The first fifteen years. In *Proceedings of the 48th Annual Meeting of the Association for Computational Linguistics*, pages 1396–1411.

Michal Novák, Anna Nedoluzhko, and Zdeněk Žabokrtský. 2013. Translation of "It" in a deep syntax framework. In *Proceedings of the Workshop on Discourse in Machine Translation*, pages 51–59, Sofia, Bulgaria. Association for Computational Linguistics.

Michal Novák. 2011. Utilization of anaphora in machine translation. In *Proceedings of the 20th Annual Conference of Doctoral Students–Contributed Papers: Part I*, WDS11, pages 155 — 160, Prague. Matfyzpress.

Kishore Papineni, Salim Roukos, Todd Ward, and Wei-Jing Zhu. 2002. BLEU: a Method for Automatic

Evaluation of Machine Translation. In *Proceedings of the 40th Annual Meeting of the Association for Computational Linguistics*, ACL'02, pages 311–318, Philadelphia, Pennsylvania. Association for Computational Linguistics.

Andrei Popescu-Belis, Thomas Meyer, Jeevanthi Liyanapathirana, Bruno Cartoni, and Sandrine Zufferey. 2012. Discourse-level annotation over europarl for machine translation: Connectives and pronouns. In *Proceedings of the 8th International Conference on Language Resources and Evaluation*, LREC'12, Istanbul, Turkey. European Language Resources Association (ELRA).

Tanya Reinhart. 1983. *Anaphora Resolution and Semantic Interpretation*. Croom Helm.

Wee Meng Soon, Hwee Tou Ng, and Daniel Chung Yong Lim. 2001. A Machine Learning Approach to Coreference Resolution of Noun Phrases. *Computational Linguistics*, 27(4):521–544.

Veselin Stoyanov, Claire Cardie, Nathan Gilbert, Ellen Riloff, David Buttler, and David Hysom. 2009. Conundrums in noun phrase coreference resolution: Making sense of the state-of-the-art. In *Proceedings of the Joint Conference of the 47th Annual Meeting of the Association for Computational Linguistics and the 4th International Joint Conference on Natural Language Processing of the Asian Federation of Natural Language Processing*, ACL-IJCNLP 2009.

Michael Strube. 2007. Corpus-based and machine learning approaches to coreference resolution. In Monika Schwarz-Friesel, Manfred Consten, and Mareile Knees, editors, *Anaphors in Text. Cognitive, Formal and Applied Approaches to Anaphoric Reference*, pages 207–222. John Benjamins Publishing Company, Amsterdam.

Bonnie Webber and Aravind Joshi. 2012. Discourse Structure and Computation: Past, Present and Future. In *Proceedings of the ACL-2012 Special Workshop on Rediscovering 50 Years of Discoveries*, ACL'12, pages 42–54, Jeju Island, Korea. Association for Computational Linguistics.

Eric Wehrli and Luka Nerima. 2009. L'analyseur syntaxique Fips. In *Proceedings of the 11th Conference on Parsing Technologies*, IWPT 09, Paris, France.

Eric Wehrli, Luka Nerima, and Yves Scherrer. 2009. Deep linguistic multilingual translation and bilingual dictionaries. In *Proceedings of the Fourth Workshop on Statistical Machine Translation*, pages 90–94.

Eric Wehrli. 2007. Fips, a "Deep" linguistic multilingual parser. In *Proceedings of the Workshop on Deep Linguistic Processing*, pages 120–127. Association for Computational Linguistics.

Jochen Stefan Weiner. 2014. Pronominal anaphora in machine translation. Master of science, Karlsruhe Institute of Technology.

Pronoun Translation and Prediction with or without Coreference Links

Ngoc Quang Luong
Idiap Research Institute
Rue Marconi 19, CP 592
1920 Martigny, Switzerland
nluong@idiap.ch

Lesly Miculicich Werlen*
Université de Neuchâtel
Institut d'Informatique
2000 Neuchâtel, Switzerland
lesly.miculicich@unine.ch

Andrei Popescu-Belis
Idiap Research Institute
Rue Marconi 19, CP 592
1920 Martigny, Switzerland
apbelis@idiap.ch

Abstract

The Idiap NLP Group has participated in both DiscoMT 2015 sub-tasks: pronoun-focused translation and pronoun prediction. The system for the first sub-task combines two knowledge sources: grammatical constraints from the hypothesized coreference links, and candidate translations from an SMT decoder. The system for the second sub-task avoids hypothesizing a coreference link, and uses instead a large set of source-side and target-side features from the noun phrases surrounding the pronoun to train a pronoun predictor.

1 Introduction

The NLP Group of the Idiap Research Institute participated in both sub-tasks of the DiscoMT 2015 Shared Task: pronoun-focused translation and pronoun prediction (Hardmeier et al., 2015). The first task aimed at evaluating the quality of pronoun translation in the output of a full-fledged machine translation (MT) system, while the second task aimed at restoring hidden pronouns in a high-quality reference translation. In our view, both sub-tasks raise the same question: given the limitations of current anaphora resolution systems, to what extent is it possible to correctly translate pronouns with unreliable knowledge of their antecedents? Although the answer depends on the translation divergencies from the source language to the target one, we explore here two different approaches to answer this question, within the DiscoMT 2015 Shared Task: one using imperfect knowledge of the antecedents of pronouns, and the other one replacing it with a large set of morphological features.

The SMT system we submitted to the pronoun-focused translation sub-task (Section 3) combines two probabilistic knowledge sources to decide the translation of the English pronouns *it* and *they* into French, namely a probability distribution obtained from an anaphora resolution system and one obtained from the SMT decoder. The classifier for the pronoun prediction sub-task (Section 4), uses morphological and positional features of source-side and target-side noun phrases surrounding the pronoun to be restored, without any hypothesis on its antecedents. System configurations are shown in Section 5, and results in Section 6.

2 Related Work

As rule-based anaphora resolution systems reached their maturity in the 1990s (Mitkov, 2002), several early attempts were made to use these methods for MT, especially in situations when pronominal issues must be addressed specifically such as EN/JP translation (Bond and Ogura, 1998; Nakaiwa and Ikehara, 1995). Following the development of statistical methods for anaphora resolution (Ng, 2010), several studies have attempted to integrate anaphora resolution with statistical MT, as reviewed by Hardmeier (2014, Section 2.3.1). Le Nagard and Koehn (2010) designed a two-pass system for EN/FR MT, first translating all possible antecedents, identifying the antecedents of pronouns using (imperfect) anaphora resolution, and constraining pronoun translation according to the features of the antecedent (with moderate improvements of MT). Other attempts along the same lines include those by Hardmeier and Federico (2010), and by Guillou (2012). Our system for the first sub-task (Section 3) enriches the approach with a probabilistic combination of constraints from anaphora resolution and pronoun candidates from the search graph generated by the MT decoder.

Another line of research attempted to post-edit pronouns in SMT output, possibly including as features the baseline translations of pro-

*Work performed while at the Idiap Research Institute.

Proceedings of the Second Workshop on Discourse in Machine Translation (DiscoMT), pages 94–100,
Lisbon, Portugal, 17 September 2015.

nouns. The approach was shown to be successful for translating discourse connectives (Meyer and Popescu-Belis, 2012). A large set of features was used within a deep neural network architecture by Hardmeier (2014, Chapters 7–9). In our system for the second sub-task, we extend the features sketched by Popescu-Belis et al. (2012).

3 Pronoun-Focused Translation

Our system for this task works in two passes. First, the source text is pre-processed and translated by a baseline MT system to acquire pronoun candidates. Then, we apply several post-editing strategies over the translations of *"it"* and *"they"*, which help in correcting erroneous instances.

3.1 Pass 1: Baseline MT Outputs

The test data is first tokenized using the tokenizer provided by the organizers. Then, we apply a baseline MT system to generate the candidate pronouns. This system is the Moses decoder (Koehn et al., 2007) with a translation and a language model trained with no additional resources other than the official data provided by the shared task organizers (including Europarl, News Commentary and Ted talks). Parameters are tuned on domain-specific Ted(dev) data set. We run the Moses decoder with the *-print-alignment-info* and *-output-search-graph* options to obtain the word alignments and the search graph plain-text representation, used for post-editing in the second pass.

3.2 Pass 2: Automatic Pronoun Post-editing

Since the pronoun-focused task concentrates on the quality of translated pronouns, in the second pass we post-edit target words aligned to *"it"* and *"they"* while keeping intact all the others. However, when translating these pronouns into French, the target pronoun is determined not only by the source word itself, but also by other contextual and grammatical factors, and most importantly by the actual gender of the antecedent. Therefore, the whole source sentence and its precedent sentences, as well as the target one, are analyzed for making decision.

3.2.1 Overview of our Approach

Our post-editing process considers the baseline translation of each pronoun *"it"* and *"they"* from the output of Pass 1. If this is one of the "complex" pronouns (e.g. *"celui"* or *"cela"*, see Section 3.2.6), then we simply accept the results from Pass 1 (baseline translation) and do not attempt to post-edit this pronoun. If this is not the case, then we check first whether it is a subject or an object pronoun. In the former case (subject pronoun), we examine two cues: the gender and number of the translation of its antecedent hypothesized by a co-reference system, along with the decoder's score for this lexical item calculated from the search graph during decoding. The selected pronoun is the one that maximizes the combined scores of these two criteria. In the latter case (object pronoun), we use a set of heuristics based on French grammar rules to seek the appropriate word. Finally, the post-edited word is substituted to the one from Pass 1 in order to generate the output of Pass 2. These steps are displayed in Figure 1.

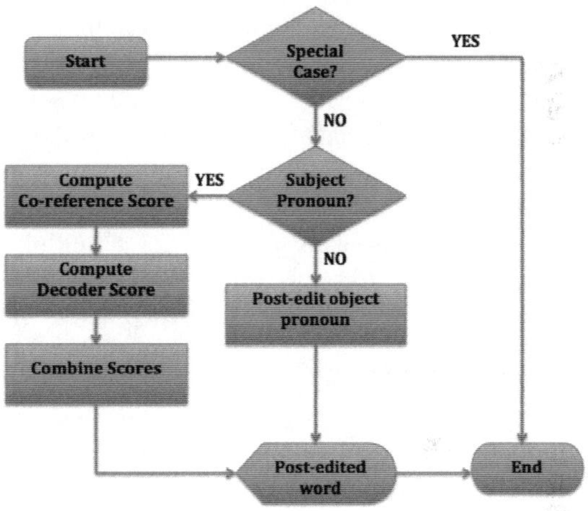

Figure 1: Flowchart of post-editing process

3.2.2 Grammatical Gender and Number

French pronouns always conform to the grammatical gender and number of their antecedent. Ignoring this contextual factor, as current phrase-based MT systems do, may generate inaccurate pronoun translations. Therefore, we consider the antecedent's gender and number as the most important criterion for pronoun translation.

We thus perform anaphora resolution on the source side, and using alignment we hypothesize the noun phrase antecedent on the target side (French), and determine its gender and number. More specifically, we first employ the Stanford Coreference system (Lee et al., 2011), which currently supports English and Chinese, for identifying the antecedents of the source pronouns (*"it"* or *"they"*). In cases where antecedent is a noun phrase with several nouns, then the head word is identified by the toolkit using syntactic features extracted from the sentence's parse tree (Raghunathan et al., 2010). It is very likely that its aligned words will be the target pronoun's antecedent. A French Part-Of-Speech (POS) tagger is then used (Morfette by Chrupala et al. (2008)) to obtain morphological tags, from which we extract the gender and number of the antecedent.

If the anaphora resolution system always identified accurately the antecedent, then the above method would perfectly post-edit pronouns, with some exceptions: e.g. the case of non-referential pronouns, or antecedents which are singular in form yet plural in meaning (e.g. *"a couple" ... they*). However, we estimate that the accuracy of the anaphora resolution system we used was around 60% only, as we found by examining 100 sentences containing 120 pronouns. Therefore, we define a confidence score for coreference resolution based on this accuracy. In other words, if the antecedent detected by the system is masculine singular, then the confidence score for a masculine singular target pronoun is 60%, and for a feminine singular one it is 40%. The decision is made by considering the decoder score presented hereafter.

3.2.3 Decoder Scores

Our motivation for using the decoder score is that the baseline SMT system generates the 1-best hypothesis based on the global feature functions score; however, this does not guarantee that the translations of every word are optimal, especially for pronouns. Hence, we calculate, for each pronoun, the number of occurrences of all its possible translations in the Search Graph (SG) built by Moses during the decoding process.

In the search graph plain-text file (generated by using the *-output-search-graph* option), each line represents a partial hypothesis and stores all its attributes. Among them, we notice two important attributes: *"covered"* (the source word's position) and *"out"* (the source word's translation). By selecting the hypotheses whose *"covered"* attribute matches the position of the source pronoun, we can list all possible candidates (in *"out"* attribute) and count the number of occurrences of each type. The decoder score (noted SG), i.e. the probability of translating the source pronoun into a specific target one, is computed as the ratio between its number of occurrences and the sum over all pronoun candidates.

3.2.4 Combination of Scores

We demonstrate the combination of coreference and decoder scores on an example, with the following source text: *"the supreme court has fallen way down from what it used to be ."* and the following MT hypothesis (with several mistakes): *"la cour suprême a chuté de manière ce qu' **il** était ."*. Here, the source word *"court"*, detected by the anaphora resolution system as the antecedent of pronoun *"it"*, is aligned to the target word *"cour"*, whose gender and number are determined as feminine and singular respectively. Thus, we consider only two singular candidates *"il"* and *"elle"* as potential translations[1], with the confidence scores computed as above: $p_{ana}(\text{"}il\text{"}) = 0.40$, $p_{ana}(\text{"}elle\text{"}) = 0.60$. In the next step, the SG enables us to compute the probability to translate *"it"* into either of these candidates, yielding: $p_{SG}(\text{"}il\text{"}) = 0.35$, $p_{SG}(\text{"}elle\text{"}) = 0.29$. The final scores are simply the averages of the two scores (*ana* and *SG*): $p(\text{"}il\text{"}) = 0.375$ and $p(\text{"}elle\text{"}) = 0.395$, and the candidate with the highest score (*"elle"* in this case) is selected, leading here to an improved output (in terms of pronoun translation, not overall quality): *"la cour suprême a chuté de manière ce qu' **elle** était ."*

3.2.5 Object Pronoun *It*

In English, *"they"* plays the role of a subject pronoun, since its antecedent is a plural noun phrase. Therefore, its translations into French are generally plural subject pronouns[2]. On the contrary, *"it"* can be used either as a subject or an object. Due to the fact that, unlike English, French singular subject and object pronouns are different, we propose post-editing rules to deal with this case.

Generally, the object pronoun *"it"* refers to the "recipient" of an action caused by the subject, and generally follows the verb. However, its position might be either right after the verb (e.g. *"I know it"*) or several words away (e.g. *"I talk about it."*). In order to detect the object pronouns, we employ Stanford parser (Chen and Manning, 2014). In the parse tree, an object pronoun is always a node of a subtree whose root is a verb phrase (VP) node, while a subject pronoun is under a noun phrase (NP) node. Therefore, we traverse up-ward from

[1]All other singular pronouns are considered as special cases, see Section 3.2.6.

[2]Except when they refer to English plural nouns which are singular in French, e.g. *"trousers"* − > *"pantalon"*.

the pronoun node to the root. If on the way we encounter "VP" node, then we consider the pronoun as an object one.

The translation of *"it"* depends on the object type (direct or indirect), which we identify by matching the verb preceding the pronoun with one of the French verbs which always have an indirect object[3]. For direct objects, the translation is *l'* if the following word starts with a vowel or a silent 'h', otherwise it is either *"le"* or *"la"* depending on the antecedent's gender (masculine or feminine, respectively). The SG score is not used for this decision. For indirect objects, the translation is *"lui"*, which is identical for both genders.

3.2.6 Special Cases

We observed on development data that our methods had difficulties with some French pronouns, which require more sophisticated constraints to determine their translation, which the above rules did not fully cover. Indeed, when applying the above rules, the judgments from annotators showed that a large part of these corrections degraded Pass 1's translation. Therefore we decided not to post-edit the results of baseline SMT (Moses) for: demonstrative pronouns (*ce* or *c'* before a vowel, *ça, celui, cela, celle, celui-là* and *celui-ci*); the indefinite pronoun *on*; and two personal pronouns specific to French which have many idiomatic uses (*y* and *en*).

3.2.7 Replacement or Insertion

Due to alignment or translation errors, sometimes a source pronoun is aligned with a non-pronoun target word, which is detrimental for post-editing. Therefore, if the word to be processed is not one of the known French pronouns, we insert the post-edited pronoun in the position preceding it, without replacing the non-pronoun word. For instance, given the following source sentence: *"I see it and then I buy it"* and the Pass 1 (incorrect) hypothesis: *"Je vois et puis j' achète"*, the MT system aligns wrongly *"see it"* with *"vois"*, and respectively *"buy it"* with *"achète"*. Our post-editing method suggests the following post-editions for the words aligned with *"it"*: *"le"* for the first occurrence , and *"l"'* for the second one. We will not alter the current target words *vois* and *achète*), since they are not known French pronouns. Instead, we add the post-editions in front of them, yielding the following post-edited target sentence: *"Je le vois et puis j' l' achète"*, which has both translations of *"it"* correct.

[3]Using the list at http://instruction2.mtsac.edu/french/liberte3/chapitre11/verbesobjINdirect.htm.

4 Cross-Lingual Pronoun Prediction

4.1 Training Datasets

The challenge in this task is to build classifiers to predict the hidden pronouns in translations, knowing the source. Four data sets of different domains were provided for development: Europarl, News Commentary (NCv9), IWSLT 2014 and TED(dev) talks. Each data set includes a series of five-element tuples: source sentence, target sentence (with pronouns substituted by placeholders), alignment information, actual pronouns and gold-standard ones (last two not given in the test data).

We first extract features for all occurrences of *"it"* and *"they"*, and then train classifiers over the feature set with various machine learning methods. In fact, to ensure an acceptable training time, we exploit entirely only the smaller data sets, and partially the larger ones: we use for constructing predictors all the occurrences of *"it"* and *"they"* of TED(dev), 10% of those of NCv9, 10% of those of IWSLT and about 1% of those of Europarl. The sizes, total numbers of *"it"* and *"they"* occurrences, and the actual number exploited are shown in Table 1.

Dataset	Size #sentences	#(it+they) provided	#(it+they) used
NCv9	182761	41227	4123
TED	1664	747	747
IWSLT	179404	77354	7730
EUROPARL	2049662	273827	2700

Table 1: Size, number of occurrences of *"it"* and *"they"*, and instances actually used for training.

4.2 Features

The goal of the submitted system is to explore the potential of morphological features for predicting target pronouns, without attempting to perform anaphora resolution, which is error prone and might not be required, in many cases, for correct pronoun prediction. Instead, we extract possible candidates for antecedents (co-referent nouns and pronouns) from the context surrounding the hidden pronoun and its source counterpart. We aim at estimating how much information we can obtain from the context words without using anaphora resolution for the prediction. We illustrate the idea on the following pair of sentences as example:

EN: *The police reported the accident to the township, but **it** didn't take action.*

FR: *La police a signalé l'accident à la commune, mais [**elle**] n'a pris aucune mesure.*

In this case the source pronoun is *"it"* and the hidden pronoun is *"elle"*, which must be determined by the system. Two out of the three nouns preceding the hidden pronoun are feminine and singular; therefore, we predict based on the majority gender and number that the pronoun translating *"it"* into French is singular and feminine, which corresponds to *"elle"*. In this example we used information of gender and number, but we added also other features that we considered to be potentially relevant.

The features were extracted from both source and target sentences. The target-side features are the 3 nouns or pronouns preceding and the 3 nouns or pronouns following the hidden pronoun. Also, we add as features the gender, number, person, and POS tag for each of these nouns or pronouns. To determine them automatically, we used the French tagger Morfette (Chrupala et al., 2008). Additionally, we included two sets of "summarized" features. The first set corresponds to the modes (i.e. majority) of gender, number and person respectively. For example, if 2 of the 3 preceding nouns or pronouns are feminine, then we indicate that the mode of the gender in the preceding part is *feminine*. Thus, we have 3 modes (gender, number, person) for the preceding nouns/pronouns and 3 for the following ones. The second set of "summarized" features indicates whether all preceding/following nouns and/or pronouns have the same gender, number or person. For example, if all preceding nouns or pronouns are feminine then the value of the feature will be *feminine*, but if only 1 or 2 of them are feminine while the rest are masculine then the value of the feature will be *not-absolute*. Similarly to the first set, we have 3 indicators for the preceding part and 3 for the following part. There are in all 42 features extracted from the French target text.

The 14 source-side features are the original pronoun, the 3 preceding and the 3 following nouns or pronouns, and their respective POS tags identified with the English tagger TreeTagger (Schmid, 1994). Additionally, for each extracted English noun or pronoun, we included their aligned words in the French text, with the same target-side features as described above (42 features). Finally, we have 98 features to analyze – which represent quite a large set, requiring a large training set for properly learning their relevance.

4.3 Pronoun Prediction

The predictors are trained using the WEKA tookit (Hall et al., 2009). We experiment with four machine learning techniques: Naive Bayes (NB) (Friedman et al., 1997), Decision Trees (DT) (Quinlan, 1986), Support Vector Machines (SVM) (Burges, 1998), and Random Forests (RF) (Breiman, 2001). With features coming from the four data sets presented above, we train the classifiers and then test them using 10-fold cross validation. For NB, SVM and RF, the default parameters are used. For DT, the "minimum number of instances per leaf" is adjusted from 5 to 15 and binary splits are applied on nominal features. The evaluation results shown in Table 2 indicate that, on all four sets, NB and DT significantly outperform SVM and RF. When comparing between NB and DT, there are cases where the former is more beneficial (e.g. on IWSLT data), but also reverse ones (e.g. on NCv9). Based on these results, we decide to employ Naive Bayes and Decision Trees for our submissions.

Dataset	NB	DT	SVM	RF
NCV9	0.421	0.453	0.401	0.386
TED	0.463	0.476	0.422	0.419
IWSLT	0.560	0.535	0.510	0498
EUROPARL	0.478	0.466	0.424	0.398

Table 2: Cross-validation results (macro-averaged F-scores) over 4 data sets and 4 types of classifiers.

The size and domain of the data are among the top factors affecting the performance of the classifiers. We prepared three composite data sets from the training data to study these factors:

- **ALL**: all data (large size)
- **IWSLT**: only data from IWSLT 2014 (7703 instances) (in-domain data with the test set)
- **SPL**: sampled data (4123 NCv9 + 7730 IWSLT + 747 TED + 2700 EUROPARL, for a total of 15,300 instances) (partially in-domain data, large size)

These sets are used for training the two most effective machine learning methods found above through cross-validation, namely NB and DT, resulting in a total of six classifiers.

5 Submissions to the Shared Task

5.1 Task 1: Pronoun-Focused Translation

Our submissions were evaluated over a test set of 2093 sentences, containing 1105 pronouns *"it"* and *"they"*, following the above method. In order to better understand the contribution of coreference information itself to improve pronoun translation, besides the system with combination of two scores as stated above (denoted as **SYS1**), we also submitted another (contrastive) system which only uses the gender of the hypothesized antecedent to correct the subject pronoun (**SYS2**).

5.2 Task 2: Pronoun Prediction

As stated above, the two most effective classifiers were applied to the test set of 2093 sentences, with 1105 instances of *"it"* and *"they"*, yielding predicted labels for each of them. Then, in order to select the two best systems for submission, we sampled a subset of 147 pronouns (*"it"* and *"they"*) and inspected the accuracy of predictions. The two systems with the highest total of accurate instances, namely *DT trained on IWSLT* and *NB trained on ALL*, were selected for submission. Moreover, we observed from these results that using in-domain data for training (i.e. from IWSLT) was more beneficial than using a mixed set. In some cases, the simple NB classifier was more effective than DT on our data.

6 Results and Discussion

The submissions to the first task were judged by human annotators (recruited by the task organizers) for the correctness of translated pronouns, using two main metrics: "Accuracy with OTHER" (all pronouns) and "Accuracy without OTHER" (only on a limited pronoun set). Our system was ranked first, with scores of, respectively, 0.657 and 0.617. Still, these scores remain slightly below the Moses baseline system provided by the organizers (trained on the same data as our system, see Section 3.1). Our scores on the more frequent pronouns (particularly *"il"* and *"elle"*) demonstrate the validity of our approach, while our (still good) scores on the rare ones reflect our strategy to avoid post-editing our baseline SMT output.

Unlike the first task, the strategy we proposed for the second one (using morphological features and no anaphora resolution) obtained rather poor results, ranking among the weakest submissions. Our two submissions scored respectively 20.62 and 16.39 in terms of fine-grained macro-averaged F-score, and respectively 32.40 and 42.53 for coarse accuracy. In fact, as for the first task, the baseline proposed by the organizers (using a language model to restore pronouns) was the best performing strategy (58.40 F-score and 68.42 accuracy). These results tend to show that the proposed features are poor predictors of the pronoun to be used, or possibly that the number of features was too large with respect to the available training data. Using hypotheses from anaphora resolution tends to improve performance, but its contribution remains below the statistical baseline. This indicates the need for additional knowledge, or higher anaphora resolution accuracy, to improve over the baseline.

7 Conclusion and Perspectives

In this paper, we proposed some ideas to enhance the translation quality of pronouns from English into French. For pronoun post-editing (Task 1), coreference scores combined with those from an SMT decoder were employed to correct the wrong pronouns generated by SMT system. Furthermore, with object pronouns, we suggested using specific grammatical rules to determine the candidate. While reaching a high rank compared to other participants, the approach still left a number of pronouns untouched. On the contrary, our rather low scores on Task 2 indicate that unstructured context information is insufficient for predicting pronouns. Therefore, integrating these predictions as an additional feature for the post-editor in Task 1 does not seem promising.

Future work will focus on a deeper analysis of the factors that are most detrimental to current predictors, the selection of co-reference features to train them, and their integration directly into the SMT decoder.

Acknowledgments

The work has been supported by the Swiss National Science Foundation through the MODERN project (`www.idiap.ch/project/modern`). We are grateful to three anonymous reviewers for their helpful comments.

References

Francis Bond and Kentaro Ogura. 1998. Reference in Japanese–English machine translation. *Machine Translation*, 13(2):107–134.

Leo Breiman. 2001. Random forests. *Machine Learning*, 45(1):5–32.

Christopher J. C. Burges. 1998. A tutorial on support vector machines for pattern recognition. *Data Mining and Knowledge Discovery*, 2:121–167.

Danqi Chen and Christopher Manning. 2014. A fast and accurate dependency parser using neural networks. In *Proceedings of the 2014 Conference on Empirical Methods in Natural Language Processing (EMNLP)*, pages 740–750, Doha, Qatar.

Grzegorz Chrupala, Georgiana Dinu, and Josef van Genabith. 2008. Learning morphology with Morfette. In *Proceedings of the 6th International Conference on Language Resources and Evaluation (LREC)*, Marrakech, Morocco.

Nir Friedman, Dan Geiger, Moises Goldszmidt, G. Provan, P. Langley, and P. Smyth. 1997. Bayesian network classifiers. In *Machine Learning*, pages 131–163.

Liane Guillou. 2012. Improving pronoun translation for statistical machine translation. In *Proceedings of EACL 2012 Student Research Workshop (13th Conference of the European Chapter of the ACL)*, pages 1–10, Avignon, France.

Mark Hall, Eibe Frank, Geoffrey Holmes, Bernhard Pfahringer, Peter Reutemann, and Ian H. Witten. 2009. The WEKA data mining software: An update. *SIGKDD Explorations Newsletter*, 11(1):10–18.

Christian Hardmeier and Marcello Federico. 2010. Modelling pronominal anaphora in statistical machine translation. In *Proceedings of International Workshop on Spoken Language Translation (IWSLT)*, Paris, France.

Christian Hardmeier, Preslav Nakov, Sara Stymne, Jörg Tiedemann, Yannick Versley, and Mauro Cettolo. 2015. Pronoun-focused MT and cross-lingual pronoun prediction: Findings of the 2015 DiscoMT shared task on pronoun translation. In *Proceedings of the Second Workshop on Discourse in Machine Translation*, pages 1–16, Lisbon, Portugal.

Christian Hardmeier. 2014. *Discourse in Statistical Machine Translation*. PhD thesis, Uppsala University, Sweden.

Philipp Koehn, Hieu Hoang, Alexandra Birch, Chris Callison-Burch, Marcello Federico, Nicola Bertoldi, Brooke Cowan, Wade Shen, Christine Moran, Richard Zens, Chris Dyer, Ondrej Bojar, Alexandra Constantin, and Evan Herbst. 2007. Moses: Open source toolkit for statistical machine translation. In *Proceedings of the 45th Annual Meeting of the Association for Computational Linguistics (ACL)*, pages 177–180, Prague, Czech Republic.

Ronan Le Nagard and Philipp Koehn. 2010. Aiding pronoun translation with co-reference resolution. In *Proceedings of the Joint 5th Workshop on Statistical Machine Translation and Metrics (MATR)*, pages 258–267, Uppsala, Sweden.

Heeyoung Lee, Yves Peirsman, Angel Chang, Nathanael Chambers, Mihai Surdeanu, and Dan Jurafsky. 2011. Stanford's multi-pass sieve coreference resolution system at the CoNLL-2011 shared task. In *Proceedings of the Fifteenth Conference on Computational Natural Language Learning (CoNLL): Shared Task*, pages 28–34, Portland, OR.

Thomas Meyer and Andrei Popescu-Belis. 2012. Using sense-labeled discourse connectives for statistical machine translation. In *Proceedings of the EACL 2012 Joint Workshop on Exploiting Synergies between IR and MT, and Hybrid Approaches to MT (ESIRMT-HyTra)*, pages 129–138, Avignon, France.

Ruslan Mitkov. 2002. *Anaphora Resolution*. Longman, London, UK.

Hiromi Nakaiwa and Satoru Ikehara. 1995. Intrasentential resolution of Japanese zero pronouns in a machine translation system using semantic and pragmatic constraints. In *Proceedings of the 6th International Conference on Theoretical and Methodological Issues in Machine Translation (TMI)*, pages 96–105, Leuven, Belgium.

Vincent Ng. 2010. Supervised noun phrase coreference research: The first fifteen years. In *Proceedings of the 48th Annual Meeting of the Association for Computational Linguistics (ACL)*, pages 1396–1411, Uppsala, Sweden.

Andrei Popescu-Belis, Thomas Meyer, Jeevanthi Liyanapathirana, Bruno Cartoni, and Sandrine Zufferey. 2012. Discourse-level Annotation over Europarl for Machine Translation: Connectives and Pronouns. In *Proceedings of the 8th International Conference on Language Resources and Evaluation (LREC)*, Istanbul, Turkey.

J. R. Quinlan. 1986. Induction of decision trees. *Machine Learning*, 1(1):81–106.

Karthik Raghunathan, Heeyoung Lee, Sudarshan Rangarajan, Nathanael Chambers, Mihai Surdeanu, Dan Jurafsky, and Christopher Manning. 2010. A multi-pass sieve for coreference resolution. In *Proceedings of the 2010 Conference on Empirical Methods in Natural Language Processing (EMNLP)*, pages 492–501, Cambridge, MA.

Helmut Schmid. 1994. Probabilistic part-of-speech tagging using decision trees. In *Proceedings of the International Conference on New Methods in Language Processing*, pages 44–49, Manchester, UK.

Predicting pronouns across languages with continuous word spaces

Ngoc-Quan Pham
Erasmus Mundus Master Program in
Language and Communication Technology
ngoc-quan.pham.14@um.edu.mt

Lonneke van der Plas
Institute of Linguistics
University of Malta
lonneke.vanderplas@um.edu.mt

Abstract

Predicting pronouns across languages from a language with less variation to one with much more is a hard task that requires many different types of information, such as morpho-syntactic information as well as lexical semantics and coreference. We assumed that continuous word spaces fed into a multi-layer perceptron enriched with morphological tags and coreference resolution would be able to capture many of the linguistic regularities we found. Our results show that the model captures most of the linguistic generalisations. Its macro-averaged F-score is among the top-3 systems submitted to the DiscoMT shared task reaching 56.5%.

1 Introduction

This paper provides the description for the classification system, submitted by the University of Malta, to the DiscoMT shared task on cross-lingual pronoun prediction (Hardmeier et al., 2015). In this task, we are concerned with finding the correct French translations for the English third-person subject pronouns *it* and *they*. An example would be the following, where we need to predict the pronoun corresponding to the placeholder "REPLACE" given in the French sentence.

- And so, if you depend on these sources, you have to have some way of getting the energy during those time periods that **it**'s not available .
- Et donc, si vous dépendez de ces sources, vous devez avoir un moyen d'obtenir de l'énergie pendant ces périodes de temps où **REPLACE** n'est pas disponible.

The task is setup in such a way that the system needs to choose between 9 classes of French pronouns : *ce, elle, elles, il, ils, ça, cela, on*, and OTHER in bitexts in which the pronoun aligned to the English pronouns *it* and *they* are substituted by placeholders [1]. The difficulty of this task lies in the fact that the French translation for a particular English pronoun is generally inconsistent and dependent on many different factors. By analysing the linguistic characteristics of this problem, we identified the factors contributing to the predictability of the pronouns, as described in Section 2.

The dependencies are modeled by using a probabilistic neural network, motivated by previous work in the field of Statistical Language Modeling and Statistic Machine Translation. Specifically, the feature words are treated through a projection layer to become continuous vectors. This approach leads to a *distributed representation* of the words, that has shown to capture morpho-syntactic and semantic information (Mikolov et al., 2013c; Köper et al., 2015). After that, the output of the network is a soft-max layer computing probabilities of the possible outputs, such as language models (Bengio et al., 2003), or translation models (Son et al., 2012). The input words can belong to one single language (language model case (Bengio et al., 2003)), or even two different languages (translation model case (Son et al., 2012)). More importantly, the size of projected vectors is much smaller than the vocabulary, aiming at a reduction of the data sparseness problem. We apply the concept in our system, by learning the probabilities of the pronouns given the word vectors in the input layer.

In the works mentioned to motivate this structure, this projection layer is learned together with the neural network parameters (Schwenk, 2007; Mikolov et al., 2010; Le et al., 2011). For the task of cross-lingual pronoun prediction, Hardmeier et al. (2013) also chose to learn the projection matrices and the neural network weights at the same

1. For more information on the task setup we refer to the introductory paper of the shared task (Hardmeier et al., 2015)

Proceedings of the Second Workshop on Discourse in Machine Translation (DiscoMT), pages 101–107,
Lisbon, Portugal, 17 September 2015.

time. We chose to train the projection matrix separately, and then train the neural network on top of the learned continuous word vectors (Mikolov et al., 2013a) to alleviate the training process.

In contrast to English, the source language in this shared task, every noun in French has a grammatical gender. Pronouns agree in gender and number with their antecedents (or postcedents). As a consequence, in many cases in which the English translation contains the pronoun *it*, we need to choose between *elle* or *il* in French depending on the gender of the nouns the pronoun is referring to. In the example above the gender of the noun *énergie* is feminine so we choose the pronoun *elle*. We included the Stanford Coreference Resolution system (Lee et al., 2013) in our model for this reason. Moreover, in an effort to compare the effectiveness of the word embeddings and handcrafted features for capturing morpho-syntactic information, we decided to use Morfette (Seddah et al., 2010) to supply information on gender and number for each French word explicitly.

2 Linguistic analysis and feature selection

We explained above that pronouns agree in gender and number with their antecedents. But apart from gender and number, there are many other factors at play. For example, there are cases where the English pronoun *they* is translated with *on*. This is usually the case when the antecedents of the pronoun are indefinite or even absent. An example from the training data is *someone can grab your ear and say what* ***they*** *have to say.* It is translated in French as *on peut attraper votre oreille et dire ce que l'* ***on*** *a à dire.*

The same happens when there is a passive in English with the pronoun *it* that is translated in French with active voice. The phrase ***It*** *was called* is translated in French with ***On*** *l' a appelé.*

It can also be translated to *il*. For example, when we find a dummy or expletive pronoun in combination with certain classes of verbs such as *pleuvoir* 'rain', *neiger* 'snow', but also with the verb *sembler* 'seem' and *être* 'be' in expressions such as ***It*** *is time to* translated to ***Il*** *est temps de.*

We could go on explaining the linguistic generalities that were attested in the training data. In summary, we concluded that most of the factors will be captured by including the following features :

1. The English pronoun. This will capture the nature of the English pronoun : is it *it* or *they*.
2. Three words in front of and three words after the English pronoun. This will capture whether the passive is used, whether we find one of the verbs that are often found with expletive pronouns etc.
3. Two words in front of and three words after the French pronoun. This will capture whether we find active or passive voice in French, whether we find one of the verbs that are often found with expletive pronouns and so on.
4. Antecedents and postcedents of the French pronoun. This will capture whether there are antecedents at all and if they are found how definite they are. We can also infer the gender of the antecedents to determine whether to use masculine of feminine forms of pronouns in French.

3 The neural network classifier

3.1 Concept

The neural network structure is described in figure 1. Overall, it resembles the feed-forward neural network structure used in the Continuous Space Translation Model (Son et al., 2012), in which the input layer contains the English words on the source side, and the French words on the target side of the bitext. By using the toolkit learning the word vectors, known as word2vec (Mikolov et al., 2013a) in Python (Řehůřek and Sojka, 2010), we trained two different projection matrices for English and French correspondingly.

A conventional Multi-Layer Perceptron (MLP) on top of the distributed representations maps the input sequences into the pronouns. It is notable that this task is much simpler than the concept used in language models and translation models, in which the output layer needs to be hierachically organised to deal with the gigantic size of the vocabulary. This pronoun prediction task only needs to deal with several pronouns of the target language. If the feature set is limited to only the target words (French), the model is almost identical to a mini language model learning the probabilities of the long n-grams predicting the pronoun class.

In order to include additional features such as the antecedents of the pronoun or morphological tags of the French words, we extend the input lay-

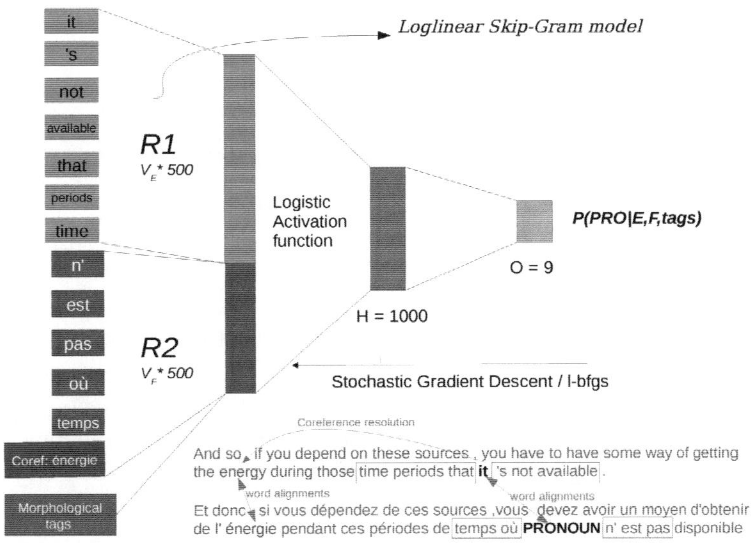

FIGURE 1 – The overview structure of the neural network classifier. The words are transformed into 500-size vectors with two projection matrices $R1$ and $R2$. The size of the hidden layer is 1000, while the output layer gives probabilities for 9 outputs.

ers with additional vectors. One difficulty of the corefence resolution is that the co-referring noun phrases have inconsistent length and might contain a headword and possibly determiners, adjectives or adverbs along with the headword. Our solution was to take only the French words aligned to the English headwords found by the coreference locator[2] for the feature. Therefore, the whole antecedent phrase representation is the average of the French word vectors composing that phrase. That vector is then concatenated to the total feature vector. An additional difficulty lies in the fact that there might be several co-referring expressions for one pronoun, we therefore averaged the projected vectors of all co-referring headwords as done in Hardmeier et al. (2013), but without the probability weighting, since the Stanford Coreference Resolution system does not provide such probabilities.

Technically, this feature is not fully utilised. Coreference resolution can only be found on 30% of the samples. Due to our time and resource limit, we only managed to investigate the antecedents by looking backward one sentence. There are samples whose antecedents are the pronouns of the previous sentences, rendering the feature useless.

As for the linguistic annotations for French morphological features, we treated the tags as one-hot vectors with the size as the total number of tags. Each tagged word is then converted to a corresponding vector, which is then integrated to the input layer of the MLP (the output of the projection layer in the figure). A similar approach was chosen for including the morphological tags of the antecedents as features, where we took the tag vectors of all words in the head-phrases and concatenate the averaged one into the ultimate feature vector.

2. These include referential links within the same sentence.

3.2 Training

As described in the introduction, we trained the system using two separate processes :

- Training the word2vec for continuous representation of English and French words
- Training the MLP classifier

The first part of the training is performed by following the log-linear model concepts proposed by Mikolov et al. (2013a). Fundamentally, word regularities are learnt by using a log-linear classifier to predict a particular word based on its surrounding words (Continuous Bag-Of-Words approach) or to predict the surrounding words based on the current words (Skip-gram approach).

The neural network classifier is trained in order to maximize the log-likelihood of the training data. Backward propagation with Stochastic Gradient Descent optimisation process is performed to obtain the model weights.

Notably, training the neural network is more demanding than training the word vectors, from a similar amount of data. Consequently, compared to the original training scheme used in language models, we are able to utilise more data for training the word vectors, thus covering a larger vocabulary than the training data provided as the bitext. The difference of the training data for the two parts, as well the parameter selection will be described in the subsequent section.

4 Experiment Setups

4.1 Corpora

The organisers provided us with three different corpora :

- The TED (IWSLT2014) corpus containing approximately 179k bi-sentences.
- The News Commentary corpus, with around 180k sentence pairs.
- The Europarl dataset, originally collected by Koehn (2005) having 2 million sentences.

All three datasets are employed for training the word vectors. Specifically, the projection matrix for each language is trained from approximately 100 million words, comprised of 20k size vocabularies. For training the MLP, we ran experiments with only the in-domain data (TED). For the final submissions of the task, we include another system trained with a larger set of data, including the TED and News Commentary corpora.

4.2 Word2vec training

Regarding architectures, since it is known in previous research (Mikolov et al., 2013a) that the Skip-gram architecture is dominating in terms of modeling the semantics of words, while the CBOW structure is better at capturing morpho-syntactic regularities, we experimented with both architectures to train the projection matrices.

Two important parameters in word2vec are negative sampling and sub-sampling. Negative sampling alters the objective function, from maximizing the corpus probability, that is from the conditional probabilities of the context words given the input words to maximizing directly the quality of the word representations, related to the joint probability of the words and the contexts (Mikolov et al., 2013b; Goldberg and Levy, 2014). "Negative Sample" indicates that, for each sample of word/context, k other samples are drawn randomly assuming they are all negative. The optimisation process only concerns the word representations, rather than the data likelihood. The k value used to generate negative samples is 10 in our setup, which is recommeneded for our corpus size in previous works (Mikolov et al., 2013b).

Sub-sampling is the act of downsampling the very frequent words, based on the intuition that distributional vectors of those words do not change much throughout the training data, plus they do not hold useful information. When sub-sampling was set to 10^{-5}, the performance on the development data was considerably reduced so we decided to leave it out for the remainder of the experiments. As we stated before, it is possible that the frequent words, such as determiners, are necessary for the task.

Our experiments were conducted to observe the impact of word vectors serving pronoun translation, using negative sampling or hierarchical softmax (which is the training method used when negative sampling is disabled). Besides, the context of each word is chosen as 10 (5 words per side). The learned vectors have the size of 500, which are 40 times smaller than the vocabularies.

4.3 Neural Network training

As aforementioned, there are three types of features fed into the MLP :

- Context words from the source side and target side of the translation. Their vectors are treated as the input of the MLP.
- The search for antecedents was performed by the Stanford Coreference Resolution system (Lee et al., 2013). The English words corresponding to the French placeholder are found based on the alignments. Afterwards, coreference resolution is done on the English side by backtracking one sentence and the word alignments help us map the English antecedents to the French counterpart. The feature for the MLP is eventually the averaged word vectors of all words in the French antecedents.
- The Morfette morphological analyser (Seddah et al., 2010) is used to tag each French word with morphological labels, indicating their number and gender properties. We represent such properties as one-hot vectors, showing the index of the tag in the tag list, whose size is 97.

Due to time limitation, we chose to tune the hyper parameters of the network by using the development data. The result of this tuning process is that the activation function is **logistic**, the training algorithm is **l-bfgs** and the hidden layer size is 1000. The experiments were conducted with the Scikit-Learn tool kit (Pedregosa et al., 2011).

5 Results

5.1 Architecture and Feature effect

TABLE 1 – *Results on development set, in macro-average F-measure (%). Comparison of features (English words(E), Coreference(C), French words (F) and Morphological tags(M)), Skip-gram and CBOW architectures, trained with Hierarchical Softmax (HS) and Negative Sampling (NS).*

Features	word2vec Architecture			
	Skip-gram		CBOW	
	HS	NS	HS	NS
English words	37.6	32.6	36.0	32.7
E+Coreference	38.2	32.9	38.0	31.9
E+C+C_MorpTags	39.2	32.7	36.1	34.7
E+C+C_M+French w.	58.4	43.1	58.1	40.6
E+C+C_M+F+F_M	**64.8**	49.7	57.2	50.0

The experimental results for feature engineering and model variations are summerised in Table 1. In total, we exploited 5 progressive feature sets, testing them with two word2vec architectures (Skip-gram and CBOW), each of which is trained with two different methods : Hierarchical Softmax (HS) and Negative Sampling (NS).

Regarding features, the antecedents are shown to be little informative. We see two main reasons for this. First, we explained in Section 3 that we implemented coreference resolution in a suboptimal way due to time restrictions. We will show in the error analysis that the largest part of the mistakes are due to suboptimal coreference handling. Second, in the setup provided for this shared task, the words surrounding the placeholder provide gender and number information already. This fact will downplay the added value of coreference resolution. In an ideal setting the context words would have been normalised. The French words, as expected, contributed greatly for the classification task. They capture many of the linguistic regularities described in Section 2 and on top of that, they often provide gender and number information in the given task setup.

Looking at the difference between the two training methods for both word2vec architectures, the word vectors trained by negative sampling surprisingly fell behind the ones with hierarchical softmax. With the best feature set (E+C+C_M+F+F_M), the HS models outperformed the NS ones by nearly 20% relatively. The reason why NS was effective in previous research is unknown (Goldberg and Levy, 2014), yet it is possible that the dataset in our experiment is preferable for HS in terms of size.

Lastly, we want to discuss the difference in ability of Skip-gram and CBOW models to capture semantic versus morpho-syntactic regularities. From Table 1, we can infer that the CBOW model is able to capture morpho-syntactic regularities, which Skip-gram cannot, which is in line with previous work (Mikolov et al., 2013a). For the Skip-gram models (for the better word vectors trained with HS), the addition of the Morfette tags always led to improvement, especially with the tags of the surrounding French words. The scenario is reversed for the CBOW models, where adding the morphological tags decreased the performance of the system (HS). On the other hand, no matter how well CBOW captures the morpho-syntactic regularities, it falls short in general as Skip-gram outperforms it in all settings (HS). In this task that requires both semantic and morpho-syntactic information, we are best off with a superior semantic model (Skip-gram) in combination with an external tool for morphological analysis.

5.2 Final results on test set

For the final submission on the test set provided by the shared task organisers, we employed the final setting consisting of the best feature set, with the word vectors trained with Skip-gram architecture and hierarchical softmax optimisation, which delivered the highest F-measure for the development set. Furthermore, we doubled the amount of training data, by adding the News Commentary corpus into the training data.

We report results for both fine-grained evaluation (9 classes) and the coarse-grained evaluation (7 classes) as provided by the official scorer. As can be seen in the comparative evaluations provided by the overview paper (Hardmeier et al., 2015), our system is in the top-three in the fine-grained evaluation. A closer look at the performance per class across systems shows that our system has particular problems keeping *cela* and *ça* apart, with an F-measure as low as 7.1% for *cela*. We will argue in the error analysis, that we found this distinction to be quite arbitrary in the given data. In the coarse-grained evaluation provided, in which *cela* has been merged with *ça* and *on* has been merged with OTHER, we outperform all competing systems.

TABLE 2 – *Results on test set with additional training data, in macro-average F-measure for both the fine-grained evaluation (9 classes) and the coarse-grained evaluation (7 classes) (%).*

Training data	Fine-g. eval.	Coarse-g. eval.
TED	56.1	**65.8**
TED + NC	**56.5**	65.4

The performance difference between the development set and the test set are large. Although we did not find a clear reason for why this is the case, we point to the overview paper that shows that the baseline also performs very differently on the two sets. They attribute this effect to the test set's better coverage of infrequent pronouns.

Adding more training data does not lead to clear improvements. One reason for that seems to be that the class distribution of the out-of-domain data is rather different from the in-domain data.

5.3 Error analysis

We inspected the output of our best system on the development data in order to find the major sources of error. We randomly selected about 2/3rd of the data. We came to the following conclusions : The model manages to capture the linguistic regularities described in Section 2 rather well. It does less well on capturing the antecedent and using this type of information for predicting the French pronoun. Approximately 50% of the errors made by our system seemed due to an improper handling of coreference. We explained that our implementation of features for coreference was suboptimal, but improving this component to handle coreference perfectly is very hard as shown in previous work (Hardmeier et al., 2013). The coreference needs to be transferred from the English to the French sentences and alignment errors are added to mistakes already present in the original English coreference chains.

On the bright side of things, we saw that approximately 10% of the errors were in fact perfectly acceptable. For example, the difference between *ça* and *cela* is merely due to differences is register, and we saw individual speakers switching back and forth between the two in one conversation. The coarse-grained evaluation proposed conflates *ça* and *cela*.

6 Conclusions

In this paper, we described a system that addresses the task of cross-lingual pronoun prediction from English to French. We show that it is a hard task that requires many different types of information, such as morpho-syntactic information as well as semantics of context words and identification of antecedents of the French pronoun.

We proposed a model that captures linguistic generalisation using word embeddings that are fed into a MLP in addition to morphological analysis and coreference resolution. Although word embeddings (CBOW) are known to capture morpho-syntactic operations quite well, we show that using a standalone morphological analyser in combination with the semantically stronger version of the continuous word space models (Skip-gram) produces the best results (56.5% on the test set). Coreference resolution showed the least beneficial in our experiments. This seems due to the suboptimal implementation of this type of information in our model and the gender and number information contained in the French context words.

The error analysis showed that half of the errors could be solved with a proper implementation of coreference resolution, which is however not trivial to do. 10% percent of the errors were in fact acceptable variations. The coarse-grained evaluation proposed conflates some of these seemingly equivalent classes and results in a 65.4%, the best score reported by participating teams. Also, performance numbers should be higher, when based on human judgements.

Acknowledgments

This research was funded by the Erasmus Mundus European Masters Program in Language and Communication Technologies (LCT) and the University of Malta and has been carried out using computational facilities procured through the European Regional Development Fund, Project ERDF-080 'A Supercomputing Laboratory for the University of Malta' (http://www.um.edu.mt/research/scienceeng/erdf_080).

References

Yoshua Bengio, Réjean Ducharme, Pascal Vincent, and Christian Janvin. 2003. A neural probabilistic language model. *The Journal of Machine Learning Research*, 3 :1137–1155.

Yoav Goldberg and Omer Levy. 2014. word2vec explained : deriving mikolov et al.'s negative-sampling word-embedding method. *arXiv preprint arXiv :1402.3722*.

Christian Hardmeier, Jörg Tiedemann, and Joakim Nivre. 2013. Latent anaphora resolution for cross-lingual pronoun prediction. In *EMNLP 2013 ; Conference on Empirical Methods in Natural Language Processing ; 18-21 October 2013 ; Seattle, WA, USA*, pages 380–391. Association for Computational Linguistics.

Christian Hardmeier, Preslav Nakov, Sara Stymne, Jörg Tiedemann, Yannick Versley, and Mauro Cettolo. 2015. Pronoun-focused MT and cross-lingual pronoun prediction : Findings of the 2015 DiscoMT shared task on pronoun translation. In *Proceedings of the Second Workshop on Discourse in Machine Translation*, Lisbon, Portugal.

Philipp Koehn. 2005. Europarl : A parallel corpus for statistical machine translation. In *MT summit*, volume 5, pages 79–86. Citeseer.

Maximilian Köper, Christian Scheible, and Sabine Schulte im Walde. 2015. Multilingual reliability and "semantic" structure of continuous word spaces. *IWCS 2015*, page 40.

Hai-Son Le, Ilya Oparin, Alexandre Allauzen, Jean-Luc Gauvain, and François Yvon. 2011. Structured output layer neural network language model. In *Acoustics, Speech and Signal Processing (ICASSP), 2011 IEEE International Conference on*, pages 5524–5527. IEEE.

Heeyoung Lee, Angel Chang, Yves Peirsman, Nathanael Chambers, Mihai Surdeanu, and Dan Jurafsky. 2013. Deterministic coreference resolution based on entity-centric, precision-ranked rules. *Computational Linguistics*, 39(4) :885–916.

Tomas Mikolov, Martin Karafiát, Lukas Burget, Jan Cernockỳ, and Sanjeev Khudanpur. 2010. Recurrent neural network based language model. In *INTERSPEECH 2010, 11th Annual Conference of the International Speech Communication Association, Makuhari, Chiba, Japan, September 26-30, 2010*, pages 1045–1048.

Tomas Mikolov, Kai Chen, Greg Corrado, and Jeffrey Dean. 2013a. Efficient estimation of word representations in vector space. *arXiv preprint arXiv :1301.3781*.

Tomas Mikolov, Ilya Sutskever, Kai Chen, Greg S Corrado, and Jeff Dean. 2013b. Distributed representations of words and phrases and their compositionality. In *Advances in neural information processing systems*, pages 3111–3119.

Tomas Mikolov, Wen-tau Yih, and Geoffrey Zweig. 2013c. Linguistic regularities in continuous space word representations. In *HLT-NAACL*, pages 746–751.

Fabian Pedregosa, Gaël Varoquaux, Alexandre Gramfort, Vincent Michel, Bertrand Thirion, Olivier Grisel, Mathieu Blondel, Peter Prettenhofer, Ron Weiss, Vincent Dubourg, et al. 2011. Scikit-learn : Machine learning in python. *The Journal of Machine Learning Research*, 12 :2825–2830.

Holger Schwenk. 2007. Continuous space language models. *Computer Speech & Language*, 21(3) :492–518.

Djamé Seddah, Grzegorz Chrupała, Özlem Çetinoğlu, Josef Van Genabith, and Marie Candito. 2010. Lemmatization and lexicalized statistical parsing of morphologically rich languages : the case of french. In *Proceedings of the NAACL HLT 2010 First Workshop on Statistical Parsing of Morphologically-Rich Languages*, pages 85–93. Association for Computational Linguistics.

Le Hai Son, Alexandre Allauzen, and François Yvon. 2012. Continuous space translation models with neural networks. In *Proceedings of the 2012 conference of the north american chapter of the association for computational linguistics : Human language technologies*, pages 39–48. Association for Computational Linguistics.

Radim Řehůřek and Petr Sojka. 2010. Software framework for topic modelling with large corpora. *Proceedings of the International Conference on Language Resources and Evaluation*.

Baseline Models for Pronoun Prediction and Pronoun-Aware Translation

Jörg Tiedemann
Department of Linguistics and Philology, Uppsala University
Department of Modern Languages, University of Helsinki
firstname.lastname@lingfil.uu.se

Abstract

This paper presents baseline models for the cross-lingual pronoun prediction task and the pronoun-focused translation task at DiscoMT 2015. We present simple yet effective classifiers for the former and discuss the impact of various contextual features on the prediction performance. In the translation task we rely on the document-level decoder Docent and a cross-sentence target language-model over selected words based on the parts-of-speech of the aligned source language words.

1 Introduction

The second workshop on discourse in machine translation (DiscoMT 2015) features a shared task on pronoun translation. Pronouns are difficult to translate due to their complex semantics. Anaphoric pronouns refer back to their antecedent and, therefore, have to agree with linguistic properties such as gender and number. The main problem for machine translation is that antecedents can be arbitrarily far away from the pronouns that refer back to them. This is not an issue if gender, number and other properties are preserved in translation and if these properties are marked in both languages. However, this is not always the case and for most language pairs there are various grammatical differences that need to be taken care of. A prototypical example is grammatical gender which is used in languages like German or French. Translations of inanimate nouns such as "the door" are assigned to a gender (feminine in the case of the German "die Tür") which is not derivable from the source. Hence, machine translation faces the problem to decide which pronoun to use in translations of "it" referring back to "the door". The task, however, is even more complex due to the frequent use of non-referential pronouns in constructions like "it is raining" where an equivalent pronoun may or may not appear in the translation. The shared task focuses on French translations of the third-person pronouns "it" and "they". The cross-lingual pronoun prediction task asks for the corresponding item in French (grouped into nine classes) for given English documents and their human-generated translations into French. The translation task requires complete translations of English documents to French and the evaluation emphasizes the translations of the two types of pronouns. The domain is translated TED talks. In the following, we first look at the prediction task and our classification approach. Thereafter, we discuss the translation model that we used in our submission (UU-TIEDEMANN).

2 Cross-Lingual Pronoun Prediction

In the pronoun prediction task, the system needs to return one of nine classes that correspond to the translation of "it" and "they" into French in given context. The classes include the pronouns *ce, cela, elle, elles, il, ils, on* and *ça* which are common translations of the given English pronouns, and another class (*OTHER*) that covers all other cases (including pleonastic uses and other cases that do not have any correspondence in French). English and French context is fully visible for the entire document with special place holders marking the space where the corresponding class is to be filled in. Note that the data (training and test data) is prepared using automatic word alignment and, therefore, includes noise.

In our submission, we were mainly interested in testing various baselines in order to test how far we can get with a rather poor feature model and minimal amounts of pre-processing. Hence, we do not attempt to run any kind of anaphora resolution to identify co-referential links nor any other kind of linguistic analyses that might help to resolve the ambiguities of the decision. We look at two types of features only:

Proceedings of the Second Workshop on Discourse in Machine Translation (DiscoMT), pages 108–114,
Lisbon, Portugal, 17 September 2015.

Local context: Surrounding words in source and target language.

Preceding noun phrases: Preceding noun phrases in the close neighborhood have a good chance to represent antecedents of given pronouns. Assuming that they may be marked with the properties we require for disambiguation (number and gender) we extract simple features from them as additional features.

Our experiments are based on standard classifiers and we use existing implementations out of the box. We tested local classification models based on maximum entropy models, averaged perceptrons (using MegaM (Daumé III, 2004)) and linear SVMs (using liblinear (Fan et al., 2008)) but also a sequence model based on conditional random fields (using crf++ (Kudo, 2013)). In our initial experiments it turned out that liblinear produces significantly better results than any of the other tools and, therefore, we only report results from applying that software. In all experiments we use L2-loss SVC dual solvers which is the standard setting in liblinear. We did not perform any optimization of the regularization parameter C and we only use IWSLT14 for training.

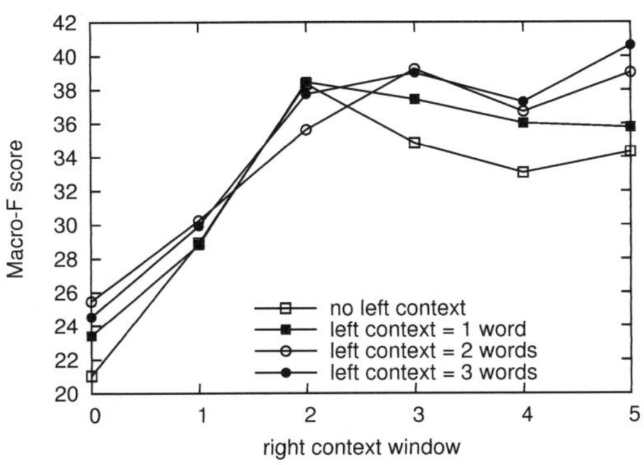

Figure 1: Various context windows in the source language (used as bag of words).

Our first batch of experiments considers various sizes of source language context. Figure 1 illustrates the impact of source language features with increasing window sizes using tokens to the left and to the right. The figure shows that context to the right seems to be more important than left-side context. Windows larger than 2 words seem to be sufficient but overall, the performance is not satisfactory.

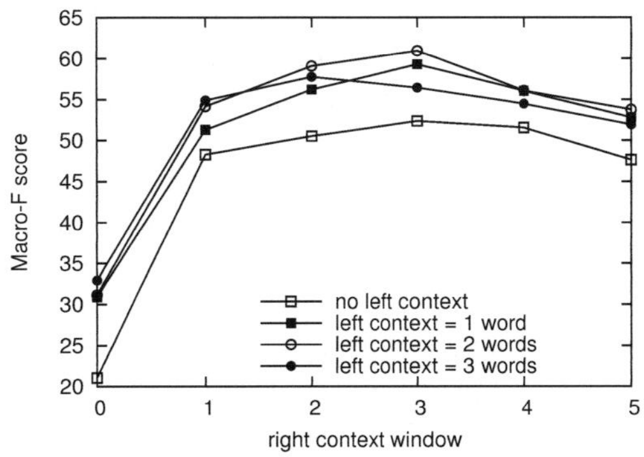

Figure 2: Various context windows in the target language (used as bag of words).

It is to be expected that target language context is more informative for the classifier decision. Figure 2 demonstrates this using the same setup as in the experiments with source language context. The overall performance in terms of macro F-scores is much higher now but similar to source language context, tokens to the right seem to be more informative for classification decisions. Small window sizes are preferred as well and the optimal performance on development data is achieved for two words to the left and three words to the right.

system	macro F	accuracy
bag-of-words		
trg2+3, 1 det	61.67	79.79
trg2+3, 2 det	61.97	79.52
trg2+3, 3 det	57.85	79.25
trg2+3, 4 det	58.54	78.98
trg2+3, 5 det	55.42	78.85
position-sensitive		
trg2+3, det 1	60.82	81.79
trg2+3, det 2	57.78	80.59
trg2+3, det 3	57.45	80.72
trg2+3, det 4	56.91	80.32
trg2+3, det 5	57.01	80.46

Table 1: Classifiers with tokens aligned to English determiners in previous context as extra features besides target language context (2 words before and 3 words after).

The results above use bag-of-words models that do not make any difference between the positions of the contextual words within the selected window. We also ran experiments with features marked with their positions relative to the predicted item but the outcome was rather inconclusive. In our next setup, we present both, position-sensitive models and bag-of-word models. The main difference in the feature model is, otherwise, the addition of long-distance contextual information. Assuming that preceding noun-phrases in the close neighborhood are good candidates of antecedents that may be marked with gender and number, we extract French tokens that are linked to English determiners and demonstratives from previous context. In order to make our approach completely independent from external tools we simply specify a fixed list of common determiners: *a, an, the, those, this, these* and *that*. The corresponding French tokens are taken from the given word alignments. Table 1 lists the classifier performances with these additional features in terms of macro F-scores and overall accuracy. We can see that the determiner information adds information that leads to modest improvements but only if one or two items are considered. We can also see that there is a discrepancy between macro F-scores and accuracy with respect to the use of positional information. Bag-of-word models produce higher F-scores for small windows but lower overall accuracy than position-sensitive models. For our final experiments, we rely on position-sensitive models assuming that macro F-scores are less stable than accuracy especially also considering the differences in class distributions between development and test set.

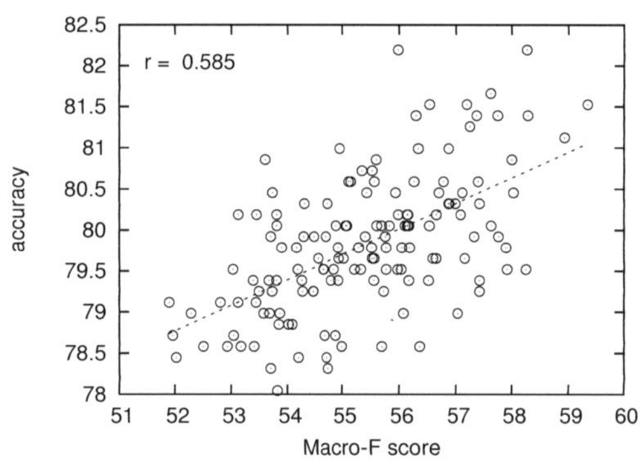

Figure 3: Correlation between macro F-score and accuracy for various context windows in source and target language (development set).

The correlation between macro F-score and accuracy is further shown in Figure 3. The plot shows the relation between these two metrics for various context windows in source and target language. From the plot we can see that there certainly is a correlation between overall accuracy and macro F-score but that this correlation is not as strong as one might expect especially with respect to these quite homogenous features.

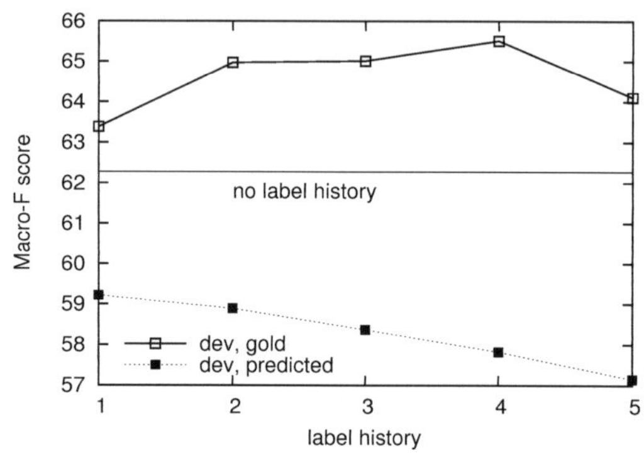

Figure 4: Using label history features: Oracle scores with gold label features and predicted labels as features besides position-sensitive local context (src1+2 and trg1+2) and tokens aligned to English determiners (det 2) tested on the development set.

Another strategy that we explored is the use of local dependencies between predicted labels. Intuitively, it should be important to know about previously used pronouns to predict the next ambiguous one. Referential pronouns are often included in larger coreferential chains and refer back to the same entity in the discourse. This fact can be exploited by sequence labeling techniques that incorporate target dependencies. However, our results with CRF that include markovian dependencies on predicted labels were quite disappointing and fall far behind the results obtained with local predictions using liblinear. Therefore, we also added a model with history features that include previous labels as additional features in local predictions. Training such models is straightforward with fully visible data sets as the ones given in the pronoun prediction task. The main problem is that the model needs to handle noisy predicted labels at testing time where gold labels of previous decisions are not available. Figure 4 plots the score obtained with history features on the DiscoMT development set. The oracle scores using gold history labels from the development set shows the capacity of these features. They significantly push the performance with over five point gains in macro F-score. Dependencies up to four labels in history seem to be beneficial. However, using a simplistic approach to incorporate predicted labels at testing time results in drastic drops leading to scores below the models without history features. These results are rather discouraging and we did not try to improve the history-based models by common techniques such as training with predicted labels using jackknifing approaches. This could, however, be interesting to explore in future work.

class	precision	recall	F
ce	80.28	92.93	86.15
cela	25.00	22.22	23.53
elle	45.65	25.30	32.56
elles	66.67	27.45	38.89
il	49.26	64.42	55.83
ils	74.50	93.12	82.78
on	70.83	45.95	55.74
ça	66.22	48.04	55.68
OTHER	88.83	91.32	90.06
micro avg	74.21	74.21	74.21
macro avg	63.03	56.75	57.91

Table 2: Final classifier result on the DiscoMT test set (submission UU-TIED).

Finally, in our submitted system we, therefore, applied a local classifier without history features and target context only. We used two words before and three words after from the local context and target language words linked to the closest source language determiner from previous context regardless of distance. Furthermore, we added the word that follows next to those linked words in the target language to add yet another feature that may help the classifier to predict gender and number correctly. The final results of this model applied to the official test set is shown in Table 2. The scores show that we cannot achieve the same quality on test data as we have seen on the development data. This is certainly to be expected but the drop is quite significant (both in macro F-score and in overall accuracy). Still, our system is the highest ranked submission according to the official macro average F-score. However, it is below the baseline model (58.4%) but significantly outperforms the baseline in overall accuracy (74.2% versus 66.3%).

The system works surprisingly well in recognizing OTHER cases and also the frequent demonstrative pronoun "ce" as well as the masculine plural "ils" works reasonably well. Most problems can be found in the predictions of the female pronouns "elle" and "elles" but also the confusion between "cela" and "ça" is noticeable. For further details of the individual mistakes done by the classifier,

	← classified as →									
	ce	cela	elle	elles	il	ils	on	ça	other	sum
ce	171	1	0	0	7	1	0	2	2	184
cela	1	6	3	0	0	0	0	11	6	27
elle	9	2	21	0	28	5	3	6	9	83
elles	1	0	0	14	2	32	0	0	2	51
il	12	2	15	1	67	0	3	2	2	104
ils	0	0	0	5	1	149	0	0	5	160
on	2	1	0	0	11	4	17	2	0	37
ça	4	11	6	0	15	2	0	49	15	102
other	13	1	1	1	5	7	1	2	326	357
sum	213	24	46	21	136	200	24	74	367	

Table 3: Confusion matrix

please look at the confusion matrix in Table 3. Here, we can see that "il" is very often misclassified as "ce" and "elle", and "elle" is often tagged as "il" – important ambiguous cases that DiscoMT tries to focus on. Looking at these results, we can conclude that the final model is only modestly successful and further work needs to be done to improve prediction quality.

3 Pronoun-Focused Translation

The pronoun-focused translation task at DiscoMT requires a full machine translation system. Our submission uses a phrase-based model with one additional document-level feature function that captures long-distance relations spanning over arbitrarily long distances within a given document and its translation. We use Docent (Hardmeier et al., 2013), a document-level decoder that supports such feature functions and test our model on the DiscoMT test set.

3.1 Document-Level Decoding

The common strategy to decode phrase-based SMT models is to use a beam search algorithm based on dynamic programming and incremental hypotheses expansion (Koehn, 2010). This approach is very efficient and successful for local features such as context-independent translation options of word sequences and n-gram-based language models. Long-distance dependencies on the target language are impossible to incorporate which makes it difficult to account for coreferential relations over arbitrary spans in order to resolve, for example, ambiguities in the translation of anaphoric pronouns. Docent implements a different decoding strategy that starts with a complete translation hypotheses of an entire document applying local changes to improve the translation according to the model it uses (Hardmeier et al., 2012). The algorithm is a stochastic variant of standard hill climbing and at each step, the decoder generates a successor of the current translation by randomly applying one of a set of state-changing operations at a random location in the document. Operations include changing the translation of a phrase, swapping positions of two phrases, moving a phrase and re-segmenting phrases. The decoder is non-deterministic but has been shown to be quite stable at least with standard features commonly used in phrase-based SMT. The decoder can be initialized using a randomly generated translation of the entire document based on translation options from the phrase table or using the beam-search decoder implemented in Moses (Koehn et al., 2007). More details about the decoder and document-level feature models can be found in (Hardmeier, 2014).

3.2 Selected Word Language Models

For the purpose of DiscoMT, we implemented a feature function that can handle n-gram language models over selected words. These n-grams can easily cross sentence boundaries within a given document d but otherwise they use the same approach as any other Markovian language model:

$$p_{swlm}(d) = p(w_{s1})p(w_{s2}|w_{s1})..p(w_{sn}|w_{sn-k+1}..w_{sn-1})$$

The *selected* words $w_{s1}..w_{sn}$ can be found using various criteria. The selection can be based on part-of-speech labels or other annotation or properties such as word length. Depending on the chosen criteria, only a small subset of words may be selected and the distance between them can be arbitrary long within the limits of the document. One problematic issue in the machine translation setup where arbitrary strings can be generated is that such a language model prefers hypotheses that include as few elements as possible if corresponding n-gram probabilities are sufficiently high. This is a typical behavior of any n-gram language model and penalty features are commonly used to penalize short hypotheses. Another possibility is to base the selection process on the given source language string which is given and fixed and to obtain the target language tokens through word alignment. In this way, the feature function includes a similar number of factors (small differences are due to different word alignment types) for each hypotheses and additional penalty features can be avoided. This is especially useful for our document-level decoder in which tuning of feature weights is not very stable.

The strategy that we like to explore in the pronoun-focused translation task is to make use of the relation between subsequent pronouns and context words that may indicate anaphoric agreement constraints such as gender and number. For this, we implemented an n-gram language model over words that are linked to English pronouns and determiners and used this feature function as the only additional long-distance feature besides standard sentence-level phrase-based SMT features. We tagged the English part of the DiscoMT training data (Europarl, IWSLT15 and News Commentary v9) with HunPos and a model trained on the Universal Dependency Treebank v1 (McDonald et al., 2013) using the coarse universal PoS tag set of Petrov et al. (2012). From the tagged corpus and the alignments to their French translations, we extracted the linked French tokens for selected words using the provided word alignments and, finally, trained a 7-gram language model with modified Kneser-Ney smoothing using KenLM (Heafield et al., 2013) from that data set.

The feature function implemented in Docent caches the target word sequence aligned to selected source language words and updates the language model score each time the hypotheses is modified and the chain is effected by the modification. Similar to the interface of the standard language model implemented in Docent, we only consider the context window that is defined by the model to allow efficient computation of the feature. The model can easily be adjusted to other word selections using parameters in the configuration file. In our case, we use a regular expression to specify the PoS labels that need to be considered:

```
<model type="selected-pos-lm" id="splm">
<p name="lm-file">/path/to/lm.kenlm</p>
<p name="selected-pos-regex">^DET|PRON$</p>
```

We did not attempt to properly tune the corresponding weight for this feature function and fixed it to a rather arbitrary value of 0.2 which seemed to perform reasonably well on development data. Table 5 lists the BLEU scores of our models with and without the additional pronoun-oriented language model. The table includes also a model that contains a language model over pronouns only (without including determiners in the context). We can see that our modified models are slightly below the baseline model in overall BLEU which is most probably due to inappropriate tuning of the

	P		R_{min}		F_{min}	R_{max}		F_{max}
ce	38/50	0.760	38/51	0.745	0.752	41/51	0.804	0.781
cela	7/8	0.875	7/47	0.149	0.255	20/47	0.426	0.573
elle	8/12	0.667	8/19	0.421	0.516	8/19	0.421	0.516
elles	3/4	0.750	3/15	0.200	0.316	5/15	0.333	0.462
il	7/23	0.304	7/22	0.318	0.311	13/22	0.591	0.402
ils	45/53	0.849	45/48	0.938	0.891	45/48	0.938	0.891
on	0/0	n/a	0/0	n/a	n/a	0/0	n/a	n/a
All pronouns	108/150	0.720	108/170	0.635	0.675			
Other	27/ 47	0.574	27/ 27	1.000	0.730			

13 instances marked as "bad translations"

	accuracy		automatic evaluation				MT scores			
	+ other	- other	pron-F	P	R	F	BLEU	NIST	TER	METEOR
Baseline	0.676	0.630	0.699	0.371	0.361	0.366	37.18	8.04	46.74	60.05
Proposed	0.643	0.590	0.675	0.386	0.353	0.369	36.92	8.02	46.93	59.92

Table 4: Official results of the pronoun-focused translation task.

additional feature weight.

system	BLEU
baseline	0.4000
+PRON-LM	0.3982
+DET+PRON-LM	0.3969

Table 5: Translation with and without pronoun language model on development data. PRON uses words linked to English pronouns and DET+PRON includes words linked to determiners as well.

In order to test our models on the specific task of translating pronouns in context, we also performed automatic evaluations of the translations we obtained for the development set. Table 6 lists the results for the three models using the evaluation approach of Hardmeier and Federico (2010). We can see that both augmented models improve the overall F1 scores mainly due to an increase in precision. The model that includes target language words linked to determiners performs best at least according to our automatic evaluation and, therefore, we selected this model as our primary submission. The differences are, however, very small and the manual evaluation of the test set translations revealed that our model could not even beat the phrase-based baseline without a pronoun-specific model. The official results of the translation task are shown in Table 4. We can see that the proposed system still scores slightly better than the baseline mode with the automatic evaluation but it is clearly below the baseline according to the manual evaluation.

	Precision	Recall	F1
baseline			
it	0,3616	0,3712	0,3663
they	0,6641	0,7227	0,6922
TOTAL	0,5000	0,5270	0,5131
+PRON-LM			
it	0,3827	0,3545	0,3681
they	0,6800	0,7143	0,6967
TOTAL	0,5237	0,5140	0,5188
+DET+PRON-LM			
it	0,3793	0,3679	0,3735
they	0,6867	0,7185	0,7023
TOTAL	0,5213	0,5233	0,5223

Table 6: Automatic evaluation of translated pronouns using the development set and its reference translation.

4 Conclusions

This paper presents the results of simple but efficient baseline classifiers that predict translations of pronouns in given context. Our experiments look at varying contexts and show that small windows of target language context are very effective. Adding information from potential antecedents leads to modest improvements. We also present a language model over pronouns and determiners integrated in document-level decoding of phrase-based machine translation. The model is promising according to automatic evaluation but manual inspection reveals that it does not lead to better translations of the selected ambiguous pronouns.

References

Hal Daumé III. 2004. Notes on CG and LM-BFGS optimization of logistic regression. Paper and implementation available at `http://www.umiacs.umd.edu/~hal/megam/`.

Rong-En Fan, Kai-Wei Chang, Cho-Jui Hsieh, Xiang-Rui Wang, and Chih-Jen Lin. 2008. LIBLINEAR: A library for large linear classification. *Journal of Machine Learning Research*, 9:1871–1874.

Christian Hardmeier and Marcello Federico. 2010. Modelling pronominal anaphora in statistical machine translation. In *Proceedings of IWSLT*, pages 283–289.

Christian Hardmeier, Joakim Nivre, and Jörg Tiedemann. 2012. Document-wide decoding for phrase-based statistical machine translation. In *Proceedings of EMNLP-CONLL*, pages 1179–1190.

Christian Hardmeier, Sara Stymne, Jörg Tiedemann, and Joakim Nivre. 2013. Docent: A document-level decoder for phrase-based statistical machine translation. In *Proceedings ACL: System Demonstrations*, pages 193–198, Sofia, Bulgaria, August.

Christian Hardmeier. 2014. *Discourse in Statistical Machine Translation*. Ph.D. thesis, Uppsala University.

Kenneth Heafield, Ivan Pouzyrevsky, Jonathan H. Clark, and Philipp Koehn. 2013. Scalable Modified Kneser-Ney Language Model Estimation. In *Proceedings of ACL*, pages 690–696.

Philipp Koehn, Hieu Hoang, Alexandra Birch, Chris Callison-Burch, Marcello Federico, Nicola Bertoldi, Brooke Cowan, Wade Shen, Christine Moran, Richard Zens, Christopher J. Dyer, Ondřej Bojar, Alexandra Constantin, and Evan Herbst. 2007. Moses: Open Source Toolkit for Statistical Machine Translation. In *Proceedings of ACL*, pages 177–180.

Philipp Koehn. 2010. *Statistical Machine Translation*. Cambridge University Press.

Taku Kudo. 2013. CRF++: Yet Another CRF toolkit. http://taku910.github.io/crfpp/. v0.58.

Ryan McDonald, Joakim Nivre, Yvonne Quirmbach-Brundage, Yoav Goldberg, Dipanjan Das, Kuzman Ganchev, Keith Hall, Slav Petrov, Hao Zhang, Oscar Täckström, Claudia Bedini, Núria Bertomeu Castelló, and Jungmee Lee. 2013. Universal Dependency Annotation for Multilingual Parsing. In *Proceedings of ACL*, pages 92–97.

Slav Petrov, Dipanjan Das, and Ryan McDonald. 2012. A Universal Part-of-Speech Tagset. In *Proceedings of LREC*, pages 2089–2096.

A Maximum Entropy Classifier for Cross-Lingual Pronoun Prediction

Dominikus Wetzel and **Adam Lopez** and **Bonnie Webber**
School of Informatics
University of Edinburgh
11 Crichton Street, Edinburgh
d.wetzel@ed.ac.uk, {alopez,bonnie}@inf.ed.ac.uk

Abstract

We present a maximum entropy classifier for cross-lingual pronoun prediction. The features are based on local source- and target-side contexts and antecedent information obtained by a co-reference resolution system. With only a small set of feature types our best performing system achieves an accuracy of 72.31%. According to the shared task's official macro-averaged F1-score at 57.07%, we are among the top systems, at position three out of 14. Feature ablation results show the important role of target-side information in general and of the resolved target-side antecedent in particular for predicting the correct classes.

1 Introduction

In this paper we focus on pronouns which pose a problem for machine translation (MT). Pronoun translation is challenging due to the fact that pronouns often refer to entities mentioned in a non-local context such as previous clauses or sentences. Furthermore, languages differ with respect to usage of pronouns, e.g. how they agree with their antecedent or whether source and target language exhibit similar patterns of pronoun usage. Since pronouns contribute an important part to the meaning of an utterance, the meaning can be changed considerably when wrongly resolved and translated.

This problem gained recent interest and work has been presented in annotating and analysing translations of pronouns in parallel corpora (Guillou et al., 2014) and MT systems focusing on translation of pronouns have been proposed (Hardmeier and Federico, 2010; Le Nagard and Koehn, 2010; Guillou, 2012; Hardmeier et al., 2014).

The DiscoMT 2015 shared task on pronoun translation (Hardmeier et al., 2015) calls for contributions to tackle this problem.We focus on the cross-lingual pronoun prediction subtask, which is set up as follows: the two English (source language) third-person subject pronouns *it* and *they* can be translated in a variety of ways into French. A common set of nine classes (*ce, cela, elle, elles, il, ils, on, ça*) is defined as possible translations including an extra class OTHER which groups together any less frequent translations, including *null*, noun translations, alignment errors. The source and target corpora both consist of human-created documents and therefore abstract away from additional difficulties that arise with noisy automatic translations.

Hardmeier et al. (2013) propose a neural-network-based approach for a similar cross-lingual pronoun prediction task. Their model jointly models anaphora resolution and pronoun prediction. Our approach builds on a maximum entropy (MaxEnt) classifier that incorporates various features based on the source pronoun and local source- and target-side contexts. Moreover, the target-side noun referent (i.e. the *antecedent*) of a pronoun is used and obtained with an automatic co-reference resolution system. Our system achieves high accuracy and performs third-best according to the official evaluation metric.

In Section 2 we present our MaxEnt classifier including a description of the features used. This is followed by Section 3 with experiments and evaluation. Furthermore, in Section 4 we discuss the results and in Section 5 we give concluding remarks.

2 Systems for Cross-Lingual Pronoun Prediction

2.1 Maximum Entropy Classification

A MaxEnt classifier can model multinomial dependent variables (discrete class labels) given a set of independent variables (i.e. observations).

Proceedings of the Second Workshop on Discourse in Machine Translation (DiscoMT), pages 115–121,
Lisbon, Portugal, 17 September 2015.

antecedent

... une *symphonie* et qu' **elle** était ...
... the *symphony* and it was ...

Figure 1: Antecedent of a pronoun within local context, which is also captured by a 5-gram language model.

Each observation is represented by a set of m features extracted from the observation. The m features can provide overlapping evidence, hence do not have to be independent of each other. The model consists of a function $f(x_i, y_i) \rightarrow \mathbb{R}^{m+1}$ that maps the i-th observation x and associated label y to a real valued vector. It also consists of a weight vector $\vec{\theta}$ of corresponding size, which contains the model parameters that are learned from the training data. The model is of the form

$$p(y|x) = \frac{exp\, \vec{\theta} \cdot f(x,y)}{Z(x)}$$

where $Z(x)$ is a normalizing factor ensuring valid probabilities.

2.2 Features

Local Context The local context around the source pronoun and target pronoun can contain the antecedent (cf. Figure 1) or other information, such as the inflection of a verb which can provide evidence for the gender or number of the target-side pronoun. Therefore, we include the tokens that are within a symmetric window of size 3 around the pronoun. We integrate this information as bag-of-words, but separate the feature space by source and target side vocabulary and whether the word occurs before or after the pronoun. Special BOS and EOS markers are included for contexts at the beginning or end of sentence, respectively. We neither remove stopwords nor normalize the tokens.

We also include as features, the *Part-of-Speech (POS) tags* in a 3-word window to each side of source and target pronouns. This gives some abstraction from the lexical surface form. For the source side we use the POS tags from Stanford CoreNLP (Manning et al., 2014) mapped to universal POS tags (Petrov et al., 2012). For the target side we use coarse-grained tags provided by Morfette (Chrupała et al., 2008).[1]

Language Model Prediction We include a target-side *Language Model (LM) prediction* as a feature for the classifier. A 5-gram LM is queried by providing the preceding four context words followed by one of the eight target-side pronouns that the class labels represent. The pronoun that has the highest prediction probability is the feature that we include in the training data. The ninth class OTHER requires special treatment, since it represents all other tokens that were observed in the aligned data and thus does not itself appear in the LM training data. To get an accurate prediction probability for this aggregate class one would have to iterate over the entire vocabulary V (excluding the other eight pronouns) and find the most likely token. Since this would require a huge amount of LM queries ($|V|\times$ number of training instances) we approximated this search by taking the 40 most frequent tokens that are observed in the training data in the position which was labelled as OTHER. The highest prediction probability is then used to compete with the probabilities of the other explicit classes. Once the most likely prediction is determined we included the predicted class label as feature.

Target-side Antecedent The *target-side noun antecedent* of the pronoun determines the morphological features the pronoun has to agree with, i.e. *number* and *gender*. We use the source-side co-reference resolution system provided by Stanford CoreNLP (Lee et al., 2013) to determine the co-reference chains in each document of the training data. We then project these chains to the target side via word-alignments (cf. Figure 2). The motivation to obtain target-side co-reference chains in that way is three-fold. First, the target side of the training data is missing most of the target-side pronouns since it is the task to predict them. Therefore, relevant parts of co-reference chains are missing and the place-holders for these pronouns will introduce noise to the resolution system. Secondly, we have a statistical machine translation (SMT) scenario in mind as an application for cross-lingual pronoun prediction. Applying a co-reference system to the noisy SMT output of already translated parts of the document is subjecting the system to much noisier data than it was originally developed for. Thirdly, resources

[1] `https://github.com/gchrupala/morfette`

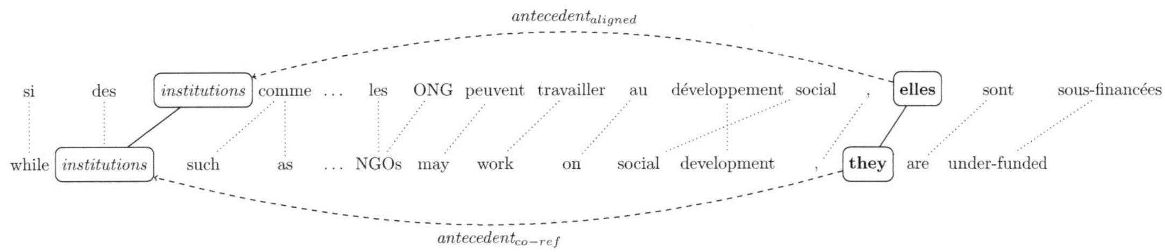

Figure 2: The $antecedent_{co-ref}$ of *they* on the English sentence (source language) is determined with a co-reference resolution system. The target-side $antecedent_{aligned}$ is obtained by following the word alignment links. In the shared task, the target pronoun *elles* has to be predicted.

and tools for automatic co-reference resolution are more easily available for English than for French.

Given the target-side co-reference chains in a document, we consider the chain the target-side pronoun is assigned to and greedily search for the closest noun token in the chain in the preceding context. This mention is included in the training data for the classifier as lexical feature. In addition, we extract morphological features from the noun (i.e. number and gender) by automatically analyzing the target-side sentences with Morfette.[2] In cases where the pronoun was not assigned to a co-reference chain, a special indicator feature was used. In addition, the word alignment can align one source token to multiple target tokens. We searched for the first noun in the aligned tokens and considered this to be the representative head antecedent of the given pronoun. If no noun could be found with this method, we resorted to taking the best representative antecedent of the source chain as determined by the Stanford co-reference system and took the aligned token as the relevant target-side antecedent. In this case *null* alignments are also possible and a special indicator feature is used for that.

Pleonastic Pronouns *Pleonastic pronouns* are a class of pronouns that do not have a referent in the discourse, e.g. in "*It* is raining". Their surface form in English is indistinguishable from referential forms. Nada (Bergsma and Yarowsky, 2011) is a tool that provides confidence estimates for pronouns whether they are referential.[3] We include these estimates as an additional feature. This should provide information especially for the French class labels that can be used as pleonastic pronouns, e.g. "*il* pleut (it is raining)" or "*ça* fait mal (it hurts)".

In addition, the rule-based detection of pleonastic pronouns is only basic in the Stanford co-reference system (Lee et al., 2013). However since they do not have a referent, they cannot be part of a co-reference chain. Therefore, we expect this feature to also counteract wrong decisions by the co-reference resolution system to a certain degree. Since Nada only provides estimates for *it*, we do not have such a feature for pleonastic uses of the other source pronoun of the task *they*.

2.3 Classifier Types

We trained classifiers in two different setups. The first setup provides all our extracted features as training data to one MaxEnt classifier, including the source pronoun as additional feature for each training instance (from now on referred to as the ALLINONE system). The second setup splits the training data into the two source pronoun cases (*it* and *they*) and trains a separate classifier for each of them (POSTCOMBINED system).

3 Experiments and Evaluation

3.1 Data

The shared task provides three corpora that can be used for training. The Europarl7 corpus, the NewsCommentary9 corpus and the IWSLT14 corpus which are transcripts of planned speech, i.e. TED talks. Only the latter two corpora come with natural text boundaries. Since these boundaries are necessary for co-reference resolution, we did not use the Europarl corpus. The test data contains 1105 classification instances within a total of

[2] Morfette's performance is quite robust and can handle sentences that contain $REPLACE\_xx$ tokens, which are the placeholders for target-side pronouns that have to be predicted. A comparison of the performance on the original sentences and the sentences with the $REPLACE\_xx$ tokens showed only minor differences.

[3] `https://code.google.com/p/nada-nonref-pronoun-detector/`

	fine Mac-F1	**coarse** Acc
BASELINE	58.40 (1)	68.42 (8)
ALLINONE	57.07 (3)	74.84 (6)
POSTCOMBINED	54.96 (7)	74.03 (7)

Table 1: Official performance on the test data. Ranks according to each metric are given in parenthesis out of 14 submitted systems (including multiple submissions per submitter and the baseline).

2093 sentences in twelve TED talk documents.

3.2 Classifier

We extract features from the training and test set and use Mallet (McCallum, 2002) to train the MaxEnt classifier.[4] The variance for regularizing the weights is set to 1 (default setting).

For the LM component of our system we use the baseline model provided for the pronoun translation subtask. This is a 5-gram modified Kneser-Ney LM trained with KenLM (Heafield, 2011).[5]

3.3 Evaluation Metrics

The official evaluation metric for the shared task is the macro-averaged F-score over all prediction classes (Mac-F1). Since this metric favours systems that perform equally well on all classes, the task puts emphasis on handling low-frequency classes well instead of only getting the frequent classes right. In addition to scores with the official metric we also report overall accuracy (Acc), i.e. the ratio between the correctly predicted classes and all test instances.

The evaluation script of the shared task provides results for the official fine-grained class separation with nine classes. It also provides a coarse-grained separation where some of the class labels are merged. Results reflect the fine-grained distinction except where stated.

3.4 Results on the Test Set

Table 1 shows the official results on the test set together with the respective ranks out of 14 submitted systems. Table 2 and Table 3 provide the per-class precision, recall and F1, overall accuracy, and overall macro-averaged F-score. Table 4 shows results of our feature ablation experiments.

[4] http://mallet.cs.umass.edu/

[5] http://kheafield.com/code/kenlm/

	Prec	Recall	F1
ce	77.78	87.50	82.35
cela	25.00	18.52	21.28
elle	51.79	34.94	41.73
elles	85.00	33.33	47.89
il	50.00	59.62	54.39
ils	76.84	91.25	83.43
on	63.64	37.84	47.46
ça	62.69	41.18	49.70
OTHER	80.95	90.48	85.45
Macro-averaged	63.74	54.96	**57.07**
Accuracy			**72.31**

Table 2: Performance of ALLINONE classifier on the **test** set.

	Prec	Recall	F1
ce	78.05	86.96	82.26
cela	9.52	7.41	8.33
elle	49.06	31.33	38.24
elles	80.00	31.37	45.07
il	51.54	64.42	57.26
ils	75.79	90.00	82.29
on	61.90	35.14	44.83
ça	64.29	44.12	52.33
OTHER	80.00	88.52	84.04
Macro-averaged	61.13	53.25	**54.96**
Accuracy			**71.40**

Table 3: Performance of POSTCOMBINED classifier on the **test** set.

4 Discussion

Confusion Matrices Table 5 and Table 6 present confusion matrices on the test set. Divergences from strong diagonal values in both tables derive in part from gender-choice errors. In addition, the morphological number of the personal pronouns is almost perfectly predicted in all cases. The OTHER class causes quite a few confusions, which is not surprising since it aggregates a heterogeneous set of possible source pronoun translations. We expect a more detailed distinction in this group to lead to better systems in general.

	ALLINONE		POSTCOMBINED	
	Mac-F1	Acc	Mac-F1	Acc
all features	57.07	72.31	54.96	71.40
all w/o antecedent features	51.59	70.14	54.15	71.13
all w/o nada	50.86	69.86	54.84	71.40
all w/o morph	54.62	71.67	54.33	71.40
all w/o language model	54.83	71.13	55.32	71.59
only src features	34.81	55.20	34.41	54.84
only tgt features	55.05	71.49	54.82	71.31

Table 4: Feature ablation for both types of classifiers on the **test** set.

classified as →	ce	cela	elle	elles	il	ils	on	ça	OTHER	*Total*
ce	161	0	1	1	11	0	0	3	7	184
cela	0	5	2	0	4	0	0	9	7	27
elle	8	1	29	0	21	3	2	5	14	83
elles	2	0	0	17	0	28	0	0	4	51
il	12	1	12	0	62	1	4	2	10	104
ils	1	0	0	1	0	146	0	0	12	160
on	2	0	3	1	5	4	14	2	6	37
ça	6	12	7	0	18	0	1	42	16	102
OTHER	15	1	2	0	3	8	1	4	323	357
Total	207	20	56	20	124	190	22	67	399	1105

Table 5: Confusion matrix for the **ALLINONE** classifier on the **test** set. Row labels are gold labels and column labels are labels as they were classified.

classified as →	ce	cela	elle	elles	il	ils	on	ça	OTHER	*Total*
ce	160	0	2	0	11	1	0	3	7	184
cela	0	2	1	1	5	0	0	8	10	27
elle	10	0	26	0	23	3	3	6	12	83
elles	2	0	1	16	0	28	0	0	4	51
il	9	1	10	1	67	1	2	2	11	104
ils	0	0	0	2	0	144	0	1	13	160
on	2	0	5	0	6	4	13	2	5	37
ça	5	14	6	0	14	0	1	45	17	102
OTHER	17	4	2	0	4	9	2	3	316	357
Total	205	21	53	20	130	190	21	70	395	1105

Table 6: Confusion matrix for the **POSTCOMBINED** classifier on the **test** set. Row labels are gold labels and column labels are labels as they were classified.

Feature Ablation In order to investigate the usefulness of the different types of features, we performed a feature ablation. When removing all features that are related to the antecedent of the target pronoun we need to predict, i.e. the antecedent itself and its number and gender, we observe a considerable drop in performance for both evaluation metrics. This is according to our expectations, since number and gender are strong cues for most of the classes. The antecedent token itself also provides enough information to the classifier to make a positive impact on the results .

When removing all features related to the target side we can observe a consistent drop in performance over all sets and classifiers.[6] This result shows the important influence the target language has on the translation of a source pronoun. Removing the source-side features does not have a strong impact on the results, which is consistent again over all settings. Both results taken together strongly indicate that the target-side features are much more important than the source-side features.

Classifier Types The overall results show a consistent preference for the ALLINONE classifier over the POSTCOMBINED one. The difference in performance seems to be mostly influenced by the fact that splitting the training data into two separate sets for the POSTCOMBINED setting also results in much smaller data sizes for each of the individual classifiers. Our feature ablation results show that particular features are useful for the former classifier, but useless or even harmful for the latter. This instability might be due to the fact that the POSTCOMBINED classifier has to learn from much smaller data sets. Incorporating more training data from the Europarl corpus could alleviate this problem and would make it possible to determine whether these differences persist.

Language Model The mixed results for the usefulness of the LM features prompt for a further investigation of how to integrate the LM. Currently we base the LM predictions on the preceding n-gram of the target pronoun. However, it is also conceivable for this task to query the LM with n-grams that are within a sliding window of tokens containing the target pronoun. Furthermore, there is a small mismatch between the trained LM which has been trained on truecased data and the preceding tokens we have from the shared task data where the case was not modified. If this difference is eliminated we expect more accurate LM predictions, which should then in turn provide more accurate features for the classifiers.

Additionally, our LM feature currently predicts OTHER with a fairly high frequency of around 80% (followed by *il* with around 15%). This might be another reason why some classifiers work better without this feature, since this distribution does not match the observed distribution of target pronouns in the training data.

[6]Features related to the target side are the LM, the target side context windows (lexical tokens and POS tags), the antecedent of the target pronoun (lexical token and morphological features).

5 Conclusion

We presented a MaxEnt classifier that can determine the French translation of the English 3rd person subject pronouns with fairly high accuracy and performs among the top systems that have been submitted for this task. The classifier only uses a small set of feature types. Target-side features contribute most to the classification quality. Potentially non-local target-side antecedent features obtained via a source-side co-reference system and projected to the target via word alignments provide useful information as well.

Acknowledgments

This paper has received funding from the European Union's Horizon 2020 research and innovation programme under grant agreement 644402 (HimL).

References

Shane Bergsma and David Yarowsky. 2011. NADA: A robust system for non-referential pronoun detection. In *Proceedings of the 8th Discourse Anaphora and Anaphor Resolution Colloquium (DAARC)*, pages 12–23, Faro, Portugal, October.

Grzegorz Chrupała, Georgiana Dinu, and Josef van Genabith. 2008. Learning morphology with Morfette. In *Proceedings of the Sixth International Conference on Language Resources and Evaluation (LREC'08)*, Marrakech, Morocco, May. European Language Resources Association (ELRA).

Liane Guillou, Christian Hardmeier, Aaron Smith, Jörg Tiedemann, and Bonnie Webber. 2014. Parcor 1.0: A parallel pronoun-coreference corpus to support statistical mt. In *Proceedings of the Ninth International Conference on Language Resources and Eval-*

uation (LREC'14), Reykjavik, Iceland, May. European Language Resources Association (ELRA).

Liane Guillou. 2012. Improving pronoun translation for statistical machine translation. In *Proceedings of the Student Research Workshop at the 13th Conference of the European Chapter of the Association for Computational Linguistics*, pages 1–10, Avignon, France, April. Association for Computational Linguistics.

Christian Hardmeier and Marcello Federico. 2010. Modelling Pronominal Anaphora in Statistical Machine Translation. In Marcello Federico, Ian Lane, Michael Paul, and François Yvon, editors, *Proceedings of the seventh International Workshop on Spoken Language Translation (IWSLT)*, pages 283–289.

Christian Hardmeier, Jörg Tiedemann, and Joakim Nivre. 2013. Latent anaphora resolution for cross-lingual pronoun prediction. In *Proceedings of the 2013 Conference on Empirical Methods in Natural Language Processing*, pages 380–391, Seattle, Washington, USA, October. Association for Computational Linguistics.

Christian Hardmeier, Sara Stymne, Jörg Tiedemann, Aaron Smith, and Joakim Nivre. 2014. Anaphora models and reordering for phrase-based smt. In *Proceedings of the Ninth Workshop on Statistical Machine Translation*, pages 122–129, Baltimore, Maryland, USA, June. Association for Computational Linguistics.

Christian Hardmeier, Preslav Nakov, Sara Stymne, Jörg Tiedemann, Yannick Versley, and Mauro Cettolo. 2015. Pronoun-focused MT and cross-lingual pronoun prediction: Findings of the 2015 DiscoMT shared task on pronoun translation. In *Proceedings of the Second Workshop on Discourse in Machine Translation*, Lisbon, Portugal. `http://www.idiap.ch/workshop/DiscoMT/shared-task`.

Kenneth Heafield. 2011. KenLM: faster and smaller language model queries. In *Proceedings of the EMNLP 2011 Sixth Workshop on Statistical Machine Translation*, pages 187–197, Edinburgh, Scotland, United Kingdom, July.

Ronan Le Nagard and Philipp Koehn. 2010. Aiding pronoun translation with co-reference resolution. In *Proceedings of the Joint Fifth Workshop on Statistical Machine Translation and MetricsMATR*, pages 252–261, Uppsala, Sweden, July. Association for Computational Linguistics.

Heeyoung Lee, Angel Chang, Yves Peirsman, Nathanael Chambers, Mihai Surdeanu, and Dan Jurafsky. 2013. Deterministic coreference resolution based on entity-centric, precision-ranked rules. *Computational Linguistics*, 39(4):885–916.

Christopher D. Manning, Mihai Surdeanu, John Bauer, Jenny Finkel, Steven J. Bethard, and David McClosky. 2014. The Stanford CoreNLP natural language processing toolkit. In *Proceedings of 52nd Annual Meeting of the Association for Computational Linguistics: System Demonstrations*, pages 55–60, Baltimore, Maryland, June. Association for Computational Linguistics.

Andrew Kachites McCallum. 2002. Mallet: A machine learning for language toolkit. `http://mallet.cs.umass.edu`.

Slav Petrov, Dipanjan Das, and Ryan McDonald. 2012. A universal part-of-speech tagset. In Nicoletta Calzolari (Conference Chair), Khalid Choukri, Thierry Declerck, Mehmet Uğur Doğan, Bente Maegaard, Joseph Mariani, Asuncion Moreno, Jan Odijk, and Stelios Piperidis, editors, *Proceedings of the Eight International Conference on Language Resources and Evaluation (LREC'12)*, Istanbul, Turkey, May. European Language Resources Association (ELRA).

Measuring 'Registerness' in Human and Machine Translation: A Text Classification Approach

Ekaterina Lapshinova-Koltunski and Mihaela Vela
Saarland University
A2.2 University Campus
D-66123 Saarbrücken
{e.lapshinova,m.vela}@mx.uni-saarland.de

Abstract

In this paper, we apply text classification techniques to prove how well translated texts obey linguistic conventions of the target language measured in terms of registers, which are characterised by particular distributions of lexico-grammatical features according to a given contextual configuration. The classifiers are trained on German original data and tested on comparable English-to-German translations. Our main goal is to see if both human and machine translations comply with the non-translated target originals. The results of the present analysis provide evidence for our assumption that the usage of parallel corpora in machine translation should be treated with caution, as human translations might be prone to errors.

1 Introduction: Motivation and Goals

In the present paper, we demonstrate that both manually and automatically translated texts differ from original texts in terms of *register*, i.e. language variation according to context (Halliday and Hasan, 1989; Quirk et al., 1985). Similar observations were made in other studies, such as those by Gellerstam (1986), Baker (1995) and Teich (2003), who show that translations tend to share a set of lexical, syntactic and/or textual features. Several studies, including (Ozdowska and Way, 2009; Baroni and Bernardini, 2006; Kurokawa et al., 2009) and (Lembersky et al., 2012), employ computational techniques to investigate these differences quantitatively, mainly applying text classification methods.

Our main aim is to show that human translations, which are extensively deployed as data for both training and evaluation of statistical machine translation (SMT), do not necessarily obey the conventions of the target language. We define these conventions as register profiles on the basis of comparable data in the form of original, non-translated texts in the target language. These register-specific profiles are based on quantitative distributions of features characterising certain registers derived from theories described in Section 2.1 below. The non-translated data set and the corresponding register-specific features are used to train classifiers, for which we apply two different classification methods (see Section 3.4). The resulting classes serve as approximation for the standards of the target language. For the test data, we use multiple translations of the same texts produced by both humans and machines. The results of this analysis provide evidence for our assumption that we should treat the application of human translations in multilingual technologies, especially SMT (for instance, its evaluation), with caution. Our results show that there is a need for new technologies which would allow a machine-translated text to be a closer approximation to the original text in terms of its register. However, we are not aiming to provide solutions for this problem in the paper, but rather to show the importance of registers for both human and machine translation.

2 Related Work

2.1 Main notions within register theory

Studies related to register theory, e.g. by Quirk et al. (1985), Halliday and Hasan (1989) or Biber (1995), are concerned with contextual variation of languages, and state that languages vary with respect to usage context within and across languages. For example, languages may vary according to the activity of the involved participants or the relationship between speaker and addressee(s). These parameters correspond to the variables of (1) *field*, (2) *tenor* and (3) *mode* de-

Proceedings of the Second Workshop on Discourse in Machine Translation (DiscoMT), pages 122–131,
Lisbon, Portugal, 17 September 2015.

fined in the framework of systemic functional linguistics (SFL), which describes language variation according to situational contexts; see, for instance, studies by Halliday and Hasan (1989) and Halliday (2004). These variables are associated with the corresponding lexico-grammatical features. Field of discourse is realised in term patterns or functional verb classes, such as activity (*approach*, *supply*, etc.), communication (*answer*, *inform*, *suggest*, etc.) and others. Tenor is realised in modality expressed by modal verbs (*can*, *may*, *must*, etc.) or stance expressions (used by speakers to convey personal attitude to the given information, e.g. adverbs like *actually*, *certainly*, *amazingly*, *importantly*). And mode is realised in information structure and textual cohesion, e.g. coreference via personal (*she*, *he*, *it*) and demonstrative (*this*, *that*) pronouns. Thus, differences between registers can be identified through the analysis of occurrence of lexico-grammatical features in these registers; see Biber's studies on linguistic variation (Biber, 1988; Biber, 1995; Biber et al., 1999). The field of discourse also includes *experiential domain* realised in the lexis. This corresponds to the notion of domain used in the machine translation community. However, it also includes colligation (morpho-syntactic preferences of words), in which grammatical categories are involved. Thus, domain is just one of the parameter features a register can have.

2.2 Register in translation

Whereas attention is paid to register settings in human translation as described by House (2014), Steiner (2004), Hansen-Schirra et al. (2012), Kruger and van Rooy (2012), De Sutter et al. (2012), Delaere and De Sutter (2013) and Neumann (2013), registers have not yet been considered much in machine translation. There are some studies in the area of SMT evaluation, e.g. those dealing with the errors in translation of new domains (Irvine et al., 2013). However, the error types concern the lexical level only, as the authors operate solely with the notion of domain (field of discourse) and not register (which includes more parameters, see Section 2.1 above). Domains reflect what a text is about, its topic. So, consideration of domain alone would classify news reporting on certain political topics together with political speeches discussing the same topics, although they belong to different registers. We expect that texts from the latter (political speeches) translated with a system trained on the former (news) would be lacking in persuasiveness, argumentation and other characteristics reflected in their lexico-grammatical features, for instance, imperative verbal constructions used to change the addressee's opinion, or interrogatives as a rhetorical means. The similarity in domains would cover only the lexical level, in most cases terminology, ignoring the lexico-grammatical patterns specific for the given register (see the discussion on domain vs. register in (Lapshinova-Koltunski and Pal, 2014)). More recently, Zampieri and Lapshinova-Koltunski (2015) and Lapshinova-Koltunski (inpress) have shown the dominance of register-specific features of translated texts over translation-method-specific ones. Although some NLP studies, for example, those employing web resources, do argue for the importance of register conventions, see (Santini et al., 2010) among others, register remain out of the focus of machine translation. One of the few works addressing the relevance of register features for machine translation is (Petrenz, 2014), in which the author uses text features to build cross-lingual register classifiers.

2.3 The impact of target and source texts in translation quality

If languages differ in their register settings (Hansen-Schirra et al., 2012; Neumann, 2013), the register profiles of the source and the target are also different. In his work on translation quality, Steiner (2004) applies 'the guiding norms' for evaluation derived from both the target language and the register properties of the source. In MT evaluation, various methods and metrics of evaluation commonly rely on reference translations, which means that the relation between machine-translated texts and human translations is considered. We believe that we cannot judge the quality of a translation by merely comparing a source and a (reference) translation. Quality assessment also requires consideration of the target language conventions, i.e. those derived from comparable texts (belonging to the same registers) in a target language.

Some recent corpus-based studies on translation (Baroni and Bernardini, 2006; Koppel and Ordan, 2011) have shown that it is possible to automatically predict whether a text is an original or a translation. Furthermore, automatic classification of original vs. translated texts found application in machine translation, especially in studies showing the impact of the nature (original vs. translation) of the text in translation and language models used in SMT. Kurokawa et al. (2009) show that for an English-to-French MT system, a translation model trained on an English-to-French data performs better than one trained on French-to-English translations. However, the 'better performance' of an SMT system is measured by BLEU scores (Papineni et al., 2002), indicating to which extend an SMT output comply with a reference, which is a translation itself. Inspired by Kurokawa et al. (2009)'s work, Lembersky et al. (2012) show that the BLEU score can be improved if they apply language models compiled from translated texts and not non-translated ones. They also show that language models trained on translated texts fit better to reference translations in terms of perplexity. In fact, this confirms the claim that machine translations comply more with translated rather than with non-translated texts produced by humans. It results in the improvement of the BLEU score, but not necessary leading to a better quality of machine translation. Several studies have confirmed the fact that BLEU scores should be treated carefully, see (Callison-Burch et al., 2006; Vela et al., 2014a; Vela et al., 2014b).

3 Methodology and Resources

3.1 Research questions

Following the assumption that translated language should normalise the linguistic features (like those described in 2.1 above) in order to adapt them to target language conventions, we use a classification method (using German original data for training, and translations for testing) to prove if register settings in translations correspond to those of the comparable originals. It is not our intention to directly measure the differences between originals and translations in the same language. This has been a common practice in numerous corpus-based translation studies that concentrate mostly on features in isolation, not paying much attention to their correlation: see Section 2.3 above.

Instead, we want to investigate if the register-related differences modelled for non-translated texts also apply for translation, and if they are sensitive to the variation according to the translation method involved. In fact, we model register classes for German non-translated texts, and test them on German translations from English source texts which are comparable to German non-translated ones in terms of registers. We expect that for some types of translations (e.g. human vs. machine), registers are identified more easily than for the others. We measure the accuracy scores (*precision, recall* and *f-measure*) which are class-specific numbers obtained for various sets of data: see details in Section 3.4.

Our classification analysis is structured according to the following questions: (1) Do translations from English into German correspond to German originals in their register settings? (2) Which translation can be classified best in terms of register? (3) Is there any difference between human (PT1 and PT2) and machine translations (RBMT and SMT), if register settings are concerned?

3.2 Feature selection

The input for the classifiers represents a set of features derived from register studies described in Section 2.1 above. These features constitute lexico-grammatical patterns of more abstract concepts, i.e. textual cohesion expressed via pronominal coreference or other cohesive devices, evaluative patterns (e.g. *it is interesting/important that*) and others. Several studies (Biber et al., 1999; Neumann, 2013), successfully employed these features for cross-lingual register analysis, showing that they reflect intra-lingual linguistic variation. In our previous work, see (Lapshinova-Koltunski, inpress), we applied a similar set of features to analyse register variation in translation.

Register features should reflect linguistic characteristics of all texts under analysis, be content-independent (do not contain terminology or keywords), be easy to interpret yielding insights on the differences between variables under analysis. So, we use groupings of nominal and verbal phrases instead of part-of-speech n-grams, as they are easier to interpret as n-grams. The set of selected features for the present analysis is outlined in Table 1. The first column denotes the extracted and analysed patterns, the second represents the corresponding linguistic features, and the third denotes the three context parameters according to register theory as previously described in Section 2.1.

The number of nominal and verbal parts-of-speech, chunks and nominalisations (*ung-*

nominalisations) reflect participants and processes in the field parameter. The distribution of abstract or general nouns and their comparison to other nouns gives information on the vocabulary (parameter of field). Modal verbs grouped according to different meanings defined by Biber et al. (1999), and evaluation patterns express modality and evaluation, i.e. the parameter of tenor. Content words and their proportion to the total number of word in a text represent lexical density, which is an indicator of the parameter of mode. Conjunctions, for which we analyse distributions of logico-semantic relations, belong to the parameter of mode as they serve as discourse-structuring elements. Reference, expressed either in nominal phrases or in pronouns, reflects textual cohesion (mode). Overall, we define 21 features[1] representing subtypes of the categories given in Table 1.

3.3 Corpus resources

German non-translated texts (GO=German originals) used as training data for classifiers are extracted from CroCo (Hansen-Schirra et al., 2012), a corpus of both parallel and comparable texts in English and German. The dataset contains 108 texts which cover seven registers: political essays (ESSAY), fictional texts (FICTION), manuals (INSTR), popular-scientific articles (POPSCI), letters to share-holders (SHARE), prepared political speeches (SPEECH), and tourism leaflets (TOU). The decision to include this wide range of registers is justified by the need for heterogeneous data for our experiment. Therefore, the dataset contains both frequently machine-translated texts, e.g. SPEECH, ESSAY and INSTR, and those, which are commonly not translated with MT systems, such as FICTION or POPSCI. The number of texts per register in GO comprises approximately 36 thousand tokens.

The translation data set is smaller (50 texts) and contains multiple German translations (both human and machine) of the same English texts, see (Lapshinova-Koltunski, 2013). Translations vary in (1) translator expertise, which differentiate them into professional (PT1), and novice (PT2) translations; and in (2) translation tools, which include rule-based (RBMT) and statistical machine translation (SMT). PT1 was exported from the above mentioned corpus CroCo (Hansen-Schirra et al., 2012), which contains not only GO but also comparable German translations from English originals covering the same registers as in GO. PT2 was produced by trainee translators with at least BA degree, who have little experience in translation. All of them produced translations using different translation memories (available via OPUS[2]) with the help of Across[3], a computer-aided translation tool which can be integrated into the usual work environment of a translator. The rule-based machine translation variant was produced with SYSTRAN6[4] (Systran, 2001), whereas for statistical machine translation, a Moses-based system was used which was trained with EUROPARL, a parallel corpus containing texts from the proceedings of the European parliament (Koehn, 2005). Every translation subcorpus has the same number of texts, as the data represent multiple translations of the same texts.

To extract the occurrences of register features described in 3.2, we annotate all subcorpora with information on token, lemma, part-of-speech (pos), syntactic chunks and sentence boundaries using Tree Tagger (Schmid, 1994). The features are then defined as linguistic patterns in form of the Corpus Query Processor regular expressions (Evert and Hardie, 2011), available within the CWB tools (CWB, 2010). As the procedures to annotate and to extract features are fully automatic, we expect them to influence some of the results, e.g. lexical density, which is entirely based on the pos categories assigned by Tree Tagger. So, the erroneous output of the tagger could also effect the results on the features. However, a gold-standard corpus is needed to evaluate the performance of the feature extraction, which is beyond the goals of the present work.

3.4 Classification methods

For our classification task, we train two different models by using two different classifiers on German original data. The applied techniques include (1) *k-nearest-neighbors* (KNN), a non-parametric method, and (2) *support vector machines* (SVM) with a linear kernel, a supervised method, both commonly used in text classification.

[1]Note that we select 18 only for the final classification, see details in Section 3.4.

[2]`http://opus.lingfil.uu.se/`

[3]`http://www.across.net/`

[4]Note that SYSTRAN6 is a rule-based system. With the release of SYSTRAN7 in 2010, SYSTRAN implemented a hybrid (rule-based/statistical) machine translation technology which is not involved in this analysis.

pattern	feature	parameter
nominal and verbal chunks	participants and processes	field
ung-nominalisations and general nouns	vocabulary and style	
modals with the meanings of permission, obligation, volition	modality	tenor
evaluative patterns	evaluation	
content vs. functional words	lexical density	mode
additive, adversative, causal, temporal, modal conjunctive relations	logico-semantic relations	
3rd person personal and demonstrative pronouns	cohesion via reference	

Table 1: Features under analysis

When using KNN, the input consists of the K closest training examples in the feature space, and the output is a class membership. This method is instance-based, where each instance is compared with existing ones using a distance metric, and the distance-weighted average of the closest neighbours is used to assign a class to the new instance (Witten et al., 2011).

For our experiments we have to determine the final number for K and the most appropriate number of features used in the classification, for which the Monte Carlo cross-validation method is used (as this method provides a less variable, but more biased estimate). Having the most significant features in the set, we calculate the distribution of errors by cross-validating 10 pairs of training-validation sets and choosing K[5] and the tuple (*numberOfFeatures=17, K=11*) is selected for our classification analysis. The classification is then performed on the translation (test) data, using the *knn* package (Ripley, 1996; Venables and Ripley, 2002).

Because the features that we select for classification have different measurement scales in our data, both the training and the test data are standardised using Formula 1 below.

$$x_s = \frac{x - Min}{Max - Min} \tag{1}$$

Applied to our corpus, the classification algorithm is supposed to store all available cases in GO (108 data points) and classify new cases in translation data (50 data points) based on a distance function measure, for which Euclidean distance is used.

[5]with in an interval between 3 and 19

When using SVM models (Vapnik and Chervonenkis, 1974), the learning algorithm tries to find the optimal boundary between classes by maximising the distance to the nearest training data of each class. Given labelled training data, the algorithm outputs an optimal hyperplane which categorises new instances. One of the reasons why SVM are used often is their robustness towards overfitting as well as their ability to map to a high-dimensional space.

We apply SVM on the same data set as for KNN, meaning that the same standardised training (108 data points) and test (50 data points) sets, as well as the same features were selected. We also apply the same procedures, training the SVM classifier on the German originals and testing the resulting model on the German translations.

First, both classifiers are tested in the 10-fold cross-validation step (Section 4.1). Judging the performance scores in terms of *precision*, *recall* and *f-measure*, we decide on classes (registers) used to answer the research questions formulated in Section 3.1. As already mentioned above, these scores are class-specific and indicate the results of automatic assignment of register labels to certain non-translated texts. In case of precision, we measure the class agreement of the data with the positive labels given by the classifier. For example, there are ten German fictional texts in our data. If the classifier assigns FICTION labels to ten texts only, and all of them really belong to FICTION, then we will achieve the precision of 100%. With recall, we measure, if all translations of a certain register were assigned to the register class they should belong to. So, if we have ten fictional texts, we would have the highest recall if all of them are assigned with the FICTION label. F-measure combines both precision and recall, and is understood as the harmonic mean of both. For the tests on translation data, we select registers for which we could achieve at least 60% of f-measure.

Next, we apply the classifiers on the translation data, which is split into different variables according to the posed research questions in Section 3.1, i.e. all translation variants or human vs. machine. As in the previous step, we also analyse the scores for precision, recall and f-measure, as our assumption is that these values would indicate if German translated texts correspond with their register settings to the non-translated German. Hence, the higher the values, the better a translation correspond to comparable originals.

4 Classification analysis

4.1 Classifier performance

In the first step, we validate the performance of our classifiers trained on German originals with the selected set of features. As we don't have comparable data in German at hand to test the classifier, we perform 10-fold cross-validation for both KNN and SVM classifiers. The results of the cross-validation are presented in Table 2.

Overall, we achieve up to 80% of precision for the classification of GO with the register features. However, the performance of the classifier is dependent on the nature of the registers involved. Some of them seem to be more difficult to model than others: e.g. compare the results for fictional texts with those for SHARE or SPEECH.

	precision		**recall**		**f-measure**	
	KNN	SVM	KNN	SVM	KNN	SVM
ESSAY	0.43	0.64	0.70	0.61	0.53	0.62
FICTION	1.00	1.00	1.00	1.00	1.00	1.00
INSTR	1.00	1.00	0.64	0.79	0.78	0.88
POPSCI	0.75	0.89	0.90	0.80	0.82	0.84
SHARE	0.67	0.71	0.36	0.46	0.47	0.56
SPEECH	0.54	0.89	0.39	0.44	0.45	0.59
TOU	0.76	0.53	0.73	0.96	0.74	0.68
AVERAGE	0.74	0.81	0.67	0.72	0.69	0.74

Table 2: Classification results for GO per register

The best results are shown for fictional texts, popular-scientific texts and instruction manuals, for which the resulting f-measure amounts between 80-100%. SPEECH and SHARE reveal the lowest scores, and thus, are excluded from further analysis.

4.2 Question 1: Translations and register

Table 3 provides an overview of the f-measure values representing basically the diagonal of the confusion matrix of all classes (registers) under analysis, for the four different translation methods and two different classifiers. The table reveals that our classification algorithms perform differently depending on the register.

The best results are achieved for FICTION with both classification methods (lower performance is observed for PT2 with KNN and RBMT with SVM), where we observe f-measures up to 100%. This means that translations of English fictional texts best match the standards of German fiction. The worst results are observed for translations of political essays and popular-scientific texts, where missing correspondence with originals is observed for machine-translated texts in terms of SVM. The KNN values, although better, achieve the maximum of 53% for RBMT-POPSCI.

Misclassification results are observed for every class, varying in the translation method involved.

The classification results with both classifiers do not demonstrate the same results, e.g. SVM performs better for FICTION and INSTR, whereas KNN's best performance is observed for ESSAY, POPSCI and TOU. Therefore, we cannot claim that certain registers are generally more difficult to be identified in translated data than others, as the performance of the classifiers vary depending not only on the register but also the translation method involved.

4.3 Question 2: The best performance

To answer the second question, we compare the average values (for all classes) for precision, recall and f-measure for each translation variant in our data, as shown in Table 4.

	precision		**recall**		**f-measure**	
	KNN	SVM	KNN	SVM	KNN	SVM
PT1	0.56	0.49	0.71	0.72	0.61	0.51
PT2	0.53	0.68	0.67	0.58	0.55	0.44
RBMT	0.43	0.24	0.61	0.56	0.50	0.32
SMT	0.50	0.32	0.61	0.53	0.54	0.34

Table 4: Average values for the classification per translation variant

Ranking translations according to the calculated values, we observe the best performance of translations by humans with both classifiers. The differences between the KNN and SVM results are caused by the differences in the approach to learning: for KNN, all K neighbours influence the classification, whereas the SVM classifier draws a line

	ESSAY		FICTION		INSTR		POPSCI		TOU	
	KNN	SVM	KNN	SVM	KNN	SVM	KNN	SVM	KNN	SVM
PT1	0.45	0.13	0.86	0.86	0.62	0.52	0.55	0.60	0.43	0.44
PT2	0.52	0.27	0.75	1.00	0.35	0.35	0.67	0.29	0.40	0.30
RBMT	0.36	0.00	0.86	0.75	0.17	0.55	0.53	0.00	0.50	0.32
SMT	0.48	0.00	0.86	0.80	0.33	0.60	0.46	0.00	0.46	0.29
AVERAGE	0.45	0.10	0.83	0.85	0.37	0.51	0.55	0.22	0.45	0.34

Table 3: F-measure scores for classification per translation variant and register

to separate the data points. Significance analysis[6] confirms that the KNN results are similar for all translation varieties, as no significant difference can be observed (p-value of 0.99). This means that all translation variants correspond to comparable originals in a similar way. By contrast, the SVM values reveal variation, as the calculated p-value equals 0.03 (which is below the significance level of 0.05). Thus, we see that PT2 comply more with the register settings of the target language.

4.4 Question 3: Human vs. machine

In the following step, we compare the values for human and machine translations, analysing them per class (register). The results (see Table 5) show that both human and machine translations perform similarly, although both classifiers perform better on human translations (with the average f-measures of 0.58 vs. 0.48 for KNN and 0.52 vs. 0.33 for SVM). Our significance tests show that the results for HU vs. MT differ in terms of SVM (p-value of 1.59e-11), and is similar in terms of KNN (p-value of 0.08).

A more detailed analysis of the calculated values (presented in Figure 1) reveals much variation across registers in the results. Human translation performs better for certain registers only, i.e. ESSAY and POPSCI (both with KNN and SVM). The results for FICTION, INSTR and TOU vary depending on the classifier used. Table 6 indicates which translation method performed better for the given registers depending on the classifier used.

register	KNN	SVM
ESSAY	HU	HU
FICTION	MT	HU
INSTR	HU	MT
POPSCI	HU	HU
TOU	MT	HU

Table 6: Performance for human and machine translation across registers

[6]We perform Pearson's chi-squared test on the evaluation data.

5 Discussion and Outlook

We have shown that translations can be classified according to register features corresponding to the target language conventions. In case of a good classification performance, translations seem to adapt these conventions. However, we also observed misclassification cases, e.g. for tourism texts or those of political essays. We suppose that the reason for this lies in the nature of translated texts which differ from comparable originals. MT systems trained with such human translations result in the same kind of non-correspondence with the register standards of the target language. This might explain the similarities in our classification results for both humans and machines. While human translation characteristics in MT are often considered to be beneficial as they can improve the BLEU scores, we believe that the application of human translation as a reference should be treated with caution. There is a need for a closer approximation of the MT outputs to the original texts in terms of register, which are possible in form of high-level language models capturing register profiles in a target language. One of the ideas here is the application of such profiles (see as conventions of the target language) to rank translated texts, which might serve as basis for new techniques of MT evaluation. However, their implementation, as well as exploitation of such profiles for MT development, need a thorough elaboration of features, which is beyond the aims of the present study. In the area of MT development, we suggest that techniques such as document-wide decoding used for other discourse phenomena in Hardmeier et al. (2012) could be promising in the improvement of register profiles in machine-translated texts.

We believe that the knowledge on the discriminative features resulting from our classification can be beneficial for natural language processing, as they indicate register-specific differences of language means. For example, Petrenz and Webber (2011) show that within a newspaper corpus, the occurrence of the word *states* as a verb

	precision				recall				f-measure			
	HU		MT		HU		MT		HU		MT	
	KNN	SVM	KNN	SVM	KNN	SVM	KNN	SVM	KNN	SVM	KNN	SVM
ESSAY	0.53	0.67	0.53	0.00	0.54	0.12	0.45	0.00	0.53	0.20	0.49	0.00
FICTION	0.68	0.88	0.75	0.80	1.00	1.00	1.00	0.83	0.80	0.93	0.86	0.78
INSTR	0.42	0.28	0.25	0.40	0.65	1.00	0.25	1.00	0.51	0.44	0.25	0.57
POPSCI	0.80	0.88	0.44	0.00	0.50	0.33	0.63	0.00	0.61	0.44	0.52	0.00
TOU	0.32	0.24	0.37	0.19	0.75	0.80	0.70	0.90	0.45	0.37	0.48	0.31
AVERAGE	0.55	0.59	0.47	0.28	0.69	0.65	0.61	0.55	0.58	0.48	0.52	0.33

Table 5: Evaluation of classification results per human and machine translation

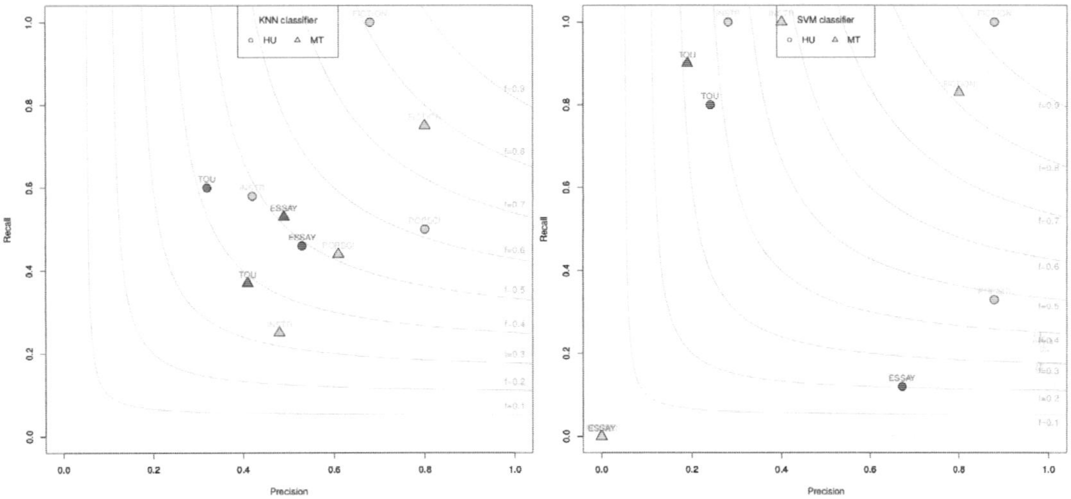

Figure 1: Evaluation of classification results per human and machine translation

is higher in letters than in editorials, and the cues on such specific features correlating with registers may impact system performance. The knowledge from confusion matrices can thus be useful for the decision if we can use an MT system trained on texts of one register and translate texts of another register which was commonly classified as the first one in our experiments. Experiments of this kind are part of our future work, which will also include inspection of the feature weights resulting from classification. The higher the weight of a feature, the more distinctive it is for a class, regardless of its positive or negative sign. A feature ranking will help us to determine the relative discriminatory force of certain features specific for a particular register, as described by (Teich et al., 2015) in their work on register diversification in scientific writing.

We also need to have a closer look at the features contributing to misclassification, as they might also serve as translation error indicators. For this, human assessments of quality is required, which involves manual evaluation of our translation data. The manual effort would also allow us to evaluate the performance of the automatic feature extraction, which might be erroneous, as stated in Section 3.3.

6 Acknowledgement

We thank Elke Teich, Erich Steiner and all anonymous reviewers for their constructive comments. We also gratefully acknowledge the help of Heike Przybyl in preparing the final version of this article. All remaining errors and misconceptions are our own.

References

Mona Baker. 1995. Corpora in translation studies: An overview and some suggestions for future research. *Target*, 7(2):223–243.

Marco Baroni and Silvia Bernardini. 2006. A new approach to the study of translationese: Machine-learning the difference between original and translated text. *Literary and Linguistic Computing*, 21(3):259–274.

Douglas Biber, Stig Johansson, Geoffrey Leech, Susan Conrad, and Edward Finegan. 1999. *Longman Grammar of Spoken and Written English*. Longman, Harlow.

Douglas Biber. 1988. *Variation Across Speech and Writing*. Cambridge University Press, Cambridge.

Douglas Biber. 1995. *Dimensions of Register Variation. A Cross Linguistic Comparison*. Cambridge University Press, Cambridge.

Chris Callison-Burch, Miles Osborne, and Philipp Koehn. 2006. Re-Evaluation the Role of Bleu in Machine Translation Research. In *Proceedings of the 11th Conference of the European Chapter of the Association for Computational Linguistics*, pages 249–256.

2010. The IMS Open Corpus Workbench. accessed February 2015.

Gert De Sutter, Isabelle Delaere, and Koen Plevoets. 2012. Lexical lectometry in corpus-based translation studies: Combining profile-based correspondence analysis and logistic regression modeling. In Michael P Oakes and Ji Meng, editors, *Quantitative Methods in Corpus-based Translation Studies: a Practical Guide to Descriptive Translation Research*, volume 51, pages 325–345. John Benjamins Publishing Company, Amsterdam, The Netherlands.

Isabelle Delaere and Gert De Sutter. 2013. Applying a multidimensional, register-sensitive approach to visualize normalization in translated and non-translated Dutch. *Belgian Journal of Linguistics*, 27:43–60.

Stefan Evert and Andrew Hardie. 2011. Twenty-first century corpus workbench: Updating a query architecture for the new millennium. In *Proceedings of the Corpus Linguistics-2011 Conference*, Birmingham, UK.

Martin Gellerstam. 1986. Translationese in Swedish novels translated from English. In L. Wollin and H. Lindquist, editors, *Translation Studies in Scandinavia*, pages 88–95. CWK Gleerup, Lund.

M.A.K. Halliday and Ruqaiya Hasan. 1989. *Language, context and text: Aspects of language in a social-semiotic perspective*. Oxford University Press, Oxford.

M.A.K. Halliday. 2004. *An Introduction to Functional Grammar*. Arnold, London.

Silvia Hansen-Schirra, Stella Neumann, and Erich Steiner. 2012. *Cross-linguistic Corpora for the Study of Translations. Insights from the Language Pair English-German*. de Gruyter, Berlin, New York.

Christian Hardmeier, Joakim Nivre, and Jörg Tiedemann. 2012. Document-wide decoding for phrase-based statistical machine translation. In *Proceedings of the 2012 Joint Conference on Empirical Methods in Natural Language Processing and Computational Natural Language Learning*, EMNLP-CoNLL'12, pages 1179–1190, Stroudsburg, PA, USA. Association for Computational Linguistics.

Juliane House. 2014. *Translation Quality Assessment. Past and Present*. Routledge.

Ann Irvine, John Morgan, Marine Carpuat, Hal Daumé III, and Dragos Stefan Munteanu. 2013. Measuring machine translation errors in new domains. *TACL*, 1:429–440.

Philipp Koehn. 2005. Europarl: A Parallel Corpus for Statistical Machine Translation. In *Conference Proceedings: the tenth Machine Translation Summit*, pages 79–86, Phuket, Thailand. AAMT.

Moshe Koppel and Noam Ordan. 2011. Translationese and its dialects. *Proceedings of the 49th Annual Meeting of the Association for Computational Linguistics (ACL-2011)*, June.

Haidee Kruger and Bertus van Rooy. 2012. Register and the Features of Translated Language. *Across Languages and Cultures*, 13(1):33–65.

David Kurokawa, Cyril Goutte, and Pierre Isabelle. 2009. Automatic detection of translated text and its impact on machine translation. In *Proceedings of MT-Summit XII*.

Ekaterina Lapshinova-Koltunski and Santanu Pal. 2014. Comparabilty of corpora in human and machine translation. In Nicoletta Calzolari, Khalid Choukri, Thierry Declerck, Hrafn Loftsson, Bente Maegaard, Joseph Mariani, Asuncion Moreno, Jan Odijk, and Stelios Piperidis, editors, *Proceedings of the Seventh Workshop on Building and Using Comparable Corpora*, Reykjavik, Iceland, May. European Language Resources Association (ELRA). LREC-2014.

Ekaterina Lapshinova-Koltunski. 2013. VARTRA: A comparable corpus for analysis of translation variation. In *Proceedings of the Sixth Workshop on Building and Using Comparable Corpora*, pages 77–86, Sofia, Bulgaria, August. Association for Computational Linguistics.

Ekaterina Lapshinova-Koltunski. *in press*. Linguistic features in translation varieties: Corpus-based analysis. In G. De Sutter, I. Delaere, and M.-A. Lefer, editors, *New Ways of Analysing Translational Behaviour in Corpus-Based Translation Studies*. Mouton de Gruyter. TILSM series.

Gennadi Lembersky, Noam Ordan, and Shuly Wintner. 2012. Language models for machine translation: Original vs. translated texts. *Computational Linguistics*, 38(4):799–825.

Stella Neumann. 2013. *Contrastive Register Variation. A Quantitative Approach to the Comparison of English and German*. De Gruyter Mouton, Berlin, Boston.

Sylwia Ozdowska and Andy Way. 2009. Optimal bilingual data for french-english pb-smt. In *EAMT 2009 – 13th Annual Conference of the European Association for Machine Translation*, Barcelona, Spain, May.

Kishore Papineni, Salim Roukus, Todd Ward, and Wei-Jing Zhu. 2002. BLEU: a method for automatic evaluation of machine translation. In *Proceedings of the 40th annual meeting on association for computational linguistics*, pages 311–318.

Philipp Petrenz and Bonnie Webber. 2011. Stable classification of text genres. *Computational Linguistics*, 37:385–393.

Philipp Petrenz. 2014. *Cross-Lingual Genre Classification*. Ph.D. thesis, School of Informatics, University of Edinburgh, Scotland.

Randolph Quirk, Sidney Greenbaum, Geoffrey Leech, and Jan Svartvik. 1985. *A Comprehensive Grammar of the English Language*. Longman, London.

Brian D. Ripley. 1996. *Pattern Recognition and Neural Networks*. Cambridge University Press.

Marina Santini, Alexander Mehler, and Serge Sharoff. 2010. Riding the rough waves of genre on the web. In A. Mehler, S. Sharoff, and M. Santini, editors, *Genres on the Web: Computational Models and Empirical Studies*, pages 3–30. Springer.

Helmut Schmid. 1994. Probabilistic Part-of-Speech Tagging Using Decision Trees. In *International Conference on New Methods in Language Processing*, pages 44–49, Manchester, UK.

Erich Steiner. 2004. *Translated Texts. Properties, Variants, Evaluations*. Peter Lang Verlag, Frankfurt/M.

Systran. 2001. Past and present. Technical report.

Elke Teich, Stefania Degaetano-Ortlieb, Peter Fankhauser, Hannah Kermes, and Ekaterina Lapshinova-Koltunski. 2015. The linguistic construal of disciplinarity: A data mining approach using register features. *Journal of the Association for Information Science and Technology*, pages n/a–n/a.

Elke Teich. 2003. *Cross-Linguistic Variation in System und Text. A Methodology for the Investigation of Translations and Comparable Texts*. Mouton de Gruyter, Berlin.

Vladimir N. Vapnik and Alexey J. Chervonenkis. 1974. *Theory of pattern recognition*. Nauka.

Mihaela Vela, Anne-Kathrin Schumann, and Andrea Wurm. 2014a. Beyond Linguistic Equivalence. An Empirical Study of Translation Evaluation in a Translation Learner Corpus. In *Proceedings of the EACL Workshop on Humans and Computer-assisted Translation (HaCat)*, pages 47–56, April.

Mihaela Vela, Anne-Kathrin Schumann, and Andrea Wurm. 2014b. Human Translation Evaluation and its Coverage by Automatic Scores. In *Proceedings of the LREC Workshop on Automatic and Manual Metrics for Operational Translation Evaluation (MTE)*, pages 20–30, May.

William N. Venables and Brian D. Ripley. 2002. *Modern Applied Statistics with S*. Statistics and Computing. Springer.

Ian H Witten, Eibe Frank, and Mark A Hall. 2011. *Data Mining: Practical machine learning tools and techniques*. Morgan Kaufmann, Burlington, Massachusetts.

Marcos Zampieri and Ekaterina Lapshinova-Koltunski. 2015. Investigating genre and method variation in translation using text classification. In Petr Sojka, Ales Horák, Ivan Kopecek, and Karel Pala, editors, *Text, Speech and Dialogue - 18th International Conference, TSD 2015, Plzen, Czech Republic, Proceedings*, Lecture Notes in Computer Science. Springer.

Translation Model Adaptation Using Genre-Revealing Text Features

Marlies van der Wees **Arianna Bisazza** **Christof Monz**
Informatics Institute, University of Amsterdam
{m.e.vanderwees,a.bisazza,c.monz}@uva.nl

Abstract

Research in domain adaptation for statistical machine translation (SMT) has resulted in various approaches that adapt system components to specific translation tasks. The concept of a *domain*, however, is not precisely defined, and most approaches rely on provenance information or manual subcorpus labels, while genre differences have not been addressed explicitly. Motivated by the large translation quality gap that is commonly observed between different genres in a test corpus, we explore the use of document-level genre-revealing text features for the task of translation model adaptation. Results show that automatic indicators of genre can replace manual subcorpus labels, yielding significant improvements across two test sets of up to 0.9 BLEU. In addition, we find that our genre-adapted translation models encourage document-level translation consistency.

1 Introduction

Statistical machine translation (SMT) systems use large bilingual corpora to train translation models, which can be used to translate unseen test sentences. Training corpora are typically collected from a wide variety of sources and therefore have varying textual characteristics such as writing style and vocabulary. The test set, on the other hand, is much smaller and usually more homogeneous. As a result, there is often a mismatch between the test data and the majority of the training data. In such situations, it is beneficial to adapt the translation system to the translation task at hand, which is exactly the challenge of domain adaptation in SMT.

The concept of a *domain*, however, is not precisely defined across existing domain adaptation methods. Different domains typically correspond to different subcorpora, in which documents exhibit a particular combination of genre and topic, and optionally other textual characteristics such as dialect and register. This definition, however, has two major shortcomings. First, subcorpus-based domains depend on provenance information, which might not be available, or on manual grouping of documents into subcorpora, which is labor intensive and often carried out according to arbitrary criteria. Second, the commonly used notion of a domain neglects the fact that topic and genre are two distinct properties of text (Stein and Meyer Zu Eissen, 2006). While this distinction has long been acknowledged in text classification literature (Lee, 2001; Dewdney et al., 2001; Lee and Myaeng, 2002), most work on domain adaptation in SMT uses in-domain and out-of-domain data that differs on both the topic and the genre level (e.g., Europarl political proceedings (Koehn, 2005) versus EMEA medical text (Tiedemann, 2009)), making it unclear whether the proposed solutions address topic or genre differences.

In this work, we follow text classification literature for definitions of the concepts topic and genre. While *topic* refers to the general subject (e.g., sports, politics or science) of a document, *genre* is harder to define since existing definitions vary. Swales (1990), for example, refers to genre as a class of communicative events with a shared set of communicative purposes, and Karlgren (2004) calls it a grouping of documents that are stylistically consistent. Based on previous definitions, Santini (2004) concludes that the term genre is pri-

Proceedings of the Second Workshop on Discourse in Machine Translation (DiscoMT), pages 132–141,
Lisbon, Portugal, 17 September 2015.

marily used as a concept complementary to topic, covering the non-topical text properties function, style, and text type. Examples of genres include editorials, newswire, or user-generated (UG) text, i.e., content written by lay-persons that has not undergone any editorial control. Within the latter we can distinguish more fine-grained subclasses, such as dialog-oriented content (e.g., SMS or chat messages), weblogs, or commentaries to news articles, all of which pose different challenges to SMT (van der Wees et al., 2015a).

Recently, we studied the impact of topic and genre differences on SMT quality using the Gen&Topic benchmark set, an Arabic-English evaluation set with controlled topic distributions over two genres; newswire and UG comments (van der Wees et al., 2015b). Motivated by the observation that translation quality varies more between the two genres than across topics, we explore in this paper the task of genre adaptation. Concretely, we incorporate genre-revealing features, inspired by previous findings in genre classification literature, into a competitive translation model adaptation approach with the aim of improving translation quality across two test sets; the first containing newswire and UG comments, and the second containing newswire and UG weblogs.

In a series of translation experiments we show that automatic indicators of genre can replace manual subcorpus labels, yielding improvements of up to 0.9 BLEU over a strong unadapted baseline. In addition, we observe small but mostly significant improvements when using the automatic genre indicators on top of manual subcorpus labels. We also find that our genre-revealing feature values can be computed on either side of the training bitext, indicating that the proposed features are to a large extent language independent. Finally, we notice that our genre-adapted translation models encourage document-level translation consistency with respect to the unadapted baseline.

2 Related work

In recent years, domain adaptation for SMT has been studied actively. Outside of SMT research, text genre classification has received considerable attention, resulting in various sets of genre-revealing features. To our knowledge, the fields have not been combined in any previous work.

2.1 Domain adaptation for SMT

Most existing domain adaptation approaches can be grouped into two categories, depending on where in the SMT pipeline they adapt the system. First, *mixture modeling* approaches learn models from different subcorpora and interpolate these linearly (Foster and Kuhn, 2007) or log-linearly (Koehn and Schroeder, 2007). Sennrich (2012) enhances the approach by interpolating up to ten models, and Bertoldi and Federico (2009) use in-domain monolingual data to automatically generate in-domain bilingual data.

Second, *instance weighting* methods prioritize training instances that are most relevant to the test data, by assigning weights to sentence pairs (Matsoukas et al., 2009) or phrase pairs (Foster et al., 2010; Chen et al., 2013). In the most extreme case, weights are binary and training instances are either selected or discarded (Moore and Lewis, 2010; Axelrod et al., 2011).

In most previous work, domains are typically hard-labeled concepts that correspond to provenance or particular topic-genre combinations. In recent years, some work has explicitly addressed *topic* adaptation for SMT (Eidelman et al., 2012; Hewavitharana et al., 2013; Hasler et al., 2014a; Hasler et al., 2014b) using latent Dirichlet allocation (Blei et al., 2003). Surprisingly, *genre* (or style) adaptation has only been addressed to a limited extent (Bisazza and Federico, 2012; Wang et al., 2012), with methods requiring the availability of clearly separable in-domain and out-of-domain training corpora.

2.2 Text genre classification

Work on text genre classification has resulted in various methods that use different sets of genre-specific text features. Karlgren and Cutting (1994) were among the first to use simple document statistics, such as common word frequencies, first-person pronoun count, and average sentence length. Kessler et al. (1997) categorize four types of genre-revealing cues: *structural cues* (e.g., part-of-speech (POS) tag counts), *lexical cues* (specific words), *character-level cues* (e.g., punctuation marks), and *derivative cues* (ratios and variation measures based on other types of cues). Dewdney et al. (2001) compare a large number of document features and show that these outperform bag-of-words approaches, which are traditionally used in topic-based text classification. Finn and Kushmerick (2006) also compare the bag-of-words approach with simple text statistics and conclude that both methods achieve high classification accuracy on fixed topic-genre combinations but perform worse when predicting topic-independent genre labels.

While mostly focused on the English language, some work has addressed language-independent (Sharoff, 2007; Sharoff et al., 2010) or cross-lingual genre classification (Gliozzo and Strapparava, 2006; Petrenz, 2012; Petrenz and Webber, 2012), indicating that a single set of genre-revealing features can generalize across multiple languages. In this paper, we examine whether genre-revealing features are also language independent when applied to translation model genre adaptation for SMT.

3 Translation model genre adaptation

For the task of genre adaptation to the genres newswire (NW) and UG comments or weblogs, we use a flexible translation model adaptation approach based on phrase pair weighting using a vector space model (VSM) inspired by Chen et al. (2013). The reason we choose an instance-weighting method rather than a mixture modeling approach is twofold: First, mixture modeling approaches intrinsically depend on subcorpus boundaries, which resemble provenance or require manual labeling. Second, Irvine et al. (2013) have shown that including relevant training data in a mixture modeling approach solves many coverage errors, but also introduces substantial amounts of new scoring errors. With phrase-pair weighting we aim to optimize phrase translation selection while keeping our training data fixed, and we can thus compare the impact of several methodological variants on genre adaptation for SMT.

3.1 VSM adaptation framework

In the selected adaptation method, each phrase pair in the training data is represented by a vector capturing information about the phrase:

$$V(\bar{f},\bar{e}) = < w_1(\bar{f},\bar{e}), \ldots, w_N(\bar{f},\bar{e}) > . \quad (1)$$

Here, $w_i(\bar{f},\bar{e})$ is the weight for phrase pair $(\bar{f},\bar{e})$ of dimension $i \in N$ in the vector space. The exact definition of dimensions $i \in N$, and hence the information captured by the vector, depends on the definition of the vector space, for which we describe different variants in Sections 3.2–3.4.

In addition to the phrase pair vectors, a single vector is created for the development set which is assumed to be similar to the test data:

$$V(dev) = < w_1(dev), \ldots, w_N(dev) >, \quad (2)$$

where weights $w_i(dev)$ are computed for the entire development set, summing over the vectors of all phrase pairs that occur in the development set:

$$w_i(dev) = \sum_{(\bar{f},\bar{e}) \in P_{dev}} c_{dev}(\bar{f},\bar{e}) \; w_i(\bar{f},\bar{e}). \quad (3)$$

Here P_{dev} refers to the set of phrase pairs that can be extracted from the development set, $c_{dev}(\bar{f},\bar{e})$ is the count of phrase pair $(\bar{f},\bar{e})$ in the development set, and $w_i(\bar{f},\bar{e})$ is the phrase pair's weight for dimension i in the vector space.

Next, for each phrase pair in the training corpus, we compute the Bhattacharyya Coefficient (BC) (Bhattacharyya, 1946) as a similarity score[1] between its vector and the development vector:

$$BC(dev;\bar{f},\bar{e}) = \sum_{i=0}^{i=N} \sqrt{p_i(dev) \cdot p_i(\bar{f},\bar{e})}, \quad (4)$$

where $p_i(dev)$ and $p_i(\bar{f},\bar{e})$ are probabilities representing smoothed normalized vector weights $w_i(dev)$ and $w_i(\bar{f},\bar{e})$, respectively.

The computed similarity is assumed to indicate the relevance of the phrase pair with respect to the development and test set and is added to the decoder as a new feature. In a similar fashion, two similarity-based decoder features $BC(dev;\bar{f},\bullet)$ and $BC(dev;\bullet,\bar{e})$ are added for the marginal counts of the source and target phrases, respectively. Further technical details can be found in (Chen et al., 2013).

The presented framework for translation model adaptation allows us to empirically compare various sets of VSM features, of which we present three in the following sections.

3.2 Genre adaptation with subcorpus labels

First, we adhere to the commonly used scenario in which adaptation is guided by manual subcorpus labels that resemble provenance of training documents. In this formulation, each weight $w_i(\bar{f},\bar{e})$ in Equation (1) is a standard *tf-idf* weight capturing the relative occurrence of phrase pair $(\bar{f},\bar{e})$ in

[1] Chen et al. (2013) compared three similarity measures and observed that the BC similarity performed best.

different subcorpora. Since our aim is to adapt to multiple genres in a test corpus, we follow Chen et al. (2013) and manually group our training data into subcorpora that reflect various genres (see Table 3). While this definition of the vector space can approximate genres at different levels of granularity, manual subcorpus labels are labor intensive to generate, particularly in the scenario where provenance information is not available, and may not generalize well to new translation tasks.

3.3 Genre adaptation with genre features

To move away from manually assigned subcorpus labels, we explore the use of genre-revealing features that have proven successful for distinguishing genres in classification tasks (Section 2.2). To this end, we construct a list of features that are directly observable in raw text, see Table 1. For each genre feature i, we first compute its raw count at the document level $c_i(d)$, which we then normalize for document length and scale to a value in range $[0, 1]$ to obtain the final document-level feature value $w_i(d)$. Next, each vector weight $w_i(\bar{f}, \bar{e})$ in Equation (1) equals the weighted average of the document-level values of genre feature i for all training instances of phrase pair $(\bar{f}, \bar{e})$:

$$w_i(\bar{f}, \bar{e}) = \frac{1}{c_{train}(\bar{f}, \bar{e})} \sum_{d \in D} c_d(\bar{f}, \bar{e})\ w_i(d). \quad (5)$$

Here, $c_{train}(\bar{f}, \bar{e})$ is the total count of phrase pair $(\bar{f}, \bar{e})$ in the training corpus, D is the number of documents in the training corpus, $c_d(\bar{f}, \bar{e})$ is the count of $(\bar{f}, \bar{e})$ in document d, and $w_i(d)$ is the document-level value of genre feature i for document d. Note that this definition differs from the standard *tf-idf* weight that is used in Section 3.2 since each genre feature has exactly one score per document, and we do not have to normalize for dissimilar subcorpus sizes.

We determine the most genre-discriminating features with a Mann-Whitney U test (Mann and Whitney, 1947) on the observed feature values for each genre in the development set. The seven most discriminative features between the genres NW and UG which we use in the remainder of this paper are shown in the top part of Table 1. The main goal of this paper is to investigate whether this type of genre-revealing features can be useful for the task of translation model genre adaptation, hence we do not attempt to fully exploit the set of possible features. Since genre-discriminating

Feature
First person pronoun count
Second person pronoun count
Repeating punctuation count ("...", "?!", etc.)
Exclamation mark count
Question mark count
Emoticons count
Numbers count
Third person pronoun count
Plural pronoun count
Average word length
Average sentence length
Total punctuation count
Quote count
Dates count
Percentages count
Long words (> 7 characters) count
Stopwords count
Unique words count

Table 1: Selection of document-level features inspired by genre-classification literature. The top seven features are most discriminative between the genres NW and UG, and are used in the genre-specific VSM approaches.

features potentially generalize across languages (Petrenz and Webber, 2012), we compute the document-level feature values $w_i(d)$ on the source as well as the target sides of our bitext, and we examine whether both are equally suitable for translation model genre adaptation.

3.4 Genre adaptation with LDA

Another type of feature that does not depend on provenance information is Latent Dirichlet allocation (LDA) (Blei et al., 2003), an unsupervised word-based approach that infers a preset number of latent dimensions in a corpus and represents documents as distributions over those dimensions. Despite its recent successes in topic adaptation for SMT, we expect such a bag-of-words approach to be insufficient to model genre accurately. Nevertheless, since many of the proposed genre-revealing features are in fact lexical features, it is worth verifying whether LDA can infer genre differences directly from raw text.

To this end, we use LDA-inferred document distributions as a third vector representation in the adaptation framework. Weights $w_i(\bar{f}, \bar{e})$ in Equation (1) are now average probabilities of latent dimension i for all training instances of phrase pair $(\bar{f}, \bar{e})$, computed as in Equation (5). We implement LDA using Gensim (Řehůřek and Sojka,

Benchmark			NW	UG	Total
Gen&Topic (1 reference)	Dev	#Sent	997	1,127	2,124
		#Tok	26.9K	25.8K	52.7K
	Test	#Sent	1,567	1,749	3,316
		#Tok	46.3K	45.5K	91.8K
NIST (4 references)	Dev	#Sent	1,033	764	1,797
		#Tok	34.4K	14.6K	49.0K
	Test	#Sent	1,399	1,274	2,673
		#Tok	46.6K	39.9K	86.6K

Table 2: Corpus statistics of the evaluation sets. Numbers of tokens are counted on the Arabic side. Note that Gen&Topic contains one reference translation per sentence, while NIST has four sets of reference translations.

Subcorpus	Genre	#Sentences	#Tokens
NIST broadcast conv.	BC	48K	1,071K
NIST broadcast news	BN	41K	923K
NIST newsgroup	NG	15K	392K
NIST newswire	NW	133K	4,545K
NIST weblog	WL	7.7K	126K
ISI newswire	NW	699K	22,231K
Web newswire	NW	376K	11,107K
Web UG comments	CM	203K	5,985K
Web editorials	ED	127K	4,341K
Web Ted talks	SP	98K	2,168K
Total	All	1.75M	52.9M

Table 3: Corpus statistics of the Arabic-English parallel training data. Tokens are counted on the Arabic side. Genre mapping: BC=broadcast conversation, BN=broadcast news, NG=newsgroup, NW=newswire, WL=UG weblogs, CM=UG comments, ED=editorials, SP=speech transcripts.

2010), with varying numbers of latent dimensions (5, 10, 20, and 50). Of these, LDA with 10 dimensions yields the best translation performance, which is consistent with findings in a related topic adaptation approach by Eidelman et al. (2012). The LDA features in this VSM variant are inferred from the source side of the training data.

4 Experimental setup

We evaluate the methods described in Section 3 on two Arabic-to-English translation tasks, both comprising the NW and UG. The first evaluation set is the Gen&Topic benchmark (van der Wees et al., 2015b), which consists of manually translated web-crawled news articles and their respective manually translated user comments, both covering five different topics. Since this evaluation set has controlled topic distributions per genre, differences in translation quality between genres can be entirely attributed to actual genre differences. The second evaluation set contains NIST OpenMT Arabic-English test sets, using NIST 2006 for tuning, and NIST 2008 and NIST 2009 combined for testing. These data sets cover the genres NW and UG weblogs but are not controlled for topic distributions. Specifications for both evaluation sets are shown in Table 2. Note that Gen&Topic contains one reference translation per sentence, while NIST has four sets of reference translations.

We perform our experiments using an in-house phrase-based SMT system similar to Moses (Koehn et al., 2007). All runs use lexicalized reordering, distinguishing between monotone, swap, and discontinuous reordering, with respect to the previous and next phrase (Koehn et al., 2005). Other features include linear distortion with limit 5, lexical weighting (Koehn et al., 2003), and a 5-gram target language model trained with Kneser-Ney smoothing (Chen and Goodman, 1999). The feature weights are tuned using pairwise ranking optimization (PRO) (Hopkins and May, 2011). For all experiments, tuning is done separately for the two genre-specific development sets.

All runs use parallel corpora made available for NIST OpenMT 2012, excluding the UN data. While LDC-distributed data sets contain substantial portions of documents within the NW genre, they only contain small portions of UG documents. To alleviate this imbalance we augment our LDC-distributed training data with a variety of web-crawled manually translated documents, containing user comments that are of a similar nature as the UG documents in the Gen&Topic, set as well as a number of other genres. Table 3 lists the corpus statistics of the training data, split by manual subcorpus labels as used for the subcorpus VSM variant (see Section 3.2). While our manually grouped subcorpora approximate those used by Chen et al. (2013), exact agreement was impossible to obtain, illustrating that it is not trivial to manually generate optimal subcorpus labels.

We tokenize all Arabic data using MADA (Habash and Rambow, 2005), ATB scheme. Word alignment was performed by running GIZA++ in both directions and generating the symmetric alignments using the 'grow-diag-final-and' heuristics. We use an adapted language model which

Method		Gen&Topic (1 reference) NW	UG	All	NIST (4 references) NW	UG	All
Baseline		21.5	17.2	19.3	55.3	40.4	48.5
VSM variants using automatic indicators of genre:							
LDA 10 topics		21.7 (+0.2)	17.3 (+0.1)	19.4$^{\triangle}$(+0.1)	55.9$^{\blacktriangle}$(+0.6)	40.7$^{\triangle}$(+0.3)	49.0$^{\blacktriangle}$(+0.5)
Genre features	Source	21.9$^{\blacktriangle}$(+0.4)	17.4$^{\triangle}$(+0.2)	19.6$^{\blacktriangle}$(+0.3)	55.7$^{\blacktriangle}$(+0.4)	41.0$^{\blacktriangle}$(+0.6)	49.0$^{\blacktriangle}$(+0.5)
	Target	21.7 (+0.2)	17.5$^{\blacktriangle}$(+0.3)	19.6$^{\blacktriangle}$(+0.3)	55.9$^{\blacktriangle}$(+0.6)	41.2$^{\blacktriangle}$(+0.8)	49.1$^{\blacktriangle}$(+0.6)
Genre+LDA	Source	**21.9$^{\blacktriangle}$(+0.4)**	**17.5$^{\blacktriangle}$(+0.3)**	**19.7$^{\blacktriangle}$(+0.4)**	56.1$^{\blacktriangle}$(+0.8)	41.2$^{\blacktriangle}$(+0.8)	49.2$^{\blacktriangle}$(+0.7)
	Target	21.8$^{\blacktriangle}$(+0.3)	17.5$^{\blacktriangle}$(+0.3)	19.6$^{\blacktriangle}$(+0.3)	**56.2$^{\blacktriangle}$(+0.9)**	**41.2$^{\blacktriangle}$(+0.8)**	**49.2$^{\blacktriangle}$(+0.7)**

Table 4: BLEU scores of the baseline system and all VSM variants using automatic indicators of genre. Significance is tested against the baseline, and the best performing VSM variant per test set is bold-faced.

is trained on 1.6B tokens and linearly interpolates different English Gigaword subcorpora with the English side of our bitext. The resulting model covers both genres in the benchmark sets, but is not varied between experiments since we want to investigate the effects of different features on translation model adaptation.

5 Results

In this section we compare a number of variants of the general VSM framework, differing in the way vectors are defined and constructed (see Sections 3.2–3.4). Translation quality of all experiments is measured with case-insensitive BLEU (Papineni et al., 2002) using the closest-reference brevity penalty. We use approximate randomization (Noreen, 1989) for significance testing (Riezler and Maxwell, 2005). Statistically significant differences are marked by $\triangle$ and $\blacktriangle$ for the $p \leq 0.05$ and the $p \leq 0.01$ level, respectively.

VSM using intrinsic text features. We first test various VSM variants that use automatic indicators of genre and do not depend on the availability of provenance information or manual subcorpus labels (Table 4). Of these, genre adaptation with LDA-based features (Section 3.4) achieves strongly significant improvements over the unadapted baseline for the NIST-NW and the complete NIST test sets, however improvements on the other test portions are very small. When manually inspecting the LDA-inferred latent dimensions, we observe that LDA is overly aggressive in considering all of the UG genre as a single thread, while latent dimensions inferred for NW are more fine-grained. While this finding can be explained by the unbalanced amount of training data per genre, it also illustrates that LDA-based features seem less suitable to capture low-resource genres.

Next, we evaluate the VSM variant that uses genre-revealing text features inspired by genre classification research (Section 3.3). This approach achieves statistically significant improvements over the baseline in all runs except one (i.e., target-side features on Gen&Topic NW). We also see that translation quality is fairly similar for features computed on either side of the bitext, indicating that the proposed genre features can generalize across languages.

Our last VSM variant in Table 4 combines genre-revealing and LDA features by using VSM similarities from both approaches as additional decoder features. This combined setting yields the largest improvements, which are all strongly significant and always equal to or better than the performance achieved by either individual feature type, suggesting that the two vector representations are to some extent complementary. Again, source and target genre feature values perform alike, with source-side genre features performing best for Gen&Topic, and target-side genre features obtaining slightly better overall results for NIST.

VSM using manual subcorpus labels. Next we compare our best performing VSM variant per test set (bold-faced in Table 4) to the originally proposed VSM variant using manual subcorpus labels (Section 3.2). The latter can be considered as an adapted baseline, however with the disadvantage that it relies on the availability of provenance information or manual grouping of documents into informative subcorpora.

Table 5 first shows the performance of VSM with manual subcorpus labels, which works well

Method	Gen&Topic (1 reference)			NIST (4 references)		
	NW	UG	All	NW	UG	All
VSM manual subcorpora	21.6	17.3	19.3	56.3	41.1	49.2
Δ *wrt unadapted baseline*	*(+0.1)*	*(+0.1)*	*(±0.0)*	*(+1.0)*$^{\blacktriangle}$	*(+0.7)*$^{\blacktriangle}$	*(+0.7)*$^{\blacktriangle}$
VSM automatic genre	21.9$^{\blacktriangle}$(+0.3)	17.5$^{\vartriangle}$(+0.2)	19.7$^{\blacktriangle}$(+0.4)	56.2 (−0.1)	41.2 (+0.1)	49.2 (±0.0)
VSM manual+automatic	21.9$^{\blacktriangle}$(+0.2)	17.4 (+0.1)	19.6$^{\blacktriangle}$(+0.3)	56.4 (+0.1)	41.4$^{\vartriangle}$(+0.3)	49.5$^{\blacktriangle}$(+0.3)

Table 5: BLEU scores of VSM with manual subcorpus labels in comparison to the best performing VSM with automatic indicators of genre per test corpus (see bold-faced results in Table 4), and the combination of manual subcorpus labels and automatic features. BLEU differences and significance for the bottom two variants are measured with respect to VSM manual subcorpora.

on NIST, confirming previously published results (Chen et al., 2013), but does not lead to significant improvements on Gen&Topic with respect to the unadapted baseline. This suggests that the success of this approach depends on a good fit between the test data distribution and the partitioning of training data into subcorpora, and that a single set of manual subcorpus labels is not guaranteed to generalize to new translation tasks.

The bottom half of the table shows that similar (for NIST) or larger (for Gen&Topic) improvements can be achieved when using the most competitive VSM variant that uses intrinsic text properties instead of manual subcorpus labels. Finally, we use intrinsic text features on top of manual subcorpus labels, i.e., we add all three proposed VSM feature types as additional decoder features. For NIST, this approach yields weakly significant improvements over the runs with only manual subcorpus labels, indicating that the automatic genre features capture additional genre information that is not contained in the manually grouped subcorpora. For Gen&Topic, including manual subcorpus labels does not increase translation performance with respect to VSM with genre and LDA features only, confirming the poor generalization of manual subcorpus labels to new translation tasks.

6 Translation consistency analysis

In the proposed translation model adaptation approach lexical choice is more tailored towards the different genres than in the baseline. We therefore hypothesize that the adapted system increases consistency of output translations within genres. To test this hypothesis, we measure translation consistency following Carpuat and Simard (2012). Their approach studies *repeated phrases*, defined

Test set	Genre	# Repeated phrases	% Consistent phrases	
			Base	VSM auto. genre
G&T	NW	7,318	43.2	47.4 (+4.2)
	UG	6,024	55.5	58.2 (+2.7)
	All	13,342	48.7	52.3 (+3.6)
NIST	NW	7,412	40.5	40.6 (+0.1)
	UG	5,431	54.5	57.1 (+2.6)
	All	12,843	46.5	47.6 (+1.1)

Table 6: Document-level translation consistency values for the baseline and best performing VSM variant using automatic genre indicators.

as source phrases p in the phrase table that occur more than once in a single test document d and contain at least one content word. For each repeated phrase, all of its 1-best output translations are compared. If these are identical except for punctuation or stopword differences, the repeated phrase is deemed *consistent*.

The results of the consistency analysis for the unadapted baseline and the best performing VSM genre+LDA variants are shown in Table 6. We observe that for both benchmark sets translation consistency is clearly lower in NW than in UG documents. This is likely due to the lower coverage of UG in the training data, which is in agreement with the finding by Carpuat and Simard that translation consistency increases for weaker systems trained on smaller amounts of training data. In line with our expectation, the results also show that document-level translation consistency increases when using the adapted system. Although Carpuat and Simard show that translation consistency does not imply higher quality, they also conclude that consistently translated phrases are more often translated correctly than inconsistently translated phrases.

Table 7 shows some examples of phrases that

Genre	Source phrase	Baseline translation(s)	VSM automatic genre translation(s)
Inconsistent in baseline, consistent in adapted system:			
UG	و هذا يدل	and this indicates / and this shows that	and this shows
UG	و الاجهاد	fatigue and stress / and the stress	and the stress
NW	القطاع الصحي	the health sector / workers in the health sector	the health sector
NW	المائة من	percent of egyptians / percent of them	percent of
Consistent in baseline, inconsistent in adapted system:			
UG	مليار دولار سنويا	billion dollars annually	billion dollars annually / billion dollars a year
UG	التطعيم	immunization	immunization / vaccination
NW	شرق افريقيا	east african countries	east african countries / east africa
NW	عالميا	worldwide	worldwide / global

Table 7: Examples of source phrases that generate inconsistent translations in the baseline and consistent translations in the adapted system (top), and vice versa (bottom).

were translated consistently in one system, but inconsistently in the other. While more phrases moved from being translated inconsistently in the baseline to consistently in the adapted system, the opposite was also observed for all benchmark sets. Looking at the examples for UG, we see that the adapted system often favors translations that are more colloquial or simplified than (some of) their counterparts in the baseline system, e.g., "shows" instead of "indicates", "a year" instead of "annually", and "vaccination" instead of "immunization". For NW, on the other hand, translations in the adapted system are often more formal (e.g., "global" instead of "worldwide") or more concise (e.g., "the health sector" instead of "workers in the health sector", and "east africa" instead of "east african countries") than in the baseline.

7 Conclusions

Domain adaptation is an active field for statistical machine translation (SMT), and has resulted in various approaches that adapt system components to specific translation tasks. However, the concept of a *domain* is not precisely defined and often confuses the notions of *topic*, *genre*, and *provenance*. Motivated by the large translation quality gap that is commonly observed between different genres, we have explored the task of translation model genre adaptation. To this end, we incorporated document-level genre-revealing features, inspired by genre classification research, into a competitive adaptation framework.

In a series of experiments across two test sets with two genres we show that automatic indicators of genre can replace manual subcorpus labels, yielding significant improvements of up to 0.9 BLEU over an unadapted baseline. In addition, we observe small improvements when using automatic genre features on top of manual subcorpus labels. We also find that the genre-revealing feature values can be computed on either side of the training bitext, indicating that our proposed features are language independent. Therefore, the advantages of using the proposed method are twofold: (i) manual subcorpus labels are not required, and (ii) the same set of features can be used successfully across different test sets and languages. Finally, we find that our genre-adapted translation models encourage document-level translation consistency with respect to the unadapted baseline.

Future work includes developing other methods for genre adaptation, on both the translation and language model level; possibly eliminating the need of a development set that is representative of the test set's genre distribution; scaling to more than two genres; and finally improving model coverage in addition to scoring.

Acknowledgments

This research was funded in part by the Netherlands Organization for Scientific Research (NWO) under project number 639.022.213.

References

Amittai Axelrod, Xiaodong He, and Jianfeng Gao. 2011. Domain adaptation via pseudo in-domain data selection. In *Proceedings of the 2011 Conference on Empirical Methods in Natural Language Processing*, pages 355–362.

Nicola Bertoldi and Marcello Federico. 2009. Domain adaptation for statistical machine translation with monolingual resources. In *Proceedings of the Fourth Workshop on Statistical Machine Translation*, pages 182–189.

Anil Bhattacharyya. 1946. On a measure of divergence between two multinomial populations. *Sankhyā: The Indian Journal of Statistics*, pages 401–406.

Arianna Bisazza and Marcello Federico. 2012. Cutting the long tail: Hybrid language models for translation style adaptation. In *Proceedings of the 13th Conference of the European Chapter of the ACL*, pages 439–448.

David Blei, Andrew Ng, and Michael Jordan. 2003. Latent dirichlet allocation. *Journal of Machine Learning Research*, 3:993–1022.

Marine Carpuat and Michel Simard. 2012. The trouble with SMT consistency. In *Proceedings of the Seventh Workshop on Statistical Machine Translation*, pages 442–449.

Stanley F. Chen and Joshua Goodman. 1999. An empirical study of smoothing techniques for language modeling. *Computer Speech and Language*, 13(4):359–393.

Boxing Chen, Roland Kuhn, and George Foster. 2013. Vector space model for adaptation in statistical machine translation. In *Proceedings of the 51st Annual Meeting of the ACL*, pages 1285–1293.

Nigel Dewdney, Carol VanEss-Dykema, and Richard MacMillan. 2001. The form is the substance: classification of genres in text. In *Proceedings of the Workshop on Human Language Technology and Knowledge Management*.

Vladimir Eidelman, Jordan Boyd-Graber, and Philip Resnik. 2012. Topic models for dynamic translation model adaptation. In *Proceedings of the 50th Annual Meeting of the ACL*, pages 115–119.

Aidan Finn and Nicholas Kushmerick. 2006. Learning to classify documents according to genre. *Journal of the American Society for Information Science and Technology*, 57:1506–1518.

George Foster and Roland Kuhn. 2007. Mixture-model adaptation for SMT. In *Proceedings of the Second Workshop on Statistical Machine Translation*, pages 128–135.

George Foster, Cyril Goutte, and Roland Kuhn. 2010. Discriminative instance weighting for domain adaptation in statistical machine translation. In *Proceedings of the 2010 Conference on Empirical Methods in Natural Language Processing*, pages 451–459.

Alfio Gliozzo and Carlo Strapparava. 2006. Exploiting comparable corpora and bilingual dictionaries for cross-language text categorization. In *Proceedings of the 21st International Conference on Computational Linguistics and 44th Annual Meeting of the ACL*, pages 553–560.

Nizar Habash and Owen Rambow. 2005. Arabic tokenization, part-of-speech tagging and morphological disambiguation in one fell swoop. In *Proceedings of the 43rd Annual Meeting of the ACL*, pages 573–580.

Eva Hasler, Phil Blunsom, Philipp Koehn, and Barry Haddow. 2014a. Dynamic topic adaptation for phrase-based MT. In *Proceedings of the 14th Conference of the European Chapter of the ACL*, pages 328–337.

Eva Hasler, Barry Haddow, and Philipp Koehn. 2014b. Dynamic topic adaptation for SMT using distributional profiles. In *Proceedings of the Ninth Workshop on Statistical Machine Translation*, pages 445–456.

Sanjika Hewavitharana, Dennis Mehay, Sankaranarayanan Ananthakrishnan, and Prem Natarajan. 2013. Incremental topic-based translation model adaptation for conversational spoken language translation. In *Proceedings of the 51st Annual Meeting of the ACL*, pages 697–701.

Mark Hopkins and Jonathan May. 2011. Tuning as ranking. In *Proceedings of the 2011 Conference on Empirical Methods in Natural Language Processing*, pages 1352–1362. ACL.

Ann Irvine, John Morgan, Marine Carpuat, Hal Daumé III, and Dragos Stefan Munteanu. 2013. Measuring machine translation errors in new domains. *Transactions of the ACL*, 1:429–440.

Jussi Karlgren and Douglas Cutting. 1994. Recognizing text genres with simple metrics using discriminant analysis. In *Proceedings of the 15th International conference on Computational Linguistics (COLING 94)*, pages 1071–1075.

Jussi Karlgren. 2004. The wheres and whyfores for studying text genre computationally. In *Workshop on Style and Meaning in Language, Art, Music, and Design*.

Brett Kessler, Geoffrey Numberg, and Hinrich Schütze. 1997. Automatic detection of text genre. In *Proceedings of the eighth conference of the European chapter of the ACL*, pages 32–38.

Philipp Koehn and Josh Schroeder. 2007. Experiments in domain adaptation for statistical machine translation. In *Proceedings of the Second Workshop on Statistical Machine Translation*, pages 224–227.

Philipp Koehn, Franz Josef Och, and Daniel Marcu. 2003. Statistical phrase-based translation. In *Proceedings of the 2003 Conference of the North American Chapter of the ACL on Human Language Technology*, pages 48–54.

Philipp Koehn, Amittai Axelrod, Alexandra Birch Mayne, Chris Callison-Burch, Miles Osborne, and David Talbot. 2005. Edinburgh system description for the 2005 IWSLT speech translation evaluation. In *Proceedings of the International Workshop on Spoken Language Translation*.

Philipp Koehn, Hieu Hoang, Alexandra Birch, Chris Callison-Burch, Marcello Federico, Nicola Bertoldi, Brooke Cowan, Wade Shen, Christine Moran, Richard Zens, Chris Dyer, Ondřej Bojar, Alexandra Constantin, and Evan Herbst. 2007. Moses: open source toolkit for statistical machine translation. In *Proceedings of the 45th Annual Meeting of the ACL on Interactive Poster and Demonstration Sessions*, pages 177–180.

Philipp Koehn. 2005. Europarl: A parallel corpus for statistical machine translation. In *Machine Translation Summit X*, pages 79–86.

Yong-Bae Lee and Sung Hyon Myaeng. 2002. Text genre classification with genre-revealing and subject-revealing features. In *Proceedings of the 25th annual international ACM SIGIR conference on Research and development in information retrieval*, pages 145–150.

David Y.W. Lee. 2001. Genres, registers, text types, domains and styles: Clarifying the concepts and navigating a path through the BNC jungle. *Language Learning & Technology*, 5(3):37–72.

Henry B. Mann and Donald R. Whitney. 1947. On a test of whether one of two random variables is stochastically larger than the other. *The annals of mathematical statistics*, pages 50–60.

Spyros Matsoukas, Antti-Veikko I. Rosti, and Bing Zhang. 2009. Discriminative corpus weight estimation for machine translation. In *Proceedings of the 2009 Conference on Empirical Methods in Natural Language Processing*, pages 708–717.

Robert C. Moore and William Lewis. 2010. Intelligent selection of language model training data. In *Proceedings of the ACL 2010 Conference (Short Papers)*, pages 220–224.

Eric W. Noreen. 1989. *Computer-Intensive Methods for Testing Hypotheses: An Introduction*. Wiley-Interscience.

Kishore Papineni, Salim Roukos, Todd Ward, and Wei-Jing Zhu. 2002. BLEU: a method for automatic evaluation of machine translation. In *Proceedings of the 40th Annual Meeting of the ACL*, pages 311–318.

Philipp Petrenz and Bonnie Webber. 2012. Robust cross-lingual genre classification through comparable corpora. In *The 5th Workshop on Building and Using Comparable Corpora*, pages 1–9.

Philipp Petrenz. 2012. Cross-lingual genre classification. In *Proceedings of the Student Research Workshop at the 13th Conference of the European Chapter of the ACL*, pages 11–21.

Radim Řehůřek and Petr Sojka. 2010. Software framework for topic modelling with large corpora. In *Proceedings of the LREC 2010 Workshop on New Challenges for NLP Frameworks*, pages 45–50.

Stefan Riezler and John T. Maxwell. 2005. On some pitfalls in automatic evaluation and significance testing for MT. In *Proceedings of the ACL Workshop on Intrinsic and Extrinsic Evaluation Measures for Machine Translation and/or Summarization*, pages 57–64.

Marina Santini. 2004. State-of-the-art on automatic genre identification. Technical Report ITRI-04-03, Information Technology Research Institute, University of Brighton.

Rico Sennrich. 2012. Perplexity minimization for translation model domain adaptation in statistical machine translation. In *Proceedings of the 13th Conference of the European Chapter of the ACL*, pages 539–549.

Serge Sharoff, Zhili Wu, and Katja Markert. 2010. The web library of babel: evaluating genre collections. In *Proceedings of the Seventh conference on International Language Resources and Evaluation*, pages 3063–3070.

Serge Sharoff. 2007. Classifying web corpora into domain and genre using automatic feature identification. In *Proceedings of the 3rd Web as Corpus Workshop*.

Benno Stein and Sven Meyer Zu Eissen. 2006. Distinguishing topic from genre. In *Proceedings of the 6th International Conference on Knowledge Management (I-KNOW 06)*, pages 449–456.

John M. Swales. 1990. *Genre Analysis*. Cambridge University Press., Cambridge, UK.

Jörg Tiedemann. 2009. News from OPUS - A collection of multilingual parallel corpora with tools and interfaces. In *Recent Advances in Natural Language Processing*, pages 237–248.

Marlies van der Wees, Arianna Bisazza, and Christof Monz. 2015a. Five shades of noise: Analyzing machine translation errors in user-generated text. In *Proceedings of the ACL 2015 Workshop on Noisy User-generated Text*, pages 28–37.

Marlies van der Wees, Arianna Bisazza, Wouter Weerkamp, and Christof Monz. 2015b. What's in a domain? Analyzing genre and topic differences in statistical machine translation. In *Proceedings of the Joint Conference of the 53rd Annual Meeting of the ACL and the 7th International Joint Conference on Natural Language Processing of the AFNLP (Short Papers)*, pages 560–566.

Wei Wang, Klaus Macherey, Wolfgang Macherey, Franz Och, and Peng Xu. 2012. Improved domain adaptation for statistical machine translation. In *Proceedings of the Tenth Conference of the Association for Machine Translation in the Americas*.

Crosslingual Annotation and Analysis of Implicit Discourse Connectives for Machine Translation

Frances Yung **Kevin Duh** **Yuji Matsumoto**
Nara Institute of Science and Technology
8916-5 Takayama, Ikoma, Nara, 630-0192 Japan
{pikyufrances-y, kevinduh, matsu}@is.naist.jp

Abstract

Usage of discourse connectives (DCs) differs across languages, thus addition and omission of connectives are common in translation. We investigate how implicit (omitted) DCs in the source text impacts various machine translation (MT) systems, and whether a discourse parser is needed as a preprocessor to explicitate implicit DCs. Based on the manual annotation and alignment of 7266 pairs of discourse relations in a Chinese-English translation corpus, we evaluate whether a preprocessing step that inserts explicit DCs at positions of implicit relations can improve MT.
Results show that, without modifying the translation model, explicitating implicit relations in the input source text has limited effect on MT evaluation scores. In addition, translation spotting analysis shows that it is crucial to identify DCs that should be explicitly translated in order to improve implicit-to-explicit DC translation.
On the other hand, further analysis reveals that the disambiguation as well as explicitation of implicit relations are subject to a certain level of optionality, suggesting the limitation to learn and evaluate this linguistic phenomenon using standard parallel corpora.

1 Introduction

Discourse relations are semantic and pragmatic relations between clauses or sentences. The relations can be explicitly expressed by surface words known as explicit 'discourse connectives' (DCs) or implicitly inferred. The markedness of discourse relations varies across languages. For example, Chinese discourse units are typically clauses separated by commas, so DCs are often implicit. Explicit and implicit DCs account for 45% and 40% of the DCs annotated in the Penn Discourse Treebank (PDTB) (Prasad et al., 2008) respectively, while in the Chinese Discourse Treebank (CDTB), they account for 22% and 76% respectively (Zhou and Xue, 2015).

Comparing with other language pairs, such as Arabic and English, it is found that discourse factors impact machine translation quality more in Chinese-to-English translation, especially when translating discourse relations that are expressed implicitly in one language but explicitly in the other (Li et al., 2014).

When translating from Chinese to English, implicit DCs are explicitated when necessary. For example, a causal relation can be inferred between the 2 clauses of the Chinese sentence below. In the English translation, the 2 clauses should be connected by an explicit DC, such as 'thus'.

- [1][出口快速增长]，(export grows rapidly) [2][成为推动经济增长的重要力量。] (become important strength in promoting the economy to grow.)

An open question in discourse for SMT is how best to handle cases where DCs are implicit in the source (e.g. Chinese) but explicit in the target (e.g. English). In this paper, we investigate how implicit DCs are translated in a translation corpus, and if explicitating implicit DCs in the source can improve MT.

2 Related Work

In translation studies, explicitation of implicit DCs is observed in translations between European languages (Becher, 2011; Zuffery and Cartoni,

Proceedings of the Second Workshop on Discourse in Machine Translation (DiscoMT), pages 142–152,
Lisbon, Portugal, 17 September 2015.

2014). On the other hand, it is also reported that certain English explicit DCs are not translated explicitly in French or German (Meyer and Webber, 2013). We hypothesize that explicitation is more common in Chinese-to-English translation.

To incorporate DC translation in SMT, explicit DCs are annotated in French-English parallel corpus and classifiers are trained to disambiguate DC senses before SMT training (Meyer et al., 2011; Meyer and Popescu-Belis, 2012). Also, translation model based on Rhetorical Structure Theory (Mann and Thompson, 1986) styled discourse parse has been used in Chinese-English SMT (Tu et al., 2013). These works focus on explicit discourse relations.

Chinese sentences can be 'discourse-like', consisting of a sequence of discourse units. Syntactic parsing of Chinese complex sentences (CCS) (Zhou, 2004) covers certain intersentential discourse relations, including both explicit and implicit relations. Tu et al. (2014) presents a CCS-tree-to-string translation model in which translation rules and language model are conditioned by automatic CCS parse. Improved BLEU scores are reported, but it is not clear how much the translation of implicit DCs has been improved.

Sense classification of implicit DCs is a hard task (Lin et al., 2009; Pitler et al., 2009; Park and Cardi, 2012). Echihabi and Marcu (2002) remove DCs in texts to create pseudo implicit DCs training instances. More useful pseudo samples can be generated by classifying ommisable and non-ommisable explicit DCs (Rutherford and Xue, 2015). Concerning the options of explicit and implicit usage, Patterson and Kehler (2013) presents a model that accurately (86.6%) predicts the choice of using an explicit or implicit DC given the discourse sense. However, human performance of the task is only 66%, implying that both choices are acceptable in some cases.

3 Crosslingual manual alignment of DCs

To investigate how DCs are translated from Chinese to English, we manually align DCs in the source to their translations on a parallel corpus. The DCs are further annotated with their nature and senses. This section describes the strategy and findings of our annotation.

3.1 Annotation scheme

The parallel corpus comes from 325 newswire articles (2353 sentences) of the the Chinese Treebank and their English translation (Palmer et al., 2005; Bies et al., 2007)[1]. The annotation was carried out by 1 professional Chinese-English translator.

We use translation spotting technique (Meyer et al., 2011) to align the DCs crosslingually, considering both explicit and implicit DCs. Annotation is carried out on the raw texts. Readers are refered to Yung et al. (2015) for details concerning the Chinese side annotation, such as definition of discourse units and annotation policy for parallel connectives. The labels used in the crosslingual annotation are defined as follows:

- **Explicit DC**: An explicit DC is a lexical expression that connects two discourse units with a relation. We do not define a close set of explicit DCs to be annotated. The list is constructed in the course of annotation. We also do not limit the syntactic categories of the DCs. In total, 227 Chinese and 152 English DCs are identified. (See Table 2)

- **Implicit DC**: An implicit DC is an implied relation between two discourse units represented by a lexical expression, e.g. '*and*' for an expansion relation. Since texts are naturally coherent, we assume that two consecutive discourse units are always related by a relation. The list of DCs that is used to annotate implicit relation is the list of 'fine senses'. (see below)

- **Redundant**: The 'redundant' tag is used when it is not grammatically acceptable to insert an implicit DC. Typically, it is annotated on either side of a DC alignment. For example, either half of a pair of parallel Chinese DCs (e.g.'因为'*because*...'所以'*therefore*) is aligned to 'redundant', as it is not grammatical to use both DCs in English.

- **AltLex**: 'AltLex' refers to the 'Alternative lexicalization' of a discourse relation that cannot be isolated from context as an explicit DC, e.g. '*it was followed by*' for a *Temporal* relation. Prepositions that mark discourse

[1]Our annotation is independent of existing monolingual discourse annotation on the Chinese Treebank such as the CDTB(Zhou and Xue, 2015) and Li et al. (2014b)

relations are also labeled 'AltLex', such as '*through*' for a *Contingency* relation. This label is defined on English side only.

- **Coarse sense**: We first group the DCs under the 4 top-level discourse senses defined in PDTB, namely *Expansion, Contingency, Comparison* and *Temporal*.

- **Fine sense**: The sense hierarchy of PDTB is always modified in comparable discourse corpora of different languages (Prasad et al., 2014). Instead of defining a list of senses that cover discourse relations of both languages, we group interchangeable explicit DCs under the same category, and the category serves as the 'fine sense' label. For example, '*besides*' ,'*moreover*' and '*in addition*' are all annotated with the fine sense '*in addition*'. Similar to DC identification, the list of fine senses is built in the course of annotation. In total, there are 74 Chinese and 75 English fine senses (See Table 2).

The discourse sense annotation and DC alignment are carried out at one pass by below procedure:

1. Explicit DCs are identified in the source Chinese sentence, and labeled with sense tags.

2. The English translation of the DC is spotted, aligned to the Chinese DC and labeled with sense tags.

3. If the Chinese DC is not translated to an English DC, the annotator first looks for 'AltLex'. If no 'AltLex' can be identified, an implicit DC is inserted. If insertion is not grammatical, the DC is aligned to 'redundant'.

4. On the Chinese side of the corpus, implicit DCs are inserted between two discourse units if they are not related by an explicit DC[2]. The implicit DC is aligned following the strategy in Step 3.

5. Any explicit DCs on the English side that are not aligned are identified. Further implicit DCs are inserted to the Chinese side for alignment. If insertion of implicit DCs is ungrammatical, they are aligned to 'redundant'.

[2]We treat each component of a paired DC independently: when only half of a paired DC occurs explicitly, the other half is inserted as an implicit DC.

Each pair of aligned DCs are thus tagged with 8 labels. Some annotation examples are shown below.

Example 1

中国必须对国有企业进行改革, **[1]**加强本身的竞争力。
China must implement reforms on state-owned enterprises so as to **[1]** improve its own competitiveness. .

	Chinese	English
[1]nature:	implicit	explicit
actual DC:	*nil*	so as to
fine sense:	来	in order to
coarse sense:	*Contingency*	*Contingency*

Example 2

[1] 在投资项目上比上年减少四百四十四件,但 **[2]**投资金额却 **[3]**比上年加一点三亿多美元。
[1] The number of investment projects dropped by 444 as compared with last year, but **[2]** the value of investments **[3]** rose by more than 130 million as compared with last year.

	Chinese	English
[1]nature:	implicit	implicit
actual DC:	*nil*	*nil*
fine sense:	其实	in fact
coarse sense:	*Expansion*	*Expansion*
[2]nature:	explicit	explicit
actual DC:	但	but
fine sense:	但是	but
coarse sense:	*Comparison*	*Comparison*
[3]nature:	explicit	redundant
actual DC:	却	*nil*
fine sense:	却	*nil*
coarse sense:	*Comparison*	*nil*

3.2 How many DCs are identified?

In total, 7266 pairs of discourse relations are aligned. Table 1 shows the distribution of coarse DC senses (*Comparison* (COM), *Contingency* (CON), *Expansion* (EXP) and *Temporal* (TEM)).

Similar to the findings in PDTB and CDTB, there are more implicit DCs than explicit DCs on the Chinese side but they are of similar proportion in English. *Comparison*, *Contingency*, and *Expansion* relations are more often expressed by implicit DCs than explicit DCs in Chinese. On the other hand, *Contingency* and *Expansion* relations are more often expressed by implicit DCs than explicit DCs in English.

Similar tendency is found in the PDTB. In CDTB, among the 9 coarse senses, *Causation*, *Entailment*, *Expansion* and *Conjunction* relations are more often implicit than explicit.

Table 2 shows the number of unique DCs and

Chi.	Explicit	Implicit		Total
COM	248 (36%)	446 (64%)		694 (9.9%)
CON	379 (20%)	1551(80%)		1930 (27.5%)
EXP	683 (18%)	3022(82%)		3705 (52.8%)
TEM	522 (76%)	165 (24%)		687 (9.8%)
Total	1832(26%)	5184(74%)		7016

Eng.	Explicit	Implicit	AltLex	Total
COM	287 (51%)	274 (48%)	6 (1%)	567 (9.3%)
CON	308 (25%)	584 (47%)	338(27%)	1230 (20.3%)
EXP	1545(42%)	1927(52%)	218 (6%)	3690 (60.8%)
TEM	408 (70%)	108 (19%)	63 (11%)	579 (9.5%)
Total	2548(42%)	2893(48%)	625(10%)	6066

Table 1: Proportion of various DCs per coarse sense. On top of above, there are 250 Chinese and 1200 English 'redundant' cases

fine senses that are identified in the annotation process. A smaller variety of DCs are used in the English translation than the Chinese source. The number of fine senses recognized in implicit DCs is smaller than that of explicit DCs, implying that some fine senses are only expressed explicitly.

Exp.	COM	CON	EXP	TEM	Total
Chi.	30(11)	63(18)	72(26)	62(19)	227(74)
Eng.	20(11)	41(13)	55(23)	40(14)	156(61)
Imp.	COM	CON	EXP	TEM	Total
Chi.	−(9)	−(15)	−(17)	−(13)	−(54)
Eng.	−(7)	−(11)	−(12)	−(9)	−(39)

Table 2: Number of unique DCs and DC fine senses (in brackets)[3]

Table 3 shows the number of alignments between discourse relations of different nature. Among the 5184 implicit DCs in Chinese, about

[3]DCs and fine senses that have multiple course senses are counted as different DCs/senses. If counted only once, the total numbers of unique DCs and DC fine senses (in brackets) are: explicit-Chinese: 200(70); explicit-English: 139(56); implicit-Chinese: (52); implicit-English: (38)

Eng. / Chi.	Explicit	Implicit	Redun.	TTL
Explicit	1332	1193	23	2548
Implicit	81	2812	0	2893
Redund.	198	775	227	1200
AltLex	221	404	0	625
TTL	1832	5184	250	7266

Table 3: Number of alignments between discourse relations of different nature

70% are not explicitly translated in English (2812 aligned to implicit DCs and 775 to 'redundant'). The rest 30% are translated to explicit DCs or other explicit lexicalization in English. We further examine the crosslingual alignment of discourse senses in Section 5.2.

Statistics of the annotated parallel corpus shows the divergence in DC usage between Chinese and English. It suggests that certain implicit Chinese DCs are explicitated in the English translation. To correctly model the translation of implicit relations, do we need a discourse parser that classifies an implicit source DC to its fine sense or coarse sense? Or will SMT robustly handle implicit-to-explicit DC translation without any discourse preprocessing? We seek to answer these questions in the next section.

4 Explicitating implicit DCs for MT based on manual annotation

With an automatic discoure parser, a discourse-tree-to-string translation model can be built. Nonetheless, state-of-the-art accuracy of implicit discourse sense classification is still low for downstream application (Rutherford and Xue, 2014). In this work, we design oracle experiments to evaluate the MT of implicit DCs assuming that the gold discourse sense is given.

4.1 Method

In our annotation scheme, implicit DCs senses are defined by DCs that are identified during explicit DC annotation. In other words, the implicit DCs are represented by explicit DC that acturally occur in Chinese discourse. We hypothize that explicitating implicit DCs in the source based on manual annotation will improve implicit-to-explicit DC translations and thus the overall MT result.

We use the annotated corpus as the *test set* for the MT experiments. The source input is preprocessed based on the manual DC annotations. We compare a number of variations of the preprocess:

- **Implicit fine sense (FIN)**: We insert the annotated lexicalized fine sense to the source text. For example, referring to Example 2 in Section 3.1, '其实 ('in fact') ' is inserted at position **[1]** in the source sentence.
- **Implicit coarse sense (COA)**: Classification up to the coarse discourse sense could be helpful enough to translate the implicit DCs. We insert the most frequent fine sense of the annotated coarse sense to the source text[4]. Referring to the same example, '而且' ('and') is inserted at position **[1]** because it is the most frequent fine sense under the coarse sense *Expansion*.
- **Most explicitated DCs (TOP)**: According to findings in translation studies, explicitation of DCs is DC-dependent (Zuffery and Cartoni, 2014). We thus preprocess the input source text by explicitating only the N most frequently explicitated implicit DCs (implicit in source but explicit in target) according to the manual annotation[5]. Referring to the same example, no DC is inserted at position **[1]** because the annotated fine sense '其实' ('in fact') is not within the top 4.
- **Same DC for all implicit relations (SAM)**: To evaluate the effect of inserting explicit DCs to the source text independent of the discourse sense, we homogenously insert the most frequently explicited DC, '而且' ('and'), to all positions where an implicit DC is annotated in the source text. Therefore, '而且' is inserted to position **[1]** of both Example 1 and Example 2 under this setting.

We compare the 4 kinds of preprocessing (FIN, COA, TOP, SAM) to see what kind of explication of implicit DCs could improve MT. For each of the 4 kinds of preprocessing, we also experimented with an additional variant 'implicit-to-explicit only' (i2e), which restrictively explicitate only those DCs that are actually aligned to explicit target DCs. This is to evaluate the importance of identifying which implicit DC has to be explicitly translated. Referring to Example 2, no DC is inserted to position **[1]** since it is not an 'implicit-to-implicit' alignment. These various versions of source texts are decoded by SMT systems.

4.2 MT Settings

We train baseline MT systems with 2.5 million sentences of bitexts through the LDC[6], including newswire, broadcast news and law genres. To see if there is any bias of DC translation to certain framework, we build 3 types of SMT systems with default settings: a phrase-based model and a hierarchical model using MOSES (Koehn et al., 2007), and a tree-to-string model using TRAVATAR (Neubig, 2013). All models use a 5-gram language model trained on the English Gigaword (Parker et al., 2011) and are tuned by MERT (Och, 2003). We use GIZA^{++} (Och and Ney, 2003) for automatic word alignment and the Stanford Parser (Levy and Manning, 2003) to parse the source text for tree-to-string MT training. Tuning and testing with the newswire portions of OpenMT08 and OpenMT06 respectively, the phrase-based, Hiero and tree-to-string systems yield BLEU scores of 26.7, 26.1 and 20.4 respectively, evaluating against 4 reference translations.

We use these SMT models to translate the source text in which implicit DCs are explicitated by the methods described in Section 4.1. 1178 sentences and 1175 sentences of the manually annotated parallel corpus are used as the tuning and test sets respectively. The systems are tuned with the tuning set preprocessed by the **FIN** method.

Note that the SMT training data is not discourse annotated and thus the translation models are not trained with any discourse markups. Nonetheless, the source side of the training data contains abundant examples of both implicit and explicit DCs and we believe that the translation model will contain translation rules for both natures. The question is whether explicitating implicit DC senses in the source input will the improve final performance.

[4]The top frequent DCs per coarse sense for *Expansion, Comparison, Contingency* and *Temporal* relations are '而且' ('and'), '但' ('but'), '然后' ('then'), and '从而' ('thus') respectively.

[5]We use the 4 most often explicitated fine senses, which are '而且' ('and'), '而' ('whearas'), '和' ('and'), '并' ('also').

[6]LDC2004T08, LDC2005E47, LDC2005T06, LDC2007T23, LDC2008T08, LDC2008T18, LDC2012T16, LDC2012T20, LDC2014T04, LDC2014T11, LDC2014T15

4.3 Result

Figure 4 shows the BLEU and METEOR scores of the SMT outputs resulting from various preprocessed test sets. Explicitation of implicit DCs in the source input generally results in evaluation scores comparable to that of the unprocessed input. Similar results are produced by the 3 SMT frameworks. Only the **SAM** preprocess results in higher evaluation scores using Hiero SMT.

To our surprise, disambiguating the implicit discourse sense up to the fine sense does not yeild better translation comparing with disambiguation up to the coarse sense. In turn, homogenously inserting '而且' ('and') without sense disambiguation yeilds even better result. Similar scores are produced by explicitating only the most frequently explicitated implicit DCs. The 'implicit-to-explicit only' restriction generally produces higher scores, suggesting that it is crucial to identify which DCs should be explicitated in translation and which should not.

Results of the oracle MT experiment show that

	PBMT		Hiero		T2S	
	B	M	B	M	B	M
original	**15.6**	**24.5**	15.6	24.4	**12.6**	**22.7**
FIN	15.5	24.4	15.3	24.4	12.3	22.6
FIN+i2e	**15.6**	24.4	15.6	24.4	12.4	22.6
COA	15.4	**24.5**	15.4	24.4	12.4	**22.7**
COA+i2e	15.5	24.4	15.5	24.4	12.5	22.6
TOP	**15.6**	**24.5**	15.6	24.5	12.5	22.6
TOP+i2e	**15.6**	24.4	15.6	24.4	12.5	**22.7**
SAM	15.4	**24.5**	**15.7**	**24.6**	12.4	**22.7**
SAM+i2e	15.5	24.4	15.5	24.4	12.4	**22.7**

Table 4: BLEU (B) and METEOR (M) scores of MT outputs resulting from various DC insertions. Highest scores of each SMT system are bolded

MT performance is hardly improved by explicitating implicit DCs even based on manual annotation. It will be more difficult to improve MT based on predicted implicit discourse senses.

5 Analysis

The negative MT results could be due to the following possibilities: (1) Improvement of DC translation is not captured by automatic evaluation scores. (2) The sense of the implicit DCs that requires explicitation is unevenly distributed, such that disambiguating the sense has limited effect. (3) The context in which a discourse relation is expressed explicitly in the source largely differs from the context in which it is expressed implicity. As a result, translation rules of actual explicit DCs cannot correctly translate artificially expliciated DCs.

We analyze these possibilities in this section.

5.1 Is the translation of implicit-to-explicit DCs improved?

Since DCs contribute to a small portion of word counts in the MT output, the difference in DC translation is not sensitive to global n-gram-based evaluation metrics. Translation of DCs can be actually improved while BLEU scores remain similar (Meyer et al., 2012).

We manually analyze 100 sentences of the baseline Hiero output, the reference translation, as well as the Hiero MT outputs produced by the preprocesses TOP and TOP with 'i2e' restriction. It is done by spotting how each implicit source DC is translated - to which explicit DC or not translated as explicit DC. Table 5 shows the proportion of different DC alignments produced by different MT systems and the reference translation.

(1)	**implicit-to-explicit rate**			
Ref.	19%			
Original	23%			
TOP	73%			
TOP+i2e	33%			
(2)	**correct**		**incorrect**	
Original	22%		78%	
TOP	23%		77%	
TOP+i2e	48%		52%	
(3)	**insert=explicit**		**nil=explicit**	
TOP	90%		10%	
TOP+i2e	44%		56%	
(4)	**correct**	**incorrect**	**correct**	**incorrect**
TOP	25%	75%	6%	94%
TOP+i2e	97%	3%	9%	91%

Table 5: Comparison of implicit DC translations in different preprocessing schemes

Part (1) of Table 5 compares the rate in which implicit source DCs are explicitated in the translation outputs. As expected, more implicit DCs are translated explicitly in the output of the preprocessed source text than that of the original source text. However, the original output already explicitates more implicit DCs than the reference does.

Part (2) of the table shows how much of the

target DCs aligned to (originally) implicit source DCs are correct translation. The explicit target DC is considered **correct** if it matches with the explicit DC in the reference translation, and **incorrect** if the explicit DC is different from the reference DC or the relation is not translated as an explicit DC in the reference. It is seen that the preprocess (23%) hardly improves the accuracy comparing with the original output (22%), unless we only explicitate source DCs that are known to be explicitly translated (48%).

Part (3) of the table shows how often explicitating source DCs actually produces explicit DC translations. '**insert=explicit**' means the target explicit DC is aligned to a source explicit DC inserted by preprocess. '**nil=explicit**' means the target explicit DC is not aligned to any source DCs (inserted or not). It is observed that implicit DCs are sometimes explicitly translated by the MT systems even without source explicitation, yet the translation accuracy is low, comparing with translation from explicitated source DCs, as shown in Part (4) of the table.

Result of this analysis supports our hypothesis that the improvement in implicit-to-explicit DC translation is not captured by MT evaluation metrics. Although the MT outputs under comparison have similar scores, implicit-to-explicit DC translation is improved under the TOP+i2e setting, but not under the other settings. In addition, the result suggests that certain implicit-to-explicit DC translation is captured by SMT even without source explicitation preprocessiing.

5.2 Which senses are more common in implicit-to-explicit aligments?

On average, 18.5 Chinese and 15.25 English fine senses are identified under each of the 4 coarse senses. Nonetheless, the oracle MT experiment suggests that classifying the implicit discourse senses more precisely does not improve MT more. A possible explanation is that the senses of implicit-to-explicit DCs only limit to a small set of senses that are already captured by coarse sense classification.

Among the 7266 aligned relations, there are 1193 implicit-explicit alignments (refer to Table 3). Table 6 shows the sense distribution of these pairs. While the sense distribution on the Chinese side is comparable to the overall sense distribution (refer to Table 1), over 80% of which are translated by explicit DCs that signal an *Expansion* sense. In fact, 88% of the implicit source DCs are aligned to the explicit target DC '*and*'.

Chi.	Chinese		English	
COM	131	11.0%	90	7.5%
CON	300	25.1%	109	9.1%
EXP	715	59.9%	958	80.3%
TEM	47	3.9%	36	3.0%
Total	1193		1193	

Table 6: Sense distribution of imp.-exp. DC

Table 7 lists the top 10 frequent implicit-explicit alignments. It shows that '*and*' is used to explicitate a range of discourse relations. On the other hand, although '*and*' ambiguously signal various senses, non-*Expansion* senses only occur marginally in PTDB, as shown in Table8. The distinct discrepancy suggests that DC usage differs between spontaneous writing and translation.

source implicit fine sense	target explicit DC	count	(coverage)
而且 'and'	and	203	(17%)
而 'whearas'	and	117	(15%)
和 'and'	and	139	(12%)
并 'also'	and	81	(11%)
从而 'thus'	and	61	(7%)
所以 'therefore'	and	46	(5%)
来 'in order to'	and	26	(4%)
因此 'therefore'	and	23	(3%)
然后 'and then'	and	18	(2%)
即 'which is'	and	18	(2%)

Table 7: Top 10 frequent imp.-exp. alignments

sense of explicit '*and*'		count	(coverage)
Conjunction	(expansion)	2543	(85%)
result	(contingency)	38	(1%)
Conjunction and *result*		138	(5%)
others		281	(9%)
sense of implicit '*and*'		**count**	**(coverage)**
Conjunction	(expansion)	891	(70%)
List	(expansion)	346	(27%)
others		35	(3%)

Table 8: Sense distribution of DC '*and*' in PDTB.

Analysis of the implicit-explicit alignments explains why more precise sense disambiguation of the source relations does not improve MT. It is because the reference translation uses *'and'* as the *'wild card'* to translate most implicit DCs 'explicitly', but without explicitating the discourse sense. This finding is similar to the analysis based on word-aligned Chinese-English translation corpus, which also reports that *'and'* is the most frequently added DC to the reference translation (Li et al., 2014a). Therefore, to improve implicit-to-explicit DC translation, an additional task should be defined to identify whether a source implicit DC is kept implicit, explicitly translated to an ambigous DC such as *'and'*, or explicitly translated to other unambiguous DCs.

Generally, it is pragmatically correct to use *'and'* to translate an implicit discourse relation, or to keep the relation implicit as in the source. Nonetheless, repetatively using this stragegy will result in excessively long sentences, as in the example below. In this case, insertion of explicit DCs to the target text is desirable, instead of duplicating the source writing style.

Source

[1][天津港保税区投入运行五年来，] [2][已建成了中国第一货物分拨中心，] [3][具备了口岸关的功能，] [4][开通了天津港保税区经西安、兰州到新疆阿拉山口口岸的铁路专用线；] [5][建立了一批集仓储、运输、销售于一体的大型物流配给中心，] [6][开办了铁路和国际集装箱多式联运，] [7][月接卸集装箱能力达六千标准箱；] [8][形成了七千门程控电话的装机能力，] [9][供电能力达二点五万千伏、日供水能力一万吨。]

Reference

[1][Since being put into operation five years ago,] [2][the Tianjin Port Bonded Area has completed the construction of China's first goods distribution center,] [3][functioned like a customs port,] [4][opened up the special use the railway line from the Tianjin Port Bonded Area passing Xi'an and Lanzhou to arrive at Xinjiang's Allah Mountain pass customs port,] [5][established a number of large-scale materials circulation distribution and supply centers integrating storage, transportation and sales,] [6][opened multiple railway and international container joint-operations] [7][with a monthly loading and unloading capacity reaching 6,000 standard containers.] [8][It has built up an installation capacity of 7,000 sets of program-controlled telephones,] [9][with a power supply capacity of 25,000 kilovolts, and a daily water supply capacity of 10,000 tons.]

5.3 Contexts of explicit/implicit DC usage

Lastly, we compare the contexts in which a particular sense is expressed explicitly or implicitly in the source. If the contexts are distinctly different, it suggests that artificially explicitated source implicit DCs cannot be captured by a translation model trained only with naturally occuring explicit DCs.

In addition, we compare the contexts in which a source implicit DC is translated into an explicit DC or by other means (by implicit DC or alternative lexicalization). If the contexts are similar, it suggests that the translation strategy could be an option independent of the context.

Following Rutherford and Xue (2015), we define the context of a discourse relation as the unigram distribution of words in the 2 arguments connected by the relation. The context of a particular discourse usage is thus the sum of the unigram distributions of all discourse relations associated with that usage. We also use the Jensen-Shannon Divergence (JSD) to evaluate the similarity of the contextual distributions (Rutherford and Xue, 2015; Hutchinson, 2005; Lee, 2001). This metric compares 2 distributions with the average. If both distributions are close to the average, it means they are close to each other as well. The metric value ranges from 0 (identical) to $\ln 2$.

Table 9 shows the difference between the context of each source sense against the context of other senses, when the discourse relation is expressed implicitly (Column [1]) and explicitly (Column [2]). The difference suggests that implicit and explict DCs are used in different contexts, supporting our hypothesis. In particular, the difference between the context of each sense against others is smaller in implicit usage, thus making implicit relations harder to disambiguate.

Comparing with the difference in context between implicit and explicit usage (Column [3]), the context of source implicit relations that are explicitated in the target is similar to the context of source implicit relations that are kept implicit (Column [4]). This suggests that to explicitate the implicit DC or not in translation is independent of the local context to certain extent.

The example below shows the optionality of DC translation. It is taken from the test data of OpenMT 06. The implicit relations between the 3 discourse units in the source are translated by different DC usage in the target. For example, the re-

	$JSD(q,r)$			
source fine sense	[1] 1 sense vs all imp	[2] 1 sense vs all exp	[3] exp vs imp	[4] imp-imp vs imp-exp
而且 'and'	.025	.149	.142	.059
而 'whearas'	.052	.111	.124	.076
和 'and'	.066	.166	.186	.106
并 'also'	.064	.052	.068	.110
从而 'thus'	.052	.182	.189	.094
所以 'therefore	.051	.238	.239	.142
来 'in order to	.053	.126	.124	.178
因此 'therefore'	.039	.164	.164	.119
然后 'and then'	.154	.286	.316	.218
即 'which is'	.131	.321	.393	.205

Table 9: Jensen-Shannon Divergence (JSD) of various discourse usage of the top imp-exp DCs

lation between Unit 1 and Unit 2 is translated to a *Temporal* DC *'as'* in Reference 1, while translated to a *Contingency* DC *'so that'* in Reference 3. In Reference 2, 4, it is kept implicit. This suggests that multiple reference are necessary for evaluation of DC translation.

Source:

[1][这厚重的历史回声,通过电视台"连线"大陆和香港],[2][南京市民与香港同胞"天涯共此时" ,] [3][共同庆祝香港回归祖国十周年。]

Reference 1:

[1][This rich echo of history connected the mainland and Hong Kong via television,] [2][***as*** the citizens of Nanjing and Hong Kong compatriots "shared the same occasion from the far corners of the earth"][3][***and*** celebrated together the tenth anniversary of Hong Kong's reversion to the motherland.]

Reference 2

[1][This echo of profound historical significance "connected" the Mainland and Hong Kong through television;][2][citizens of Nanjing and their fellow countrymen in Hong Kong "shared this moment with the entire world" together][3][***celebrating*** the 10th anniversary of Hong Kong's handover to the motherland]

Reference 3

[1][The sophisticated echo of history "connected" the mainland and Hong Kong through a TV channel,] [2][***so that*** Nanjing citizens and Hong Kong compatriots "shared the moments across the land"][3][***to*** celebrate together the 10th anniversary of Hong Kong's return to the motherland.]

Reference 4

[1][The heavy historical echo "connected" the Mainland with Hong Kong through television station.][2][Residents of Nanjing shared the moment with Hong Kong compatriots from afar][3][***to*** celebrate the 10th Anniversary of the return of Hong Kong to its motherland together.]

6 Conclusion

Motivated by the difference in DC usage between Chinese and English, we investigate the translation of implicit to explicit DCs given the gold crosslingual DC senses. We present a scheme to annotate and align DCs crosslingually and annotate 7266 relations in a Chinese-English translation corpus.

To simulate the incorporation of implicit DC information to MT, we explicitate the implicit DCs in the input source text based on annotation, and decode the preprocessed input by baseline, non-discourse-aware SMT models. Results show that artificially explicitating source implicit DCs in the input text alone does not improve the MT performance significantly.

Further analysis by translation spotting suggests that discourse usage as well as sense disambiguation can be subject to a certain level of optionality. In our annotated corpus, explicitation of implicit source DCs in translation is suppressed, either by traslation not using an explicit DC, or by translation using an ambiguous, sense-neutral explicit DC.

Nonetheless, our analysis is based on written-text in the news domain, while the discrepancy of Chinese-English DC usage is different in conversation dialogues and other domains (Steele and Specia, 2014). The suppression in explicitation of implicit DC could be due to the fact that subjective interpretation is avoided in news report. The future direction of our work is thus to exploit data from other domains, and to identify implicit DC relations that require explicitation in translation. The annotation used in this work is openly released on `http://cl.naist.jp/nldata/zhendisco`.

References

Viktor Becher. 2011. When and why do translators add connectives? a corpus-based study. *Target*, 23(1).

Ann Bies, Martha Palmer, Justin Mott, and Colin Warner. 2007. English chinese translation treebank v1.0 (ldc2007t02).

Ben Hutchinson. 2005. Modelling the similarity of

discourse connectives. *Proceedings of the Annual Meeting of the Cognitive Science Society*.

Philipp Koehn, Hieu Hoang, Alexandra Birch, Chris Callison-Burch, Marcello Federico, Nicola Bertoldi, Brooke Cowan, Wade Shen, Christine Moran, Richard Zens, Chris Dyer, Ondrej Bojar, Alexandra Constantin, and Evan Herbst. 2007. Moses: Open source toolkit for statistical machine translation. *Proceedings of the Annual Meeting of the Association for Computational Linguistics*.

Lillian Lee. 2001. On the effectiveness of the skew divergence for statistical language analysis. *Artificial Intelligence and Statistics*.

Roger Levy and Christopher Manning. 2003. Is it harder to parse chinese, or the chinese treebank. *Proceedings of the Annual Meeting of the Association for Computational Linguistics*.

Junyi Jessy Li, Marine Carpuat, and Ani Nenkova. 2014. Assessing the discourse factors that influence the quality of machine translation. *Proceedings of the Annual Meeting of the Association for Computational Linguistics*.

Junyi Jessy Li, Marine Carpuat, and Ani Nenkova. 2014a. Cross-lingual discourse relation analysis: A corpus study and a semi-supervised classifacation system. *Proceedings of the International Conference on Computational Linguistics*.

Yancui Li, Wenhi Feng, Jing Sun, Fang Kong, and Guodong Zhou. 2014b. Building chinese discourse corpus with connective-driven dependency tree structure. *Proceedings of the Conference on Empirical Methods on Natural Language Processing*.

Ziheng Lin, Minyen Kan, and Hwee Tou Ng. 2009. Recognizing implicit discourse relations in the penn discourse treebank. *Proceedings of the Conference on Empirical Methods on Natural Language Processing*.

William C Mann and Sandra A Thompson. 1986. Rhetorical structure theory: Description and construction of text structures. Technical report, DTIC Document.

Daniel Marcu and Abdessamad Echihabi. 2002. An unsupervised approach to recognizing discourse relations. *Proceedings of the Annual Meeting of the Association for Computational Linguistics*.

Thomas Meyer and Andrei Popescu-Belis. 2012. Using sense-labeled discourse connectives for statistical machine translation. *Proceedings of the Workshop on Hybrid Approaches to Machine Translation*.

Thomas Meyer and Bonnie Webber. 2013. Implicitation of discourse connectives in (machine) translation. *Proceedings of the Discourse in Machine Translation Workshop*.

Thomas Meyer, Andrei Popescu-Belis, Sandrine Zufferey, and Bruno Cartoni. 2011. Multilingual annotation and disambiguation of discourse connectives for machine translation. *Proceedings of the Annual Meeting of the Special Interest Group on Discourse and Dialogue*.

Thomas Meyer, Andrei Popescu-Belis, and Najeh Hajlaoui. 2012. Machine translation of labeled discourse connectives. *Proceedings of the Biennial Conference of the Association for Machine Translation in the Americas*.

Graham Neubig. 2013. Travatar: A forest-to-string machine translation engine based on tree transducers. *Proceedings of the Annual Meeting of the Association for Computational Linguistics (Demonstration Track)*.

Franz Josef Och and Hermann Ney. 2003. A systematic comparison of various statistical alignment models. *Computational Linguistics*.

Franz Josef Och. 2003. Minimum error rate training in statistical machine translation. *Proceedings of the Annual Meeting of the Association for Computational Linguistics*.

Martha Palmer, Fu-Dong Chiou, Nianwen Xue, and Tsan-Kuang Lee. 2005. Chinese treebank 5.0 (ldc2005t01).

Joonsuk Park and Claire Cardi. 2012. Improving implicit discourse relation recognition through feature set optimization. *Proceedings of Annual Meeting on Discourse and Dialogue*.

Robert Parker, David Graff, Junbo Kong, Ke Chen, and Kazuaki Maeda. 2011. English gigaword fifth edition ldc2011t07. Linguistic Data Consortium.

Gary Patterson and Andrew Kehler. 2013. Predicting the presence of discourse connectives. *Proceedings of the Conference on Empirical Methods on Natural Language Processing*.

Emily Pitler, Annie Louis, and Ani Nenkova. 2009. Automatic sense prediction for implicit discourse relations in text. *Proceedings of the Annual Meeting of the Association for Computational Linguistics and the International Joint Conference on Natural Language Processing*.

Rashmi Prasad, Nikhit Dinesh, Alan Lee, Eleni Miltsakaki, Livio Robaldo, Aravind Joshi, and Bonnie Webber. 2008. The penn discourse treebank 2.0. *Proceedings of the Language Resource and Evaluation Conference*.

Rashmi Prasad, Bonnie Webber, and Aravind Joshi. 2014. Reflections on the penn discourse treebank, comparable corpora, and complementary annotation. *Computational Linguistics*.

Attapol Rutherford and Nianwen Xue. 2014. Discovering implicit discourse relations through brown cluster pair representation and coreference patterns. *Proceedings of the Conference of the European Chapter of the Association for Computational Linguistics.*

Attapol Rutherford and Nianwen Xue. 2015. Improving the inference of implicit discourse relations via classifying explicit discourse connectives. *Proceedings of the North American Chapter of the Association of Computational Linguistics.*

David Steele and Lucia Specia. 2014. Divergences in the usage of discourse markers in english and mandarin chinese. *Text, Speech and Dialogue.*

Mei Tu, Yu Zhou, and Chengqing Zong. 2013. A novel translation framework based on rhetori- cal structure theory. *Proceedings of the Annual Meeting of the Association for Computational Linguistics.*

Mei Tu, Yu Zhou, and Chengqing Zong. 2014. Enhancing grammatical cohesion: Generating transitional expressions for smt. *Proceedings of the Annual Meeting of the Association for Computational Linguistics.*

Frances Yung, Kevin Duh, and Yuji Matsumoto. 2015. Sequential annotation and chunking of chinese discourse structure. *The SIGHAN Workshop on Chinese Language Processing.*

Yuping Zhou and Nianwen Xue. 2015. The chinese discourse treebank: a chinese corpus annotated with discourse relations. *Language Resources and Evaluation*, 49(2):397–431.

Qiang Zhou. 2004. Annotation scheme for chinese treebank. *Journal of Chinese Information Processing.*

Sandrine Zuffery and Bruno Cartoni. 2014. A multifactorial analysis of explicitation in translation. *Target*, 26(3).

Novel Document Level Features for Statistical Machine Translation

Rong Zhang and Abraham Ittycheriah
IBM T.J. Watson Research Center
Yorktown Heights, NY 10598, USA
{zhangr, abei}@us.ibm.com

Abstract

In this paper, we introduce document level features that capture necessary information to help MT system perform better word sense disambiguation in the translation process. We describe enhancements to a Maximum Entropy based translation model, utilizing long distance contextual features identified from the span of entire document and from both source and target sides, to improve the likelihood of the correct translation for words with multiple meanings, and to improve the consistency of the translation output in a document setting. The proposed features have been observed to achieve substantial improvement of MT performance on a variety of standard test sets in terms of *TER/BLEU* score.

1 Introduction

Most statistical machine translation (MT) systems use sentence as the processing unit for both training and decoding. This strategy, mainly the result of pursuing efficiency, assumes that each sentence is independent, and therefore suffers the loss of missing many kinds of "global" information, such as domain, topic and inter-sentence dependency, which are particularly important for word sense disambiguation (Chan et al., 2007) and need be learned from the span of entire document.

Table 1 shows the MT output of our sentence level Arabic-to-English translation engine on two sentences excerpted from a news article discussing middle-east politics. The Arabic sentences are displayed in Romanized form. The Arabic word *mrsy* denotes the name of the former Egyptian president *Morsi* in both sentences. In the first sentence it is translated together with prior word *mHmd*(Mohamed) as a phrase and mapped to the name correctly. In the second sentence, where no relevant local context is present, it is incorrectly translated into the word *thank*, which is the most frequent English word aligned to *mrsy* in our training data. This example shows that for ambiguous words like *mrsy*, utilizing only local features is insufficient to find them the correct translation hypotheses. This example also illustrates another weakness of sentence level MT. It has been observed that a word tends to keep same meaning within one document (Gale et al., 1992; Carpuat , 2009). However, such consistency can't be maintained by MT system working on isolated sentences since all decisions are made locally.

AR:	Alr}ys AlmSry AlmEzwl mHmd mrsy ysf nfsh b⟩nh r}ys Aljmhwryp
MT:	The deposed Egyptian president Mohamed Morsi describes himself as the president of the republic
AR:	mrsy ytHdY AlqADy fy mHAkmth bthmp Alhrwb mn Alsjn
MT:	Thank you defy the judge in his trial on charges of escaping from prison

Table 1: Sentence level MT results of two sentences excerpted from same document

To address these issues, this paper investigates document level features to utilize useful information from wider context. Three types of document level features, including source and target side long distance context, and "quasi-topic", are integrated into our MT system via the framework of Maximum Entropy, and lead to substantial improvement of translation performance.

2 A Practical Scheme to Approximate Document Level Machine Translation

Let D_f denote a document in source language f consisting of N sentences: $D_f =< \mathbf{f}_1, \mathbf{f}_2, ..., \mathbf{f}_N >$. The goal of document level MT is to search the best document hypothesis D_e^* in target language e that maximizes the translation probability:

$$D_e^* = \arg\max_{D_e} \Pr(D_e|D_f) \qquad (1)$$

Proceedings of the Second Workshop on Discourse in Machine Translation (DiscoMT), pages 153–157,
Lisbon, Portugal, 17 September 2015. ©2015 Association for Computational Linguistics.

We require that the number of sentences in D_f and D_e to be equal: $D_e =< \mathbf{e}_1, \mathbf{e}_2, ..., \mathbf{e}_N >$. Using chain rule, $\Pr(D_e|D_f)$ is estimated as follows:

$$\Pr(D_e|D_f) = \prod_{i=1}^{N} \Pr(\mathbf{e}_i|\mathbf{f}_i, D_{f,\bar{i}}, D_{e,i-}) \quad (2)$$

where $D_{f,\bar{i}}$ denotes the source document excluding the current sentence $\mathbf{f}_i$, and $D_{e,i-} =< \mathbf{e}_1, \mathbf{e}_2, ..., \mathbf{e}_{i-1} >$ which is the MT output up to previous sentence. If we keep the i.i.d. assumption of sentence generation that $D_{f,\bar{i}}$ and $D_{e,i-}$ are irrelevant to $< \mathbf{f}_i, \mathbf{e}_i >$, Eq. (2) backs off to standard sentence level translation that

$$\Pr(D_e|D_f) = \prod_{i=1}^{N} \Pr(\mathbf{e}_i|\mathbf{f}_i) \quad (3)$$

In our document level MT experiments, the estimate of $\Pr(\mathbf{e}_i|\mathbf{f}_i, D_{f,\bar{i}}, D_{e,i-})$ is divided into three separate modules combined by a normalization function:

$$\Pr(\mathbf{e}_i|\mathbf{f}_i, D_{f,\bar{i}}, D_{e,i-}) = \Theta\{\Pr(\mathbf{e}_i|\mathbf{f}_i), \Pr(\mathbf{e}_i|D_{f,\bar{i}}), \Pr(\mathbf{e}_i|\mathbf{f}_i, D_{e,i-})\} \quad (4)$$

Eq. (4) provides a scheme to integrate document level context features into translation process. In (4), $\Pr(\mathbf{e}_i|\mathbf{f}_i)$ is the standard sentence level translation model, $\Pr(\mathbf{e}_i|D_{f,\bar{i}})$ models how source side long distance features, e.g. feature regarding document topic or trigger word not in current sentence, impact the generation of $\mathbf{e}_i$, and $\Pr(\mathbf{e}_i|\mathbf{f}_i, D_{e,i-})$ can be viewed as a module exploring target side cross-sentence dependency between $\mathbf{e}_i$ and $D_{e,i-}$ to maintain translation consistency. $\Theta(.)$ is a normalized combination function that incorporates the three modules together to generate a probabilistic estimate for each hypothesis. Please note that in consideration of decoding speed, the proposed scheme does not search optimal hypothesis from document space directly, but rather enhance sentence translation by utilizing "global" information not limited to current sentence $\mathbf{f}_i$.

3 Document Level Context Features

The MT system adopted in our experiments is a direct translation model that utilizes the framework of Maximum Entropy to combine multiple types of lexical and syntactic features into translation (Ittycheriah and Roukos , 2007). The model has the following form:

$$\Pr(\mathbf{t}, j|\mathbf{s}) = \frac{\Pr_0(\mathbf{t}, j|\mathbf{s})}{Z} \exp \sum_k \alpha_k \phi_k(\mathbf{s}, \mathbf{t}) \quad (5)$$

where $\mathbf{s}$ is a source side word or phrase, $\mathbf{t}$ is the corresponding word or phrase translation, j is the transition distance from last translated word, $\Pr_0$ is a prior distribution related to phrase to phrase translation model and distortion model, and Z is a normalizing term. In Eq. (5), feature $\phi_k(\mathbf{s}, \mathbf{t})$ can be viewed as a binary question regarding lexical and syntactic attributes of $\mathbf{s}$ and $\mathbf{t}$, e.g. the question can be asked as if $\mathbf{s}$ and $\mathbf{t}$ share same POS class. Weight α_k is estimated using Iterative Scaling algorithm. Testing results from many evaluation tasks have shown that the MaxEnt system performs significantly better than regular phrase system and equally well to hierarchical system.

This section introduces three new types of document level features to model $\Pr(\mathbf{e}_i|D_{f,\bar{i}})$ and $\Pr(\mathbf{e}_i|\mathbf{f}_i, D_{e,i-})$. All the three types of features can be expressed as a triplet that $\phi_k(\mathbf{s}, \mathbf{t}) =< \mathbf{s}, c, \mathbf{t} >$, where c denotes a source or target side context word, identified from the span of entire document, which works as a *bridge* to connect $\mathbf{s}$ and $\mathbf{t}$. Please note that ϕ_k is still a binary feature which indicates if a particular context word c of certain type exists for $\mathbf{s}$ and $\mathbf{t}$.

3.1 Source Side Long Distance Context Feature

The first type of document level feature is motivated by the example shown in Table 1. The ambiguous Arabic word *mrsy* in the second sentence is mistranslated to English word *thank* because there is no local evidence to suggest it is a person name rather than a verb which is more common in training data and thus has higher translation probability in prior phrase model $\Pr_0$. In this case, if the words co-occurring with *mrsy* in the first sentence, i.e. *mHmd*(Mohamed), can be identified and passed to subsequent sentences, the probability of *mrsy* in the same document being translated into *Morsi* is likely to be increased.

ϕ_{LDC}, the long distance context (LDC) feature, is implemented as follows in training stage. Suppose the questioned source word w_f occur in sentence i with translation w_e. To identify the relevant LDC word c_f, the entire document excluding current sentence i is analyzed to find if the alignment (w_f, w_e) also occurs in other sentences. If yes, the source words within a window centered by w_f at that place are collected as the candidates for c_f. For instance, if the two Arabic sentences of Table 1 are in training data, the words *mHmd*(Mohamed) and *AlmSry*(Egyptian) in the first sentence will be viewed as the LDC word for *mrsy* in the second sentence, which results in two ϕ_{LDC} features i.e. $<$ *mrsy*, $mHmd$, *Morsi* $>$ and $<$ *mrsy*, $AlmSry$, *Morsi* $>$. As illustrated in Eq. (5), the two features can boost the translation probability of $\Pr(\textit{Morsi}|\textit{mrsy})$ for entire document if their weights are properly learned.

In training stage the check of aligned target word w_e is to ensure that only words with same meaning can be grouped together to share context features. In decoding where true w_e is unknown, we only use w_f instead of (w_f, w_e) to identify LDC word c_f. In our experiment function words are not allowed to be c_f, and $tf * idf$ score is used to filter out irrelevant context word.

3.2 Target Side Long Distance Context Feature

In order to improve the consistency of word choice in hypothesis generation, ϕ_{LDC} can be extended to target side to utilize the correlation between $D_{e,i-}$, the translation up to previous sentences, and $\mathbf{e}_i$, the translation of current sentence.

In training stage, ϕ_{tLDC}, the target side long distance context (tLDC) feature, is implemented in the following way. For a questioned source word w_f which is aligned to target word w_e in sentence i, we search their occurrence in all previous sentences from 1 to i-1. If exists, the *target* side words within the window centered by w_e in that sentence are identified as the candidates of tLDC word c_e for w_f. For the example used before, the English side words *Mohamed* and *president* are expected to make ϕ_{tLDC} features for the word *mrsy* in the second sentence.

The feature in decoding stage is implemented similarly by remembering previous translation $D_{e,i-}$ and its alignment to source words. Please note we don't use the hypothesized translation w_e itself as the tLDC word for w_f. This is because if it is an incorrect translation, such error can be spread to subsequent sentences to cause duplicated errors.

3.3 LSA based Quasi-Topic Feature

LDC and tLDC features are effective for repeated words. For words occurring once in a document, quasi-topic (QT) feature ϕ_{QT} is proposed as a back-off model which utilizes underlying topic information to eliminate ambiguity for these words.

In training stage, Latent Semantic Analysis (LSA) is performed on bilingual corpus consisting of a large set of documents with parallel sentences. Both source and target side words are mapped to vectors locating in a unified high dimensional space. For a questioned word w_f, its QT feature words are selected as follows. First all source side content words in the same document are calculated $tf * idf$ score, and sorted by their values from high to low. The top *L* words are then collected as the indicators of the underlying document topic. Next semantic similarity is measured between w_f and each of the *L* candidates based on Cosine metric. Only words showing strong correlation are selected as the QT feature c_t for w_f.

In decoding stage, MaxEnt model, as shown in Eq. (5), is utilized to estimate the probability of a hypothesis w_e being generated from w_f and QT feature words c_t. Our preliminary experiments found MaxEnt model performs better than commonly used vector based similarity metric. Generally speaking the QT features provide an implicit way for topic adaptation. When applied to translation, it changes the lexical distribution of target words to prefer the one more relevant to the hidden topic represented by c_t.

4 Related Work

Recent years witness a growing interest in exploiting long distance dependency to improve MT performance (Wong and Kit , 2012; Hardmeier et al., 2013). Domain adaptation and topic adaptation have attracted considerable attentions (Eidelman et al., 2012; Chen et al., 2013; Hewavitharana et al., 2013; Xiong and Zhang, 2013a; Hasler et al., 2014). There are also efforts that explore lexical cohesions with the help of WordNet to describe semantic co-occurrence from document span (Ben et al., 2013; Xiong et al., 2013b). Translation consistency, related to the observation of *one sense per discourse* (Gale et al., 1992; Carpuat , 2009; Guillou , 2013), has been discussed recently as an additional metric to evaluate translation quality (Xiao et al., 2011; Ture et al., 2012). There are also efforts for Arabic proper name disambiguation (Hermjakob et al., 2008). This paper investigates novel document level features to utilize lexical and semantic dependencies between sentences. In contrast to (Ben et al., 2013; Xiong et al., 2013b), our work doesn't need external resources e.g. WordNet or human efforts to identify word cohesion and isn't limited to certain word type. The advantage makes the proposed

Model	MT03		MT04		MT05		MT06		MT08		MT09	
Baseline	39.19	57.01	37.15	56.12	35.46	58.71	41.16	51.79	42.60	50.62	42.27	51.53
+LDC	38.99	57.58	37.19	56.43	35.41	59.20	41.29	52.27	42.45	**51.45**	42.18	52.02
+tLDC	39.02	57.32	37.16	56.41	35.32	58.91	41.12	52.03	42.56	51.14	42.16	51.77
+QT	39.10	57.16	37.03	56.23	35.37	58.79	41.14	51.80	42.52	50.75	42.22	51.68
+LDC+tLDC	**38.46**	**57.83**	36.83	56.50	34.97	59.64	40.91	52.23	42.25	51.26	41.92	52.26
+L+tL+QT	38.54	57.73	**36.73**	**56.75**	**34.84**	**59.75**	**40.68**	**52.40**	**42.05**	51.42	**41.82**	**52.47**

Table 2: MT performance on MT03-MT09 in terms of TER and BLEU.

features more suited to low-resource languages.

5 Experiments

Our system is primarily built for an Arabic dialect to English MT task. The training data contains LDC-released parallel corpora for the BOLT project. There are totally 6.9M sentence pairs with 207M Arabic ATB tokens and 201M English words, respectively. Three types of word alignments, maximum entropy, GIZA++ and HMM alignment, are used to generate phrase pairs as the prior model in Eq. (5). Approximately 1.8M in-domain sentence pairs distributed in 106K documents, consisting of 36M Arabic ATB tokens and 38M English words, are selected to learn sentence and document level MaxEnt features. The tuning set contains 3700 sentences in 350 documents which are mainly weblog and dialect data. Module weights for prior model, sentence and document level features, LM, and other components are tuned with PRO algorithm (Hopkins and May , 2011) to minimize the score of *(TER-BLEU)*.

We select NIST Arabic MT03-MT09 as the test sets. Results are shown in Table 2. The two numbers in each score column are TER followed by BLEU. The best performance is illustrated in bold. The result of MT system using only sentence level features is listed as the baseline. The integrations of the three document features are denoted as +LDC, +tLDC and +QT, respectively. Table 2 shows that substantial improvements of translation quality, measured by both TER and BLEU, are achieved for most of the test sets.

To understand the effectiveness of document features on different type of data, we further split MT09 set into newswire and weblog, and conduct test on them. Table 3 shows that long distance context features, ϕ_{LDC} and ϕ_{tLDC}, perform better on newswire than on weblog respecting to the relative improvement of TER and BLEU. One reason to explain this is that the rate of content word repetition is different on the two types of data. According to our calculation, about 19% content words in newswire repeat themselves while the ratio on weblog is about 13%.

Model	MT09-nw		MT09-wl	
Baseline	33.85	61.15	50.46	41.35
+LDC+tLDC	33.38	61.98	50.23	42.02

Table 3: MT performance on MT09 newswire and weblog in terms of TER and BLEU.

Table 4 shows the new MT output of the two example sentences. Three LDC features are fired for *mrsy* in the 2nd sentence: ⟨*mrsy,AlmSry,Morsi*⟩, ⟨*mrsy,mHmd,Morsi*⟩ and ⟨*mrsy,ySf,Morsi*⟩ where the 3rd one is a false alarm. Items in the triplets correspond to source word, context word and hypothesized word, respectively. Three tLDC features are also fired including ⟨*mrsy,Egyptian,Morsi*⟩, ⟨*mrsy,Mohamed,Morsi*⟩ and ⟨*mrsy,describes,Morsi*⟩ where the 3rd one is also a false alarm. To our surprise, word *Alr}ys* and its translation *president* aren't fired as context feature. Analysis found that this is due to the fact that our LDC training data was collected before Dr. Morsi was elected as president in 2012. Therefore no relevant feature is learned into MaxEnt model.

AR:	Alr}ys AlmSry AlmEzwl mHmd mrsy ysf nfsh b⟩nh r}ys Aljmhwryp
MT:	The deposed Egyptian president Mohamed Morsi describes himself as the president of the republic
AR:	mrsy ytHdY AlqADy fy mHAkmth bthmp Alhrwb mn Alsjn
MT:	Morsi defies the judge in his trial on charges of escaping from prison

Table 4: New MT results using document level features

References

Guosheng Ben, Deyi Xiong, Zhiyang Teng, Yajuan Lu and Qun Liu. 2013. Bilingual Lexical Cohesion Trigger Model for Document-Level Machine Translation. in *Proceedings of the 51st Annual Meeting of the Association for Computational Linguistics*. Sofia, Bulgaria.

Marine Carpuat. 2009. One Translation per Discourse. in *Proceedings of the NAACL HLT Workshop on Semantic Evaluations: Recent Achievements and Future Directions*. Boulder, USA.

Yee Seng Chan, Hwee Tou Ng, and David Chiang. 2007. Word Sense Disambiguation Improves Statistical Machine Translation. in *Proceedings of the 45th Annual Meeting of the Association for Computational Linguistics*. Prague, Czech.

Boxing Chen, Roland Kuhn and George Foster. 2013. Vector Space Model for Adaptation in Statistical Machine Translation. in *Proceedings of the 51th Annual Meeting of the Association for Computational Linguistics*. Sofia, Bulgaria.

Vladimir Eidelman, Jordan Boyd-Graber and Philip Resnik. 2012. Topic Models for Dynamic Translation Model Adaptation. in *Proceedings of the 50th Annual Meeting of the Association for Computational Linguistics*. Jeju Island, Korea.

William A. Gale, Kenneth W. Church, and David Yarowsky. 1992. One sense per discourse. in *Proceedings of the workshop on Speech and Natural Language, HLT-91*.

Liane Guillou. 2013. Analysing Lexical Consistency in Translation. in *ACL Proceedings of the Workshop on Discourse in Machine Translation*.

Christian Hardmeier, Sara Stymne, Jrg Tiedemann and Joakim Nivre. 2013. Docent: A Document-Level Decoder for Phrase-Based Statistical Machine Translation. in *Proceedings of the 51st Annual Meeting of the Association for Computational Linguistics*. Sofia, Bulgaria.

Eva Hasler, Phil Blunsom, Philipp Koehn, and Barry Haddow. 2014. Dynamic Topic Adaptation for Phrase-based MT. in *Proceedings of the 14th Conference of the European Chapter of the Association for Computational Linguistics*. Gothenburg, Sweden.

Ulf Hermjakob, Kevin Knight and Hal Daume III. 2008. Name Translation in Statistical Machine Translation Learning When to Transliterate. in *Proceedings of ACL-08: HLT*. Columbus, Ohio, USA.

Sanjika Hewavitharana, Dennis N. Mehay, Sankaranarayanan Ananthakrishnan and Prem Natarajan. 2013. Incremental Topic-Based Translation Model Adaptation for Conversational Spoken Language Translation. in *Proceedings of the 51st Annual Meeting of the Association for Computational Linguistics*. Sofia, Bulgaria.

Mark Hopkins and Jonathan May. 2011. Tuning as Ranking. in *Proceedings of the 2011 Conference on Empirical Methods in Natural Language Processing*. Edinburgh, UK.

Abraham Ittycheriah and Salim Roukos. 2007. Direct Translation Model 2. in *Proceedings of NAACL HLT 2007*. Rochester, NY.

Ferhan Ture, Douglas W. Oard and Philip Resnik. 2012. Encouraging Consistent Translation Choices. in *Proceedings of the 2012 Conference of the North American Chapter of the Association for Computational Linguistics: Human Language Technologies*. Montral, Canada.

Billy T. M. Wong and Chunyu Kit. 2012. Extending Machine Translation Evaluation Metrics with Lexical Cohesion To Document Level. in *Proceedings of the 2012 Joint Conference on Empirical Methods in Natural Language Processing and Computational Natural Language Learning*. Jeju Island, Korea.

Tong Xiao, Jingbo Zhu, Shujie Yao, and Hao Zhang. 2011. Document-level Consistency Verification in Machine Translation. in *Machine Translation Summit XIII*. Xiamen, China.

Deyi Xiong and Min Zhang. 2013. A Topic-Based Coherence Model for Statistical Machine Translation. in *Proceedings of the Twenty-Seventh AAAI Conference on Artificial Intelligence*. Bellevue, USA.

Deyi Xiong, Ding Yang, Min Zhang and Chew Lim Tan. 2013. Lexical Chain Based Cohesion Models for Document-Level Statistical Machine Translation. in *Proceedings of the 2013 Conference on Empirical Methods in Natural Language Processing*. Seattle, USA.

Exploration of Inter- and Intralingual Variation of Discourse Phenomena

Ekaterina Lapshinova-Koltunski
Saarland University
FR4.6, University Campus, D-66123 Saarbrücken
e.lapshinova@mx.uni-saarland.de

Abstract

In this paper, we analyse cross-linguistic variation of discourse phenomena, i.e. coreference, discourse relations and modality. We will show that contrasts in the distribution of these phenomena can be observed across languages, genres, and text production types, i.e. translated and non-translated ones. Translations, regardless of the method they were produced with, are different from their source texts and from the comparable originals in the target language, as it was stated in studies on *translationese*. These differences can be automatically detected and analysed with exploratory and automatic clustering techniques. The extracted frequency-based profiles of variables under analysis (languages, genres, text production types) can be used in further studies, e.g. in the development and enhancement of MT systems, or in further NLP applications.

1 Introduction

Although considerable research aiming at enhancing machine-translated texts with discourse properties achieved positive results in recent years, see e.g. (Webber et al., 2013; Hardmeier, 2014) or (Meyer et al., 2015), some document-wide properties of automatically translated texts still require improvement, as translation models are induced from stand-alone pairs of sentences. Moreover, target language models approximate the target language on the string level only, whereas target texts have properties that go beyond those of their individual sentences and that reveal themselves in the frequency and distribution of certain structures. These frequency- and distribution-based properties of translated and non-translated texts are in focus of corpus-based translation studies. However, these properties (in form of higher-level language models) may also be useful for natural language processing (NLP), including machine translation (MT).

In this paper, we show an example of a corpus-based analysis of interlingual (between English and German) and intralingual (across different genres) variation of discourse properties in translated and non-translated texts. In particular, this paper will focus on various types of discourse relational devices, pronominal referring expressions, as well as modal meanings expressed with particular modal verbs. The frequencies of these discourse features will be automatically extracted from English-German comparable corpora which also contain multiple translations produced with several methods, including manual and automatic ones. We will compare the distributions of these features in both languages, as well as in translations from English to German, paying attention to their variation across genres available in the dataset. We will also consider differences in their distributions in human and machine translation. For our analysis, we apply exploratory and unsupervised classification techniques. The obtained information on the frequency-based interlingual and intralingual differences may be valuable for linguistic studies on language contrasts, human translation, and may find application in NLP and especially MT.

2 Related Work

2.1 Discourse properties in English and German

Various discourse phenomena have been in focus of several translation studies and those on language contrasts dealing with English and German. Recent years have seen an increase in the number of works employing corpus-based methods for their analysis. However, multilingual stud-

Proceedings of the Second Workshop on Discourse in Machine Translation (DiscoMT), pages 158–167,
Lisbon, Portugal, 17 September 2015.

ies are mostly concerned with individual phenomena in particular genres, see e.g. (Bührig and House, 2004) for particular cohesive conjunctions or adverbs in prepared speeches, (Zinsmeister et al., 2012) for abstract anaphora in parliament debates, and (Taboada and Gómez-González, 2012) for particular coherence relations. The latter, however, considers two modes: spoken and written, and states that the differences between modes are more prominent than between languages. Kunz and Lapshinova-Koltunski (2015) and Kunz et al. (2015) show that distributions of different discourse phenomena are not only mode- but also genre-dependent. The authors show this for a number of textual phenomena, analysing structural and functional subtypes of coreference, substitution, discourse connectives and ellipsis. Their dataset includes several genres, and they are able to identify contrasts and commonalities across languages (English and German) and genres with respect to the subtypes of all textual phenomena under analysis, showing that these languages differ as to the degree of variation between individual genres. Moreover, there is more variation in the realisation of discourse devices in German than English. The authors attested the main differences in terms of preferred meaning relations: a preference for explicitly realising logico-semantic relations by discourse markers and a tendency to realise relations of identity by coreference. Interestingly, similar meaning relations are realised by different subtypes of discourse phenomena in different languages and genres.

2.2 Discourse properties in human and machine translation

Cross-lingual contrasts stated on the basis of non-translated data are also of great importance for translation. Kunz et al. (2015) suggest preferred translation strategies on the basis of contrastive interpretations for the results of their quantitative analysis, which show that language contrasts are even more pronounced if we compare languages per genre. These contrasts exist in the features used for creating textual relations. Therefore, they suggest that, for instance, when translating popular science texts from English into German translators should more extensively use linguistic means expressing textual relations. Overall, they claim that translators should use more explicit devices translating from English into German, e.g. demonstrative pronouns should be used more often instead of personal pronouns (e.g. *dies/das* instead of *es/it*). The opposite translation strategies should be used when translating from German to English.

However, studies of translated language show that translators do not necessarily apply such strategies. For instance, Zinsmeister et al. (2012) demonstrate that translations in general tend to preserve the source language anaphor's categories, functions and positions, which results in the *shining through* effect (shining through of the source language preferences, see (Teich, 2003)) in both translation directions. Additionally, due to the tendency to explicate textual relations, translators tend to use more nominal coreference instead of pronominal one. *Explicitation* (tendency of translations to be more explicit than their sources, see (Vinay and Darbelnet, 1958) and (Blum-Kulka, 1986)) along with *shining through* belong to the characteristics of translated texts caused by peculiarities of translation process. A number of works on discourse connectives, e.g. (Becher, 2011; Bisiada, 2014; Meyer and Webber, 2013) and (Li et al., 2014), show implicit/explicit discourse expression divergence in both human and machine translation. There are several studies that attempt to incorporate information on discourse relations or other discourse properties into MT, see for instance, those by Le Nagard and Koehn (2010), Hardmeier and Federico (2010) and Guillou (2012), or those presented within the first DiscoMT workshop, see (Webber et al., 2013). Most of them employ parallel corpora, thus, the approximation of the target language is based on translations, which, however, possess characteristics that differ them from non-translated texts originally written in a target language, also in terms of discourse properties. This paper will consider discourse-related characteristics that differ translation from non-translated texts, and also differentiate human from machine translations.

3 Methodology

3.1 Data

As we focus on variation of discourse phenomena in English and German, as well as English-German translations, our data should contain both English-German parallel texts and non-translated comparable texts in German. Furthermore, as we are also interested in linguistic variation in terms of genre, the texts should be from different genres. For this reason, we had to dismiss the typical corpora used in MT, e.g. Europarl (Koehn, 2005) or TED talks, as translated texts in these resources are not comparable. The latter contains multilingual subtitles which are produced under different restrictions than those of translations. We also expect that some of the phenomena under analysis might be omitted in the subtitles, as this is recommended in the guidelines[1]. So, we select two corpora which contain English-German parallel and comparable texts from different genres. English and German originals (EO and GO) were extracted from CroCo (Hansen-Schirra et al., 2012), whereas German translations originate from the VARTRA corpus (Lapshinova-Koltunski, 2013), as it contains multiple translations of the CroCo English originals produced both manually and automatically (HU and MT).

The whole dataset totals 406 texts which cover seven genres: political essays (ESS), fictional texts (FIC), instruction manuals (INS), popular-scientific articles (POP), letters to shareholders (SH), prepared political speeches (SP), and tourism leaflets (TOU). The decision to include this wide range of genres is justified by the need for heterogeneous data for our experiment. The number of words per genre in comprises ca. 36 thousand tokens. We tag both English and German data with the TreeTagger tools (Schmid, 1994).

3.2 Feature selection

Linguistic relations between textual elements help recipients in their cognitive interpretation as to how different thematic concepts are connected. These relations are indicated by particular structures that language producers employ, e.g. grammatical items such as connectives, personal and demonstrative pronouns, substitute forms, elliptical constructions and lexical items, such as nouns, verbs and adjectives. As already mentioned in Section 1 above, we will analyse discourse relations, coreference and modality.

For discourse relations, we will analyse connectives classified according to the semantic relations they convey. Our classification is based on semantic relations defined by Halliday and Hasan (1976) and includes additive (relation of addition, e.g. *and, in addition, moreover*), adversative (relation of contrast/alternative, e.g. *yet, although, by contrast*), causal (relation of causality/dependence, e.g. *because, therefore, that's why*), temporal (temporal relation between events such as *after, afterwards, at the same time*) and modal relations (expressing rather a pragmatic meaning, in which evaluation of the speaker is involved, e.g. *unfortunately, surely*).

Demonstrative and personal pronouns (such as *this, that, she, his, theirs, it*, etc.) will serve as triggers of coreference. We also consider distributions of general nouns, e.g. *plan, case, fact*, which commonly function as abstract anaphora (Zinsmeister et al., 2012). For the analysis of modality, we consider frequencies of modal verbs grouped according to the modal meanings defined by Biber et al. (1999): permission (*can/could, may/might*), volition (*will, would, shall*) and obligation (*must, ought to, should, need to, have got to, suppose to*).

feature pattern	discourse property
permission obligation volition	modality
additive adversative causal temporal modal	discourse relations
general.nouns perspron dempron	coreference

Table 1: Features under analysis

The set of 11 selected features is outlined in Table 1. The first column denotes the extracted and analysed feature patterns, the second represents the corresponding discourse property. For the extraction of the frequencies of these feature patterns, we use a number of regular expressions based on string, part-of-speech and chunk tags, as well as further constraints, e.g. position in a sentence or in a text. Frequency information is collected both per text, and per subcorpus (e.g. per genre in a certain language).

3.3 Methods

For our analysis, we use exploratory and also unsupervised classification (automatic clustering) techniques which will allow us to observe differences between groups of texts and subcorpora, and also to discriminate between them on the basis of discourse features described in Section 3.2.

We apply correspondence analysis (CA) (Venables and Smith, 2010; Baayen, 2008; Greenacre,

[1]See the subtitling guidelines http://translations.ted.org/wiki/How_to_Compress_Subtitles

2007) that is conceptually similar to principal component analysis (PCA), with the difference that the data is scaled so that rows and columns are treated equivalently. Thus, this technique will help us to see not only which variables (e.g. languages or genres) have similarities, but also possible correlation of these variables with discourse features contributing to these similarities, as distances between between dependent and independent variables are calculated. These distances are then represented in a two-dimensional map, and the larger the differences between subcorpora or texts, the further apart they are on the map. Likewise, dissimilar categories of discourse phenomena are further apart. Proximity between subcorpora and discourse features in the merged map is as good an approximation as possible of the correlation between them. In computing this low-dimensional approximation, CA transforms the correlations between rows and columns of our table into a set of uncorrelated variables, called principal axes or dimensions. These dimensions are computed in such a way that any subset of k dimensions accounts for as much variation as possible in one dimension, the first two principal axes account for as much variation as possible in two dimensions, and so on. In this way, we can identify new meaningful underlying variables, which ideally correlate with such variables as language or genre, indicating the reasons for the similarities or differences between these subcorpora. The length of the arrows in the graph indicates how pronounced a discourse feature is, see (Jenset and McGillivray, 2012) for details. The position of the points in relation to the arrows indicates the relative importance of a feature for a subcorpus. The arrows pointing in the direction of an axis indicate a high correlation with the respective dimension, and thus, a high contribution of the feature to this dimension.

The results of automatic clustering will indicate differences and similarities between the languages (English and German) and their varieties (genres). Moreover, we can also discover differences between non-translated and (manually or automatically) translated texts. We decide for unsupervised techniques, in favour of different genres contained in our data, and supervised classification performs better with single genre data, so that in a supervised scenario, we would need to perform several classification tasks. We apply *hierarchical cluster analysis* (HCA), see (Hothorn and Everitt, 2014) and (Everitt et al., 2011). This clustering technique is connectivity-based as its core idea is that objects are more related to nearby objects than to objects farther away. Objects, in our case texts and subcorpora, are connected to form clusters based on their distance measured here on the basis of the feature distributions. We calculate the distance by the Euclidean distance which is one of the most straightforward and generally accepted ways of computing distances between objects in a multi-dimensional space. The results of hierarchical clusters are represented graphically in a dendrogram, which is a branching diagram that represents the relationships of similarity among a group of entities. The arrangement of the branches tells us which texts/subcorpora (on leaves) are most similar to each other. The height of the branch points indicates how similar or different they are from each other. Ward's method (also called Ward's minimum variance method) is employed to perform clustering. This method minimises the total within-cluster variance after merging.

The main drawback of this technique is that the number of clusters needs to be specified in advance. Therefore, we apply a technique based on bootstrap resampling, with the help of which we are able to produce *p-value*-based clusters, i.e. that are highly supported by the data will have large *p-values*[2]. The output dendrogram demonstrates two types of p-values: AU (Approximately Unbiased) p-value and BP (Bootstrap Probability) value. AU p-value, which is computed by multi-scale bootstrap resampling, is a better approximation to unbiased p-value than BP value computed by normal bootstrap resampling.

4 Analyses

4.1 Discourse properties in English and German

First, we analyse English and German non-translated texts, to define the differences between these languages in terms of discourse properties. We perform CA on the subset of data containing originals only. In the first step, the dataset is labelled with text IDs only (e.g. EO_001, GO_010, etc.).

In Table 2, we present the Eigenvalues calculated for each dimension to assess how well our

[2]We use pvclust() package available in the R environment (version 3.0.2; (Team, 2013)).

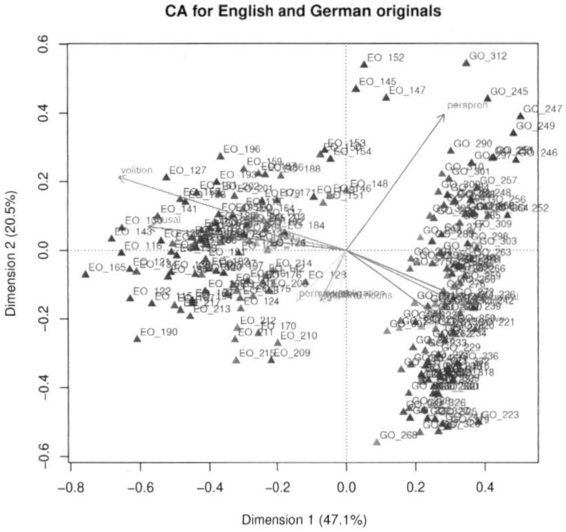

Figure 1: Variation of discourse phenomena across languages

data is represented in the graph[3]. The cumulative value for dimensions allow us to analyse how well our data is represented in the graph.

dim	value	%	cum%
1	0.109830	47.1	47.1
2	0.047842	20.5	67.6
3	0.018943	8.1	75.7
4	..		
Total:	0.233192	100.0	

Table 2: Contribution of dimensions for variation across languages

We plot the results in a two-dimensional graph in Figure 1, representing the first two dimensions, which explain 67.60% (cumulative value) of the data inertia. The second dimension although covering only 20,50% is also important for our analysis if we want to explain more than 50% of the data variation. The rest of inertia remain unexplained with the two-dimensional representation[4].

Concerning dimension 1 (47,10% of inertia), we see a clear distinction between English and German texts (along the x-axis on the left and on the right from zero respectively). So, the distinction along this dimension reflects language contrasts in the use of particular discourse features, i.e. different types of discourse relations via connectives for German, and coreference via demonstrative pronouns, modal meaning of volition and causal logico-semantic relations for English. The assumption is that the second dimension indicates distinction between genres available in our dataset, which is not seen in the data labelled with text IDs only.

For the sake of the visualisation of results, we perform the same analyses labelling our dataset with genres, and also reducing it to subcorpora corresponding to different genres and languages (e.g. EO_ESS containing all texts of English political essays, etc.), see the resulting plot in Figure 2.

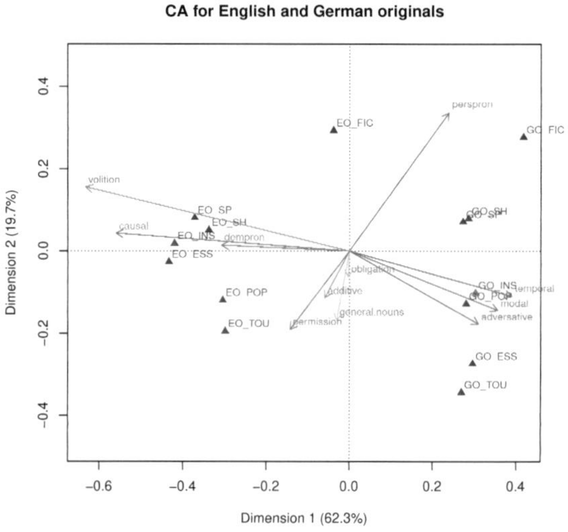

Figure 2: Variation of discourse phenomena across genres

This time, we achieve a cumulative value of 82%, with the first dimension covering over 60% of the data variance, see Table 3.

dim	value	%	cum%
1	0.103453	62.3	62.3
2	0.032665	19.7	81.9
3	0.012870	7.7	89.7
4	..		
Total:	0.166179	100.0	

Table 3: Contribution of dimensions for variation across genres

As in the previous graph, this dimension still indicates language contrasts in the dataset, with the same features contributing to these differences. The second dimension (the *y*-axis) clearly indicates language-independent differences in genres:

[3]'dim' lists dimensions, 'value' – Eigenvalues converted to percentages of explained variation in '%' and calculated as cumulative explained variation with the addition of each dimension in 'cum'.

[4]This means that we are not able to explain ca. 30% of the variation in our data, which might indicate differences to further parameters, e.g. according to individual authors or translators.

tourism, essays and popular-scientific texts grouping together below zero (with additives, modality and general nouns as features), and fiction, political speeches and letters to shareholders above zero. The features of instruction manuals seem to be language-dependent, as the English and the German INS subcorpora are positioned on the opposite axis sides. Fictional texts of both languages are positioned at the edge of the genre axis, with personal pronouns contributing to this grouping, which coincides with the results obtained by Kunz and Lapshinova-Koltunski (2015) and Kunz et al. (2015) showing that fiction is best distinguished from the other genres for both languages with supervised classification techniques.

Automatic clustering deliver similar results, see Figure 3, with the exception of English fictional texts, which are classified along with the German fictional texts into the cluster of German subcorpora.

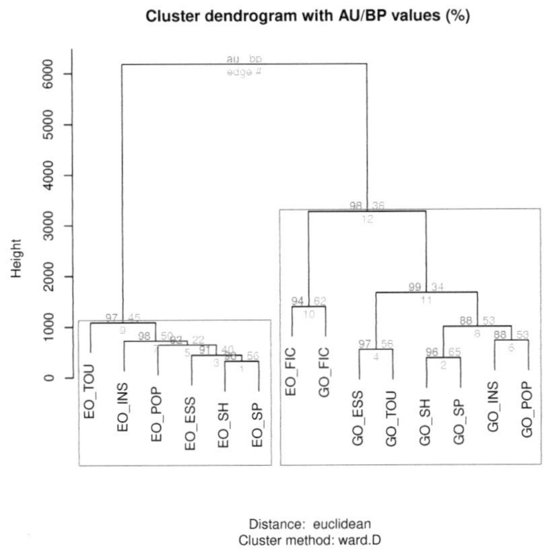

Figure 3: Classification of English and German subcorpora

4.2 Originals and translations

In the next step, we include translated texts into our analysis. The translation data is labelled with HU and MT, indicating manual or automatic method of translation, whereas digits indicate translation variants. Thus, MT1 and MT2 are produced with two different SMT systems, and HU1 and HU2 were produced by two different groups of translators. The results of the bootstrap resampling[5] suggests two classes in our data, illustrated in Figure 4.

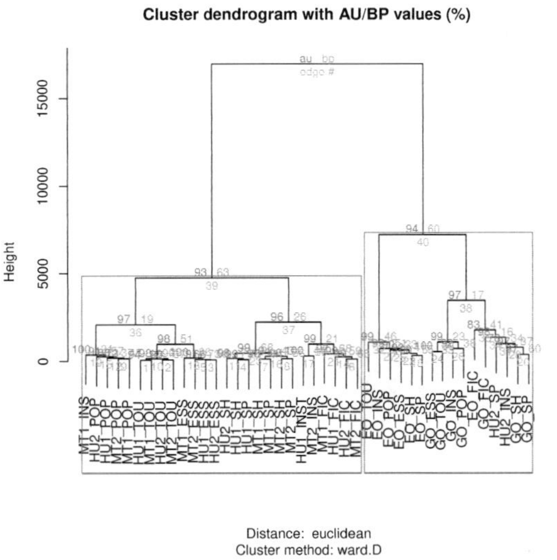

Figure 4: Classification of originals and translations

As seen from the graph, our dataset is clustered into originals (on the right side) and translations (on the left side), which is apparently the most prominent difference in this data. This coincides with the statements of the theory of *translationese*, see (Gellerstam, 1986) or (Baker, 1993), that translations have their specific feature differing them from the source texts and comparable originals in the target language. A number of studies have shown that these features can be used to automatically discriminate between translated and non-translated texts, such as (Baroni and Bernardini, 2006; Ilisei et al., 2010; Koppel and Ordan, 2011). Our results show that this discrimination is also possible with discourse features, which means that translations differ from originals also in these properties.

The only exceptions in our results are manually produced translations of political speeches (HU2-SP) and instruction manuals (HU2-INS) classified together with political speeches and letters to shareholders originally written in German. Most of the smaller clusters within the bigger 'non-translated' class are grouped rather according to languages than genres, e.g. political essays, tourism texts, manuals and popular-scientific arti-

[5]We achieve a good classification performance with an average error rate of 0,06.

cles.

Next, we want to prove if the observed difference between originals and translations is dependent on the source or the target language (which would indicate the phenomenon of shining through or normalisation). For this reason, we perform two classification experiments applying the same clustering technique and including German translation data and their English sources in the first experiment (Figure 5), and the same German translations together with German comparable non-translated texts in the second (Figure 6). The results show that in both cases, the data is separated into translations and originals, with the same two subcorpora as exceptions. So, no shining through/normalisation effect can be detected.

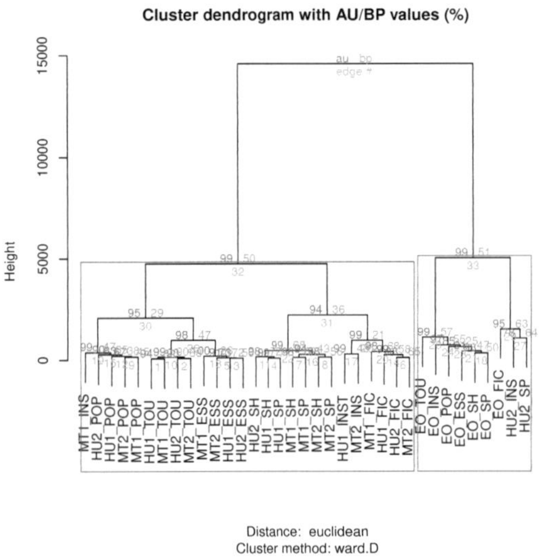

Figure 5: German translations and non-translated English source texts

4.3 Human and machine translations

Finally, we perform classification on the data subset containing translations only. The resulting dendrogram in Figure 7 reveals four heterogeneous classes of translations, all containing both manually and automatically produced outputs. The two human translations that were classified with the non-translated data in previous experiments in Section 4.2 form a cluster on their own. This is the only cluster containing one type of translations in the whole data subset. The other three clusters consist of a mixture of human and machine translations. They presumably form genre-sensitive

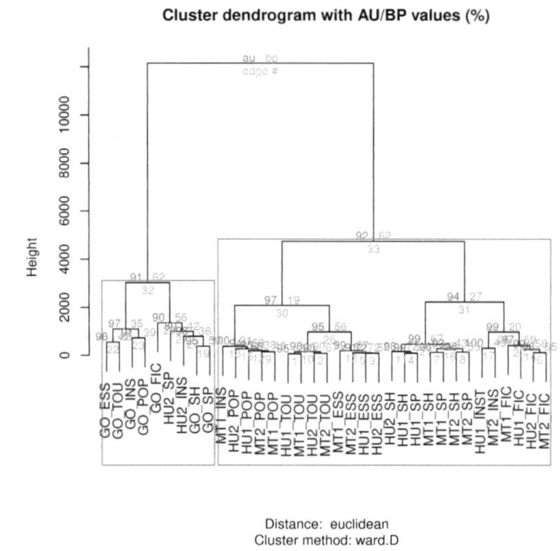

Figure 6: German translations and comparable German non-translated texts

clusters, as we observe groupings of translations of the same genres on smaller cluster nodes.

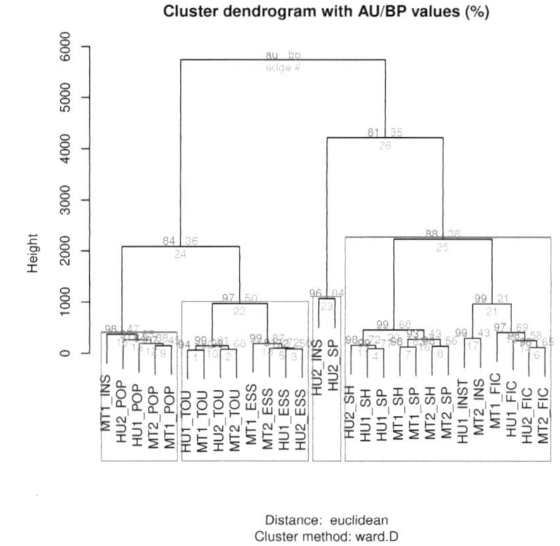

Figure 7: Human and machine translations

On the one hand, this suggests that genre is more prominent than translation method, i.e. there are more differences between various genres than between human and machine translations in the data under analysis, if discourse properties are concerned. On the other hand, the results may also indicate that discourse features are more informative in genre classification than in the distinction into human vs. machine. Similar results were shown by Zampieri and Lapshinova-Koltunski (2015) who were able to achieve better results in the classification between genres than between translation methods, operating with delexicalised n-grams and using supervised classification techniques. Therefore, we claim that the distributions of the discourse features under analysis are genre-dependent, which coincides with the results of the previous analyses within a number of multilingual genre studies.

As seen in the analyses above (see Figures 4, 5, 6 and 7), political speeches and letters to shareholders are always clustered together in translated data. Similar observations were also made in (Lapshinova-Koltunski, inpress) for a different set of features. According to Neumann (2013), these two registers seem to be closer in English than in German, and so, their commonalities in our translation data might indicate the influence of the source texts. However, CA performed on German and English originals reveal that these register are similar not only within each language, but also cross-lingually, as they are situated on the same level of the y-axis, see Figure 2. As a result, translations also reveal these similarities.

5 Conclusion and Discussion

We have demonstrated an example of a corpus-based analysis of discourse properties in a multilingual dataset which contains both translated and non-translated texts, using exploratory and automatic clustering techniques. The results show that discourse-related features vary depending on the languages and genres involved. Languages, even such closely related ones as English and German, have different preferences in the usage of discourse properties, which are also prone to interlingual variation in terms of genres. This knowledge on contrasts will be valuable not only for contrastive linguistics and translation studies, but also for natural language processing including statistical MT, as it is available in form of frequency-based information and can be used for language models. The observed variation of discourse properties is also influenced by the nature of the texts (translated vs. non-translated). Both human and machine translations have constellations of discourse properties different from those of their underlying originals, and from comparable non-translated texts in the target language.

Comparing machine-translated texts with those translated by humans, we stated that genre-membership of translations determines more prominent differences between them than the methods they were translated with (manual vs. automatic). This points to the fact that machine translations resemble rather human translations than non-translated texts in both the source and the target languages, if discourse features are considered. On the one hand, this confirms the hypothesis of *levelling out* indicating that individual translated texts are more alike than individual original texts, in both source and target languages[6]. On the other hand, our results conform to those obtained by Rabinovich and Wintner (2015) who show that multi-genre data is more difficult to be classified with translationese (translation-specific) features.

Furthermore, the results seem to contradict the findings in (Guzman et al., 2014), which used discourse information to develop automatic MT evaluation metrics. However, we believe that the differences in the outcome are caused by the nature of the dataset: translations in the present study originate from multiple genres, whereas Guzman et al. (2014) use news texts only. Intralingual variation in both English and German imply that if a model is applicable for a certain genre in one language, it is not necessarily applicable to a different genre of the same language, as the distributions of the underlying phenomena differ (sometimes) tremendously.

The contrasts between translated and non-translated texts suggest that we need more research on how to incorporate discourse-based language models induced from comparable and not parallel data. In this way, we might achieve a closer approximation of machine translation to non-translated texts in a target language. This is relevant not only for the development of machine translation systems but also for their evaluation, as the similarities between a reference and an MT output might be confounding in the quality judgement, if discourse phenomena are concerned. In the future, experiments could be planned that apply the present results for the development and evaluation of MT. Moreover, it would be interesting to learn if the differences between translated and original text affect perception of the quality of the text, for which experiments involving human judgements are required.

[6]Variation in individual translators is not considered.

References

R. Harald Baayen. 2008. *Analyzing Linguistic Data. A Practical Introduction to Statistics Using R.* Cambridge University Press.

Mona Baker. 1993. Corpus linguistics and translation studies: Implications and applications. In G. Francis Baker M. and E. Tognini-Bonelli, editors, *Text and Technology: in Honour of John Sinclair*, pages 233–250. Benjamins, Amsterdam.

Marco Baroni and Silvia Bernardini. 2006. A new approach to the study of translationese: Machine-learning the difference between original and translated text. *Literary and Linguistic Computing*, 21(3):259–274.

Viktor Becher. 2011. *Explicitation and implicitation in translation. A corpus-based study of English-German and German-English translations of business texts.* Ph.D. thesis, Universität Hamburg.

Douglas Biber, Stig Johansson, Geoffrey Leech, Susan Conrad, and Edward Finegan. 1999. *Longman Grammar of Spoken and Written English.* Longman, Harlow.

Mario Bisiada. 2014. Lösen sie Schachtelsätze möglichst auf: The impact of editorial guidelines on sentence splitting in german business article translations. *Applied Linguistics*, 3.

Shoshana Blum-Kulka. 1986. Shifts of cohesion and coherence in translation. In Juliane House and Shoshana Blum-Kulka, editors, *Interlingual and intercultural communication*, pages 17–35. Gunter Narr, Tübingen.

Kristin Bührig and Juliane House. 2004. Connectivity in translation: Transitions from orality to literacy. In J. House and J. Rehbein, editors, *Multilingual Communication*, pages 87–114. Benjamins, Amsterdam.

Brian S. Everitt, Sabine Landau, Morven Leese, and Daniel Stahl. 2011. *Cluster Analysis.* Wiley series in probability and statistics. Wiley.

Martin Gellerstam. 1986. Translationese in Swedish novels translated from English. In L. Wollin and H. Lindquist, editors, *Translation Studies in Scandinavia*, pages 88–95. CWK Gleerup, Lund.

Michael J. Greenacre. 2007. *Correspondence analysis in practice.* Chapman & Hall/CRC, Boca Raton.

Liane Guillou. 2012. Improving pronoun translation for statistical machine translation. In *EACL 2012, 13th Conference of the European Chapter of the Association for Computational Linguistics, Avignon, France, April 23-27, 2012*, pages 1–10.

Francisco Guzman, Shafiq Joty, Lluís Màrquez, and Preslav Nakov. 2014. Using discourse structure improves machine translation evaluation. In *Proceedings of the 52nd Annual Meeting of the Association for Computational Linguistics (Volume 1: Long Papers)*, pages 687–698. Association for Computational Linguistics.

M.A.K. Halliday and Ruqaiya Hasan. 1976. *Cohesion in English.* Longman, London, New York.

Silvia Hansen-Schirra, Stella Neumann, and Erich Steiner. 2012. *Cross-linguistic Corpora for the Study of Translations. Insights from the Language Pair English-German.* de Gruyter, Berlin, New York.

Christian Hardmeier and Marcello Federico. 2010. Modelling pronominal anaphora in statistical machine translation. In *IWSLT (International Workshop on Spoken Language Translation); Paris, France; December 2nd and 3rd, 2010.*, pages 283–289.

Christian Hardmeier. 2014. *Discourse in statistical machine translation.* Ph.D. thesis, Uppsala: Acta Universitatis Upsaliensis.

Torsten Hothorn and Brian S. Everitt. 2014. *A Handbook of Statistical Analyses Using R.* Chapman & Hall/CRC Press, 3rd edition.

Iustina Ilisei, Diana Inkpen, Gloria Corpas Pastor, and Ruslan Mitkov. 2010. Identification of translationese: A machine learning approach. In *Computational linguistics and intelligent text processing*, pages 503–511. Springer Berlin Heidelberg.

Gard B. Jenset and Barbara McGillivray. 2012. Multivariate analyses of affix productivity in translated english. In Michael P. Oakes and Meng Ji, editors, *Quantitative Methods in Corpus-Based Translation Studies*, pages 301–324. John Benjamins.

Philipp Koehn. 2005. Europarl: A Parallel Corpus for Statistical Machine Translation. In *Conference Proceedings: the tenth Machine Translation Summit*, pages 79–86, Phuket, Thailand. AAMT.

Moshe Koppel and Noam Ordan. 2011. Translationese and its dialects. *Proceedings of the 49th Annual Meeting of the Association for Computational Linguistics (ACL-2011)*, June.

Kerstin Kunz and Ekaterina Lapshinova-Koltunski. 2015. Cross-linguistic analysis of discourse variation across registers. *Special Issue of Nordic Journal of English Studies*, 14(1):258–288.

Kerstin Kunz, Stefania Degaetano-Ortlieb, Ekaterina Lapshinova-Koltunski, Katrin Menzel, and Erich Steiner. 2015. Gecco – an empirically-based comparison of english-german cohesion. In G. De Sutter, I. Delaere, and M.-A. Lefer, editors, *New Ways of Analysing Translational Behaviour in Corpus-Based Translation Studies.* Mouton de Gruyter. TILSM series.

Ekaterina Lapshinova-Koltunski. 2013. Vartra: A comparable corpus for analysis of translation variation. In *Proceedings of the Sixth Workshop on Building and Using Comparable Corpora*, pages 77–86,

Sofia, Bulgaria, August. Association for Computational Linguistics.

Ekaterina Lapshinova-Koltunski. *in press*. Linguistic features in translation varieties: Corpus-based analysis. In G. De Sutter, I. Delaere, and M.-A. Lefer, editors, *New Ways of Analysing Translational Behaviour in Corpus-Based Translation Studies*. Mouton de Gruyter. TILSM series.

Ronan Le Nagard and Philipp Koehn. 2010. Aiding pronoun translation with co-reference resolution. In *Proceedings of the Joint Fifth Workshop on Statistical Machine Translation and MetricsMATR*, WMT '10, pages 252–261, Stroudsburg, PA, USA. Association for Computational Linguistics.

Junyi Jessy Li, Marine Carpuat, and Ani Nenkova. 2014. Cross-lingual discourse relation analysis: A corpus study and a semi-supervised classification system. In *Proceedings of COLING 2014, the 25th International Conference on Computational Linguistics: Technical Papers*, pages 577–587, Dublin, Ireland, August 23-29.

Thomas Meyer and Bonnie Webber. 2013. Implicitation of discourse connectives in (machine) translation. In *Proceedings of the Workshop on Discourse in Machine Translation*, pages 19–26, Sofia, Bulgaria, August. Association for Computational Linguistics.

Thomas Meyer, N. Hajlaoui, and Andrei Popescu-Belis. 2015. Disambiguating discourse connectives for statistical machine translation. *Audio, Speech, and Language Processing, IEEE/ACM Transactions on*, 23(7):1184–1197, July.

Stella Neumann. 2013. *Contrastive Register Variation. A Quantitative Approach to the Comparison of English and German*. De Gruyter Mouton, Berlin, Boston.

Ella Rabinovich and Shuly Wintner. 2015. Unsupervised identication of translationese. *Transactions of the Association for Computational Linguistics*, 3.

Helmut Schmid. 1994. Probabilistic Part-of-Speech Tagging Using Decision Trees. In *International Conference on New Methods in Language Processing*, pages 44–49, Manchester, UK.

Maite Taboada and MLA Gómez-González. 2012. Discourse markers and coherence relations: Comparison across markers, languages and modalities. *Linguistics and the Human Sciences*, 6 (1-3):17–41.

R Core Team. 2013. R: A language and environment for statistical computing. Technical report, R Foundation for Statistical Computing, Vienna, Austria.

Elke Teich. 2003. *Cross-Linguistic Variation in System und Text. A Methodology for the Investigation of Translations and Comparable Texts*. Mouton de Gruyter, Berlin.

William N. Venables and David M. Smith. 2010. *An Introduction to R. Notes on R: A Programming Environment for Data Analysis and Graphics*.

Jean P. Vinay and Jean Darbelnet. 1958. *Stylistique Comparée du Français et de l'Anglais. Méthode de Traduction*. Didier, Paris.

Bonnie Webber, Andrei Popescu-Belis, Katja Markert, and Jörg Tiedemann, editors. 2013. *Proceedings of the Workshop on Discourse in Machine Translation*. Association for Computational Linguistics, Sofia, Bulgaria, August.

Marcos Zampieri and Ekaterina Lapshinova-Koltunski. 2015. Investigating genre and method variation in translation using text classification. In Petr Sojka, Ales Horák, Ivan Kopecek, and Karel Pala, editors, *Text, Speech and Dialogue - 18th International Conference, TSD 2015, Plzen, Czech Republic, Proceedings*, Lecture Notes in Computer Science. Springer.

Heike Zinsmeister, Stefanie Dipper, and Melanie Seiss. 2012. Abstract pronominal anaphors and label nouns in german and english: selected case studies and quantitative investigations. *Translation: Computation, Corpora, Cognition*, 2(1).

On Statistical Machine Translation and Translation Theory

Christian Hardmeier
Uppsala University
Department of Linguistics and Philology
Box 635, 751 26 Uppsala, Sweden
first.last@lingfil.uu.se

Abstract

The translation process in statistical machine translation (SMT) is shaped by technical constraints and engineering considerations. SMT explicitly models translation as search for a target-language equivalent of the input text. This perspective on translation had wide currency in mid-20th century translation studies, but has since been superseded by approaches arguing for a more complex relation between source and target text. In this paper, we show how traditional assumptions of translational equivalence are embodied in SMT through the concepts of *word alignment* and *domain* and discuss some limitations arising from the word-level/corpus-level dichotomy inherent in these concepts.

1 Introduction

The methods used in present-day statistical machine translation (SMT) have their foundation in specific assumptions about the nature of the translation process. These assumptions are seldom discussed or even made explicit in the SMT literature, but they have a strong influence on the way SMT models implement translation. This paper studies the relation between current approaches to SMT and major developments in translation studies. We begin with a brief overview of the most important milestones in translation theory and show that the concept of *word alignment* embodies a view of translation that is strongly related to notions of *translational equivalence* popular among translation theorists of the 1960s and 1970s. Defined in terms of an equivalence relation, translation is seen as an essentially "transparent" operation that recodes a text in a different linguistic representation without adding anything of its own, a view that ignores much of the complexity of the decision making processes involved in translation. We show how SMT works around this problem by using the concept of *domain* as a corpus-level catch-all variable and discuss why this approximation may not always be sufficient.

2 Perspectives on Translation

It has been recognised since antiquity that word-by-word translation is generally inadequate and that a higher level of understanding is necessary to translate a text adequately into another language. The fourth century church father and bible translator Jerome made a conceptual distinction between translating "word for word" and "sense for sense" (Jerome, 1979), which remained fundamental for theoretical discussions of translation until the first half of the 20th century (Bassnett, 2011).

Until the 1990s, translation was seen as an act of *transcoding* ("Umkodierung"), whereby elements of one linguistic sign vocabulary are substituted with signs of another linguistic sign vocabulary (Koller, 1972, 69–70). The principal constraint in this substitution is the concept of *equivalence* between the source language (SL) input and the TL output:

> Translating consists in reproducing in the receptor language the closest natural equivalent of the SL message, first in terms of meaning and secondly in terms of style. (Nida and Taber, 1969, 12)

Nida and Taber (1969, 12) emphasise that the primary aim of translation must be "reproducing the message", not the words of the source text. According to them, translators "must strive for equivalence rather than identity" (Nida and Taber, 1969, 12). They stress the importance of *dynamic equivalence*, a concept of functional rather than formal equivalence that is "defined in terms of the degree to which the receptors of the message in the receptor language respond to it in substantially the same manner as the receptors in the source language" (Nida and Taber, 1969, 24). Koller (1972)

Proceedings of the Second Workshop on Discourse in Machine Translation (DiscoMT), pages 168–172,
Lisbon, Portugal, 17 September 2015.

adopts a similar position. Instead of highlighting the message of the source text, he focuses on *understandability* and defines translation as the act of making the target text receptor understand the source text (Koller, 1972, 67).

The end of the last century brought about an important change of viewpoint in translation studies, which has been named the *cultural turn* (Lefevere and Bassnett, 1995; Snell-Hornby, 2010). Equivalence as a purely linguistic concept was criticised as deeply problematic because it fails to recognise the contextual parameters of the act of translating; it was called an "illusion" by Snell-Hornby (1995, 80), who also pointed out that the formal concept of equivalence "proved more suitable at the level of the individual word than at the level of the text" (Snell-Hornby, 1995, 80). A key feature of more recent theoretical approaches to translation is their emphasis on the communicative aspects of translation. Translation is seen as a "communicative process which takes place within a social context" (Hatim and Mason, 1990, 3). Instead of seeking for the TL text that is most closely equivalent to the SL input, the goal of translation is to perform an appropriate communicative act in the target community, and the target text is just a means of achieving this goal. Hatim and Mason (1990, 3) point out that doing so requires the study of *procedures* to find out "which techniques produce which effects" in the source and target community.

Interestingly enough, Lefevere and Bassnett (1995, 4) blame the shortcomings of earlier theoretical approaches oriented towards linguistic equivalence on the influence of MT research and its demands for simple concepts that are easy to capture formally. Whether or not this explanation is true, it is striking how firmly even modern SMT techniques are rooted in traditional assumptions of translational equivalence and indeed how apt much of the criticism against such theories of translation is when applied to standard methods in SMT.

Beyond the additional dependencies on pragmatic and cultural knowledge that more recent theories of translation posit, a crucial innovation is that they view translation as an intentional process in its own right. While equivalence-based accounts of translation assume that the best translation of a given input text is somehow predetermined and the translator's responsibility is just to find it, more recent theories recognise that the cultural context and the intended purpose of a translation are not necessarily equal to those of the source text and must therefore be considered as additional variables affecting the desired outcome of the translation process.

3 Word Alignment and Equivalence

The basis of all current SMT methods is the concept of word alignment, which was formalised by Brown et al. (1990; 1993) in the form still used today. Word alignments are objects of elaborate statistical and computational methods, but their linguistic meaning is defined simply by appealing to intuition:

> For simple sentences, it is reasonable to think of the French translation of an English sentence as being generated from the English sentence word by word. Thus, in the sentence pair (*Jean aime Marie*|*John loves Mary*) we feel that *John* produces *Jean*, *loves* produces *aime*, and *Mary* produces *Marie*. We say that a word is *aligned* with the word that it produces.
> (Brown et al., 1990, 80–81)

The authors do not even try to elucidate the status or significance of word alignments in more complex sentences, where the correspondence between source and target words is less intuitive than in the examples cited. In practical applications, word alignments are essentially defined by what is found by the statistical alignment models used, and the issue of interpreting them is usually evaded.

The cross-linguistic relation defined by word alignments is a sort of translational equivalence relation. It maps linguistic elements of the SL to elements of the TL that are presumed to have the same meaning, or convey the same message. The same is true of the phrase pairs of phrase-based SMT (Koehn et al., 2003) and the synchronous context-free grammar rules of hierarchical SMT (Chiang, 2007), which are usually created from simple word alignments with mostly heuristic methods. None of these approaches exploits any procedural knowledge about linguistic techniques and their effects in the source and target community. Instead, it is assumed that each source text has an equivalent target text, possibly dependent on a set of context variables generally subsumed under the concept of *domain*, and that this target text can be constructed compositionally in a bottom-up fashion.

The generation of word alignments is generally governed by two effects: A statistical dictionary or translation table allows the word aligner to spot word correspondences that are very specific in the sense that the occurrence of a particular word in the SL strongly predicts the occurrence of a certain word in the corresponding TL segment. In addition, there is a prior assumption that the word order of the SL and the TL will be at least locally similar, so that the presence of nearby aligned word pairs counts as evidence in favour of aligning two words, even if the link is only weakly supported by the translation table. While the equivalence relation between content words may be strong, it is often more doubtful whether aligned function words really fill exactly the same role in both languages, making these alignments less reliable.

4 Domain as a Catch-All Category

In SMT, the notion of *domain* is used to encode knowledge about the procedural aspects of translation referred to by Hatim and Mason (1990). Domain can be seen as a variable that all the probability distributions learnt by an SMT system are implicitly conditioned on, and it is assumed that if the domain of the system's training data matches the domain to which it will be applied, then the system will output contextually appropriate translations. If there is a mismatch between the training domain and the test domain, the performance of the system can be improved with domain adaptation techniques.

Although there is a great deal of literature on domain adaptation, few authors care to define exactly what a domain is. Frequently, a corpus of data from a single source, or a collection of corpora from similar sources, is referred to as a domain, so that researchers will refer to the "News" domain (referring to diverse collections of news documents from one or more sources such as news agencies or newspapers) or the "Europarl" domain (referring to the collection of documents from the proceedings of the European parliament published in the Europarl corpus) (Koehn, 2005) without investigating the homogeneity of these data sources in detail.

Koehn (2010, 53) briefly discusses the domain concept. He seems to use the word as a synonym of "text type", characterised by (at least) the dimensions of "modality" (spoken or written language) and "topic". Bungum and Gambäck (2011) present an interesting study of how the term is used in SMT research and how it relates to similar concepts in cognitive linguistics. In general, however, the term is used in a rather vague way and can encompass a variety of corpus-level features connected with genre conventions or the circumstances of text use. There is a clear tendency in current SMT to treat all aspects of a text either as very local, n-gram-style features that can easily be handled with the standard decoding algorithm or as corpus-level "domain" features that can conveniently be taken care of at training time.

5 Implications

The use of word-level alignments in SMT is very close to requiring a word-by-word correspondence of the type criticised already by the earliest translation theorists. SMT is a bit more flexible because the dictionaries it uses are created by a relatively unprejudiced statistical algorithm that may include word correspondences a traditional lexicographer would not necessarily agree with even though there is statistical evidence of a correspondence in the training corpus.

The definition of domain as a catch-all corpus-level category is very useful from a technical point of view since it effectively removes all pragmatic aspects from the training procedure itself and replaces them with a single, albeit very strong, assumption of corpus homogeneity. Its downside is that it is quite inflexible. The system cannot adapt easily to different language use in one and the same corpus, for instance when quoted passages differ in style from the surrounding context. Also, it can learn tendencies, but not actual dependencies. As an example, if a target language distinguishes between different levels of formality in its forms of address, domain easily captures which forms are generally preferred in a particular corpus, but it offers no help to decide which form should be selected in each individual case.

In addition, there are circumstances in which the intentionality of the translation process cannot be ignored completely. This happens mostly when the intention of the translation differs from that of the original text. A few such examples are mentioned in the literature. Stymne et al. (2013) describe an SMT system that combines translation with text simplification to cater to target groups with reading difficulties of various types. One of their main problems is the lack of training data having the desired properties on the TL side. However, even if such training data is available, SMT training is not necessarily successful. A case in point is the translation of film subtitles, where the target side is often shortened as well as translated (Pedersen, 2007; Fishel et al., 2012). Anecdotal evidence suggests that MT systems easily learn the length ratio, but truncate the texts in an erratic way that has a negative effect on translation quality.

6 Some Suggestions

Most current approaches to SMT are founded on word alignments in the spirit of Brown et al. (1990). These word alignments have no clear theoretical status, but they can be seen as an embodiment of a fairly traditional concept of translational equivalence. Equivalence in SMT is strongly surface-oriented, and SMT technology has traditionally eschewed all abstract representations of meaning, mapping tokens of the input directly into tokens of the output. This has worked well, demonstrating that much linguistic information is indeed accessible with surface-level processing. However, the SMT system often does not know exactly what it is doing. For instance, based on observational evidence from the training corpus, an SMT system might translate an active sentence in the input with a passive sentence in the output, or a personal construction in the SL with an impersonal construction in the TL without being aware of it. It is difficult to envisage consistently correct translation of complex linguistic phenomena based on such an impoverished representation.

If our goal is to promote progress towards high-quality MT, we should investigate the creation of more expressive cross-lingual representations. The challenge is, then, to do so without compromising the undeniable strength of surface-based SMT. One of its strongest points is its robust descriptive nature that learns as much as possible from data while imposing only very few and general *a priori* constraints. Rather than advocating transfer systems based on specific linguistic theories, we believe that this philosophy should be upheld as much as possible as we explore more expressive transfer representations.

The concept of word alignment works well for content words, and we see no necessity to give it up completely. However, translating function words by mapping them into the TL through word alignments is a more doubtful enterprise, and we suggest that the production of function words should be approached as a problem of generation, or prediction, rather than as a word-level mapping task.

We further believe that it is useful to focus on the correctness of individual structures rather than trying to improve the "average" correctness of an entire text and hoping that individual structures will somehow fall into place automatically. This applies to both translation and evaluation. At translation time, domain adaptation techniques increase the likelihood of correct translations on average, but they do not provide the MT system with any information to support decision-making in particular cases. Therefore, domain adaptation does not appear to be promising as a method to impress a deeper linguistic understanding on SMT; instead, we should strive to overcome the strict dichotomy between word-level and corpus-level modelling and create an additional layer of modelling between the two extremes.

Our stance on evaluation is similar. Aggregating evaluation methods like BLEU (Papineni et al., 2002) give a useful overview of the quality of a translation, but they do not afford specific information and leave too many details to chance. One possible alternative is the creation of test suites with carefully selected examples permitting quick, targeted manual evaluation of specific phenomena in the development phase.

7 Conclusions

Current SMT rests on assumptions of straightforward translational equivalence that oversimplify the complexity of the translation process. Most fundamentally, the central concept of word alignment works well for content words, but is problematic for function words. This leads to problems with controlling the semantics and pragmatics of the translation. Moreover, the intentionality of the translation process is entirely neglected, which causes difficulties particularly when the translation task is combined with some other objective such as text simplification or condensation. This should be borne in mind when designing such translation tasks, but for most applications of SMT, the first problem is clearly more pressing.

The development of new methods in SMT is usually driven by considerations of technical feasibility rather than linguistic theory. This has produced good results, and we expect that it will remain the predominant methodology in the foreseeable future. We consider that it is effective and appropriate to proceed in this way, but from time to time it makes sense to pause and examine the theoretical implications and limitations of the work accomplished, as we have attempted to do for the current standard methods in SMT in this paper.

Acknowledgements

This work was supported by the Swedish Research Council under project 2012-916 *Discourse-Oriented Statistical Machine Translation.*

References

Susan Bassnett. 2011. The translator as cross-cultural mediator. In Kirsten Malmkjær and Kevin Windle, editors, *The Oxford Handbook of Translation Studies*, pages 94–107. Oxford University Press, Oxford.

Peter F. Brown, John Cocke, Stephen A. Della Pietra, Vincent J. Della Pietra, Frederick Jelinek, John D. Lafferty, Robert L. Mercer, and Paul S. Roossin. 1990. A statistical approach to machine translation. *Computational linguistics*, 16(2):79–85.

Peter F. Brown, Stephen A. Della Pietra, Vincent J. Della Pietra, and Robert L. Mercer. 1993. The mathematics of statistical machine translation. *Computational linguistics*, 19(2):263–311.

Lars Bungum and Björn Gambäck. 2011. A survey of domain adaptation in machine translation: Towards a refinement of domain space. In *Proceedings of the India-Norway Workshop on Web Concepts and Technologies*, Trondheim (Norway).

David Chiang. 2007. Hierarchical phrase-based translation. *Computational linguistics*, 33(2):201–228.

Mark Fishel, Yota Georgakopoulou, Sergio Penkale, Volha Petukhova, Matej Rojc, Martin Volk, and Andy Way. 2012. From subtitles to parallel corpora. In *Proceedings of the 16th Conference of the European Association for Machine Translation (EAMT)*, pages 3–6, Trento (Italy).

Basil Hatim and Ian Mason. 1990. *Discourse and the Translator*. Language in Social Life Series. Longman, London.

Jerome. 1979. Letter LVII: To Pammachius on the best method of translating. In *St. Jerome: Letters and Select Works*, volume VI of *A Select Library of Nicene and Post-Nicene Fathers of the Christian Church, Second Series*, pages 112–119. Eerdmans, Grand Rapids.

Philipp Koehn, Franz Josef Och, and Daniel Marcu. 2003. Statistical phrase-based translation. In *Proceedings of the 2003 Conference of the North American Chapter of the Association for Computational Linguistics on Human Language Technology*, pages 48–54, Edmonton (Canada).

Philipp Koehn. 2005. Europarl: A corpus for statistical machine translation. In *Proceedings of MT Summit X*, pages 79–86, Phuket (Thailand). AAMT.

Philipp Koehn. 2010. *Statistical Machine Translation*. Cambridge University Press, Cambridge.

Werner Koller. 1972. *Grundprobleme der Übersetzungstheorie, unter besonderer Berücksichtigung schwedisch-deutscher Übersetzungsfälle*, volume 9 of *Acta Universitatis Stockholmiensis. Stockholmer germanistische Forschungen*. Francke, Bern.

André Lefevere and Susan Bassnett. 1995. Introduction: Proust's grandmother and the thousand and one nights: The 'cultural turn' in translation studies. In Susan Bassnett and André Lefevere, editors, *Translation, History and Culture*, pages 1–14. Cassell, London.

Eugene A. Nida and Charles R. Taber. 1969. *The theory and practice of translation*, volume 8 of *Helps for translators*. Brill, Leiden.

Kishore Papineni, Salim Roukos, Todd Ward, and Wei-Jing Zhu. 2002. BLEU: A method for automatic evaluation of machine translation. In *Proceedings of the 40th Annual Meeting of the Association for Computational Linguistics*, pages 311–318, Philadelphia (Pennsylvania, USA). ACL.

Jan Pedersen. 2007. *Scandinavian subtitles. A comparative study of subtitling norms in Sweden and Denmark with a focus on extralinguistic cultural references*. Ph.D. thesis, Stockholm University, Department of English.

Mary Snell-Hornby. 1995. Linguistic transcoding or cultural transfer? A critique of translation theory in Germany. In Susan Bassnett and André Lefevere, editors, *Translation, History and Culture*, pages 79–86. Cassell, London.

Mary Snell-Hornby. 2010. The turns of translation studies. In *Handbook of Translation Studies*, volume 1, pages 366–370. John Benjamins, Amsterdam.

Sara Stymne, Jörg Tiedemann, Christian Hardmeier, and Joakim Nivre. 2013. Statistical machine translation with readability constraints. In Stephan Oepen, Kristin Hagen, and Janne Bondi Johannesse, editors, *Proceedings of the 19th Nordic Conference of Computational Linguistics (NODALIDA 2013)*, pages 375–386, Oslo (Norway).

Author Index

Aziz, Wilker, 52

Bisazza, Arianna, 132

Callin, Jimmy, 59
Cettolo, Mauro, 1

Duh, Kevin, 142

Evers-Vermeul, Jacqueline, 41

Fishel, Mark, 47

Gong, Zhengxian, 33
Guillou, Liane, 24, 65

Hardmeier, Christian, 1, 59, 72, 168
Hoek, Jet, 41

Ittycheriah, Abraham, 153

Lapshinova-Koltunski, Ekaterina, 122, 158
Loáiciga, Sharid, 78, 86
Lopez, Adam, 115
Luong, Ngoc Quang, 94

Mascarell, Laura, 47
Matsumoto, Yuji, 142
Miculicich Werlen, Lesly, 94
Monz, Christof, 132

Nakov, Preslav, 1
Novák, Michal, 17

Oele, Dieke, 17

Pham, Ngoc-Quan, 101
Popescu-Belis, Andrei, 94

Sanders, Ted J.M., 41
Sim Smith, Karin, 52
Specia, Lucia, 52
Stymne, Sara, 1

Tiedemann, Jörg, 1, 59, 108

van der Plas, Lonneke, 101
van der Wees, Marlies, 132
van Noord, Gertjan, 17
Vela, Mihaela, 122
Versley, Yannick, 1
Volk, Martin, 47

Webber, Bonnie, 24, 115
Wehrli, Eric, 86
Wetzel, Dominikus, 115

Yung, Frances, 142

Zhang, Min, 33
Zhang, Rong, 153
Zhou, Guodong, 33

Association for Computational Linguistics
209 N. Eighth Street
Stroudsburg, Pennsylvania 18360

CURRAN ASSOCIATES INC.
proceedings
.com

ISBN 978-1-5108-1192-8